Essential Essays

BY ADRIENNE RICH

Collected Poems 1950–2012

Later Poems: Selected and New, 1971–2012

Tonight No Poetry Will Serve: Poems 2007–2010

A Human Eye: Essays on Art and Society, 1997–2008

Poetry & Commitment: An Essay

Telephone Ringing in the Labyrinth: Poems 2004–2006

The School Among the Ruins: Poems 2000–2004

What Is Found There: Notebooks on Poetry and Politics

The Fact of a Doorframe: Poems 1950–2001

Fox: Poems 1998–2000

Arts of the Possible: Essays and Conversations

Midnight Salvage: Poems 1995–1998

Dark Fields of the Republic: Poems 1991–1995

Collected Early Poems 1950–1970

An Atlas of the Difficult World: Poems 1988–1991

Time's Power: Poems 1985–1988

Blood, Bread, and Poetry: Selected Prose 1979–1985

Your Native Land, Your Life: Poems

Sources

A Wild Patience Has Taken Me This Far: Poems 1978–1981

On Lies, Secrets, and Silence: Selected Prose 1966–1978

The Dream of a Common Language: Poems 1974–1977

Twenty-One Love Poems

Of Woman Born: Motherhood as Experience and Institution

Poems: Selected and New, 1950–1974

Diving into the Wreck: Poems 1971–1972

The Will to Change: Poems 1968–1970

Leaflets: Poems 1965–1968

Necessities of Life

Snapshots of a Daughter-in-Law: Poems 1954–1962

The Diamond Cutters and Other Poems

A Change of World

Essential Essays

CULTURE, POLITICS, AND THE ART OF POETRY

Adrienne Rich

Edited and with an Introduction by Sandra M. Gilbert

W. W. NORTON & COMPANY

Independent Publishers Since 1923

New York | London

For information about permission to reproduce selections from this book, write to
Permissions, W. W. Norton & Company, Inc., 500 Fifth Avenue, New York, NY 10110

For information about special discounts for bulk purchases, please contact
W. W. Norton Special Sales at specialsales@wwnorton.com or 800-233-4830

Manufacturing by Quad Graphics Fairfield
Book design by Chris Welch Design
Production manager: Julia Druskin

ISBN 978-0-393-65236-9

W. W. Norton & Company, Inc., 500 Fifth Avenue, New York, N.Y. 10110
www.wwnorton.com

W. W. Norton & Company Ltd., 15 Carlisle Street, London W1D 3BS

1 2 3 4 5 6 7 8 9 0

Contents

On Lies, Secrets, and Silence: Selected Prose 1966–1978

Uncollected

Of Woman Born: Motherhood as Experience and Institution (1976)

Blood, Bread, and Poetry: Selected Prose 1979–1985

What Is Found There: Notebooks on Poetry and Politics (1993, 2003)

Arts of the Possible (2001)

A Human Eye (2009)

A Note on the Text

The texts for Adrienne Rich's prose printed here are taken from the most recent versions published by W. W. Norton during her life. Where Rich updated an earlier essay with new notes or additions (for example, "Compulsory Heterosexuality and Lesbian Experience" in 1986 or "The Distance Between Language and Violence" in 2003) that later text is used.

Introduction

The Treasures That Prevail

Toward the end of "Diving into the Wreck," one of her most renowned poems, Adrienne Rich explains the goals of her underwater journey:

> I came to explore the wreck.
> The words are purposes.
> The words are maps.
> I came to see the damage that was done
> and the treasures that prevail.
> I stroke the beam of my lamp
> slowly along the flank
> of something more permanent
> than fish or weed
>
> the thing I came for:
> the wreck and not the story of the wreck
> the thing itself and not the myth

Here, she says, is the imperative of investigation, needful research into "the damage that was done / and the treasures that prevail." Arguably, as she confided she had discovered sometime in the sixties, such research into reality—"the thing itself and not the myth"—was a major aim of her work as a poet. But perhaps it hasn't yet been clearly enough understood how crucially her writings in prose complemented, supplemented, enriched, and, yes, inspired her writing in verse. For in these writings she was not just one of many contemporary poets "illuminating" her verse through confessional glosses but a major memoirist, essayist, theorist, and scholar.

As an undergraduate at Radcliffe, Rich has said, she was enthralled by the poems of W. B. Yeats, from whose lucid cadences she took what she needed to enhance her aesthetic craft. As she confides in "Blood, Bread, and Poetry," the "dialogue between art and politics . . . excited me in his work, along with the sound of his language." To be sure, there are countless differences between these two writers, in particular large gaps between the Irish artist's problematic sexual politics and Rich's radical reimaginings of gender as well as between Yeats's eccentric (and aristocratic) mysticism and Rich's social realism. (She was never, she notes, interested in "his elaborate mythological systems.") Yet what links the two, at different ends of the twentieth century and of the political spectrum, is a fierce urge toward personal and poetic refashioning, along with an increasingly powerful sense of communal responsibility. For if Yeats spoke for Ireland—once telling an unruly Abbey Theater audience that "the author of *Countess Cathleen* speaks to you"—Rich spoke just as passionately for women, and more specifically for lesbians, for Black women, for working-class women, for Jews, and in a larger sense for the dispossessed, for those whom the poet Anne Winters has called "the displaced of capital."

In time, as she grew into the intense feminism that was to shape both her life and her work, Rich was increasingly drawn—as so many of us were in the sixties and seventies—to female forebears, who took the place of the "masters" she had studied in college. Like Virginia Woolf, who famously declared "We think back through our mothers, if we are women," Rich assembled a visionary company of ancestresses whose arts and ideas she meticulously analyzed. Prominent among these was the multifaceted American poet Muriel Rukeyser, whose own ongoing "dialogue between art and politics" became as inspiring to the mature Rich as Yeats had been to the Radcliffe undergraduate. Rukeyser, Rich explained in an essay I've included here, "spoke as a poet, first and foremost; but she spoke also as a thinking activist, biographer, traveler, explorer of her country's psychic geography." She had first read Rukeyser, Rich noted, in the early fifties, because, "like her, I had won the Yale Younger Poets Prize at the age of twenty-one, and I was curious to see what a woman poet, at my age, now ahead of me on the path, had written in her first book." Though she still remembered "the extraordinary force of the first poem in *Theory of Flight,* how it broke over me, and my envy of the sweeping lines, the authority" in that work, she confessed that she wasn't yet prepared to learn from Rukeyser. "I came to [her] in my maturity, as my own life opened out [and] I found her to be the poet I most needed in the struggle to make my poems and live my life." For indeed, like Rukeyser, Rich became "a thinking activist" and—throughout her career, but especially in such works as "Blood, Bread, and Poetry" and *An Atlas of the Difficult World*—a sensitive "explorer of her country's psychic geography."

To reread and to rethink Rich's prose as a complete oeuvre is to encounter a major public intellectual: responsible, self-questioning, and morally passionate. For those of us who came of age during feminism's fabled "second wave" in the seventies, texts like "When We Dead Awaken" and "Compulsory Heterosexuality and Lesbian Existence" were key proclamations of ideas that we desperately needed to guide us on our way. Equally important to us was the powerful blend of research, theory, and self-reflection that Rich produced in her landmark study *Of Woman Born: Motherhood as Experience and Institution.* Later, as we matured into the nineties and the twenty-first century, Rich's analyses of poetry—her own art and the arts of others—as in *What Is Found There,* helped us, especially those of us who were poets and devoted readers of poetry, to sort through a canon that needed reexamination. And throughout her career the political keenness and candor that energized such writings as "Why I Refused the National Medal for the Arts" grounded us in a dissent that was both firm and formidable.

What is perhaps most compelling about Rich's prose, however, isn't just its grounding in dissent but its origin in disclosure. Although she herself often claimed that she disliked the "personal" or "confessional"—considering them "therapeutic" genres that evaded edgier social contexts—her prose writings, even more than her verse, mine a richly autobiographical vein. By the time one has read

through some of her strongest essays, one comes to know her ambitious, sometimes tyrannical Jewish father, Arnold Rich, and her genteel, gentile southern mother, Helen Rich, as if they were figures in
Proust. The daughter here is nothing but honest, and her personal
interpolations significantly illuminate her political interventions.
Neither a confessional writer nor a memoirist—she was always private about the failure of her marriage and about the lives of her
children—she nevertheless profiled Baltimore (in the forties) and
Cambridge (in the fifties) in such precise detail that we feel present
at a kind of documentary.

Even *Of Woman Born: Motherhood as Experience and Institution*,
begun as a research project, offers comparable portraits of what was,
and how it changed. At the same time it was, and is, a groundbreaking feminist study that brilliantly exemplifies the innovative scholarship energized by what has come to be called "the second wave"
of the women's movement. That Rich, never a professional academic
or graduate student, was such a leader in this field, working with
rigorous lucidity, makes me wish I could leap into a time machine,
go back into the past, and remind dissenters—for instance, Midge
Decter, "the anti-feminist woman" of one of Rich's essays—how
much thought from how many serious thinkers inspired marches,
meetings, and manifestoes. In fact, it was the serious and dedicated thought of seventies feminism that not only transformed Rich
from a Yeatsian acolyte to a Rukeyser disciple but also motivated
her own "will to change" from a writer of intelligent, casual reviews
to an "activist thinker." In her eloquent "Arts of the Possible," she
recounted that metamorphic time. "The women's liberation movement embodied for a while the kind of creative space a liberatory
political movement can make possible: 'a visionary relation to reality.' Why this happens has something to do with the sheer power
of a collective imagining of change and a sense of collective hope."
Also, of course, it has something—maybe everything!—to do with the
ways in which liberatory political movements must inevitably find
poets and prophets who can articulate their collective hopes. Such a
spokesperson was Adrienne Rich, as both her poems and her prose
writings reveal.

•

One of the first essays that Rich published was a review of D. H. Lawrence's *Collected Poems*, in *Poetry* magazine, 1963. Sophisticated and incisive, the piece clearly reveals the readerly intelligence with which Rich approached the writings of a poet-novelist whose verse was at that time significantly underappreciated, even while it also demonstrates that she herself was a keen practitioner of her aesthetic craft. Analyzing Lawrence's poems in the context of his own lyric manifesto, "Poetry of the Present," she dramatized, even then, her awareness that a poet's prose writings are also, in a sense, part of her poetic canon. After that she wrote a few other reviews for *Poetry* and, in the early seventies, briefly became a columnist for the *American Poetry Review*. By the time she reviewed Lawrence's poems, however, Rich had already published two collections of her own: *A Change of World* (1951), which won the Yale Younger Poets Prize when, like Rukeyser, she was just twenty-one, and *The Diamond Cutters* (1955).

Of the first book, W. H. Auden, then editor for the Yale series, wrote in a notoriously patronizing preface that the poems "are neatly and modestly dressed, speak quietly but do not mumble, respect their elders but are not cowed by them, and do not tell fibs." A few years later, in a review of *The Diamond Cutters*, Randall Jarrell thickened the plot, claiming that the author of the book seems "to us a sort of princess in a fairy tale." But the Adrienne Cecile Rich (for so she signed her first two books) of whom these masterful poets were speaking seems to have been largely a figment of their imaginations. True, her parents had bestowed on her a somewhat flowery name, but along with that they'd given her an education in aspiration and expertise. Her father was a distinguished pathologist, her mother a former concert pianist. The elder of two sisters, Adrienne was the son the couple wanted and never had. Home-schooled until fourth grade, she was taught verse forms along with Bach and Mozart while ranging freely through her father's extensive library. After that, she went on to an excellent private school for girls and then to Radcliffe/Harvard, from which she returned after her freshman year "flaming with new insights, new information" as "the daughter who has gone out into the world, to the pinnacle of intellectual prestige . . . fulfilling my father's hopes for me, but also exposed to dangerous influences."

"Dangerous influences." Beneath a veneer of decorum, the stubborn poet had begun to stir. But given her specialized upbringing, she had to rebel on several fronts. In secret, she confided in a letter to a longtime friend, she had as a teenager "spent hours writing imitations of cosmetic advertising and illustrating them copiously" and "mercifully," she recalled in print, she "discovered *Modern Screen, Photoplay*, Jack Benny, 'Your Hit Parade,' Frank Sinatra," and other icons of popular culture. Worse still, though from her father's perspective she was "satisfyingly precocious," she had "early been given to tics and tantrums." Even in the years when Auden and Jarrell were captivated by what they saw as her dutiful command of versification ("I was exceptionally well grounded in formal technique," she herself admitted, "and I loved the craft"), she was "groping for . . . something larger." Her first act of overt rebellion against a father whom she once defined as "Papa Brontë" was to marry "a divorced graduate student" from an observant, eastern European Jewish family, a background that Arnold Rich, a secular (and atheistic) Jew, disliked. Her parents refused to attend the wedding, which was held at Hillel House in Cambridge.

After that, as she recalled, she began to write what her father defined as "'modern,' 'obscure,' 'pessimistic' poetry" and eventually she had "the final temerity to get pregnant." Another young woman poet who visited Cambridge at this time discerned what Auden, Jarrell, and Arnold Rich had failed to grasp. Sylvia Plath was fiercely rivalrous toward Rich but described her, with some respect, as "all vibrant short black hair, great sparkling black eyes and a tulip-red umbrella; honest, pink, *forthright* and even *opinionated* [ital. added]." But at the same time, curiously enough, in rebelling against her father's plans for her intellectual career Rich had entrapped herself in what Betty Friedan has called the "feminine mystique" of the fifties. She gave birth to three sons before she was thirty, and, as *Of Woman Born* testifies, her experience of motherhood as a social and cultural institution was utterly life-changing. "Motherhood radical-ized me," she declared, for both the experience and the institution had forced her to attend to the powerful gender distinctions that shape and sometimes shatter women's worlds.

"Anger and tenderness," the phrase with which Rich titled the first chapter of that book, marked her career in the nearly two decades of her marriage, when she and her husband Alfred Conrad, a Harvard professor of economics, were bringing up their boys, in both Cambridge and New York. For much of this time Rich was rel-atively silent as a poet: there is a gap of nearly a decade between her publication of *The Diamond Cutters* and her next, groundbreaking, proto-feminist book *Snapshots of a Daughter-in-Law* (1963), though for the rest of her career she was to publish nearly a collection a year.

During the tumultuous sixties, Rich's marriage to Conrad began to disintegrate, as the couple moved to New York and Rich herself turned increasingly to the intellectual activism that reshaped her art and thought. In 1970, in the midst of personal and political tur-moil, Conrad drove to Vermont near where the family had a country house and took his own life, with a gunshot. Shocked, Rich went on to become, as she called herself in one poem, "a survivor." A few years after her husband's death, she ruefully described its aftermath:

> Next year it would have been 20 years
> and you are wastefully dead
> who might have made the leap
> we talked, too late, of making
>
> which I live now
> not as a leap
> but a succession of brief, amazing movements
>
> each one making possible the next.

By the seventies, in one of those amazing movements, she had com-mitted herself to a "lesbian existence" that she defined as "womanly, powerful."

•

In 1976 Rich began her lifelong partnership with the Jamaican-born novelist and poet Michelle Cliff, and her major essay on "Compulsory Heterosexuality and Lesbian Existence" appeared in 1980. Then in "Split at the Root" (1982) and the long poem "Sources" (1982) she began to reclaim her Jewish heritage. In 1983, she went to Nicaragua to try to understand the Sandinistas and, further, "to get a sense of what art might mean in a society committed to values other than profit and consumerism." By the time she published her ambitious, Whitmanesque "Atlas of the Difficult World" (1991) she was "bent on fathoming what it means to love my country," affirming that a "patriot is one who wrestles for the soul of her country / as she wrestles for her own being." One amazing movement after another had brought her to the center of public discourse, where she wrote of blood, bread, and poetry in an effort to critique racism, misogyny, antisemitism, heterosexism, consumerism, and class privilege, with anger and tenderness. These wellsprings of art, along with the craft to shape them into powerful language, were arguably the treasures that prevailed, after she had investigated the wreck of her marriage and the culture that had deformed it.

•

"I first started writing prose about poetry," Rich explained to an interviewer in 1991, noting that after the reviews she did for *Poetry,* she had been asked to write a foreword to an edition of Anne Bradstreet. Still, she said, "I didn't think of myself as an essayist, and I didn't pursue writing prose on my own, except in my journals." Here she might have added that she was also a prolific letter writer, whose lively and witty correspondence continued throughout her life and from which a selection may soon, one hopes, appear in print. The practice of prose—in letters and journals—was thus an integral part of her relationship to language. From a professional perspective, however, she speculated "that it was finally involvement in politics that got me writing prose more, as a part of life, as a regular part of my writing. And very often it was because somebody asked me to speak or asked for an essay." Nonetheless, she continued, though her prose "has always been initiated from an exterior point, it wasn't an exterior point that was irrelevant to what was happening to me, in my life, or even in my poetry. I was writing poems out of a lot of the same things which I discussed in the essay 'When We Dead Awaken,' and I have a poem with the same title. Certainly a lot of my other essays have points of intersection with poems, probably none so much as 'Split at the Root' with 'Sources'—which I was writing at about the same time."

To a certain point, my principles of selection in this book have been inevitably governed by the arc of the poetry/prose career that the poet herself describes in these remarks. It was, of course, essential to open the book with "When We Dead Awaken," an essay that is as hortatory as it is revelatory, so much so that it functions as a kind of manifesto for the rest of the writer's career. And interestingly, some of the strongest prose from this period is precisely the kind of "re-visionary" literary criticism that Rich's manifesto inspired from other feminist thinkers in the seventies, notably her brilliant essays on *Jane Eyre* and Emily Dickinson, which many of us still remember reading with wonder when they first came out. From this period, I have also included two uncollected pieces, the "Statement at a Poetry Reading" that Albert and Barbara Gelpi have long included in a Norton Critical Edition though it was never published in any of Rich's own prose volumes, and her well-known column in the *American Poetry Review* taking Robert Lowell to task for what she regarded as his betrayal of Elizabeth Hardwick in some of his "confessional" verse.

Of Woman Born presents the editor of a prose selection with difficult problems, since the book is really a seamless project of research and argumentation, but I have tried to represent what I hope Rich herself would regard as some of its most crucial and original sections, in particular the self-searching "Anger and Tenderness" chapter and, then, the chapter she considered "the core of the book," "Motherhood and Daughterhood." From this point on, as Rich remarked, "involvement in politics" inspired much of her prose, notably "Compulsory Heterosexuality," "Split at the Root,"

"Blood, Bread, and Poetry," along with the later essays from *Arts of the Possible* and *A Human Eye*. Even literary essays—a review of Elizabeth Bishop's *Collected Poems,* an introduction to Muriel Rukeyser's writings, and excerpts from *What Is Found There*—remind us that for Rich, as for so many feminists of her generation and later ones (including my own), the personal, the poetical, and the political were one. At the same time, her extraordinary critical expertise and wide-ranging aesthetic knowledge should also remind us that, as she understatedly put it, she was "exceptionally well grounded in formal technique" and truly loved her craft.

Marianne Moore—never one of Rich's favorite poets—once famously declared, "Omissions are not accidents," and so any editor must also confess. When choosing what to reprint and what to omit from such a complex oeuvre, however, an editor must also confide that omissions are absences. I wish I had had twice as much space to devote to Rich's prose. Still, in seeking to trace this writer's ongoing lifelong research into "the thing I came for: / the wreck and not the story of the wreck / the thing itself and not the myth," I hope I will have offered readers a useful selection of—yes—the many treasures that prevail.

On Lies, Secrets, and Silence

Selected Prose
1966–1978

WHEN WE DEAD AWAKEN

Writing as Re-Vision (1971)

Ibsen's *When We Dead Awaken* is a play about the use that the male artist and thinker—in the process of creating culture as we know it—has made of women, in his life and in his work; and about a woman's slow struggling awakening to the use to which her life has been put. Bernard Shaw wrote in 1900 of this play:

> [Ibsen] shows us that no degradation ever devized or permitted is as disastrous as this degradation; that through it women can die into luxuries for men and yet can kill them; that men and women are becoming conscious of this; and that what remains to be seen as perhaps the most interesting of all imminent social developments is what will happen "when we dead awaken."[1]

It's exhilarating to be alive in a time of awakening consciousness; it can also be confusing, disorienting, and plainful. This awakening of dead or sleeping consciousness has already affected the lives of millions of women, even those who don't know it yet. It is also affecting the lives of men, even those who deny its claims upon them. The argument will go on whether an oppressive economic class system is responsible for the oppressive nature of male/female relations, or whether, in fact, patriarchy—the domination of males—is the original model of oppression on which all others are based. But in the last few years the women's movement has drawn inescapable and illuminating connections between our sexual lives and our political institutions. The sleepwalkers are coming awake, and for the first

Written in 1971, the essay first appeared in *College English* 34, no. 1 (October 1972).

time this awakening has a collective reality; it is no longer such a lonely thing to open one's eyes.

Re-vision—the act of looking back, of seeing with fresh eyes, of entering an old text from a new critical direction—is for women more than a chapter in cultural history: it is an act of survival. Until we can understand the assumptions in which we are drenched we cannot know ourselves. And this drive to self-knowledge, for women, is more than a search for identity: it is part of our refusal of the self-destructiveness of male-dominated society. A radical critique of literature, feminist in its impulse, would take the work first of all as a clue to how we live, how we have been living, how we have been led to imagine ourselves, how our language has trapped as well as liberated us, how the very act of naming has been till now a male prerogative, and how we can begin to see and name—and therefore live—afresh. A change in the concept of sexual identity is essential if we are not going to see the old political order reassert itself in every new revolution. We need to know the writing of the past, and know it differently than we have ever known it; not to pass on a tradition but to break its hold over us.

For writers, and at this moment for women writers in particular, there is the challenge and promise of a whole new psychic geography to be explored. But there is also a difficult and dangerous walking on the ice, as we try to find language and images for a consciousness we are just coming into, and with little in the past to support us. I want to talk about some aspects of this difficulty and this danger.

Jane Harrison, the great classical anthropologist, wrote in 1914 in a letter to her friend Gilbert Murray:

> By the by, about "Women," it has bothered me often—why do women never want to write poetry about Man as a sex—why is Woman a dream and a terror to man and not the other way around? . . . Is it mere convention and propriety, or something deeper?[2]

I think Jane Harrison's question cuts deep into the myth-making tradition, the romantic tradition; deep into what women and men have been to each other; and deep into the psyche of the woman writer. Thinking about that question, I began thinking of the work of two twentieth-century women poets, Sylvia Plath and Diane Wakoski. It strikes me that in the work of both Man appears as, if not a dream, a fascination and a terror; and that the source of the fascination and the terror is, simply, Man's power—to dominate, tyrannize, choose, or reject the woman. The charisma of Man seems to come purely from his power over her and his control of the world by force, not from anything fertile or life-giving in him. And, in the work of both these poets, it is finally the woman's sense of *herself*— embattled, possessed—that gives the poetry its dynamic charge, its rhythms of struggle, need, will, and female energy. Until recently this female anger and this furious awareness of the Man's power over her were not available materials to the female poet, who tended to write of Love as the source of her suffering, and to view that victimization by Love as an almost inevitable fate. Or, like Marianne Moore and Elizabeth Bishop, she kept sexuality at a measured and chiseled distance in her poems.

One answer to Jane Harrison's question has to be that historically men and women have played very different parts in each others' lives. Where woman has been a luxury for man, and has served as the painter's model and the poet's muse, but also as comforter, nurse, cook, bearer of his seed, secretarial assistant, and copyist of manuscripts, man has played a quite different role for the female artist. Henry James repeats an incident which the writer Prosper Mérimée described, of how, while he was living with George Sand,

> he once opened his eyes, in the raw winter dawn, to see his companion, in a dressing-gown, on her knees before the domestic hearth, a candlestick beside her and a red *madras* round her head, making bravely, with her own hands the fire that was to enable her to sit down betimes to urgent pen and paper. The story represents him as having felt that the spectacle chilled his ardor and tried his taste; her appearance was unfortunate, her occupation an inconsequence, and her industry a reproof—the result of all which was a lively irritation and an early rupture.[3]

The specter of this kind of male judgment, along with the misnaming and thwarting of her needs by a culture controlled by males, has created problems for the woman writer: problems of contact with herself, problems of language and style, problems of energy and survival.

In rereading Virginia Woolf's *A Room of One's Own* (1929) for the first time in some years, I was astonished at the sense of effort, of pains taken, of dogged tentativeness, in the tone of that essay. And I recognized that tone. I had heard it often enough, in myself and in other women. It is the tone of a woman almost in touch with her anger, who is determined not to appear angry, who is *willing* herself to be calm, detached, and even charming in a roomful of men where things have been said which are attacks on her very integrity. Virginia Woolf is addressing an audience of women, but she is acutely conscious—as she always was—of being overheard by men: by Morgan and Lytton and Maynard Keynes and for that matter by her father, Leslie Stephen.[4] She drew the language out into an exacerbated thread in her determination to have her own sensibility yet protect it from those masculine presences. Only at rare moments in that essay do you hear the passion in her voice; she was trying to sound as cool as Jane Austen, as Olympian as Shakespeare, because that is the way the men of the culture thought a writer should sound.

No male writer has written primarily or even largely for women, or with the sense of women's criticism as a consideration when he chooses his materials, his theme, his language. But to a lesser or greater extent, every woman writer has written for men even when, like Virginia Woolf, she was supposed to be addressing women. If we have come to the point when this balance might begin to change, when women can stop being haunted, not only by "convention and propriety" but by internalized fears of being and saying themselves, then it is an extraordinary moment for the woman writer—and reader.

I have hesitated to do what I am going to do now, which is to use myself as an illustration. For one thing, it's a lot easier and less dangerous to talk about other women writers. But there is something else. Like Virginia Woolf, I am aware of the women who are not with us here because they are washing the dishes and looking after the children. Nearly fifty years after she spoke, that fact remains largely unchanged. And I am thinking also of women whom she left out of the picture altogether—women who are washing other people's dishes and caring for other people's children, not to mention women who went on the streets last night in order to feed their children. We seem to be special women here, we have liked to think of ourselves as special, and we have known that men would tolerate, even romanticize us as special, as long as our words and actions didn't threaten their privilege of tolerating or rejecting us and our work according to *their* ideas of what a special woman ought to be. An important insight of the radical women's movement has been how divisive and how ultimately destructive is this myth of the special woman, who is also the token woman. Every one of us here in this room has had great luck—we are teachers, writers, academicians; our own gifts could not have been enough, for we all know women whose gifts are buried or aborted. Our struggles can have meaning and our privileges—however precarious under patriarchy—can be justified only if they can help to change the lives of women whose gifts—and whose very being—continue to be thwarted and silenced.

My own luck was being born white and middle-class into a house full of books, with a father who encouraged me to read and write. So for about twenty years I wrote for a particular man, who criticized and praised me and made me feel I was indeed "special." The obverse side of this, of course, was that I tried for a long time to please him, or rather, not to displease him. And then of course there were other men—writers, teachers—the Man, who was not a terror or a dream but a literary master and a master in other ways less easy to acknowledge. And there were all those poems about women, written by men: it seemed to be a given that men wrote poems and women frequently inhabited them. These women were almost always beautiful, but threatened with the loss of beauty, the loss of youth—the fate worse than death. Or, they were beautiful and died young, like Lucy and Lenore. Or, the woman was like Maud Gonne, cruel and disastrously mistaken, and the poem reproached her because she had refused to become a luxury for the poet.

A lot is being said today about the influence that the myths and images of women have on all of us who are products of culture. I think it has been a peculiar confusion to the girl or woman who tries to write because she is peculiarly susceptible to language. She goes to poetry or fiction looking for *her* way of being in the world, since she too has been putting words and images together; she is looking eagerly for guides, maps, possibilities; and over and over in the "words' masculine persuasive force" of literature she comes up against something that negates everything she is about: she meets the image of Woman in books written by men. She finds a terror and a dream, she finds a beautiful pale face, she finds La Belle Dame Sans Merci, she finds Juliet or Tess or Salomé, but precisely what she does not find is that absorbed, drudging, puzzled, sometimes inspired creature, herself, who sits at a desk trying to put words together.

So what does she do? What did I do? I read the older women poets with their peculiar keenness and ambivalence: Sappho, Christina Rossetti, Emily Dickinson, Elinor Wylie, Edna Millay, H.D. I discovered that the woman poet most admired at the time (by men) was Marianne Moore, who was maidenly, elegant, intellectual, discreet. But even in reading these women I was looking in them for the same things I had found in the poetry of men, because I wanted women poets to be the equals of men, and to be equal was still confused with sounding the same.

I know that my style was formed first by male poets: by the men I was reading as an undergraduate—Frost, Dylan Thomas, Donne, Auden, MacNiece, Stevens, Yeats. What I chiefly learned from them was craft.[5] But poems are like dreams: in them you put what you don't know you know. Looking back at poems I wrote before I was twenty-one, I'm startled because beneath the conscious craft are glimpses of the split I even then experienced between the girl who wrote poems, who defined herself in writing poems, and the girl who was to define herself by her relationships with men. "Aunt Jennifer's Tigers" (1951), written while I was a student, looks with deliberate detachment at this split.[6]

Aunt Jennifer's tigers stride across a screen,
Bright topaz denizens of a world of green.
They do not fear the men beneath the tree;
They pace in sleek chivalric certainty.

Aunt Jennifer's fingers fluttering through her wool
Find even the ivory needle hard to pull.
The massive weight of Uncle's wedding band
Sits heavily upon Aunt Jennifer's hand.

When Aunt is dead, her terrified hands will lie
Still ringed with ordeals she was mastered by.
The tigers in the panel that she made
Will go on striding, proud and unafraid.

In writing this poem, composed and apparently cool as it is, I thought
I was creating a portrait of an imaginary woman. But this woman
suffers from the opposition of her imagination, worked out in tap-
estry, and her life-style, "ringed with ordeals she was mastered by."
It was important to me that Aunt Jennifer was a person as distinct
from myself as possible—distanced by the formalism of the poem, by
its objective, observant tone—even by putting the woman in a different generation.

In those years formalism was part of the strategy—like asbestos
gloves, it allowed me to handle materials I couldn't pick up bare-
handed. A later strategy was to use the persona of a man, as I did in
"The Loser" (1958):

*A man thinks of the woman he once loved: first, after her wedding,
and then nearly a decade later.*

I
I kissed you, bride and lost, and went
home from that bourgeois sacrament,
your cheek still tasting cold upon
my lips that gave you benison

with all the swagger that they knew—
as losers somehow learn to do.

Your wedding made my eyes ache; soon
the world would be worse off for one
more golden apple dropped to ground
without the least protesting sound,
and you would windfall lie, and we
forget your shimmer on the tree.

Beauty is always wasted: if
not Mignon's song sung to the deaf,
at all events to the unmoved.
A face like yours cannot be loved
long or seriously enough.
Almost, we seem to hold it off.

II
Well, you are tougher than I thought.
Now when the wash with ice hangs taut
this morning of St. Valentine,
I see you strip the squeaking line,
your body weighed against the load,
and all my groans can do no good.

Because you are still beautiful,
though squared and stiffened by the pull
of what nine windy years have done.
You have three daughters, lost a son.
I see all your intelligence
flung into that unwearied stance.

My envy is of no avail.
I turn my head and wish him well
who chafed your beauty into use
and lives forever in a house

lit by the friction of your mind.
You stagger in against the wind.

I finished college, published my first book by a fluke, as it seemed to me, and broke off a love affair. I took a job, lived alone, went on writing, fell in love. I was young, full of energy, and the book seemed to mean that others agreed I was a poet. Because I was also determined to prove that as a woman poet I could also have what was then defined as a "full" woman's life, I plunged in my early twenties into marriage and had three children before I was thirty. There was nothing overt in the environment to warn me: these were the fifties, and in reaction to the earlier wave of feminism, middle-class women were making careers of domestic perfection, working to send their husbands through professional schools, then retiring to raise large families. People were moving out to the suburbs, technology was going to be the answer to everything, even sex; the family was in its glory. Life was extremely private; women were isolated from each other by the loyalties of marriage. I have a sense that women didn't talk to each other much in the fifties—not about their secret emptinesses, their frustrations. I went on trying to write; my second book and first child appeared in the same month. But by the time that book came out I was already dissatisfied with those poems, which seemed to me mere exercises for poems I hadn't written. The book was praised, however, for its "gracefulness"; I had a marriage and a child. If there were doubts, if there were periods of null depression or active despairing, these could only mean that I was ungrateful, insatiable, perhaps a monster.

About the time my third child was born, I felt that I had either to consider myself a failed woman and a failed poet, or to try to find some synthesis by which to understand what was happening to me. What frightened me most was the sense of drift, of being pulled along on a current which called itself my destiny, but in which I seemed to be losing touch with whoever I had been, with the girl who had experienced her own will and energy almost ecstatically at times, walking around a city or riding a train at night or typing in a student room. In a poem about my grandmother I wrote (of myself):

"A young girl, thought sleeping, is certified dead" ("Halfway"). I was writing very little, partly from fatigue, that female fatigue of suppressed anger and loss of contact with my own being; partly from the discontinuity of female life with its attention to small chores, errands, work that others constantly undo, small children's constant needs. What I did write was unconvincing to me; my anger and frustration were hard to acknowledge in or out of poems because in fact I cared a great deal about my husband and my children. Trying to look back and understand that time I have tried to analyze the real nature of the conflict. Most, if not all, human lives are full of fantasy—passive day-dreaming which need not be acted on. But to write poetry or fiction, or even to think well, is not to fantasize, or to put fantasies on paper. For a poem to coalesce, for a character or an action to take shape, there has to be an imaginative transformation of reality which is in no way passive. And a certain freedom of the mind is needed—freedom to press on, to enter the currents of your thought like a glider pilot, knowing that your motion can be sustained, that the buoyancy of your attention will not be suddenly snatched away. Moreover, if the imagination is to transcend and transform experience it has to question, to challenge, to conceive of alternatives, perhaps to the very life you are living at that moment. You have to be free to play around with the notion that day might be night, love might be hate; nothing can be too sacred for the imagination to turn into its opposite or to call experimentally by another name. For writing is re-naming. Now, to be maternally with small children all day in the old way, to be with a man in the old way of marriage, requires a holding-back, a putting-aside of that imaginative activity, and demands instead a kind of conservatism. I want to make it clear that I am *not* saying that in order to write well, or think well, it is necessary to become unavailable to others, or to become a devouring ego. This has been the myth of the masculine artist and thinker; and I do not accept it. But to be a female human being trying to fulfill traditional female functions in a traditional way *is* in direct conflict with the subversive function of the imagination. The word traditional is important here. There must be ways, and we will be finding out more and more about them, in which the energy of creation and the energy of relation can be united. But in those years I always felt the conflict as a failure of love in myself. I had thought I was choosing a full life: the life available to most men, in which sexuality, work, and parenthood could coexist. But I felt, at twenty-nine, guilt toward the people closest to me, and guilty toward my own being.

I wanted, then, more than anything, the one thing of which there was never enough: time to think, time to write. The fifties and early sixties were years of rapid revelations: the sit-ins and marches in the South, the Bay of Pigs, the early antiwar movement, raised large questions—questions for which the masculine world of the academy around me seemed to have expert and fluent answers. But I needed to think for myself—about pacifism and dissent and violence, about poetry and society, and about my own relationship to all these things. For about ten years I was reading in fierce snatches, scribbling in notebooks, writing poetry in fragments; I was looking desperately for clues, because if there were no clues then I thought I might be insane. I wrote in a notebook about this time:

> Paralyzed by the sense that there exists a mesh of relationships—e.g., between my anger at the children, my sensual life, pacifism, sex (I mean sex in its broadest significance, not merely sexual desire)—an interconnectedness which, if I could see it, make it valid, would give me back myself, make it possible to function lucidly and passionately. Yet I grope in and out among these dark webs.

I think I began at this point to feel that politics was not something "out there" but something "in here" and of the essence of my condition.

In the late fifties I was able to write, for the first time, directly about experiencing myself as a woman. The poem was jotted in fragments during children's naps, brief hours in a library, or at 3:00 A.M. after rising with a wakeful child. I despaired of doing any continuous work at this time. Yet I began to feel that my fragments and scraps had a common consciousness and a common theme, one which I would have been very unwilling to put on paper at an earlier time because I had been taught that poetry should be "universal," which meant, of course, nonfemale. Until then I had tried very much *not* to identify myself as a female poet. Over two years I wrote a ten-part poem called "Snapshots of a Daughter-in-Law" (1958–1960), in a longer looser mode than I'd ever trusted myself with before. It was an extraordinary relief to write that poem. It strikes me now as too literary, too dependent on allusion; I hadn't found the courage yet to do without authorities, or even to use the pronoun "I"—the woman in the poem is always "she." One section of it, No. 2, concerns a woman who thinks she is going mad; she is haunted by voices telling her to resist and rebel, voices which she can hear but not obey.

2.
Banging the coffee-pot into the sink
she hears the angels chiding, and looks out
past the raked gardens to the sloppy sky.
Only a week since They said: *Have no patience.*

The next time it was: *Be insatiable.*
Then: *Save yourself; others you cannot save.*
Sometimes she's let the tapstream scald her arm,
a match burn to her thumbnail,

or held her hand above the kettle's snout
right in the woolly steam. They are probably angels,
since nothing hurts her anymore, except
each morning's grit blowing into her eyes.

The poem "Orion," written five years later, is a poem of reconnection with a part of myself I had felt I was losing—the active principle, the energetic imagination, the "half-brother" whom I projected, as I had for many years, into the constellation Orion. It's no accident that the words "cold and egotistical" appear in this poem, and are applied to myself.

Far back when I went zig-zagging
through tamarack pastures
you were my genius, you
my cast-iron Viking, my helmed
lion-heart king in prison.
Years later now you're young

my fierce half-brother, staring
down from that simplified west
your breast open, your belt dragged down
by an oldfashioned thing, a sword
the last bravado you won't give over
though it weighs you down as you stride

and the stars in it are dim
and maybe have stopped burning.
But you burn, and I know it;
as I throw back my head to take you in
an old transfusion happens again:
divine astronomy is nothing to it.

Indoors I bruise and blunder,
break faith, leave ill enough
alone, a dead child born in the dark.
Night cracks up over the chimney,
pieces of time, frozen geodes
come showering down in the grate.

A man reaches behind my eyes
and finds them empty
a woman's head turns away
from my head in the mirror
children are dying my death
and eating crumbs of my life.

Pity is not your forte.
Calmly you ache up there
pinned aloft in your crow's nest,
my speechless pirate!
You take it all for granted
and when I look you back

it's with a starlike eye
shooting its cold and egotistical spear
where it can do least damage.
Breathe deep! No hurt, no pardon
out here in the cold with you
you with your back to the wall.

The choice still seemed to be between "love"—womanly, maternal love, altruistic love—a love defined and ruled by the weight of an entire culture; and egotism—a force directed by men into creation, achievement, ambition, often at the expense of others, but justifiably so. For weren't they men, and wasn't that their destiny as womanly, selfless love was ours? We know now that the alternatives are false ones—that the word "love" is itself in need of re-vision.

There is a companion poem to "Orion," written three years later, in which at last the woman in the poem and the woman writing the poem become the same person. It is called "Planetarium," and it was written after a visit to a real planetarium, where I read an account of the work of Caroline Herschel, the astronomer, who worked with her brother William, but whose name remained obscure, as his did not.

Thinking of Caroline Herschel, 1750–1848, astronomer, sister of William; and others

A woman in the shape of a monster
a monster in the shape of a woman
the skies are full of them

a woman   "in the snow
among the Clocks and instruments
or measuring the ground with poles"

in her 98 years to discover
8 comets

she whom the moon ruled
like us
levitating into the night sky
riding the polished lenses

Galaxies of women, there
doing penance for impetuousness
ribs chilled
in those spaces   of the mind

An eye,
          "virile, precise and absolutely certain"
          from the mad webs of Uranisborg
                                        encountering the NOVA

every impulse of light exploding
from the core
as life flies out of us
                    Tycho whispering at last
                    "Let me not seem to have lived in vain"

What we see, we see
and seeing is changing

the light that shrivels a mountain
and leaves a man alive

Heartbeat of the pulsar
heart sweating through my body

The radio impulse
pouring in from Taurus

      I am bombarded yet   I stand

I have been standing all my life in the
direct path of a battery of signals
the most accurately transmitted most
untranslateable language in the universe
I am a galactic cloud so deep   so invo-
luted that a light wave could take 15
years to travel through me   And has
taken   I am an instrument in the shape
of a woman trying to translate pulsations
into images   for the relief of the body
and the reconstruction of the mind.

In closing I want to tell you about a dream I had last summer. I dreamed I was asked to read my poetry at a mass women's meeting, but when I began to read, what came out were the lyrics of a blues song. I share this dream with you because it seemed to me to say something about the problems and the future of the woman writer, and probably of women in general. The awakening of consciousness is not like the crossing of a frontier—one step and you are in another country. Much of woman's poetry has been of the nature of the blues song: a cry of pain, of victimization, or a lyric of seduction.[7] And today, much poetry by women—and prose for that matter—is charged with anger. I think we need to go through that anger, and we will betray our own reality if we try, as Virginia Woolf was trying, for an objectivity, a detachment, that would make us sound more like Jane Austen or Shakespeare. We know more than Jane Austen or Shakespeare knew: more than Jane Austen because our lives are more complex, more than Shakespeare because we know more about the lives of women—Jane Austen and Virginia Woolf included.

Both the victimization and the anger experienced by women are real, and have real sources, everywhere in the environment, built into society, language, the structures of thought. They will go on being tapped and explored by poets, among others. We can neither deny them, nor will we rest there. A new generation of women poets is already working out of the psychic energy released when women begin to move out towards what the feminist philosopher Mary Daly has described as the "new space" on the boundaries of patriarchy.[8] Women are speaking to and of women in these poems, out of a newly released courage to name, to love each other, to share risk and grief and celebration.

To the eye of a feminist, the work of Western male poets now writing reveals a deep, fatalistic pessimism as to the possibilities of change, whether societal or personal, along with a familiar and threadbare use of women (and nature) as redemptive on the one hand, threatening on the other; and a new tide of phallocentric sadism and overt woman-hating which matches the sexual brutality of recent films. "Political" poetry by men remains stranded amid the struggles for power among male groups; in condemning U.S. imperialism or the Chilean junta the poet can claim to speak for the oppressed while remaining, as male, part of a system of sexual oppression. The enemy is always outside the self, the struggle somewhere else. The mood of isolation, self-pity, and self-imitation that pervades "nonpolitical" poetry suggests that a profound change in masculine consciousness will have to precede any new male poetic—or other—inspiration. The creative energy of patriarchy is fast running out; what remains is its self-generating energy for destruction. As women, we have our work cut out for us.

JANE EYRE

The Temptations of a Motherless Woman (1973)

Like Thackeray's daughters, I read *Jane Eyre* in childhood, carried away "as by a whirlwind." Returning to Charlotte Brontë's most famous novel, as I did over and over in adolescence, in my twenties, thirties, now in my forties, I have never lost the sense that it contains, through and beyond the force of its creator's imagination, some nourishment I needed then and still need today. Other novels often ranked greater, such as *Persuasion, Middlemarch, Jude the Obscure, Madame Bovary, Anna Karenina, The Portrait of a Lady*—all offered their contradictory and compelling versions of what it meant to be born a woman. But *Jane Eyre* has for us now a special force and survival value.

Comparing *Jane Eyre* to *Wuthering Heights*, as people tend to do, Virginia Woolf had this to say:

> The drawbacks of being Jane Eyre are not far to seek. Always to be a governess and always to be in love is a serious limitation in a world which is full, after all, of people who are neither one nor the other. . . . [Charlotte Brontë] does not attempt to solve the problems of human life; she is even unaware that such problems exist; all her force, which is the more tremendous for being constricted, goes into the assertion, "I love," "I hate," "I suffer" . . .[1]

She goes on to state that Emily Brontë is a greater poet than Charlotte because "there is no 'I' in *Wuthering Heights*. There are no gov-

First given as a lecture at Brandeis University in 1972, the essay was first published in *Ms.* 2, no. 4 (October 1973).

ernesses. There are no employers. There is love, but not the love of men and women." In short, and here I would agree with her, *Wuthering Heights* is mythic. The bond between Catherine and Heathcliff is the archetypal bond between the split fragments of the psyche, the masculine and feminine elements ripped apart and longing for reunion. But *Jane Eyre* is different from *Wuthering Heights*, and not because Charlotte Brontë lodged her people in a world of governesses and employers, of the love between men and women. *Jane Eyre* is not a novel in the Tolstoyan, the Flaubertian, even the Hardyesque sense. *Jane Eyre* is a tale.

The concern of the tale is not with social mores, though social mores may occur among the risks and challenges encountered by the protagonist. Neither is it an anatomy of the psyche, the fated chemistry of cosmic forces. It takes its place between the two: between the realm of the given, that which is changeable by human activity, and the realm of the fated, that which lies outside human control: between realism and poetry. The world of the tale is above all a "vale of soul-making," and when a novelist finds herself writing a tale, it is likely to be because she is moved by that vibration of experience which underlies the social and political, though it constantly feeds into both of these.

In her essay on *Jane Eyre*, critic Q. D. Leavis perceives the novel's theme as ". . . an exploration of how a woman comes to maturity in the world of the writer's youth."[2] I would suggest that a novel about how a man "comes to maturity in the world of the writer's youth"— *Portrait of the Artist*, for example—would not be dismissed as lacking in range, or, in Woolf's words, a sense of "human problems." I would suggest further, that Charlotte Brontë is writing—not a *Bildungsroman*—but the life story of a woman who is *incapable* of saying *I am Heathcliff* (as the heroine of Emily's novel does) because she feels so unalterably herself. Jane Eyre, motherless and economically powerless, undergoes certain traditional female temptations, and finds that each temptation presents itself along with an alternative—the image of a nurturing or principled or spirited woman on whom she can model herself, or to whom she can look for support.

II

In *Women and Madness* Phyllis Chesler notes that "women are motherless children in patriarchal society." By this she means that women
have had neither power nor wealth to hand on to their daughters;
they have been dependent on men as children are on women; and
the most they can do is teach their daughters the tricks of surviving
in the patriarchy by pleasing, and attaching themselves to, powerful or economically viable men:[3] Even the heiress in nineteenth-
century fiction is incomplete without a man; her wealth, like
Dorothea Brooke's or Isabel Archer's, must be devoted to the support
of some masculine talent or dilettantism; economically the heiress
is, simply, a "good match" and marriage her only real profession. In
nineteenth-century England the poor and genteel woman had one
possible source of independence if she did not marry: the profession
of governess. But, as I have suggested, Jane Eyre is *not* "always a
governess." She addresses us first as a literally motherless, and also
fatherless child, under the guardianship of her aunt, Mrs. Reed,
who despises and oppresses her. The tale opens with images of coldness, bleakness, banishment. Jane is seated behind the curtains in a
window-embrasure, trying to conceal herself from her aunt, her two
girl cousins, and her boorish boy cousin John. With the icy coldness
of the winter landscape outside on one hand, this chilly family circle
on the other, she looks at a book of engravings of Arctic wastes and
legendary regions of winter.

III

Moments after the novel begins, John Reed provokes Jane's childish
rage by striking her in the face and taunting her with her poverty
and dependency. Thus, immediately, the political/social circumstances of Jane's life are established: as a female she is exposed
to male physical brutality and whim; as an economically helpless
person she is vulnerable in a highly class-conscious society. Her
response to John's gratuitous cruelty is to "fly at him" and threat to

be dragged off and locked into the "Red Room," where her uncle had died and which is rumored to be a haunted chamber.

Here begins the ordeal which represents Jane's first temptation. For a powerless little girl in a hostile household, where both psychic and physical violence are used against her, used indeed to punish her very spiritedness and individuality, the temptation of victimization is never far away. To see herself as the sacrificial lamb or scapegoat of this household, and act out that role, or conversely to explode into violent and self-destructive hysterics which can only bring on more punishment and victimization, are alternatives all too ready at hand.

In the Red Room, Jane experiences the bitter isolation of the outsider, the powerlessness of the scapegoat to please, the abjectness of the victim. But above all, she experiences her situation as unnatural:

> Unjust—unjust! said my reason, forced by the agonizing stimulus into precocious though transitory power; and Resolve, equally wrought up, instigated some strange expedient to achieve escape from insupportable oppression—as running away, or if that could not be effected, never eating or drinking more, and letting myself die.

I want to recall to you that the person who is going through this illumination—for "dark" and "turbid" as her feelings are, they are illuminating—is a girl of ten, without material means or any known recourse in the outer world, dependent on the household she lives in for physical support and whatever strands of human warmth she can cling to. She is, even so, conscious that it could be otherwise; she imagines alternatives, though desperate ones. It is at this moment that the germ of the person we are finally to know as Jane Eyre is born: a person determined to live, and to choose her life with dignity, integrity, and pride.

Jane's passion in the Red Room comes to its climax; she hallucinates, screams, is thrust back into the dreaded death-chamber, and blacks out. Her ensuing illness, like much female illness, is an acting-out of her powerlessness and need for affection, and a psychic crisis induced by these conditions. During her convalescence from this "fit," she experiences for the first time the decency of the family apothecary and the gentle and caring side of the sharp-tongued young servant Bessie. Bessie is the first woman to show Jane affection; and it is partly the alliance with her that makes it possible for the child Jane to maintain her hope for the future, her will to survive; which prevents her from running away—a self-destructive act under the circumstances—or from relapsing into mere hysteria or depression. It is this, too, which helps her retain the self-respect and the spirit of rebellion in which she finally confronts her aunt:

> Shaking from head to foot, thrilled with ungovernable excitement, I continued—

> "I am glad you are no relation of mine. I will never call you aunt again as long as I live. I will never come to see you when I am grown up; and if anyone asks me how I liked you, and how you treated me, I will say the very thought of you makes me sick, and that you treated me with miserable cruelty."

> . . . Ere I had finished this reply, my soul began to expand, to exult, with the strangest sense of freedom, of triumph, I ever felt. It seemed as if an invisible bond had burst and that I had struggled out into unhoped-for liberty.

This outburst, like much anger of the powerless, leaves Jane only briefly elated. The depressive, self-punishing reaction sets in; she is only pulled out of it by Bessie's appearance and a confirmed sense of Bessie's affection and respect for her. Bessie tells her that she must not act afraid of people, because it will make them dislike her—an odd aslant bit of counsel, yet Jane's precocious courage is able to respond. The next chapter finds Jane on her way to Lowood Insitution.

IV

Lowood is a charity school for the poor or orphaned genteel female destined to become a governess. It is a school for the poor controlled by the rich, an all-female world presided over by the hollow, Pharisaical male figure of Mr. Brocklehurst. He is the embodiment of class and sexual double-standards and of the hypocrisy of the powerful, using religion, charity, and morality to keep the poor in their place and to repress and humiliate the young women over whom he is set in charge. He is absolute ruler of this little world. However, within it, and in spite of his sadistic public humiliation of her, Jane finds two women unlike any she has ever met: the superintendent Miss Temple, and the older student Helen Burns.

Miss Temple has no power in the world at large, or against Mr. Brocklehurst's edicts; but she has great personal attractiveness, mental and spiritual charm and strength. Unlike the Reeds, she is of gentle birth yet not a snob; unlike Bessie she is not merely sympathetic but admirable. She cannot change the institution she is hired to administer but she does quietly try to make life more bearable for its inmates. She is maternal in a special sense: not simply sheltering and protective, but encouraging of intellectual growth. Of her Jane says later in the novel:

> . . . to her instruction, I owed the best part of my acquirements; her friendship and society had been my continual solace; she had stood me in the stead of mother, governess, and latterly, companion.

Helen Burns is strong of will, awkward and blundering in the practical world yet intellectually and spiritually mature beyond her years. Severe, mystical, convinced of the transitory and insignificant nature of earthly life, she still responds to Jane's hunger for contact with a humane and sisterly concern. She is consumptive, soon to die, burning with an other-worldly intensity. Jane experiences Helen's religious asceticism as something impossible for herself, tinged with "an inexpressible sadness"; yet Helen gives her a glimpse of female character without pettiness, hysteria, or self-repudiation; it is Helen who tells her,

> "If all the world hated you, and believed you wicked, while your own conscience approved you, and absolved you from guilt, you would not be without friends."

Both Miss Temple's self-respect and sympathy, and Helen's transcendent philosophical detachment, are needed by Jane after her early humiliation by Mr. Brocklehurst. For if at Gateshead Hall Jane's temptations were victimization and hysteria, at Lowood, after her public ordeal, they are self-hatred and self-immolation.

Jane is acutely conscious of her need for love: she expresses it passionately to Helen Burns.

> ". . . to gain some real affection from you, or Miss Temple, or any other whom I truly love, I would willingly submit to have the bone of my arm broken, or to let a bull toss me, or to stand behind a kicking horse, and let it dash its hoof at my chest—"

Her need for love is compounded with a female sense that love must be purchased through suffering and self-sacrifice; the images that come to her are images of willing submission to violence, of masochism. Helen calms her, tells her she thinks "too much of the love of human beings," calls on her to think beyond this life to the reward God has prepared for the innocent beyond the grave. Like Simone Weil, like St. Teresa, like Héloïse, Helen Burns substitutes a masculine God for the love of earthly men (or women)—a pattern followed by certain gifted imaginative women in the Christian era.

The discipline of Lowood and the moral and intellectual force of Helen and Miss Temple combine to give the young Jane a sense of her own worth and of ethical choice. Helen dies of consumption with Jane in her arms held like "a little child"; Miss Temple later marries an "excellent clergyman" and leaves Lowood. Thus Jane loses her first real mothers. Yet her separation from these two women enables Jane to move forward into a wider realm of experience.

My world had for some years been in Lowood: my experience had been of its rules and systems; now I remembered that the real world was wide ...

I desired liberty; for liberty I gasped; for liberty I uttered a prayer; it seemed scattered on the wind then faintly blowing. I abandoned it and framed a humbler supplication. For change, stimulus. That petition, too, seemed swept off into vague space. "Then," I cried, half desperate, "grant me at least a new servitude!"

One of the impressive qualities of Charlotte Brontë's heroines, the quality which makes them more valuable to the woman reader than Anna Karenina, Emma Bovary, and Catherine Earnshaw combined, is their determined refusal of the romantic. They are not immune to it; in fact, they are far more tempted by it than are the cooler-headed heroines of Jane Austen; there is far more in their circumstances of orphaned wandering and intellectual eroticism to heat their imaginations—they *have*, in fact, more imagination. Jane Eyre is a passionate girl and woman; but she displays early an inner clarity which helps her to distinguish between intense feelings which can lead to greater fulfillment, and those which can only lead to self-destructiveness. The thrill of masochism is not for her, though it is one of her temptations as we have seen; having tasted a drop of it, she rejects it. In the central episode of the novel, her meeting with Mr. Rochester at Thornfield, Jane, young, inexperienced, and hungry for experience, has to confront the central temptation of the female condition—the temptation of romantic love and surrender.

V

It is interesting that the Thornfield episode is often recalled or referred to as if it *were* the novel *Jane Eyre*. So truncated and abridged, that novel would become the following: A young woman arrives as governess at a large country house inhabited by a small French girl and an older housekeeper. She is told that the child is the ward of the master of the house, who is traveling abroad. Presently the master comes home and the governess falls in love with him, and he with her. Several mysterious and violent incidents occur in the house which seem to center around one of the servants, and which the master tells the governess will all be explained once they are married. On the wedding day, it is revealed that he has a wife still alive, a madwoman who is kept under guard in the upper part of the house and who is the source of the sinister incidents. The governess decides that her only course of action is to leave her lover forever. She steals away from the house and settles in another part of the country. After some time she returns to the manor house to find it has burned to the ground, the madwoman is dead, and her lover, though blinded and maimed by the fire, is free to marry her.

Thus described, the novel becomes a blend of Gothic horror and Victorian morality. That novel might have been written by many a contributor to ladies' magazines, but it is not the novel written by Charlotte Brontë. If the Thornfield episode is central, it is because in it Jane comes to womanhood and to certain definitive choices about what it means to her to be a woman. There are three aspects of this episode: the house, Thornfield itself; Mr. Rochester, the Man; and the madwoman, Jane's alter ego.

Charlotte Brontë gives us an extremely detailed and poetically convincing vision of Thornfield. Jane reaches its door by darkness, after a long journey; she scarcely knows what the house is like till the next day when Mrs. Fairfax, the housekeeper, takes her through it on a tour which ends in the upper regions, on the rooftop. The reader's sense of its luxury, its isolation, and its mysteries is precisely Jane's, seen with the eyes of a young woman just come from the dormitory of a charity school—a young woman of strong sensuality. But it is the upper regions of the house which are of crucial importance—the part of the house Jane lives in least, yet which most affects her life. Here she first hears that laugh—"distinct, formal, mirthless"—which is ascribed to the servant Grace Poole and which she will later hear outside her own bedroom door. Here, too, standing on the roof, or walking up and down in the corridor, close to the very door behind which the madwoman is kept hidden, she gives silent vent to those feelings which are introduced by the telling phrase: "Anybody may blame me who likes . . ."

The phrase introduces a passage which is Charlotte Brontë's feminist manifesto. Written one hundred and twenty-six years ago, it is still having to be written over and over today, in different language but with essentially the same sense that sentiments of this kind are still unacceptable to many, and that in uttering them one lays oneself open to blame and to entrenched resistance:

> It is in vain to say human beings ought to be satisfied with tranquility: they must have action; and they will make it if they cannot find it. Millions are condemned to a stiller doom than mine, and millions are in silent revolt against their lot. Nobody knows how many rebellions besides political rebellions ferment in the masses of life which people earth. Women are supposed to be very calm generally; but women feel just as men feel; they need exercise for their faculties, and a field for their efforts as much as their brothers do; they suffer from too rigid a restraint, too absolute a stagnation, precisely as men would suffer; and it is narrow-minded in their more privileged fellow-creatures to say that they ought to confine themselves to making puddings and knitting stockings, to playing on the piano and embroidering bags. It is thoughtless to condemn them, or laugh at them, if they seek to do more or learn more than custom has pronounced necessary for their sex.

Immediately thereafter we are made to hear again the laugh of the madwoman. I want to remind you of another mad wife who appears in a novel of our own time—the woman Lynda in Doris Lessing's *The Four-Gated City*, who inhabits not the upper story but the cellar, and with whom the heroine Martha (like Jane Eyre an employee and in love with her employer) finally goes to live, experiencing her madness with her.

For Jane Eyre, the upper regions are not what Gaston Bachelard calls in *The Poetics of Space* "the rationality of the roof" as opposed to the unconscious and haunted world of the cellar.[4] Or, the roof is where Jane is visited by an expanding vision, but this vision, this illumination, brings her close to the madwoman captive behind the door. In Lessing's novel the madwoman is herself a source of illumination. Jane has no such contact with Bertha Rochester. Yet Jane's sense of herself as a woman—as equal to and with the same needs as a man—is next-door to insanity in England in the 1840s. Jane never feels herself to be going mad, but there is a madwoman in the house who exists as her opposite, her image horribly distorted in a warped mirror, a threat to her happiness. Just as her instinct for self-preservation saves her from earlier temptations, so it must save her from becoming this woman by curbing her imagination at the limits of what is bearable for a powerless woman in the England of the 1840s.

VI

We see little of Bertha Rochester; she is heard and sensed rather than seen. Her presence is revealed by three acts when she escapes into the inhabited part of the house. Two of these are acts of violence against men—the attempted burning of Mr. Rochester in his bed-chamber, and the stabbing of her brother when he visits Thornfield. The third act is the visit to Jane's bedroom on the night before her wedding and the tearing of the wedding veil, the symbol of matrimony. (She does not, interestingly enough, attack Jane.) Only after Bertha's existence is publicly revealed is Jane taken into the mad-woman's chamber and sees again, waking, "that purple face—those bloated features." Bertha is described as big, corpulent, virile, with a "grizzled mane" of hair like an animal's; earlier Jane had seen her as resembling "the foul German spectre—the Vampyr." In all this she is the antithesis of Jane, as Mr. Rochester points out:

> "That is *my wife*," said he. "Such is the sole conjugal embrace I
> am ever to know—such are the endearments which are to solace
> my leisure hours! And *this* is what I wished to have" (laying his
> hand on my shoulder) "this young girl, who stands so grave and

quiet at the mouth of hell, looking collectedly at the gambols of
a demon . . ."

In his long account of the circumstances of his marriage to
Bertha—a marriage arranged for financial reasons by his father, but
which he undertook for Bertha's dark sensual beauty—Rochester
makes no pretense that he was not acting out of lust. Yet he repeatedly asserts *her* coarseness, "at once intemperate and unchaste," as
the central fact of his loathing for her. Once she is pronounced mad,
he has her locked up, and goes forth on a life of sexual adventures,
one result of which has been the child Adèle, daughter of his French
mistress. Rochester's story is part Byronic romance, but it is based
on a social and psychological reality: the nineteenth-century loose
woman might have sexual feelings, but the nineteenth-century *wife*
did not and must not; Rochester's loathing of Bertha is described
repeatedly in terms of her physical strength and her violent will—
both unacceptable qualities in the nineteenth-century female, raised
to the nth degree and embodied in a monster.

VII

Mr. Rochester is often seen as the romantic Man of Fate, Byronic,
brooding, sexual. But his role in the book is more interesting: he is
certainly that which culture sees as Jane's fate, but he is not the fate
she has been seeking. When she leaves Lowood for Thornfield, when
she stands on the roof of Thornfield or walks across its fields longing for a wider, more expansive life, she is not longing for a man.
We do not know what she longs for, she herself does not know; she
uses terms like liberty, a new servitude, action. Yet the man appears,
romantically and mysteriously, in the dusk, riding his horse—and
slips and falls on the ice, so that Jane's first contact with him is with
someone in need of help; he has to lean on her to regain his seat
on horseback. Again at the novel's end it is she who must lead him,
blinded by fire. There is something more working here than the
introduction of a stock romantic hero.

Mr. Rochester offers Jane wider horizons than any she has known; travel, riches, brilliant society. Throughout the courtship there is a tension between her growing passion for him and her dislike of and uneasiness with the *style* of his love-making. It is not Rochester's sensuality that brings her up short, but his tendency to make her his object, his creature, to want to dress her up, lavish jewels on her, remake her in another image. She strenuously resists being romanticized as a beauty or a houri; she will, she tells him, be no part of his harem.

In his determination to possess Jane, Rochester is arrogant enough to lie to her three times. During the house party at which Jane, as governess, has to suffer the condescension and contempt of the ladies of the neighborhood, Rochester, disguised as an old Gypsy woman, comes to the door to read fortunes, and he attempts to trick Jane into revealing her feelings for him. It is clear, in this scene, that Rochester is well aware of the strength of Jane's character and is uneasy as to the outcome of his courtship and the kind of marriage he is going to propose to her. In making as if to read Jane's fate in her features, he tells her:

> ". . . that brow professes to say—'I can live alone, if self-respect and circumstances require me to do so. I need not sell my soul to buy bliss. I have an inward treasure born with me, which can keep me alive if all the extraneous delights should be withheld, or offered only at a price I cannot afford to give.'"

Abruptly, at the end of this scene, he reveals himself. But he continues to carry on a flirtation with the heiress Miss Ingram, in order to arouse Jane's jealousy; he pretends to the last possible moment that he intends to marry Miss Ingram, till Jane, in turmoil at the prospect, confesses her grief at having to leave him. Her grief—but also, her anger at the position in which she has been placed:

> "I tell you I must go!" I retorted, roused to something like passion. "Do you think I can stay to become nothing to you? Do you think I am automaton?—a machine without feelings? . . . Do

you think because I am poor, obscure, plain, and little, I am soulless and heartless? You think wrong!—I have as much soul as you—and full as much heart! . . . I am not talking to you now through the medium of custom, conventionalities, nor even of mortal flesh: it is my spirit that addresses your spirit; just as if both had passed through the grave and we stood at God's feet, equal—as we are!"

(Always a governess and always in love? Had Virginia Woolf really read this novel?)

VIII

Jane's parting interview with Mr. Rochester is agonizing; he plays on every chord of her love, her pity and sympathy, her vulnerability. On going to bed, she has a dream. Carried back to the Red Room, the scene of her first temptation, her first ordeal, in the dream, Jane is reminded of the "syncope," or swoon, she underwent there, which became a turning point for her; she is then visited by the moon, symbol of the matriarchal spirit and the "Great Mother of the night sky."[5]

I watched her come—watched with the strangest anticipation; as though some word of doom were to be written on her disc. She broke forth as moon never yet burst from cloud: a hand first penetrated the sable folds and waved them away; then, not a moon, but a white human form shone in the azure, inclining a glorious brow earthward. It gazed and gazed on me. It spoke to my spirit: immeasurably distant was the tone, yet so near, it whispered in my heart—

"My daughter, flee temptation."

"Mother, I will."

Her dream is profoundly, imperiously, archetypal. She is in danger, as she was in the Red Room; but her own spiritual consciousness is stronger in womanhood than it was in childhood; she is in touch with the matriarchal aspect of her psyche which now warns and protects her against that which threatens her integrity. Bessie, Miss Temple, Helen Burns, even at moments the gentle housekeeper Mrs. Fairfax, have acted as mediators for her along the way she has come thus far; even, it may be said, the terrible figure of Bertha has come between Jane and a marriage which was not yet ripe, which would have made her simply the dependent adjunct of Mr. Rochester instead of his equal. Individual women have helped Jane Eyre to the point of her severest trial; at that point she is in relation to the Great Mother herself. On waking from this dream, she leaves Thornfield, with a few pieces of clothing and twenty shillings in her purse, to set forth on foot to an unknown destination.

Jane's rebellion against Rochester's arrogance—for in pleading with her to stay with him against the laws of her own integrity, he is still arrogant—forces her to act on her own behalf even if it causes him intense suffering, even though she still loves him. Like many women in similar circumstances, she feels that such an act of self-preservation requires her to pay dearly. She goes out into the world without a future, without money, without plans—a "poor, obscure, plain, and little" figure of a woman, risking exposure to the elements, ostracism, starvation. By an act which one can read as a final unconscious sacrificial gesture, she forgets her purse with its few shillings in the stagecoach, and thus is absolutely destitute, forced to beg for the leftovers a farmer's wife is about to feed to her pig. In this whole portion of the novel, in which Jane moves through the landscape utterly alone, there is a strong counterpull between female self-immolation—the temptation of passive suicide—and the will and courage which are her survival tools.

She is literally saved from death by two sisters, Diana and Mary, living in a parsonage with their brother, the clergyman St. John Rivers. Diana and Mary bear the names of the pagan and Christian aspects of the Great Goddess—Diana or Artemis, the Virgin huntress, and Mary the Virgin Mother. These women are unmarried bluestockings; they delight in learning; in their remote parsonage they study German and read poetry aloud. They live as intellectual equals with their brother; yet with Jane, in her illness and convalescence, they are maternally tender and sensitive. As time passes and Jane recovers and begins to teach in the village school, Diana and Mary become her friends; for the first time since the death of Helen Burns she has an intellectually sympathetic companionship with young women of her own age.

Once again, a man offers her marriage. St. John has been observing her for his own purposes, and finding her "docile, diligent, disinterested, faithful, constant, and courageous; very gentle, and very heroic" he invites her to accompany him as his fellow-missionary to India, where he intends to live and die in the service of his God. He needs a helpmate to work among Indian women; he offers her marriage without love, a marriage of duty and service to a cause. The cause is of course defined by him; it is the cause of patriarchal religion: self-denying, stern, prideful, and ascetic. In a sense he offers her the destiny of Milton's Eve: "He for God only, she for God in him." What St. John offers Jane is perhaps the deepest lure for a spiritual woman, that of adopting a man's cause or career and making it her own. For more than one woman, still today, the felt energy of her own existence is still diffuse, the possibilities of her life vague; the man who pressures to define it for her may be her most confusing temptation. *He* will give shape to her search for meaning, her desire for service, her feminine urge toward self-abnegation: in short—as Jane becomes soon aware—he will *use* her.

But St. John is offering Jane this "meaning" under the rubric of marriage—and from this "use" of herself she draws back in healthy repulsion.

> Can I receive from him the bridal ring, endure all the forms of love (which I doubt not he would scrupulously observe) and know that the spirit was quite absent? Can I bear the consciousness that every endearment he bestows is a sacrifice made on principle? No: such martyrdom would be monstrous. . . .

As his curate, his comrade, all would be right: I would cross
oceans with him in that capacity; toil under Eastern suns, in
Asian deserts with him . . . admire and emulate his courage and
devotion . . . smile undisturbed at his ineradicable ambition;
discriminate the Christian from the man; profoundly esteem
the one, and freely forgive the other. . . . But as his wife—at his
side always, and always restrained, and always checked—forced
to keep the fire of my nature continually low . . . *this* would be
unendurable. . . .

"If I were to marry you, you would kill me. You are killing me
now" [she tells him].

His lips and cheeks turned white—quite white.

I should kill you—I am killing you? Your words are such as
ought not to be used—they are violent, unfeminine [*sic!*] and
untrue . . ."

So she refuses his cause; and so he meets her refusal. In the mean-
time she has inherited an income; she has become independent; and
at this point an extrasensory experience calls her back to Thornfield.

IX

"Reader, I married him." These words open the final chapter of
Jane Eyre. The question is, how and why is this a happy ending?
Jane returns to Thornfield to find it "a blackened ruin"; she discovers Rochester, his left hand amputated and his eyes blinded by the
fire in which he vainly attempted to save the life of his mad wife.
Rochester has paid his dues; a Freudian critic would say he has been
symbolically castrated. Discarding this phallic-patriarchal notion of
his ordeal, we can then ask, what kind of marriage is possible for a
woman like Jane Eyre?

Certainly not marriage with a castrate, psychic or physical. (St.
John repels Jane in part because he is *emotionally* castrated.) The

wind that blows through this novel is the wind of sexual equality—spiritual and practical. The passion that Jane feels as a girl of twenty or as a wife of thirty is the same passion—that of a strong spirit demanding its counterpart in another. Mr. Rochester needs Jane now—

> ". . . to bear with my infirmities . . . to overlook my deficiencies."

> "Which are none, sir, to me."

She feels, after ten years of marriage, that "I am my husband's life as fully as he is mine." This feeling is not that of romantic love or romantic marriage.

> To be together is for us to be at once as free as in solitude, as gay as in company. We talk—I believe, all day long; to talk to each other is but a more animated and an audible thinking.

Coming to her husband in economic independence and by her free choice, Jane can become a wife without sacrificing a grain of her Jane Eyre-ity. Charlotte Brontë sets up the possibility of this relationship in the early passages of the Thornfield episode, the verbal sparring of this couple who so robustly refuse to act out the paradigms of romantic, Gothic fiction. We believe in the erotic and intellectual sympathy of this marriage because it has been prepared by the woman's refusal to accept it under circumstances which were mythic, romantic, or sexually oppressive. The last paragraphs of the novel concern St. John Rivers: whose ambition is that of "the high master-spirit, which aims to a place in the first rank of those who are redeemed from the earth—who stand without fault before the throne of God, who share the last victories of the Lamb, who are called, and chosen, and faithful." We can translate St. John's purism into any of a number of kinds of patriarchal arrogance of our own day, whether political, intellectual, aesthetic, or religious. It is clear that Charlotte Brontë believes that human relations require something quite different: a transaction between people which is "without painful shame or damping humiliation" and in which nobody is made into an object for the use of anybody else.

In telling the tale of Jane Eyre, Charlotte Brontë was quite conscious, as she informed her publisher, that she was not telling a moral tale. Jane is not bound by orthodoxy, though superficially she is a creature of her time and place. As a child, she rejects the sacredness of adult authority; as a woman, she insists on regulating her conduct by the pulse of her own integrity. She will not live with Rochester as his dependent mistress because she knows that relationship would become destructive to her; she would live unmarried with St. John as an independent co-worker; it is he who insists this would be immoral. The beauty and depth of the novel lie in part in its depiction of alternatives—to convention and traditional piety, yes, but also to social and cultural reflexes internalized within the female psyche. In *Jane Eyre*, moreover, we find an alternative to the stereotypical rivalry of women; we see women in real and supportive relationship to each other, not simply as points on a triangle or as temporary substitutes for men. Marriage is the completion of the life of Jane Eyre, as it is for Miss Temple and Diana and Mary Rivers; but for Jane at least it is marriage radically understood for its period, in no sense merely a solution or a goal. It is not patriarchal marriage in the sense of a marriage that stunts and diminishes the woman; but a continuation of this woman's creation of herself.

VESUVIUS AT HOME

The Power of Emily Dickinson (1975)

I am traveling at the speed of time, along the Massachusetts Turn-pike. For months, for years, for most of my life, I have been hovering like an insect against the screens of an existence which inhabited Amherst, Massachusetts, between 1830 and 1886. The methods, the exclusions, of Emily Dickinson's existence could not have been my own; yet more and more, as a women poet finding my own methods, I have come to understand her necessities, could have been witness in her defense.

"Home is not where the heart is," she wrote in a letter, "but the house and the adjacent buildings." A statement of New England realism, a directive to be followed. Probably no poet ever lived so much and so purposefully in one house; even, in one room. Her niece Martha told of visiting her in her corner bedroom on the second floor at 280 Main Street, Amherst, and of how Emily Dickinson made as if to lock the door with an imaginary key, turned, and said: "Matty: here's freedom."

I am traveling at the speed of time, in the direction of the house and buildings.

Western Massachusetts: the Connecticut Valley: a countryside still full of reverberations: scene of Indian uprisings, religious revivals, spiritual confrontations, the blazing-up of the lunatic fringe of the Puritan coal. How peaceful and how threatened it looks from Route 91, hills gently curled above the plain, the tobacco barns

This essay was read in its earliest form as a lecture at Brandeis University, and in its present version as one of the Lucy Martin Donnelly lectures at Bryn Mawr College. It was first printed in *Parnassus: Poetry in Review* 5, no. 1 (Fall–Winter 1976).

standing in fields sheltered with white gauze from the sun, and the sudden urban sprawl: ARCO, McDonald's, shopping plazas. The country that broke the heart of Jonathan Edwards, that enclosed the genius of Emily Dickinson. It lies calmly in the light of May, cloudy skies breaking into warm sunshine, light-green spring softening the hills, dogwood and wild fruit-trees blossoming in the hollows.

From Northampton bypass there's a four-mile stretch of road to Amherst—Route 9—between fruit farms, steakhouses, supermarkets. The new University of Massachusetts rears its skyscrapers up from the plain against the Pelham Hills. There is new money here, real estate, motels. Amherst succeeds on Hadley almost without notice. Amherst is green, rich-looking, secure; we're suddenly in the center of town, the crossroads of the campus, old New England college buildings spread around two village greens, a scene I remember as almost exactly the same in the dim past of my undergraduate years when I used to come there for college weekends.

Left on Seelye Street, right on Main; driveway at the end of a yellow picket fence. I recognize the high hedge of cedars screening the house, because twenty-five years ago I walked there, even then drawn toward the spot, trying to peer over. I pull into the driveway behind a generous nineteenth-century brick mansion with wings and porches, old trees and green lawns. I ring at the back door—the door through which Dickinson's coffin was carried to the cemetery a block away.

For years I have been not so much envisioning Emily Dickinson as trying to visit, to enter her mind, through her poems and letters, and through my own intimations of what it could have meant to be one of the two mid–nineteenth-century American geniuses, and a woman, living in Amherst, Massachusetts. Of the other genius, Walt Whitman, Dickinson wrote that she had heard his poems were "disgraceful." She knew her own were unacceptable by her world's standards of poetic convention, and of what was appropriate, in particular, for a woman poet. Seven were published in her lifetime, all edited by other hands; more than a thousand were laid away in her bedroom chest, to be discovered after her death. When her sister discovered them, there were decades of struggle over the manuscripts, the manner of their presentation to the world, their suitability for publication, the poet's own final intentions. Narrowed-down by her early editors and anthologists, reduced to quaintness or spinsterish oddity by many of her commentators, sentimentalized, fallen-in-love with like some gnomic Garbo, still unread in the breadth and depth of her full range of work, she was, and is, a wonder to me when I try to imagine myself into that mind.

I have a notion that genius knows itself; that Dickinson chose her seclusion, knowing she was exceptional and knowing what she needed. It was, moreover, no hermetic retreat, but a seclusion which included a wide range of people, of reading and correspondence. Her sister Vinnie said, "Emily is always looking for the rewarding person." And she found, at various periods, both women and men: her sister-in-law Susan Gilbert, Amherst visitors and family friends such as Benjamin Newton, Charles Wadsworth, Samuel Bowles, editor of the Springfield *Republican*, and his wife; her friends Kate Anthon and Helen Hunt Jackson, the distant but significant figures of Elizabeth Barrett, the Brontës, George Eliot. But she carefully selected her society and controlled the disposal of her time. Not only the "gentlewomen in plush" of Amherst were excluded; Emerson visited next door but she did not go to meet him; she did not travel or receive routine visits; she avoided strangers. Given her vocation, she was neither eccentric nor quaint; she was determined to survive, to use her powers, to practice necessary economies.

Suppose Jonathan Edwards had been born a woman; suppose William James, for that matter, had been born a woman? (The invalid seclusion of his sister Alice is suggestive.) Even from men, New England took its psychic toll; many of its geniuses seemed peculiar in one way or another, particularly along the lines of social intercourse. Hawthorne, until he married, took his meals in his bedroom, apart from the family. Thoreau insisted on the values both of solitude and of geographical restriction, boasting that "I have traveled much in Concord." Emily Dickinson—viewed by her bemused contemporary Thomas Higginson as "partially cracked," by the twentieth century as fey or pathological—has increasingly struck me as a practical woman, exercising her gift as she had to, making choices.

I have come to imagine her as somehow too strong for her environment, a figure of powerful will, not at all frail or breathless, someone whose personal dimensions would be felt in a household. She was her father's favorite daughter though she professed being afraid of him. Her sister dedicated herself to the everyday domestic labors which would free Dickinson to write. (Dickinson herself baked the bread, made jellies and gingerbread, nursed her mother through a long illness, was a skilled horticulturalist who grew pomegranates, calla lilies, and other exotica in her New England greenhouse.)

Upstairs at last: I stand in the room which for Emily Dickinson was "freedom." The best bedroom in the house, a corner room, sunny, overlooking the main street of Amherst in front, the way to her brother Austin's house on the side. Here, at a small table with one drawer, she wrote most of her poems. Here she read Elizabeth Barrett's *Aurora Leigh*, a woman poet's narrative poem of a woman poet's life; also George Eliot; Emerson; Carlyle; Shakespeare; Charlotte and Emily Brontë. Here I become, again, an insect, vibrating at the frames of windows, clinging to panes of glass, trying to connect. The scent here is very powerful. Here in this white-curtained, high-ceilinged room, a red-haired woman with hazel eyes and a contralto voice wrote poems about volcanoes, deserts, eternity, suicide, physical passion, wild beasts, rape, power, madness, separation, the daemon, the grave. Here, with a darning needle, she bound these poems—heavily emended and often in variant versions—into booklets, secured with darning thread, to be found and read after her death. Here she knew "freedom," listening from above-stairs to a visitor's piano-playing, escaping from the pantry where she was mistress of the household bread and puddings, watching, you feel, watching ceaselessly, the life of sober Main Street below. From this room she glided downstairs, her hand on the polished bannister, to meet the complacent magazine editor, Thomas Higginson, unnerve him while claiming she herself was unnerved. "Your scholar," she signed herself in letters to him. But she was an independent scholar, used his criticism selectively, saw him rarely and always on *her* premises. It was a life deliberately organized on her terms. The terms she had been handed by society—Calvinist Protestantism, Romanticism, the nineteenth-century corseting of women's bodies, choices, and sexuality—could spell insanity to a woman genius. What this one had to do was retranslate her own unorthodox, subversive, sometimes volcanic propensities into a dialect called metaphor: her native language. "Tell all the Truth—but tell it Slant—." It is always what is under pressure in us, especially under pressure of concealment—that explodes in poetry.

The women and men in her life she equally converted into metaphor. The masculine pronoun in her poems can refer simultaneously to many aspects of the "masculine" in the patriarchal world—the god she engages in dialogue, again on *her* terms; her own creative powers, unsexing for a woman, the male power-figures in her immediate environment—the lawyer Edward Dickinson, her brother Austin, the preacher Wadsworth, the editor Bowles—it is far too limiting to trace that "He" to some specific lover, although that was the chief obsession of the legend-mongers for more than half a century. Obviously, Dickinson was attracted by and interested in men whose minds had something to offer her; she was, it is by now clear, equally attracted by and interested in women whose minds had something to offer. There are many poems to and about women, and some which exist in two versions with alternate sets of pronouns. Her latest biographer, Richard Sewall, rejecting an earlier Freudian biographer's theory that Dickinson was essentially a psychopathological case, the by-product of which happened to be poetry, creates a context in which the importance, and validity, of Dickinson's attachments to women may now, at last, be seen in full. She was always stirred by the existences of women like George Eliot or Elizabeth Barrett, who possessed strength of mind, articulateness, and energy. (She once characterized Elizabeth Fry and Florence Nightingale as "holy"—one suspects she merely meant, "great.")

But of course Dickinson's relationships with women were more than intellectual. They were deeply charged, and the sources both of passionate joy and pain. We are only beginning to be able to consider then in a social and historical context. The historian Carroll Smith-Rosenberg has shown that there was far less taboo on intense, even passionate and sensual, relationships between women in the

American nineteenth-century "female world of love and ritual," as she terms it, than there was later in the twentieth century. Women expressed their attachments to other women both physically and verbally; a marriage did not dilute the strength of a female friend-ship, in which two women often shared the same bed during long visits, and wrote letters articulate with both physical and emotional longing. The nineteenth-century close woman friend, according to the many diaries and letters Smith-Rosenberg has studied, might be a far more important figure in a woman's life than the nineteenth-century husband. None of this was perceived or condemned as "les-bianism."[1] We will understand Emily Dickinson better, read her poetry more perceptively, when the Freudian imputation of scandal and aberrance in women's love for women has been supplanted by a more informed, less misogynistic attitude toward women's experi-ences with each other.

But who, if you read through the seventeen hundred and seventy-five poems—who—woman or man—could have passed through that imagination and not come out transmuted? Given the space created by her in that corner room, with its window-light, its potted plants and work-table, given that personality, capable of imposing its terms on a household, on a whole community, what single theory could hope to contain her, when she'd put it all together in that space?

"Matty: here's freedom," I hear her saying as I speed back to Boston along the turnpike, as I slip the ticket into the toll-collector's hand. I am thinking of a confined space in which the genius of the nineteenth-century female mind in America moved, inventing a lan-guage more varied, more compressed, more dense with implications, more complex of syntax, than any American poetic language to date; in the trail of that genius my mind has been moving, and with its language and images my mind still has to reckon, as the mind of a woman poet in America today.

In 1971, a postage stamp was issued in honor of Dickinson; the portrait derives from the one existing daguerrotype of her, with straight, center-parted hair, eyes staring somewhere beyond the camera, hands poised around a nosegay of flowers, in correct nineteenth-century style. On the first-day-of-issue envelope sent

als—One—imperial—Thunderbolt—
at scalps your naked Soul—

hen Winds take Forests in their Paws—
e Universe—is still—

15)

uch energy has been invested in trying to identify a con-
, flesh-and-blood male lover whom Dickinson is supposed to
renounced, and to the loss of whom can be traced the secret
er seclusion and the vein of much of her poetry. But the real
tion, given that the art of poetry is an art of transformation, is
this woman's mind and imagination may have used the mas-
e element in the world at large, or those elements personified
asculine—including the men she knew; how her relationship
is reveals itself in her images and language. In a patriarchal
ure, specifically the Judeo-Christian, quasi-Puritan culture of
teenth-century New England in which Dickinson grew up, still
med with religious revivals, and where the sermon was still
ctive, if perishing, literary form, the equation of divinity with
eness was so fundamental that it is hardly surprising to find
inson, like many an early mystic, blurring erotic with religious
erience and imagery. The poem I just read has intimations both
eduction and rape merged with the intense force of a religious
erience. But are these metaphors for each other, or for something
e intrinsic to Dickinson? Here is another:

He put the Belt around my life—
heard the Buckle snap—
And turned away, imperial,
My Lifetime folding up—
Deliberate, as a Duke would do
A Kingdom's Title Deed—
Henceforth, a Dedicated sort—
A member of the Cloud.

me by a friend there is, besides the postage stamp
of the poet as popular fancy has preferred her, in a
and with hair as bouffant as if she had just stepped
beauty-parlor. The poem chosen to represent her wo
ican public is engraved, alongside a dew-gemmed
portrait:

> If I can stop one heart from breaking
> I shall not live in vain
> If I can ease one life the aching
> Or cool one pain
> Or help one fainting robin
> Unto his nest again
> I shall not live in vain.

Now, this is extremely strange. It is a fact that, in 186
inson wrote this verse; and it is a verse which a hu
nineteenth-century versifiers could have written. I
guished language, as in its conventional sentiment, it
untypical of the poet. Had she chosen to write many
one we would have no "problem" of nonpublication, of
mating the poet at her true worth. Certainly the sen
tented and unambiguous altruism—is one which even
some quarters be accepted as fitting from a female ve
of Girl Scout prayer. But we are talking about the wom

> He fumbles at your Soul
> As Players at the Keys
> Before they drop full Music on—
> He stuns you by degrees—
> Prepares your brittle Nature
> For the Ethereal Blow
> By fainter Hammers—further heard—
> Then nearer—Then so slow
> Your breath has time to straighten—
> Your brain—to bubble Cool—

Yet not too far to come at call—
And do the little Toils
That make the Circuit of the Rest—
And deal occasional smiles
To lives that stoop to notice mine—
And kindly ask it in—
Whose invitation, know you not
For Whom I must decline?

(#273)

These two poems are about possession, and they seem to me a poet's poems—that is, they are about the poet's relationship to her own power, which is exteriorized in masculine form, much as masculine poets have invoked the female Muse. In writing at all—particularly an unorthodox and original poetry like Dickinson's—women have often felt in danger of losing their status as women. And this status has always been defined in terms of relationship to men—as daughter, sister, bride, wife, mother, mistress, Muse. Since the most powerful figures in patriarchal culture have been men, it seems natural that Dickinson would assign a masculine gender to that in herself which did not fit in with the conventional ideology of womanliness. To recognize and acknowledge our own interior power has always been a path mined with risks for women; to acknowledge that power and commit oneself to it as Emily Dickinson did was an immense decision.

Most of us, unfortunately, have been exposed in the schoolroom to Dickinson's "little-girl" poems, her kittenish tones, as in "I'm Nobody! Who Are You?" (a poem whose underlying anger translates itself into archness) or

I hope the Father in the skies
Will lift his little girl—
Old fashioned—naughty—everything—
Over the stile of "Pearl."

(#70)

or the poems about bees and robins. One critic—Richard Chase—
has noted that in the nineteenth century "one of the careers open
to women was perpetual childhood." A strain in Dickinson's letters and some—though by far a minority—of her poems was a
self-diminutivization, almost as if to offset and deny—or even
disguise—her actual dimensions as she must have experienced them.
And this emphasis on her own "littleness," along with the deliberate strangeness of her tactics of seclusion, have been, until recently,
accepted as the prevailing character of the poet: the fragile poetess
in white, sending flowers and poems by messenger to unseen friends,
letting down baskets of gingerbread to the neighborhood children
from her bedroom window; writing, but somehow naively. John
Crowe Ransom, arguing for the editing and standardization of Dickinson's punctuation and typography, calls her "a little home-keeping
person" who, "while she had a proper notion of the final destiny of
her poems . . . was not one of those poets who had advanced to that
later stage of operations where manuscripts are prepared for the
printer, and the poet's diction has to make concessions to the publisher's style-book." (In short, Emily Dickinson did not wholly know
her trade, and Ransom believes a "publisher's style-book" to have the
last word on poetic diction.) He goes on to print several of her poems,
altered by him "with all possible forbearance." What might, in a
male writer—a Thoreau, let us say, or a Christopher Smart or William Blake—seem a legitimate strangeness, a unique intention, has
been in one of our two major poets devalued into a kind of naiveté,
girlish ignorance, feminine lack of professionalism, just as the poet
herself has been made into a sentimental object. ("Most of us are half
in love with this dead girl," confesses Archibald MacLeish. Dickinson was fifty-five when she died.)

It is true that more recent critics, including her most recent biographer, have gradually begun to approach the poet in terms of her
greatness rather than her littleness, the decisiveness of her choices
instead of the surface oddities of her life or the romantic crises of her
legend. But unfortunately anthologists continue to plagiarize other
anthologies, to reprint her in edited, even bowdlerized versions;

the popular image of her and of her work lags behind the changing consciousness of scholars and specialists. There still does not exist a selection from her poems which depicts her in her fullest range. Dickinson's greatness cannot be measured in terms of twenty-five or fifty or even five hundred "perfect" lyrics; it has to be seen as the accumulation it is. Poets, even, are not always acquainted with the full dimensions of her work, or the sense one gets, reading in the one-volume complete edition (let alone the three-volume variorum edition) of a mind engaged in a lifetime's musing on essential problems of language, identity, separation, relationship, the integrity of the self; a mind capable of describing psychological states more accurately than any poet except Shakespeare. I have been surprised at how narrowly her work, still, is known by women who are writing poetry, how much her legend has gotten in the way of her being repossessed, as a source and a foremother.

I know that for me, reading her poems as a child and then as a young girl already seriously writing poetry, she was a problematic figure. I first read her in the selection heavily edited by her niece which appeared in 1937; a later and fuller edition appeared in 1945 when I was sixteen, and the complete, unbowdlerized edition by Johnson did not appear until fifteen years later. The publication of each of these editions was crucial to me in successive decades of my life. More than any other poet, Emily Dickinson seemed to tell me that the intense inner event, the personal and psychological, was inseparable from the universal; that there was a range for psychological poetry beyond mere self-expression. Yet the legend of the life was troubling, because it seemed to whisper that a woman who undertook such explorations must pay with renunciation, isolation, and incorporeality. With the publication of the *Complete Poems*, the legend seemed to recede into unimportance beside the unquestionable power and importance of the mind revealed there. But taking possession of Emily Dickinson is still no simple matter.

The 1945 edition, entitled *Bolts of Melody*, took its title from a poem which struck me at the age of sixteen and which still, thirty years later, arrests my imagination:

I would not paint—a picture—
I'd rather be the One
Its bright impossibility
To dwell—delicious—on—
And wonder how the fingers feel
Whose rare—celestial—stir
Evokes so sweet a Torment—
Such sumptuous—Despair—

I would not talk, like Cornets—
I'd rather be the One
Raised softly to the Ceilings—
And out, and easy on—
Through Villages of Ether
Myself endured Balloon
By but a lip of Metal
The pier to my Pontoon—

Nor would I be a Poet—
It's finer—own the Ear—
Enamored—impotent—content—
The License to revere,
A privilege so awful
What would the Dower be,
Had I the Art to stun myself
With Bolts of Melody!

(#505)

This poem is about choosing an orthodox "feminine" role: the receptive rather than the creative; viewer rather than painter, listener rather than musician; acted-upon rather than active. Yet even while ostensibly choosing this role she wonders "how the fingers feel/ whose rare-celestial—stir—/ Evokes so sweet a Torment—" and the "feminine" role is praised in a curious sequence of adjectives: "Enamored—*impotent*—content—." The strange paradox of this poem—its exquisite irony—is that it is about choosing not to be a poet, a poem which is gainsaid by no fewer than one thousand seven hundred and seventy-five poems made during the writer's life, including itself. Moreover, the images of the poem rise to a climax (like the Balloon she evokes) but the climax happens as she describes, not what it is to be the receiver, but the maker and receiver at once: "A Privilege so awful/ What would the Dower be/ Had I the Art to stun myself/ With Bolts of Melody!"—a climax which recalls the poem: "He fumbles at your Soul/ As Players at the Keys/ Before they drop full Music on—" And of course, in writing those lines she possesses herself of that privilege and that Dower. I have said that this is a poem of exquisite ironies. It is, indeed, though in a very different mode, related to Dickinson's "little-girl" strategy. The woman who feels herself to be Vesuvius at home has need of a mask, at least, of innocuousness and of containment.

On my volcano grows the Grass
A meditative spot—
An acre for a Bird to choose
Would be the General thought—

How red the Fire rocks below—
How insecure the sod
Did I disclose
Would populate with awe my solitude.
(#1677)

Power, even masked, can still be perceived as destructive.

A still—Volcano—Life—
That flickered in the night—
When it was dark enough to do
Without erasing sight—

A quiet—Earthquake style—
Too subtle to suspect
By natures this side Naples—
The North cannot detect

The Solemn—Torrid—Symbol—
The lips that never lie—
Whose hissing Corals part—and shut—
And Cities—ooze away—
(#601)

Dickinson's biographer and editor Thomas Johnson has said that she often felt herself possessed by a daemonic force, particularly in the years 1861 and 1862 when she was writing at the height of her drive. There are many poems besides "He put the Belt around my Life" which could be read as poems of possession by the daemon—poems which can also be, and have been, read, as poems of possession by the deity, or by a human lover. I suggest that a woman's poetry about her relationship to her daemon—her own active, creative power—has in patriarchal culture used the language of heterosexual love or patriarchal theology. Ted Hughes tells us that

> the eruption of [Dickinson's] imagination and poetry followed when she shifted her passion, with the energy of desperation, from [the] lost man onto his only possible substitute,—the Universe in its Divine aspect. . . . Thereafter, the marriage that had been denied in the real world, went forward in the spiritual . . . just as the Universe in its Divine aspect became the mirror-image of her "husband," so the whole religious dilemma of New England, at that most critical moment in history, became the mirror-image of her relationship to him, of her "marriage" in fact.[2]

This seems to me to miss the point on a grand scale. There are facts we need to look at. First, Emily Dickinson did not marry. And her nonmarrying was neither a pathological retreat as John Cody sees it, nor probably even a conscious decision; it was a fact in her life as in her contemporary Christina Rossetti's; both women had more primary needs. Second: unlike Rossetti, Dickinson did not become a religiously dedicated woman; she was heretical, heterodox, in her religious opinions, and stayed away from church and dogma.

What, in fact, *did* she allow to "put the Belt around her Life"—what *did* wholly occupy her mature years and possess her? For "Whom" did she decline the invitations of other lives? The writing of poetry. Nearly two thousand poems. Three hundred and sixty-six poems in the year of her fullest power. What was it like to be writing poetry you knew (and I am sure she did know) was of a class by itself—to be fueled by the energy it took first to confront, then to condense that range of psychic experience into that language; then to copy out the poems and lay them in a trunk, or send a few here and there to friends or relatives as occasional verse or as gestures of confidence? I am sure she knew who she was, as she indicates in this poem:

Myself was formed—a Carpenter—
An unpretending time
My Plane—and I, together wrought
Before a Builder came—

To measure our attainments
Had we the Art of Boards
Sufficiently developed—He'd hire us
At Halves—

My Tools took Human—Faces—
The Bench, where we had toiled—
Against the Man—persuaded—
We—Temples Build—I said—
(#488)

This a poem of the great year 1862, the year in which she first sent a few poems to Thomas Higginson for criticism. Whether it antedates or postdates that occasion is unimportant; it is a poem of knowing one's measure, regardless of the judgments of others.

There are many poems which carry the weight of this knowledge. Here is another one:

I'm ceded—I've stopped being Theirs—
The name They dropped upon my face
With water, in the country church
Is finished using, now,
And They can put it with my Dolls,
My childhood, and the string of spools,
I've finished threading—too—

Baptized before, without the choice,
But this time, consciously, of Grace—
Unto supremest name—
Called to my Full—The Crescent dropped—
Existence's whole Arc, filled up,
With one small Diadem.

My second Rank—too small the first—
Crowned—Crowing—on my Father's breast—
A half unconscious Queen—
But this time—Adequate—Erect—
With Will to choose, or to reject—
And I choose, just a Crown—
(#508)

Now, this poem partakes of the imagery of being "twice-born" or, in Christian liturgy, "confirmed"—and if this poem had been written by Christina Rossetti I would be inclined to give more weight to a theological reading. But it was written by Emily Dickinson, who used the Christian metaphor far more than she let it use her. This is a poem of great pride—not pridefulness, but *self*-confirmation— and it is curious how little Dickinson's critics, perhaps misled by her diminutives, have recognized the will and pride in her poetry. It is a poem of movement from childhood to womanhood, of transcending the patriarchal condition of bearing her father's name and "crowing—on my Father's breast—." She is now a conscious Queen "Adequate—Erect/ With Will to choose, or to reject—."

There is one poem which is the real "onlie begetter" of my thoughts here about Dickinson; a poem I have mused over, repeated to myself, taken into myself over many years. I think it is a poem about possession by the daemon, about the dangers and risks of such possession if you are a woman, about the knowledge that power in a woman can seem destructive, and that you cannot live without the daemon once it has possessed you. The archetype of the daemon as masculine is beginning to change, but it has been real for women up until now. But this woman poet also perceives herself as a lethal weapon:

My life had stood—a Loaded Gun—
In Corners—till a Day
The Owner passed—identified—
And carried Me away—

And now We roam in Sovereign Woods—
And now We hunt the Doe—
And every time I speak for Him—
The Mountains straight reply—

And do I smile, such cordial light
Upon the Valley glow—
It is as a Vesuvian face
Had let its pleasure through—

And when at Night—Our good Day done—
I guard My Master's Head—
'Tis better than the Eider-Duck's
Deep Pillow—to have shared—

To foe of His—I'm deadly foe—
None stir the second time—
On whom I lay a Yellow Eye—
Or an emphatic Thumb—

Though I than He—may longer live
He longer must—than I—
For I have but the power to kill,
Without—the power to die—
(#754)

Here the poet sees herself as split, not between anything so simple
as "masculine" and "feminine" identity but between the hunter,
admittedly masculine, but also a human person, an active, willing
being, and the gun—an object, condemned to remain inactive until
the hunter—the *owner*—takes possession of it. The gun contains an
energy capable of rousing echoes in the mountains and lighting up
the valleys; it is also deadly, "Vesuvian"; it is also its owner's defender
against the "foe." It is the gun, furthermore, who *speaks for him.*
If there is a female consciousness in this poem it is buried deeper
than the images: it exists in the ambivalence toward power, which is
extreme. Active willing and creation in women are forms of aggression, and aggression is both "the power to kill" and punishable by
death. The union of gun with hunter embodies the danger of identifying and taking hold of her forces, not least that in so doing she
risks defining herself—and being defined—as aggressive, as unwomanly ("and now we hunt the Doe"), and as potentially lethal. That
which she experiences in herself as energy and potency can also be
experienced as pure destruction. The final stanza, with its precarious balance of phrasing, seems a desperate attempt to resolve the
ambivalence; but, I think, it is no resolution, only a further extension
of ambivalence.

Though I than He—may longer live
He longer must—than I—
For I have but the power to kill,
Without—the power to die—

The poet experiences herself as loaded gun, imperious energy; yet
without the Owner, the possessor, she is merely lethal. Should that

possession abandon her—but the thought is unthinkable: "He longer *must* than I." The pronoun is masculine; the antecedent is what Keats called "The Genius of Poetry."

I do not pretend to have—I don't even wish to have—explained this poem, accounted for its every image; it will reverberate with new tones long after my words about it have ceased to matter. But I think that for us, at this time, it is a central poem in understanding Emily Dickinson, and ourselves, and the condition of the woman artist, particularly in the nineteenth century. It seems likely that the nineteenth-century woman poet, especially, felt the medium of poetry as dangerous, in ways that the woman novelist did not feel the medium of fiction to be. In writing even such a novel of elemental sexuality and anger as *Wuthering Heights*, Emily Brontë could at least theoretically separate herself from her characters; they were, after all, fictitious beings. Moreover, the novel is or can be a construct, planned and organized to deal with human experiences on one level at a time. Poetry is too much rooted in the unconscious; it presses too close against the barriers of repression; and the nineteenth-century woman had much to repress. It is interesting that Elizabeth Barrett tried to fuse poetry and fiction in writing *Aurora Leigh*—perhaps apprehending the need for fictional characters to carry the charge of her experience as a woman artist. But with the exception of *Aurora Leigh* and Christina Rossetti's "Goblin Market"—that extraordinary and little-known poem drenched in oral eroticism—Emily Dickinson's is the only poetry in English by a woman of that century which pierces so far beyond the ideology of the "feminine" and the conventions of womanly feeling. To write it at all, she had to be willing to enter chambers of the self in which

Ourself behind ourself, concealed—
Should startle most—

and to relinquish control there, to take those risks, she had to create a relationship to the outer world where she could feel in control.

It is an extremely painful and dangerous way to live—split

between a publicly acceptable persona, and a part of yourself that you perceive as the essential, the creative and powerful self, yet also as possibly unacceptable, perhaps even monstrous.

> Much Madness is divinest Sense—
> To a discerning Eye—
> Much Sense—the starkest Madness—
> 'Tis the Majority
> In this, as All, prevail—
> Assent—and you are sane—
> Demur—you're   straightway   dangerous—
> And handled with a Chain—
> *(#435)*

For many women the stresses of this splitting have led, in a world so ready to assert our innate passivity and to deny our independence and creativity, to extreme consequences: the mental asylum, self-imposed silence, recurrent depression, suicide, and often severe loneliness.

Dickinson is *the* American poet whose work consisted in exploring states of psychic extremity. For a long time, as we have seen, this fact was obscured by the kinds of selections made from her work by timid if well-meaning editors. In fact, Dickinson was a great psychologist; and like every great psychologist, she began with the material she had at hand: herself. She had to possess the courage to enter, through language, states which most people deny or veil with silence.

> The first Day's Night had come—
> And grateful that a thing
> So terrible—had been endured—
> I told my Soul to sing—
>
> She said her Strings were snapt—
> Her Bow—to Atoms blown—
> And so to mend her—gave me work
> Until another Morn—

And then—a Day as huge
As Yesterdays in pairs,
Unrolled its horror in my face—
Until it blocked my eyes—

My Brain—begun to laugh—
I mumbled—like a fool—
And tho' 'tis Years ago—that Day—
My Brain keeps giggling—still.

And Something's odd—within—
That person that I was—
And this One—do not feel the same—
Could it be Madness—this?
(#410)

Dickinson's letters acknowledge a period of peculiarly intense personal crisis; her biographers have variously ascribed it to the pangs of renunciation of an impossible love, or to psychic damage deriving from her mother's presumed depression and withdrawal after her birth. What concerns us here is the fact that she chose to probe the nature of this experience in language:

The Soul has Bandaged moments—
When too appalled to stir—
She feels some ghastly Fright come up
And stop to look at her—

Salute her—with long fingers—
Caress her freezing hair—
Sip, Goblin, from the very lips
The Lover—hovered—o'er—
Unworthy, that a thought so mean
Accost a Theme—so—fair—

The soul has moments of Escape—
When bursting all the doors—
She dances like a Bomb, abroad,
And swings upon the Hours. . . .

The Soul's retaken moments—
When, Felon led along,
With shackles on the plumed feet,
And staples, in the Song,

The Horror welcomes her, again,
These, are not brayed of Tongue—
(#512)

In this poem, the word "Bomb" is dropped, almost carelessly, as a correlative for the soul's active, liberated states—it occurs in a context of apparent euphoria, but its implications are more than euphoric—they are explosive, destructive. The Horror from which in such moments the soul escapes has a masculine, "Goblin" form, and suggests the perverse and terrifying rape of a "Bandaged" and powerless self. In at least one poem, Dickinson depicts the actual process of suicide:

He scanned it—staggered—
Dropped the Loop
To Past or Period—
Caught helpless at a sense as if
His mind were going blind—

Groped up, to see if God was there—
Groped backward at Himself—
Caressed a Trigger absently
And wandered out of Life.
(#1062)

The precision of knowledge in this brief poem is such that we must assume that Dickinson had, at least in fantasy, drifted close to that state in which the "Loop" that binds us to "Past or Period" is "Dropped" and we grope randomly at what remains of abstract notions of sense, God, or self, before—almost absent-mindedly— reaching for a solution. But it's worth noting that this is a poem in which the suicidal experience has been distanced, refined, trans- formed through a devastating accuracy of language. It is not suicide that is studied here, but the dissociation of self and mind and world which precedes.

Dickinson was convinced that a life worth living could be found within the mind and against the grain of external circumstance: "Reverse cannot befall/ That fine prosperity/ Whose Sources are interior—" (#395). The horror, for her, was that which set "Staples in the Song"—the numbing and freezing of the interior, a state she describes over and over:

There is a Languor of the Life
More imminent than Pain—
'Tis Pain's Successor—When the Soul
Has suffered all it can—

A Drowsiness—diffuses—
A Dimness like a Fog
Envelopes Consciousness—
As Mists—obliterate a Crag.

The Surgeon—does not blanch—at pain—
His Habit—is severe—
But tell him that it ceased to feel—
The creature lying there—

And he will tell you—skill is late—
A Mightier than He—
Has ministered before Him—
There's no Vitality.

(#396)

I think the equation surgeon-artist is a fair one here; the artist can work with the materials of pain; she cuts to probe and heal; but she is powerless at the point where

> After great pain, a formal feeling comes—
> The Nerves sit ceremonious, like Tombs—
> The stiff Heart questions was it He, that bore,
> And Yesterday, or Centuries before?
>
> The Feet, mechanical, go round—
> Of Ground, or Air, or Ought—
> A Wooden way
> Regardless grown,
> A Quartz contentment, like a stone—
>
> This is the Hour of Lead
> Remembered, if outlived
> As Freezing persons, recollect the Snow—
> First—Chill—then Stupor—then the letting go—
> (#341)

For the poet, the terror is precisely in those periods of psychic death, when even the possibility of work is negated; her "occupation's gone." Yet she also describes the unavailing effort to numb emotion:

> Me from Myself—to banish—
> Had I Art—
> Impregnable my Fortress
> Unto All Heart—
>
> But since Myself—assault Me—
> How have I peace
> Except by subjugating
> Consciousness?

And since We're mutual Monarch
How this be
Except by Abdication—
Me—of Me?
(*#642*)

The possibility of abdicating oneself—of ceasing to be—remains.

Severer Service of myself
I—hastened to demand
To fill the awful Longitude
Your life had left behind—

I worried Nature with my Wheels
When Hers had ceased to run—
When she had put away Her Work
My own had just begun.

I strove to weary Brain and Bone—
To harass to fatigue
The glittering Retinue of nerves—
Vitality to clog

To some dull comfort Those obtain
Who put a Head away
They knew the Hair to—
And forget the color of the Day—

Affliction would not be appeased—
The Darkness braced as firm
As all my stratagem had been
The Midnight to confirm—

No Drug for Consciousness—can be—
Alternative to die
Is Nature's only Pharmacy
For Being's Malady—
(#786)

Yet consciousness—not simply the capacity to suffer, but the capacity to experience intensely at every instant—creates of death not a blotting-out but a final illumination:

This Consciousness that is aware
Of Neighbors and the Sun
Will be the one aware of Death
And that itself alone

Is traversing the interval
Experience between
And most profound experiment
Appointed unto Men—

How adequate unto itself
Its properties shall be
Itself unto itself and none
Shall make discovery.

Adventure most unto itself
The Soul condemned to be—
Attended by a single Hound
Its own identity.
(#822)

The poet's relationship to her poetry has, it seems to me—and I am not speaking only of Emily Dickinson—a twofold nature. Poetic language—the poem on paper—is a concretization of the poetry of the world at large, the self, and the forces within the self; and those forces are rescued from formlessness, lucidified, and integrated in the act of writing poems. But there is a more ancient concept of the poet, which is that she is endowed to speak for those who do not have the gift of language, or to see for those who—for whatever reasons—are less conscious of what they are living through. It is as though the risks of the poet's existence can be put to some use beyond her own survival.

> The Province of the Saved
> Should be the Art—To save—
> Through Skill obtained in Themselves—
> The Science of the Grave
>
> No Man can understand
> But He that hath endured
> The Dissolution—in Himself—
> That Man—be qualified
>
> To qualify Despair
> To Those who failing new—
> Mistake Defeat for Death—Each time—
> Till acclimated—to—
> (#539)

The poetry of extreme states, the poetry of danger, can allow its readers to go further in our own awareness, take risks we might not have dared; it says, at least: "Someone has been here before."

> The Soul's distinct Connection
> With immortality
> Is best disclosed by Danger
> Or quick Calamity—
>
> As Lightning on a Landscape
> Exhibits Sheets of Place—
> Not yet suspected—but for Flash—
> And Click—and Suddenness.
> (#974)

Crumbling is not an instant's Act
A fundamental pause
Dilapidation's processes
Are organized Decays.

'Tis first a Cobweb on the Soul
A Cuticle of Dust
A Borer in the Axis
An Elemental Rust—

Ruin is formal—Devil's work
Consecutive and slow—
Fail in an instant—no man did
Slipping—is Crash's law.
(#997)

I felt a Cleaving in my Mind
As if my Brain had split—
I tried to match it—Seam by Seam—
But could not make them fit.

The thought behind, I strove to join
Unto the thought before—
But Sequence ravelled out of Sound
Like Balls—upon a Floor.
(#937)

There are many more Emily Dickinsons than I have tried to call up here. Wherever you take hold of her, she proliferates. I wish I had time here to explore her complex sense of Truth; to follow the thread we unravel when we look at the numerous and passionate poems she wrote to or about women; to probe her ambivalent feelings about fame, a subject pursued by many male poets before her; simply to examine the poems in which she is directly apprehending the natural world. No one since the seventeenth century had reflected more variously or more probingly upon death and dying. What I have tried to do here is follow through some of the origins and consequences of her choice to be, not only a poet but a woman who explored her own mind, without any of the guidelines of orthodoxy. To say "yes" to her powers was not simply a major act of nonconformity in the nineteenth century; even in our own time it has been assumed that Emily Dickinson, not patriarchal society, was "the problem." The more we come to recognize the unwritten and written laws and taboos underpinning patriarchy, the less problematical, surely, will seem the methods she chose.

Uncollected

POETRY AND EXPERIENCE

Statement at a Poetry Reading (1964)

What a poem used to be for me, what it is today.

In the period in which my first two books were written I had a much more absolutist approach to the universe than I now have. I also felt—as many people still feel—that a poem was an arrangement of ideas and feelings, pre-determined, and it said what I had already decided it should say. There were occasional surprises, occasions of happy discovery that an unexpected turn could be taken, but control, technical mastery and intellectual clarity were the real goals, and for many reasons it was satisfying to be able to create this kind of formal order in poems.

Only gradually, within the last five or six years, did I begin to feel that these poems, even the ones I liked best and in which I felt I'd said most, were queerly limited; that in many cases I had suppressed, omitted, falsified even, certain disturbing elements, to gain that perfection of order. Perhaps this feeling began to show itself in a poem like "Rural Reflections," in which there is an awareness already that experience is always greater and more unclassifiable than we give it credit for being.

Today, I have to say that what I know I know through making poems. Like the novelist who finds that his characters begin to have a life of their own and to demand certain experiences, I find that I can no longer go to write a poem with a neat handful of materials and express those materials according to a prior plan: the poem itself

Transcribed by Rich and first published in "Adrienne Rich and the Poetics of Change" by Albert Gelpi, in *American Poetry Since 1960*, edited by Robert Shaw (Carcanet Press, 1973). Reprinted by permission of the publisher.

engenders new sensations, new awareness in me as it progresses. Without for one moment turning my back on conscious choice and selection, I have been increasingly willing to let the unconscious offer its materials, to listen to more than the one voice of a single idea. Perhaps a simple way of putting it would be to say that instead of poems *about* experiences I am getting poems that *are* experiences, that contribute to my knowledge and my emotional life even while they reflect and assimilate it. In my earlier poems I told you, as precisely and eloquently as I knew how, about something; in the more recent poems something is happening, something has happened to me and, if I have been a good parent to the poem, something will happen to you who read it.

from CARYATID

A Column (1973)

. . . . . .

I have just been reading three (two revised) volumes by Robert
Lowell, published by Farrar, Straus and Giroux. The first, called
History, is a reworking of the (already reworked) poems in the
second edition of *Notebook,* with 80 new poems added. From *Notebook* Lowell has lifted a group of poems dealing with his second marriage and his daughter, and published them separately in a volume
called *For Lizzie and Harriet.* These poems have also been revised
since they appeared in the *Notebook* versions. The third volume, *The
Dolphin,* consists of new poems which delineate Lowell's love-affair
with his present wife, his divorce and remarriage. Of these seventy-
odd poems, a number are placed in italics or quotation marks and are
presumably based on letters written to Lowell by his wife, the writer
Elizabeth Hardwick, during the period after he left her and through
the time of their divorce.

I don't know why Lowell felt he wanted to go on revising and
republishing old poems; why not let them stand and proceed on,
since life itself goes on? Perhaps, as he says, "the composition was
jumbled" in *Notebook;* but he chose, as a mature poet, to publish that
jumbled composition, and it represents his poetic and human choices
of that time. What does it mean to revise a poem? For every poet the

In 1973, *American Poetry Review*'s second year of publication, Rich contributed three
short pieces under the title "Caryatid" as regular columns in three successive issues.
The first two, "Vietnam and Sexual Violence" and "Natalya Gorbanevskaya," were
reprinted in *On Lies, Secrets, and Silence: Selected Prose 1966–1978.*

process must be different; but it is surely closer to pruning a tree than retouching a photograph. However, the intention behind *History* is clearly to produce a major literary document encompassing the élite Western sensibility of which Lowell is a late representative; a work to stand in competition with the great long poems of the past.

The lesson of *Notebook/History* is that brilliant language, powerful images, are not enough, and that they can become unbelievably boring in the service of an encapsulated ego. I remember *Notebook* as a book whose language sometimes dazzled even though it often seemed intentionally to blur and evade meaning, even though Lowell's own rather pedantic notion of surrealism led to a kind of image-making out of the intellect rather than the unconscious. I remember saying to a friend that in poem after poem, at the moment when you thought Lowell was about to cut to the bone, he veered off, lost the thread, abandoned the poem he'd begun in a kind of verbal *coitus interruptus*. In *History* it strikes me that this is poetry constructed in phrases, each hacked-out, hewn, tooled, glazed or burnished with immense expertise . . . but one gets tired of these phrases, they hammer on after awhile with a fearful and draining monotony. It becomes a performance, a method, language divorced from its breathing, vibrating sources to become, as Lowell himself says, a marble figure.

History is a book filled with people: Robespierre, Timur, Allen Tate, old classmates, old lovers, relatives, Che Guevara, Anne Boleyn, King David, poets dead and alive, Kennedys and kings. Or perhaps I should say that for his poetry Lowell *uses* real people, versifies and fictionalizes them at will, and thus attempts to reduce or dominate them. They are face-cards in a game of solitaire, but solitaire is what it remains.

There's a kind of aggrandized and merciless masculinity at work in these books, particularly the third, symptomatic of the dead-end destructiveness that masculine privilege has built for itself into all institutions, including poetry. I sense that the mind behind these poems knows—being omnivorously well-read—that "someone has suffered"—the Jews, Achilles, Sylvia Plath, his own wife—but is incapable of a true identification with the sufferers which might illuminate their condition for us. The poet's need to dominate and objectify the characters in his poems leaves him in an appalling way invulnerable. And the poetry, for all its verbal talent and skill, remains emotionally shallow.

Finally, what does one say about a poet who, having left his wife and daughter for another marriage, then titles a book with their names, and goes on to appropriate his ex-wife's letters written under the stress and pain of desertion, into a book of poems nominally addressed to the new wife? If this kind of question has nothing to do with art, we have come far from the best of the tradition Lowell would like to vindicate—or perhaps it cannot be vindicated. At the end of *The Dolphin* Lowell writes:

> I have sat and listened to too many
> words of the collaborating muse,
> and plotted perhaps too freely with my life
> not avoiding injury to others,
> not avoiding injury to myself—
> to ask compassion . . . this book, half fiction,
> an eelnet made by man for the eel fighting—
> my eyes have seen what my hand did.

I have to say that I think this is bullshit elequence, a poor excuse for a cruel and shallow book, that it is presumptuous to balance injury done to others with injury done to oneself—and that the question remains, after all—to what purpose? The inclusion of the letter-poems stands as one of the most vindictive and mean-spirited acts in the history of poetry, one for which I can think of no precedent; and the same unproportioned ego that was capable of this act is damagingly at work in all three of Lowell's books. . . .

Of Woman Born

Motherhood as Experience and Institution (1976)

FOREWORD

All human life on the planet is born of woman. The one unifying, incontrovertible experience shared by all women and men is that months-long period we spent unfolding inside a woman's body. Because young humans remain dependent upon nurture for a much longer period than other mammals, and because of the division of labor long established in human groups, where women not only bear and suckle but are assigned almost total responsibility for children, most of us first know both love and disappointment, power and tenderness, in the person of a woman.

We carry the imprint of this experience for life, even into our dying. Yet there has been a strange lack of material to help us understand and use it. We know more about the air we breathe, the seas we travel, than about the nature and meaning of motherhood. In the division of labor according to gender, the makers and sayers of culture, the namers, have been the sons of the mothers. There is much to suggest that the male mind has always been haunted by the force of the idea of *dependence on a woman for life itself,* the son's constant effort to assimilate, compensate for, or deny the fact that he is "of woman born."

Women are also born of women. But we know little about the effect on culture of that fact, because women have not been makers and sayers of patriarchal culture. Woman's status as childbearer has been made into a major fact of her life. Terms like "barren" or "childless" have been used to negate any further identity. The term "nonfather" does not exist in any realm of social categories.

Because the fact of physical motherhood is so visible and dramatic, men recognized only after some time that they, too, had a part in generation. The meaning of "fatherhood" remains tangential, elusive. To "father" a child suggests above all to beget, to provide the sperm which fertilizes the ovum. To "mother" a child implies a continuing presence, lasting at least nine months, more often for years. Motherhood is earned, first through an intense physical and psychic rite of passage—pregnancy and childbirth—then through learning to nurture, which does not come by instinct.

A man may beget a child in passion or by rape, and then disappear; he need never see or consider child or mother again. Under such circumstances, the mother faces a range of painful, socially weighted choices: abortion, suicide, abandonment of the child, infanticide, the rearing of a child branded "illegitimate," usually in poverty, always outside the law. In some cultures she faces murder by her kinsmen. Whatever her choice, her body has undergone irreversible changes, her mind will never be the same, her future as a woman has been shaped by the event.

Most of us were raised by our mothers, or by women who for love, necessity, or money took the place of our biological mothers. Throughout history women have helped birth and nurture each others' children. Most women have been mothers in the sense of tenders and carers for the young, whether as sisters, aunts, nurses, teachers, foster-mothers, stepmothers. Tribal life, the village, the extended family, the female networks of some cultures, have included the very young, very old, unmarried, and infertile women in the process of "mothering." Even those of us whose fathers played an important part in our early childhood rarely remember them for their patient attendance when we were ill, their doing the humble tasks of feeding and cleaning us; we remember scenes, expeditions, punishments, special occasions. For most of us a woman provided the continuity and stability—but also the rejections and refusals—of our early lives, and it is with a woman's hands, eyes, body, voice, that we associate our primal sensations, our earliest social experience.

2

Throughout this book I try to distinguish between two meanings of motherhood, one superimposed on the other: the *potential relationship* of any woman to her powers of reproduction and to children; and the *institution*, which aims at ensuring that that potential—and all women—shall remain under male control. This institution has been a keystone of the most diverse social and political systems. It has withheld over one-half the human species from the decisions affecting their lives; it exonerates men from fatherhood in any authentic sense; it creates the dangerous schism between "private" and "public" life; it calcifies human choices and potentialities. In the most fundamental and bewildering of contradictions, it has alienated women from our bodies by incarcerating us in them. At certain points in history, and in certain cultures, the idea of woman-as-mother has worked to endow all women with respect, even with awe, and to give women some say in the life of a people or a clan. But for most of what we know as the "mainstream" of recorded history, motherhood as institution has ghettoized and degraded female potentialities.

The power of the mother has two aspects: the biological potential or capacity to bear and nourish human life, and the magical power invested in women by men, whether in the form of Goddess-worship or the fear of being controlled and overwhelmed by women. We do not actually know much about what power may have meant in the hands of strong, prepatriarchal women. We do have guesses, longings, myths, fantasies, analogues. We know far more about how, under patriarchy, female possibility has been literally massacred on the site of motherhood. Most women in history have become mothers without choice, and an even greater number have lost their lives bringing life into the world.

Women are controlled by lashing us to our bodies. In an early and classic essay, Susan Griffin pointed out that "rape is a form of mass terrorism, for the victims of rape are chosen indiscriminately, but the propagandists for male supremacy broadcast that it is women who cause rape by being unchaste or in the wrong place at the

wrong time—in essence, by behaving as though they were free. . . .
The fear of rape keeps women off the streets at night. Keeps women
at home. Keeps women passive and modest for fear that they be
thought provocative."[1] In a later development of Griffin's analysis,
Susan Brownmiller suggests that enforced, indentured motherhood
may originally have been the price paid by women to the men who
became their "protectors" (and owners) against the casual violence
of other men.[2] If rape has been terrorism, motherhood has been
penal servitude. *It need not be.*

This book is not an attack on the family or on mothering, *except
as defined and restricted under patriarchy.* Nor is it a call for a mass
system of state-controlled child-care. Mass child-care in patriarchy
has had but two purposes: to introduce large numbers of women
into the labor force, in a developing economy or during a war, and to
indoctrinate future citizens.[3] It has never been conceived as a means
of releasing the energies of women into the mainstream of culture, or
of changing the stereotypic gender-images of both women and men.

3

I told myself that I wanted to write a book on motherhood because
it was a crucial, still relatively unexplored, area for feminist theory.
But I did not choose this subject; it had long ago chosen me.

This book is rooted in my own past, tangled with parts of my life
which stayed buried even while I dug away at the strata of early
childhood, adolescence, separation from parents, my vocation as
a poet; the geographies of marriage, spiritual divorce, and death,
through which I entered the open ground of middle age. Every journey into the past is complicated by delusions, false memories, false
naming of real events. But for a long time, I avoided this journey back
into the years of pregnancy, child-bearing, and the dependent lives of
my children, because it meant going back into pain and anger that I
would have preferred to think of as long since resolved and put away.
I could not begin to think of writing a book on motherhood until I
began to feel strong enough, and unambivalent enough in my love for
my children, so that I could dare to return to a ground which seemed

to me the most painful, incomprehensible, and ambiguous I had ever traveled, a ground hedged by taboos, mined with false-namings.

I did not understand this when I started to write the book. I only knew that I had lived through something which was considered central to the lives of women, fulfilling even in its sorrows, a key to the meaning of life; and that I could remember little except anxiety, physical weariness, anger, self-blame, boredom, and division within myself: a division made more acute by the moments of passionate love, delight in my children's spirited bodies and minds, amazement at how they went on loving me in spite of my failures to love them wholly and selflessly.

It seemed to me impossible from the first to write a book of this kind without being often autobiographical, without often saying "I." Yet for many months I buried my head in historical research and analysis in order to delay or prepare the way for the plunge into areas of my own life which were painful and problematical, yet from the heart of which this book has come. I believe increasingly that only the willingness to share private and sometimes painful experience can enable women to create a collective description of the world which will be truly ours. On the other hand, I am keenly aware that any writer has a certain false and arbitrary power. It is *her* version, after all, that the reader is reading at this moment, while the accounts of others—including the dead—may go untold.

This is in some ways a vulnerable book. I have invaded various professional domains, broken various taboos. I have used the scholarship available to me where I found it suggestive, without pretending to make myself into a specialist. In so doing, the question, *But what was it like for women?* was always in my mind, and I soon began to sense a fundamental perceptual difficulty among male scholars (and some female ones) for which "sexism" is too facile a term. It is really an intellectual defect, which might be named "patrivincialism" or "patriochialism": the assumption that women are a subgroup, that "man's world" is the "real" world, that patriarchy is equivalent to culture and culture to patriarchy, that the "great" or "liberalizing" periods of history have been the same for women as for men, that generalizations about "man," "humankind," "children,"

"Blacks," "parents," "the working class" hold true for women, mothers, daughters, sisters, wet-nurses, infant girls, and can include them with no more than a glancing reference here and there, usually to some specialized function like breastfeeding. The new historians of "family and childhood," like the majority of theorists on child-rearing, pediatricians, psychiatrists, are male. In their work, the question of motherhood as an institution or as an idea in the heads of grown-up male children is raised only where "styles" of mothering are discussed and criticized. Female sources are rarely cited (yet these sources exist, as the feminist historians are showing); there are virtually no primary sources from women-as-mothers; and all this is presented as objective scholarship.

It is only recently that feminist scholars such as Gerda Lerner, Joan Kelly, and Carroll Smith-Rosenberg have begun to suggest that, in Lerner's words: "the key to understanding women's history is in accepting—painful though it may be—that it is the history of the *majority* of mankind. . . . History, as written and perceived up to now, is the history of a minority, who may well turn out to be the 'subgroup.'"[4]

I write with a painful consciousness of my own Western cultural perspective and that of most of the sources available to me: painful because it says so much about how female culture is fragmented by the male cultures, boundaries, groupings in which women live. However, at this point any broad study of female culture can be at best partial, and what any writer hopes—and knows—is that others like her, with different training, background, and tools, are putting together other parts of this immense half-buried mosaic in the shape of a woman's face.

ANGER AND TENDERNESS

> ... to understand is always an ascending movement; that
> is why comprehension ought always to be concrete. (one
> is never got out of the cave, one comes out of it.)
> —SIMONE WEIL, *First and Last Notebooks*

Entry from my journal, November 1960

My children cause me the most exquisite suffering of which
I have any experience. It is the suffering of ambivalence:
the murderous alternation between bitter resentment and
raw-edged nerves, and blissful gratification and tenderness.
Sometimes I seem to myself, in my feelings toward these tiny
guiltless beings, a monster of selfishness and intolerance. Their
voices wear away at my nerves, their constant needs, above all
their need for simplicity and patience, fill me with despair at my
own failures, despair too at my fate, which is to serve a function for which I was not fitted. And I am weak sometimes from
held-in rage. There are times when I feel only death will free us
from one another, when I envy the barren woman who has the
luxury of her regrets but lives a life of privacy and freedom.*

And yet at other times I am melted with the sense of their helpless, charming and quite irresistible beauty—their ability to go
on loving and trusting—their staunchness and decency and
unselfconsciousness. *I love them.* But it's in the enormity and
inevitability of this love that the sufferings lie.

---

* The term "barren woman" was easy for me to use, unexamined, fifteen years ago.
As should be clear throughout this book, it seems to me now a term both tendentious
and meaningless, based on a view of women which sees motherhood as our only
positive definition.

April 1961

A blissful love for my children engulfs me from time to time and seems almost to suffice—the aesthetic pleasure I have in these little, changing creatures, the sense of being loved, however dependently, the sense too that I'm not an utterly unnatural and shrewish mother—much though I am!

May 1965

To suffer with and for and against a child—maternally, egotistically, neurotically, sometimes with a sense of helplessness, sometimes with the illusion of learning wisdom—but always, everywhere, in body and soul, *with* that child—because that child is a piece of oneself.

To be caught up in waves of love and hate, jealousy even of the child's childhood; hope and fear for its maturity; longing to be free of responsibility, tied by every fibre of one's being.

That curious primitive reaction of protectiveness, the beast defending her cub, when anyone attacks or criticizes him—And yet no one more hard on him than I!

September 1965

Degradation of anger. Anger at a child. How shall I learn to absorb the violence and make explicit only the caring? Exhaustion of anger. Victory of will, too dearly bought—far too dearly!

March 1966

Perhaps one is a monster—an anti-woman—something driven and without recourse to the normal and appealing consolations of love, motherhood, joy in others . . .

Unexamined assumptions: First, that a "natural" mother is a person without further identity, one who can find her chief gratification in being all day with small children, living at a pace tuned to theirs; that the isolation of mothers and children together in the home must be taken for granted; that maternal love is, and should be, quite literally selfless; that children and mothers are the "causes" of each others' suffering. I was haunted by the stereotype of the mother whose love is "unconditional"; and by the visual and literary images of motherhood as a single-minded identity. If I knew parts of myself existed that would never cohere to those images, weren't those parts then abnormal, monstrous? And—as my eldest son, now aged twenty-one, remarked on reading the above passages: "You seemed to feel you ought to love us all the time. But there *is* no human relationship where you love the other person at every moment." Yes, I tried to explain to him, but women—above all, mothers—have been supposed to love that way.

From the fifties and early sixties, I remember a cycle. It began when I had picked up a book or began trying to write a letter, or even found myself on the telephone with someone toward whom my voice betrayed eagerness, a rush of sympathetic energy. The child (or children) might be absorbed in busyness, in his own dreamworld; but as soon as he felt me gliding into a world which did not include him, he would come to pull at my hand, ask for help, punch at the typewriter keys. And I would feel his wants at such a moment as fraudulent, as an attempt moreover to defraud me of living even for fifteen minutes as myself. My anger would rise; I would feel the futility of any attempt to salvage myself, and also the inequality between us: my needs always balanced against those of a child, and always losing. I could love so much better, I told myself, after even a quarter-hour of selfishness, of peace, of detachment from my children. A few minutes! But it was as if an invisible thread would pull taut between us and break, to the child's sense of inconsolable abandonment, if I moved—not even physically, but in spirit—into a realm beyond our tightly circumscribed life together. It was as if my placenta had begun to refuse him oxygen. Like so many women, I waited with impatience for the moment when their father would return from work, when for an hour or two at least the circle drawn around mother and children would grow looser, the intensity between us slacken, because there was another adult in the house.

I did not understand that this circle, this magnetic field in which we lived, was not a natural phenomenon.

Intellectually, I must have known it. But the emotion-charged, tradition-heavy form in which I found myself cast as the Mother seemed, then, as ineluctable as the tides. And, because of this form—this microcosm in which my children and I formed a tiny, private emotional cluster, and in which (in bad weather or when someone was ill) we sometimes passed days at a time without seeing another adult except for their father—there *was* authentic need underlying my child's invented claims upon me when I seemed to be wandering away from him. He was reassuring himself that warmth, tenderness, continuity, solidity were still there for him, in my person. My singularity, my uniqueness in the world as *his mother*—perhaps more dimly also as Woman—evoked a need vaster than any single human being could satisfy, except by loving continuously, unconditionally, from dawn to dark, and often in the middle of the night.

2

In a living room in 1975, I spent an evening with a group of women poets, some of whom had children. One had brought hers along, and they slept or played in adjoining rooms. We talked of poetry, and also of infanticide, of the case of a local woman, the mother of eight, who had been in severe depression since the birth of her third child, and who had recently murdered and decapitated her two youngest, on her suburban front lawn. Several women in the group, feeling a direct connection with her desperation, had signed a letter to the local newspaper protesting the way her act was perceived by the press and handled by the community mental health system. Every woman in that room who had children, every poet, could identify with her. We spoke of the wells of anger that her story cleft open in us. We spoke of our own moments of murderous anger at our children, because there was no one and nothing else on which to discharge anger. We spoke in the sometimes tentative, sometimes rising, sometimes bitterly witty, unrhetorical tones and language of women who had met together over our common work, poetry, and who found another common ground in an unacceptable, but undeniable anger. The words are being spoken now, are being written down; the taboos are being broken, the masks of motherhood are cracking through.

For centuries no one talked of these feelings. I became a mother in the family-centered, consumer-oriented, Freudian-American world of the 1950s. My husband spoke eagerly of the children we would have; my parents-in-law awaited the birth of their grandchild. I had no idea of what *I* wanted, what *I* could or could not choose. I only knew that to have a child was to assume adult womanhood to the full, to prove myself, to be "like other women."

To be "like other women" had been a problem for me. From the age of thirteen or fourteen, I had felt I was only acting the part of a feminine creature. At the age of sixteen my fingers were almost constantly ink-stained. The lipstick and high heels of the era were difficult-to-manage disguises. In 1945 I was writing poetry seriously, and had a fantasy of going to postwar Europe as a journalist, sleeping among the ruins in bombed cities, recording the rebirth of civilization after the fall of the Nazis. But also, like every other girl I knew, I spent hours trying to apply lipstick more adroitly, straightening the wandering seams of stockings, talking about "boys." There were two different compartments, already, to my life. But writing poetry, and my fantasies of travel and self-sufficiency, seemed more real to me; I felt that as an incipient "real woman" I was a fake. Particularly was I paralyzed when I encountered young children. I think I felt men could be—wished to be—conned into thinking I was truly "feminine"; a child, I suspected, could see through me like a shot. This sense of acting a part created a curious sense of guilt, even though it was a part demanded for survival.

I have a very clear, keen memory of myself the day after I was married: I was sweeping a floor. Probably the floor did not really need to be swept; probably I simply did not know what else to do with myself. But as I swept that floor I thought: "Now I am a woman.

This is an age-old action, this is what women have always done." I felt I was bending to some ancient form, too ancient to question. *This is what women have always done.*

As soon as I was visibly and clearly pregnant, I felt, for the first time in my adolescent and adult life, not-guilty. The atmosphere of approval in which I was bathed—even by strangers on the street, it seemed—was like an aura I carried with me, in which doubts, fears, misgivings, met with absolute denial. *This is what women have always done.*

Two days before my first son was born, I broke out in a rash which was tentatively diagnosed as measles, and was admitted to a hospital for contagious diseases to await the onset of labor. I felt for the first time a great deal of conscious fear, and guilt toward my unborn child, for having "failed" him with my body in this way. In rooms near mine were patients with polio; no one was allowed to enter my room except in a hospital gown and mask. If during pregnancy I had felt in any vague command of my situation, I felt now totally dependent on my obstetrician, a huge, vigorous, paternal man, abounding with optimism and assurance, and given to pinching my cheek. I had gone through a healthy pregnancy, but as if tranquilized or sleep-walking. I had taken a sewing class in which I produced an unsightly and ill-cut maternity jacket which I never wore; I had made curtains for the baby's room, collected baby clothes, blotted out as much as possible the woman I had been a few months earlier. My second book of poems was in press, but I had stopped writing poetry, and read little except household magazines and books on child-care. I felt myself perceived by the world simply as a pregnant woman, and it seemed easier, less disturbing, to perceive myself so. After my child was born the "measles" were diagnosed as an allergic reaction to pregnancy.

Within two years, I was pregnant again, and writing in a notebook:

November 1956

Whether it's the extreme lassitude of early pregnancy or something more fundamental, I don't know; but of late I've felt,

toward poetry,—both reading and writing it—nothing but boredom and indifference. Especially toward my own and that of my
immediate contemporaries. When I receive a letter soliciting
mss., or someone alludes to my "career," I have a strong sense of
wanting to deny all responsibility for and interest in that person
who writes—or who wrote.

If there is going to be a real break in my writing life, this is as
good a time for it as any. I have been dissatisfied with myself,
my work, for a long time.

My husband was a sensitive, affectionate man who wanted children and who—unusual in the professional, academic world of the
fifties—was willing to "help." But it was clearly understood that this
"help" was an act of generosity; that *his* work, *his* professional life,
was the real work in the family; in fact, this was for years not even an
issue between us. I understood that my struggles as a writer were a
kind of luxury, a peculiarity of mine; my work brought in almost no
money: it even cost money, when I hired a household helper to allow
me a few hours a week to write. "Whatever I ask he tries to give me,"
I wrote in March 1958, "but always the initiative has to be mine." I
experienced my depressions, bursts of anger, sense of entrapment, as
burdens my husband was forced to bear because he loved me; I felt
grateful to be loved in spite of bringing him those burdens.

But I was struggling to bring my life into focus. I had never really
given up on poetry, nor on gaining some control over my existence.
The life of a Cambridge tenement backyard swarming with children,
the repetitious cycles of laundry, the night-wakings, the interrupted
moments of peace or of engagement with ideas, the ludicrous dinner
parties at which young wives, some with advanced degrees, all seriously and intelligently dedicated to their children's welfare and their
husbands' careers, attempted to reproduce the amenities of Brahmin Boston, amid French recipes and the pretense of effortlessness—
above all, the ultimate lack of seriousness with which women were
regarded in that world—all of this defied analysis at that time, but
I *knew* I had to remake my own life. I did not then understand that

we—the women of that academic community—as in so many middle-class communities of the period—were expected to fill both the part of the Victorian Lady of Leisure, the Angel in the House, and also of the Victorian cook, scullery maid, laundress, governess, and nurse. I only sensed that there were false distractions sucking at me, and I wanted desperately to strip my life down to what was essential.

June 1958

> These months I've been all a tangle of irritations deepening to anger: bitterness, disillusion with society and with myself; beating out at the world, rejecting out of hand. What, if anything, has been positive? Perhaps the attempt to remake my life, to save it from mere drift and the passage of time . . .

> The work that is before me is serious and difficult and not at all clear even as to plan. Discipline of mind and spirit, uniqueness of expression, ordering of daily existence, the most effective functioning of the human self—these are the chief things I wish to achieve. So far the only beginning I've been able to make is to waste less time. That is what some of the rejection has been all about.

By July of 1958 I was again pregnant. The new life of my third—and, as I determined, my last—child, was a kind of turning for me. I had learned that my body was not under my control; I had not intended to bear a third child. I knew now better than I had ever known what another pregnancy, another new infant, meant for my body and spirit. Yet, I did not think of having an abortion. In a sense, my third son was more actively chosen than either of his brothers; by the time I knew I was pregnant with him, I was not sleepwalking any more.

August 1958 (Vermont)

I write this as the early rays of the sun light up our hillside and eastern windows. Rose with [the baby] at 5:30 A.M. and have fed him and breakfasted. This is one of the few mornings on which I haven't felt terrible mental depression and physical exhaustion.

... I have to acknowledge to myself that I would not have chosen to have more children, that I was beginning to look to a time, not too far off, when I should again be free, no longer so physically tired, pursuing a more or less intellectual and creative life.... The *only* way I can develop now is through much harder, more continuous, connected work than my present life makes possible. Another child means postponing this for some years longer—and years at my age are significant, not to be tossed lightly away.

And yet, somehow, something, call it Nature or that affirming fatalism of the human creature, makes me aware of the inevitable as already part of me, not to be contended against so much as brought to bear as an additional weapon against drift, stagnation and spiritual death. (For it is really death that I have been fearing—the crumbling to death of that scarcely-born physiognomy which my whole life has been a battle to give birth to—a recognizable, autonomous self, a creation in poetry and in life.)

If more effort has to be made then I will make it. If more despair has to be lived through, I think I can anticipate it correctly and live through it.

Meanwhile, in a curious and unanticipated way, we really do welcome the birth of our child.

There was, of course, an economic as well as a spiritual margin which allowed me to think of a third child's birth not as my own death-warrant but as an "additional weapon against death." My body, despite recurrent flares of arthritis, was a healthy one; I had good prenatal care; we were not living on the edge of malnutrition; I knew that all my children would be fed, clothed, breathe fresh air; in fact it did not occur to me that it could be otherwise. But, in another sense, beyond that physical margin, I knew I was fighting for my life through, against, and with the lives of my children, though very little else was clear to me. I had been trying to give birth to myself; and in some grim, dim way I was determined to use even pregnancy and parturition in that process.

Before my third child was born I decided to have no more children, to be sterilized. (Nothing is removed from a woman's body during this operation; ovulation and menstruation continue. Yet the language suggests a cutting- or burning-away of her essential womanhood, just as the old word "barren" suggests a woman eternally empty and lacking.) My husband, although he supported my decision, asked whether I was sure it would not leave me feeling "less feminine." In order to have the operation at all, I had to present a letter, counter-signed by my husband, assuring the committee of physicians who approved such operations that I had already produced three children, and stating my reasons for having no more. Since I had had rheumatoid arthritis for some years, I could give a reason acceptable to the male panel who sat on my case; my own judgment would not have been acceptable. When I awoke from the operation, twenty-four hours after my child's birth, a young nurse looked at my chart and remarked coldly: "Had yourself spayed, did you?"

The first great birth-control crusader, Margaret Sanger, remarks that of the hundreds of women who wrote to her pleading for contraceptive information in the early part of the twentieth century, all spoke of wanting the health and strength to be better mothers to the children they already had; or of wanting to be physically affectionate to their husbands without dread of conceiving. None was refusing

motherhood altogether, or asking for an easy life. These women—
mostly poor, many still in their teens, all with several children—
simply felt they could no longer do "right" by their families, whom
they expected to go on serving and rearing. Yet there always has
been, and there remains, intense fear of the suggestion that women
shall have the final say as to how our bodies are to be used. It is as
if the suffering of the mother, the primary identification of woman
as the mother—were so necessary to the emotional grounding of
human society that the mitigation, or removal, of that suffering, that
identification, must be fought at every level, including the level of
refusing to question it at all.

3

"Vous travaillez pour l'armée, madame?" (You are working for the
army?), a Frenchwoman said to me early in the Vietnam war, on
hearing I had three sons.

April 1965

> Anger, weariness, demoralization. Sudden bouts of weeping. A
> sense of insufficiency to the moment and to eternity . . .

> Paralyzed by the sense that there exists a mesh of relations,
> between e.g. my rejection and anger at [my eldest child], my
> sensual life, pacifism, sex (I mean in its broadest significance,
> not merely physical desire)—an interconnectedness which, if I
> could see it, make it valid, would give me back myself, make it
> possible to function lucidly and passionately—Yet I grope in and
> out among these dark webs—

> I weep, and weep, and the sense of powerlessness spreads like
> a cancer through my being.

August 1965, 3:30 A.M.

> Necessity for a more unyielding discipline of my life.
> Recognize the uselessness of blind anger.
> Limit society.
> Use children's school hours better, for work & solitude.
> Refuse to be distracted from own style of life.
> Less waste.
> Be harder & harder on poems.

Once in a while someone used to ask me, "Don't you ever write poems about your children?" The male poets of my generation did write poems about their children—especially their daughters. For me, poetry was where I lived as no-one's mother, where I existed as myself.

The bad and the good moments are inseparable for me. I recall the times when, suckling each of my children, I saw his eyes open full to mine, and realized each of us was fastened to the other, not only by mouth and breast, but through our mutual gaze: the depth, calm, passion, of that dark blue, maturely focused look. I recall the physical pleasure of having my full breast suckled at a time when I had no other physical pleasure in the world except the guilt-ridden pleasure of addictive eating. I remember early the sense of conflict, of a battleground none of us had chosen, of being an observer who, like it or not, was also an actor in an endless contest of wills. This was what it meant to me to have three children under the age of seven. But I recall too each child's individual body, his slenderness, wiriness, softness, grace, the beauty of little boys who have not been taught that the male body must be rigid. I remember moments of peace when for some reason it was possible to go to the bathroom alone. I remember being uprooted from already meager sleep to answer a childish nightmare, pull up a blanket, warm a consoling bottle, lead a half-asleep child to the toilet. I remember going back to bed starkly awake, brittle with anger, knowing that my broken sleep would make next day a hell, that there would be more nightmares, more need for consolation, because out of my weariness I would rage at those children for no reason they could understand. I remember thinking I would never dream again (the unconscious of the young mother— where does it entrust its messages, when dream-sleep is denied her for years?)

For many years I shrank from looking back on the first decade of my children's lives. In snapshots of the period I see a smiling young woman, in maternity clothes or bent over a half-naked baby; gradually she stops smiling, wears a distant, half-melancholy look, as if she were listening for something. In time my sons grew older, I began changing my own life, we began to talk to each other as equals. Together we lived through my leaving the marriage, and through their father's suicide. We became survivors, four distinct people with strong bonds connecting us. Because I always tried to tell them the truth, because their every new independence meant new freedom for me, because we trusted each other even when we wanted different things, they became, at a fairly young age, self-reliant and open to the unfamiliar. Something told me that if they had survived my angers, my self-reproaches, and still trusted my love and each others', they were strong. Their lives have not been, will not be, easy; but their very existences seem a gift to me, their vitality, humor, intelligence, gentleness, love of life, their separate life-currents which here and there stream into my own. I don't know how we made it from their embattled childhood and my embattled motherhood into a mutual recognition of ourselves and each other. Probably that mutual recognition, overlaid by social and traditional circumstance, was always there, from the first gaze between the mother and the infant at the breast. But I do know that for years I believed I should never have been anyone's mother, that because I felt my own needs acutely and often expressed them violently, I was Kali, Medea, the sow that devours her farrow, the unwomanly woman in flight from womanhood, a Nietzschean monster. Even today, rereading old journals, remembering, I feel grief and anger; but their objects are no longer myself and my children. I feel grief at the waste of myself in those years, anger at the mutilation and manipulation of the relationship between mother and child, which is the great original source and experience of love.

On an early spring day in the 1970s, I meet a young woman friend on the street. She has a tiny infant against her breast, in a bright cotton sling; its face is pressed against her blouse, its tiny hand clutches a piece of the cloth. "How old is she?" I ask. "Just two weeks old," the mother tells me. I am amazed to feel in myself a passionate longing to have, once again, such a small, new being clasped against my body. The baby belongs there, curled, suspended asleep between her mother's breasts, as she belonged curled in the womb. The young mother—who already has a three-year-old—speaks of how quickly one forgets the pure pleasure of having this new creature, immaculate, perfect. And I walk away from her drenched with memory, with envy. Yet I know other things: that her life is far from simple; she is a mathematician who now has two children under the age of four; she is living even now in the rhythms of other lives—not only the regular cry of the infant but her three-year-old's needs, her husband's problems. In the building where I live, women are still raising children alone, living day in and day out within their individual family units, doing the laundry, herding the tricycles to the park, waiting for the husbands to come home. There is a baby-sitting pool and a children's playroom, young fathers push prams on weekends, but child-care is still the individual responsibility of the individual woman. I envy the sensuality of having an infant of two weeks curled against one's breast; I do not envy the turmoil of the elevator full of small children, babies howling in the laundromat, the apartment in winter where pent-up seven- and eight-year-olds have one adult to look to for their frustrations, reassurances, the grounding of their lives.

4

But, it will be said, this is the human condition, this interpenetration of pain and pleasure, frustration and fulfillment. I might have told myself the same thing, fifteen or eighteen years ago. But the ˙ˑrchal institution of motherhood is not the "human condition" any more than rape, prostitution, and slavery are. (Those who speak largely of the human condition are usually those most exempt from its oppressions—whether of sex, race, or servitude.)

Motherhood—unmentioned in the histories of conquest and serfdom, wars and treaties, exploration and imperialism—has a history, it has an ideology, it is more fundamental than tribalism or nationalism. My individual, seemingly private pains as a mother, the individual, seemingly private pains of the mothers around me and before me, whatever our class or color, the regulation of women's reproductive power by men in every totalitarian system and every socialist revolution, the legal and technical control by men of contraception, fertility, abortion, obstetrics, gynecology, and extrauterine reproductive experiments—all are essential to the patriarchal system, as is the negative or suspect status of women who are not mothers.

Throughout patriarchal mythology, dream-symbolism, theology, language, two ideas flow side by side: one, that the female body is impure, corrupt, the site of discharges, bleedings, dangerous to masculinity, a source of moral and physical contamination, "the devil's gateway." On the other hand, as mother the woman is beneficent, sacred, pure, asexual, nourishing; and the physical potential for motherhood—that same body with its bleedings and mysteries— is her single destiny and justification in life. These two ideas have become deeply internalized in women, even in the most independent of us, those who seem to lead the freest lives.

In order to maintain two such notions, each in its contradictory purity, the masculine imagination has had to divide women, to see us, and force us to see ourselves, as polarized into good or evil, fertile or barren, pure or impure. The asexual Victorian angel-wife and the Victorian prostitute were institutions created by this double thinking, which had nothing to do with women's actual sensuality and everything to do with the male's subjective experience of women. The political and economic expediency of this kind of thinking is most unashamedly and dramatically to be found where sexism and racism become one. The social historian A. W. Calhoun describes the encouragement of the rape of Black women by the sons of white planters, in a deliberate effort to produce more mulatto slaves, mulattos being considered more valuable. He quotes two mid-nineteenth-century southern writers on the subject of women:

> "The heaviest part of the white racial burden in slavery was the African woman of strong sex instincts and devoid of a sexual conscience, at the white man's door, in the white man's dwelling." . . . "Under the institution of slavery, the attack against the integrity of white civilization was made by the insidious influence of the lascivious hybrid woman at the point of weakest resistance. In the uncompromising purity of the white mother and wife of the upper classes lay the one assurance of the future purity of the race."[1]

The motherhood created by rape is not only degraded; the raped woman is turned into the criminal, the *attacker*. But who brought the Black woman to the white man's door, whose absence of a sexual conscience produced the financially profitable mulatto children? Is it asked whether the "pure" white mother and wife was not also raped by the white planter, since she was assumed to be devoid of "strong sexual instinct?" In the American South, as elsewhere, it was economically necessary that children be produced; the mothers, Black and white, were a means to this end.

Neither the "pure" nor the "lascivious" woman, neither the so-called mistress nor the slave woman, neither the woman praised for reducing herself to a brood animal nor the woman scorned and penalized as an "old maid" or a "dyke," has had any real autonomy or selfhood to gain from this subversion of the female body (and hence of the female mind). Yet, because short-term advantages are often the only ones visible to the powerless, we, too, have played our parts in continuing this subversion.

5

Most of the literature of infant care and psychology has assumed that the process toward individuation is essentially the *child's* drama, played out against and with a parent or parents who are, for better or worse, givens. Nothing could have prepared me for the realization that I *was* a mother, one of those givens, when I knew I was still in a state of uncreation myself. That calm, sure, unambivalent woman who moved through the pages of the manuals I read seemed as unlike me as an astronaut. Nothing, to be sure, had prepared me for the intensity of relationship already existing between me and a creature I had carried in my body and now held in my arms and fed from my breasts. Throughout pregnancy and nursing, women are urged to relax, to mime the serenity of madonnas. No one mentions the psychic crisis of bearing a first child, the excitation of long-buried feelings about one's own mother, the sense of confused power and powerlessness, of being taken over on the one hand and of touching new physical and psychic potentialities on the other, a heightened sensibility which can be exhilarating, bewildering, and exhausting. No one mentions the strangeness of attraction—which can be as single-minded and overwhelming as the early days of a love affair—to a being so tiny, so dependent, so folded-in to itself—who is, and yet is not, part of oneself.

From the beginning the mother caring for her child is involved in a continually changing dialogue, crystallized in such moments as when, hearing her child's cry, she feels milk rush into her breasts; when, as the child first suckles, the uterus begins contracting and returning to its normal size, and when later, the child's mouth, caressing the nipple, creates waves of sensuality in the womb where it once lay; or when, smelling the breast even in sleep, the child starts to root and grope for the nipple.

The child gains her first sense of her own existence from the mother's responsive gestures and expressions. It's as if, in the mother's eyes, her smile, her stroking touch, the child first reads the message: *You are there!* And the mother, too, is discovering her own existence newly. She is connected with this other being, by the most mundane and the most invisible strands, in a way she can be connected with no one else except in the deep past of her infant connection with her own mother. And she, too, needs to struggle from that one-to-one intensity into new realization, or reaffirmation, of her being-unto-herself.

The act of suckling a child, like a sexual act, may be tense, physically painful, charged with cultural feelings of inadequacy and guilt; or, like a sexual act, it can be a physically delicious, elementally soothing experience, filled with a tender sensuality. But just as lovers have to break apart after sex and become separate individuals again, so the mother has to wean herself from the infant and the infant from herself. In psychologies of child-rearing the emphasis is placed on "letting the child go" for the child's sake. But the mother needs to let it go as much or more for her own.

Motherhood, in the sense of an intense, reciprocal relationship with a particular child, or children, is *one part* of female process; it is not an identity for all time. The housewife in her mid-forties may jokingly say, "I feel like someone out of a job." But in the eyes of society, once having been mothers, what are we, if not always mothers? The process of "letting-go"—though we are charged with blame if we do not—is an act of revolt against the grain of patriarchal culture. But it is not enough to let our children go; we need selves of our own to return to.

To have borne and reared a child is to have done that thing which patriarchy joins with physiology to render into the definition of femaleness. But also, it can mean the experiencing of one's own body and emotions in a powerful way. We experience not only physical, fleshly changes but the feeling of a change in character. We learn, often through painful self-discipline and self-cauterization, those qualities which are supposed to be "innate" in us: patience, self-sacrifice, the willingness to repeat endlessly the small, routine chores of socializing a human being. We are also, often to our amazement, flooded with feelings both of love and violence intenser and fiercer than any we had ever known. (A well-known pacifist, also a mother, said recently on a platform: "If anyone laid a hand on *my* child, I'd murder him.")

These and similar experiences are not easily put aside. Small wonder that women gritting their teeth at the incessant demands of child-care still find it hard to acknowledge their children's growing independence of them; still feel they must be at home, on the *qui vive*, be that ear always tuned for the sound of emergency, of being needed. Children grow up, not in a smooth ascending curve, but jaggedly, their needs inconstant as weather. Cultural "norms" are marvelously powerless to decide, in a child of eight or ten, what gender s/he will assume on a given day, or how s/he will meet emergency, loneliness, pain, hunger. One is constantly made aware that a human existence is anything but linear, long before the labyrinth of puberty; because a human being of six is still a human being.

In a tribal or even a feudal culture a child of six would have serious obligations; ours have none. But also, the woman at home with children is not believed to be doing serious work; she is just supposed to be acting out of maternal instinct, doing chores a man would never take on, largely uncritical of the meaning of what she does. So child and mother alike are depreciated, because only grown men and women in the paid labor force are supposed to be "productive."

The power-relations between mother and child are often simply a reflection of power-relations in patriarchal society: "You will do this because I know what is good for you" is difficult to distinguish from "You will do this because I can *make* you." Powerless women have always used mothering as a channel—narrow but deep—for their own human will to power, their need to return upon the world what it has visited on them. The child dragged by the arm across the room to be washed, the child cajoled, bullied, and bribed into taking "one more bite" of a detested food, is more than just a child which must be reared according to cultural traditions of "good mothering." S/he is a piece of reality, of the world, which can be acted on, even modified, by a woman restricted from acting on anything else except inert materials like dust and food.*

---

* 1986: the work of the Swiss psychotherapist Alice Miller has made me reflect further on the material in this chapter and in Chapters IX and X. Miller identifies the "hidden cruelty" in child-rearing as the repetition of "poisonous pedagogy" inflicted by the parents of the generation before and as providing the soil in which obedience to authoritarianism and fascism take root. She notes that "there is one taboo that has withstood all the recent efforts at demystification: the idealization of mother love" (*The Drama of the Gifted Child: How Narcissistic Parents Form and Deform the Emotional Lives of Their Talented Children* [New York: Harper & Row, 19⌐⌐ ⁀ Her work traces the damages of that idealization (of both parents, but e the mother) upon children forbidden to name or protest their suffering, ⸱

6

When I try to return to the body of the young woman of twenty-six, pregnant for the first time, who fled from the physical knowledge of her pregnancy and at the same time from her intellect and vocation, I realize that I was effectively alienated from my real body and my real spirit by the institution—not the fact—of motherhood. This institution—the foundation of human society as we know it—allowed me only certain views, certain expectations, whether embodied in the booklet in my obstetrician's waiting room, the novels I had read, my mother-in-law's approval, my memories of my own mother, the Sistine Madonna or she of the Michelangelo *Pietà*, the floating notion that a woman pregnant is a woman calm in her fulfillment or, simply, a woman waiting. Women have always been seen as waiting: waiting to be asked, waiting for our menses, in fear lest they do or do not come, waiting for men to come home from wars, or from work, waiting for children to grow up, or for the birth of a new child, or for menopause.

In my own pregnancy I dealt with this waiting, this female fate, by denying every active, powerful aspect of myself. I became dissociated both from my immediate, present, bodily experience and from my reading, thinking, writing life. Like a traveler in an airport

---

with their parents against themselves. Miller notes, "I cannot listen to my child with empathy if I am inwardly preoccupied with being a good mother; I cannot be open to what she is telling me" (*For Your Own Good: Hidden Cruelty in Child-rearing and the Roots of Violence* [New York: Farrar, Straus & Giroux, 1983], p. 258). Miller explores the sources of what has been defined as *child abuse*—i.e., physical violation and sadistic punishment—but she is equally concerned with the "gentle violence" of child-rearing, including that of "antiauthoritarian" or "alternative" prescriptions, based on the denial and suppression of the child's own vitality and feelings. Miller does not consider the predominance of women as primary care-givers, the investment of authoritarian or fascist systems in perpetuating male control of women's sexuality and reproductivity, or the structural *differences* between father-as-parent and mother-as-parent. She does acknowledge that in America, women especially "have discovered the power of their knowledge. They do not shrink from pointing out the poisonous nature of false information, even though it has been well-concealed for millennia behind sacrosanct and well-meaning labels" (*For Your Own Good*, p. xii).

where her plane is several hours delayed, who leafs through magazines she would never ordinarily read, surveys shops whose contents do not interest her, I committed myself to an outward serenity and a profound inner boredom. If boredom is simply a mask for anxiety, then I had learned, as a woman, to be supremely bored rather than to examine the anxiety underlying my Sistine tranquility. My body, finally truthful, paid me back in the end: I was allergic to pregnancy.

I have come to believe, as will be clear throughout this book, that female biology—the diffuse, intense sensuality radiating out from clitoris, breasts, uterus, vagina; the lunar cycles of menstruation; the gestation and fruition of life which can take place in the female body—has far more radical implications than we have yet come to appreciate. Patriarchal thought has limited female biology to its own narrow specifications. The feminist vision has recoiled from female biology for these reasons; it will, I believe, come to view our physicality as a resource, rather than a destiny. In order to live a fully human life we require not only *control* of our bodies (though control is a prerequisite); we must touch the unity and resonance of our physicality, our bond with the natural order, the corporeal ground of our intelligence.

The ancient, continuing envy, awe, and dread of the male for the female capacity to create life has repeatedly taken the form of hatred for every other female aspect of creativity. Not only have women been told to stick to motherhood, but we have been told that our intellectual or aesthetic creations were inappropriate, inconsequential, or scandalous, an attempt to become "like men," or to escape from the "real" tasks of adult womanhood: marriage and childbearing. To "think like a man" has been both praise and prison for women trying to escape the body-trap. No wonder that many intellectual and creative women have insisted that they were "human beings" first and women only incidentally, have minimized their physicality and their bonds with other women. The body has been made so problematic for women that it has often seemed easier to shrug it off and travel as a disembodied spirit.

But this reaction against the body is now coming into synthesis with new inquiries into the actual—as opposed to the culturally warped—power inherent in female biology, however we choose to use it, and by no means limited to the maternal function.

My own story, which is woven throughout this book, is only one story. What I carried away in the end was a determination to heal—insofar as an individual woman can, and as much as possible with other women—the separation between mind and body; never again to lose myself both psychically and physically in that way. Slowly I came to understand the paradox contained in "my" experience of motherhood; that, although different from many other women's experiences it was not unique; and that only in shedding the illusion of my uniqueness could I hope, as a woman, to have any authentic life at all.

MOTHERHOOD AND DAUGHTERHOOD

Mother
I write home
I am alone and
give me my body back.
—SUSAN GRIFFIN

A folder lies open beside me as I start to write, spilling out references and quotations, all relevant probably, but none of which
can help me to begin. This is the core of my book, and I enter it as a
woman who, born between her mother's legs, has time after time
and in different ways tried to return to her mother, to repossess her
and be repossessed by her, to find the mutual confirmation from and
with another woman that daughters and mothers alike hunger for,
pull away from, make possible or impossible for each other.

The first knowledge any woman has of warmth, nourishment, tenderness, security, sensuality, mutuality, comes from her mother. That
earliest enwrapment of one female body with another can sooner or
later be denied or rejected, felt as choking possessiveness, as rejection, trap, or taboo; but it is, at the beginning, the whole world. Of
course, the male infant also first knows tenderness, nourishment,
mutuality from a female body. But institutionalized heterosexuality
and institutionalized motherhood demand that the girl-child trans-
fer those first feelings of dependency, eroticism, mutuality, from
her first woman to a man, if she is to become what is defined as a
"normal" woman—that is, a woman whose most intense psychic and
physical energies are directed towards men.*

---

* At the risk of seeming repetitious, I will note here, again, that the *institution* of
heterosexuality, with its social rewards and punishments, its role-playing, and its
sanctions against "deviance," is not the same thing as a human experience freely
chosen and lived.

1986: See my essay, "Compulsory Heterosexuality and Lesbian Existence," in
Blood, Bread, and Poetry: Selected Prose 1979–1985 (New York: Norton, 1986).

I saw my own mother's menstrual blood before I saw my own. Hers was the first female body I ever looked at, to know what women were, what I was to be. I remember taking baths with her in the hot summers of early childhood, playing with her in the cool water. As a young child I thought how beautiful she was; a print of Botticelli's Venus on the wall, half-smiling, hair flowing, associated itself in my mind with her. In early adolescence I still glanced slyly at my mother's body, vaguely imagining: I too shall have breasts, full hips, hair between my thighs—whatever that meant to me then, and with all the ambivalence of such a thought. And there were other thoughts: I too shall marry, have children—but *not like her.* I shall find a way of doing it all differently.

My father's tense, narrow body did not seize my imagination, though authority and control ran through it like electric filaments. I used to glimpse his penis dangling behind a loosely tied bathrobe. But I had understood very early that he and my mother were different. It was his voice, presence, style, that seemed to pervade the household. I don't remember when it was that my mother's feminine sensuousness, the reality of her body, began to give way for me to the charisma of my father's assertive mind and temperament; perhaps when my sister was just born, and he began teaching me to read.

My mother's very name had a kind of magic for me as a child: Helen. I still think it one of the most beautiful of names. Reading Greek mythology, while very young, I somehow identified Helen my mother with Helen of Troy; or perhaps even more with Poe's "Helen," which my father liked to quote:

Helen, thy beauty is to me
Like those Nicean barks of yore,
That gently, o'er a perfumed sea,
The weary, wayworn wanderer bore
To his own native shore . . .

She was, Helen my mother, *my* native shore of course; I think that in that poem I first heard my own longings, the longings of the female child, expressed by a male poet, in the voice of a man—my father.

My father talked a great deal of beauty and the need for perfection. He felt the female body to be impure; he did not like its natural smells. His incorporeality was a way of disengaging himself from that lower realm where women sweated, excreted, grew bloody every month, became pregnant. (My mother became aware, in the last months of pregnancy, that he always looked away from her body.) He was perhaps very Jewish in this, but also very southern: the "pure" and therefore bloodless white woman was supposed to be a kind of gardenia, blanched by the moonlight, staining around the edges when touched.

But the early pleasure and reassurance I found in my mother's body was, I believe, an imprinting never to be wholly erased, even in those years when, as my father's daughter, I suffered the obscure bodily self-hatred peculiar to women who view themselves through the eyes of men. I trusted the pleasures I could get from my own body even at a time when masturbation was an unspeakable word. Doubtless my mother would have actively discouraged such pleasures had she known about them. Yet I cannot help but feel that I finally came to love my own body through first having loved hers, that this was a profound matrilineal bequest. I knew I was not an incorporeal intellect. My mind and body might be divided, as if between father and mother; but *I had both.*

Mothers and daughters have always exchanged with each other—beyond the verbally transmitted lore of female survival—a knowledge that is subliminal, subversive, preverbal: the knowledge flowing between two alike bodies, one of which has spent nine months inside the other. The experience of giving birth stirs deep reverberations of her mother in a daughter; women often dream of their mothers during pregnancy and labor. Alice Rossi suggests that in first breast-feeding her own child a woman may be stirred by the remembered smell of her own mother's milk. About menstruation, some daughters feel a womanly closeness with their mothers even where the relationship is generally painful and conflicted.[1]

2

It is hard to write about my own mother. Whatever I do write, it is my story I am telling, my version of the past. If she were to tell her own story other landscapes would be revealed. But in my landscape or hers, there would be old, smoldering patches of deep-burning anger. Before her marriage, she had trained seriously for years both as a concert pianist and a composer. Born in a southern town, mothered by a strong, frustrated woman, she had won a scholarship to study with the director at the Peabody Conservatory in Baltimore, and by teaching at girls' schools had earned her way to further study in New York, Paris, and Vienna. From the age of sixteen, she had been a young belle, who could have married at any time, but she also possessed unusual talent, determination, and independence for her time and place. She read—and reads—widely and wrote—as her journals from my childhood and her letters of today reveal—with grace and pungency.

She married my father after a ten years' engagement during which he finished his medical training and began to establish himself in academic medicine. Once married, she gave up the possibility of a concert career, though for some years she went on composing, and she is still a skilled and dedicated pianist. My father, brilliant, ambitious, possessed by his own drive, assumed that she would give her life over to the enhancement of his. She would manage his household with the formality and grace becoming to a medical professor's wife, though on a limited budget; she would "keep up" her music, though there was no question of letting her composing and practice conflict with her duties as a wife and mother. She was supposed to bear him two children, a boy and a girl. She had to keep her household books to the last penny—I still can see the big blue gray ledgers, inscribed in her clear, strong hand; she marketed by streetcar, and later, when they could afford a car, she drove my father to and from his laboratory or lectures, often awaiting him for hours. She raised two children, and taught us all our lessons, including music. (Neither of us was sent to school until the fourth grade.) I am sure that she was made to feel responsible for all our imperfections.

My father, like the transcendentalist Bronson Alcott, believed that he (or rather, his wife) could raise children according to his unique moral and intellectual plan, thus proving to the world the values of enlightened, unorthodox child-rearing. I believe that my mother, like Abigail Alcott, at first genuinely and enthusiastically embraced the experiment, and only later found that in carrying out my father's intense, perfectionist program, she was in conflict with her deep instincts as a mother. Like Abigail Alcott, too, she must have found that while ideas might be unfolded by her husband, their daily, hourly practice was going to be up to her. (" 'Mr. A. aids me in general principles, but nobody can aid me in the detail,' she mourned. . . . Moreover her husband's views kept her constantly wondering if she were doing a good job. 'Am I doing what is right? Am I doing enough? Am I doing too much?' " The appearance of "temper" and "will" in Louisa, the second Alcott daughter, was blamed by her father on her inheritance from her mother.)[2] Under the institution of motherhood, the mother is the first to blame if theory proves unworkable in practice, or if anything whatsoever goes wrong. But even earlier, my mother had failed at one part of the plan: she had not produced a son.

For years, I felt my mother had chosen my father over me, had sacrificed me to his needs and theories. When my first child was born, I was barely in communication with my parents. I had been fighting my father for my right to an emotional life and a selfhood beyond his needs and theories. We were all at a draw. Emerging from the fear, exhaustion, and alienation of my first childbirth, I could not admit even to myself that I wanted my mother, let alone tell her how much I wanted her. When she visited me in the hospital neither of us could uncoil the obscure lashings of feeling that darkened the room, the tangled thread running backward to where she had labored for three days to give birth to me, and I was not a son. Now, twenty-six years later, I lay in a contagious hospital with my allergy, my skin covered with a mysterious rash, my lips and eyelids swollen, my body bruised and sutured, and, in a cot beside my bed, slept the perfect, golden, male child I had brought forth. How could I have interpreted her feelings when I could not begin to decipher my own? My body had spoken all too eloquently, but it was, medically, just my body.

I wanted her to mother me again, to hold my baby in her arms as she had once held me; but that baby was also a gauntlet flung down: *my son.* Part of me longed to offer him for her blessing; part of me wanted to hold him up as a badge of victory in our tragic, unnecessary rivalry as women.

But I was only at the beginning. I know now as I could not possibly know then, that among the tangle of feelings between us, in that crucial yet unreal meeting, was her guilt. Soon I would begin to understand the full weight and burden of maternal guilt, that daily, nightly, hourly, *Am I doing what is right? Am I doing enough? Am I doing too much?* The institution of motherhood finds all mothers more or less guilty of having failed their children; and my mother, in particular, had been expected to help create, according to my father's plan, a perfect daughter. This "perfect" daughter, though gratifyingly precocious, had early been given to tics and tantrums, had become permanently lame from arthritis at twenty-two; she had finally resisted her father's Victorian paternalism, his seductive charm and controlling cruelty, had married a divorced graduate student, had begun to write "modern," "obscure," "pessimistic" poetry, lacking the fluent sweetness of Tennyson, had had the final temerity to get pregnant and bring a living baby into the world. She had ceased to be the demure and precocious child or the poetic, seducible adolescent. Something, in my father's view, had gone terribly wrong. I can imagine that whatever else my mother felt (and I know that part of her *was* mutely on my side) she also was made to feel blame. Beneath the "numbness" that she has since told me she experienced at that time, I can imagine the guilt of Everymother, because I have known it myself.

But I did not know it yet. And it is difficult for me to write of my mother now, because I have known it too well. I struggle to describe what it felt like to be her daughter, but I find myself divided, slipping under her skin; a part of me identifies too much with her. I know deep reservoirs of anger toward her still exist: the anger of a four-year-old locked in the closet (my father's orders, but my mother carried them out) for childish misbehavior; the anger of a six-year-old kept too long at piano practice (again, at his insistence, but it was she who gave the lessons) till I developed a series of facial tics. (As a mother I know what a child's facial tic is—a lancet of guilt and pain running through one's own body.) And I still feel the anger of a daughter, pregnant, wanting my mother desperately and feeling she had gone over to the enemy.

And I know there must be deep reservoirs of anger in her; every mother has known overwhelming, unacceptable anger at her children. When I think of the conditions under which my mother became a mother, the impossible expectations, my father's distaste for pregnant women, his hatred of all that he could not control, my anger at her dissolves into grief and anger *for* her, and then dissolves back again into anger at her: the ancient, unpurged anger of the child.

My mother lives today as an independent woman, which she was always meant to be. She is a much-loved, much-admired grandmother, an explorer in new realms; she lives in the present and future, not the past. I no longer have fantasies—they are the unhealed child's fantasies, I think—of some infinitely healing conversation with her, in which we could show all our wounds, transcend the pain we have shared as mother and daughter, say everything at last. But in writing these pages, I am admitting, at least, how important her existence is and has been for me.

For it was too simple, early in the new twentieth-century wave of feminism, for us to analyze our mothers' oppression, to understand "rationally"—and correctly—why our mothers did not teach us to be Amazons, why they bound our feet or simply left us. It was accurate and even radical, that analysis; and yet, like all politics narrowly interpreted, it assumed that consciousness knows everything. There was, is, in most of us, a girl-child still longing for a woman's nurture, tenderness, and approval, a woman's power exerted in our defense, a woman's smell and touch and voice, a woman's strong arms around us in moments of fear and pain. Any of us would have longed for a mother who had chosen, in Christabel Pankhurst's words, that "reckoning the cost [of her suffragist activism] in advance, Mother prepared to pay it, for women's sake."[3] It was not enough to *understand* our mothers; more than ever, in the effort to touch our own strength as women, we *needed* them. The cry of that female child in us need not be shameful or regressive; it is the germ of our desire to create a world in which strong mothers and strong daughters will be a matter of course.

We need to understand this double vision or we shall never understand ourselves. Many of us were mothered in ways we cannot yet even perceive; we only know that our mothers were in some incalculable way on our side. But if a mother had deserted us, by dying, or putting us up for adoption, or because life had driven her into alcohol or drugs, chronic depression or madness, if she had been forced to leave us with indifferent, uncaring strangers in order to earn our food money, because institutional motherhood makes no provision for the wage-earning mother; if she had tried to be a "good mother" according to the demands of the institution and had thereby turned into an anxious, worrying, puritanical keeper of our virginity; or if she had simply left us because she needed to live without a child—whatever our rational forgiveness, whatever the individual mother's love and strength, the child in us, the small female who grew up in a male-controlled world, still feels, at moments, wildly unmothered. When we can confront and unravel this paradox, this contradiction, face to the utmost in ourselves the groping passion of that little girl lost, we can begin to transmute it, and the blind anger and bitterness that have repetitiously erupted among women trying to build a movement together can be alchemized. Before sisterhood, there was the knowledge—transitory, fragmented, perhaps, but original and crucial—of mother-and-daughterhood.

3

This cathexis between mother and daughter—essential, distorted, misused—is the great unwritten story. Probably there is nothing in human nature more resonant with charges than the flow of energy between two biologically alike bodies, one of which has lain in amniotic bliss inside the other, one of which has labored to give birth to the other. The materials are here for the deepest mutuality and the most painful estrangement. Margaret Mead offers the possibility of "deep biochemical affinities between the mother and the female child, and contrasts between the mother and the male child, of which we now know nothing."[4] Yet this relationship has been minimized and trivialized in the annals of patriarchy. Whether in theological doctrine or art or sociology or psychoanalytic theory, it is the mother and son who appear as the eternal, determinative dyad. Small wonder, since theology, art, and social theory have been produced by sons. Like intense relationships between women in general, the relationship between mother and daughter has been profoundly threatening to men.

A glance at ancient texts would suggest that daughters barely existed. What the son means to the father is abundantly expressed, in the Upanishads:

> [The woman] nourishes her husband's self, the son, within her. . . . The father elevates the child even before the birth, and immediately after, by nourishing the mother and by performing ceremonies. When he thus elevates the child . . . he really elevates his second self, for the continuation of these worlds. . . . This is his second birth.

Aten, or Atum, is hailed in the Egyptian hymn:

> Creator of seed in women,
> Thou who makes fluid into man,
> Who maintainest the son in the womb of the mother. . . .

And Jewish traditional lore has it that a female soul is united with a male sperm, resulting in, of course, a "man-child."[5]

Daughters have been nullified by silence, but also by infanticide, of which they have everywhere been the primary victims. "Even a rich man always exposes a daughter." Lloyd deMause suggests that the statistical imbalance of males over females from antiquity into the Middle Ages resulted from the routine practice of killing off female infants. Daughters were destroyed not only by their fathers, but by their mothers. A husband of the first century B.C. writes to his wife as a matter of course: "If, as well may happen, you give birth to a child, if it is a boy let it live; if it is a girl, expose it."*⁶ Given the long prevalence of this practice, it is no wonder if a mother dreaded giving birth to a female like herself. While the father might see himself as "twice-born" in his son, such a "second birth" was denied the mothers of daughters.

In *To the Lighthouse* Virginia Woolf created what is still the most complex and passionate vision of mother-daughter schism in modern literature. It is significantly, one of the very few literary documents in which a woman has portrayed her mother as a central figure. Mrs. Ramsay is a kaleidoscopic character, and in successive readings of the novel, she changes, almost as our own mothers alter in perspective as we ourselves are changing. The feminist scholar Jane Lilienfeld has pointed out that during Virginia's early years her mother, Julia Stephen, expended almost all her maternal energies in caring for her husband and his lifework, the *Dictionary of National Biography*. Both Virginia and her sister Vanessa were later to seek each other for mothering, and Lilienfeld suggests that Leonard Woolf was to provide Virginia with the kind of care and vigilance that her mother had given her father.⁷ In any case, Mrs. Ramsay, with her "strange severity, her extreme courtesy" her attentiveness to others' needs (chiefly those of men), her charismatic attractiveness, even as a woman of fifty who had borne eight children—Mrs. Ramsay is no simple idealization. She is the "delicious fecundity . . . [the] fountain and spray of life [into which] the fatal sterility of the male plunged itself"; at the same time that "she felt this thing that she called life terrible, hostile, and quick to pounce on you if you gave it a chance."

She perceives "without hostility, the sterility of men," yet as Lilienfeld notes, she doesn't like women very much, and her life is spent in attunement to male needs. The young painter Lily Briscoe, sitting with her arms clasped around Mrs. Ramsay's knees, her head on her lap, longs to become one with her, in "the chambers of the mind

---

* It can be argued that, just as infanticide in general was a form of population control and even of eugenics (twins, infants who were undersized, malformed, or otherwise abnormal were destroyed, whatever their sex), female infanticide was a way of limiting births, since females were seen primarily as breeders. Still, the implicit devaluation of the female was hardly a message to be lost on women.

and heart of the woman who was, physically, touching her. . . . Could loving, as people called it, make her and Mrs. Ramsay one? for it was not knowledge but unity that she desired, not inscriptions on tablets, nothing that could be written in any language known to men, but intimacy itself . . ."

Yet nothing happens. Mrs. Ramsay is not available to her. And since Woolf has clearly transcribed herself into Lily Briscoe, the scene has a double charge: the daughter seeking intimacy with her own mother, the woman seeking intimacy with another woman, not her mother but toward whom she turns those passionate longings. Much later she understands that it is only in her work that she can "stand up to Mrs. Ramsay" and her "extraordinary power." In her work, she can reject the grouping of Mrs. Ramsay and James, "mother and son," as a pictorial subject. Through her work, Lily is independent of men, as Mrs. Ramsay is not. In the most acute, unembittered ways, Woolf pierces the shimmer of Mrs. Ramsay's personality; she needs men as much as they need her, her power and strength are founded on the dependency, the "sterility" of others.

It is clear that Virginia the daughter had pondered Julia her mother for years before depicting her in *To the Lighthouse*. Again, that fascinated attention is ascribed to Lily Briscoe:

> Fifty pairs of eyes were not enough to get around that one woman with, she thought. Among them, must be one that was stone blind to her beauty. One wanted some most secret sense, fine as air, with which to steal through keyholes and surround her where she sat knitting, talking, sitting silent in the window alone; which took to itself and treasured up like the air which held the smoke of the steamer, her thoughts, her imaginations, her desires. What did the hedge mean to her, what did the garden mean to her, what did it mean to her when a wave broke?[8]

And this, precisely, is what Virginia the artist achieved; but the achievement is testimony not merely to the power of her art but to the passion of the daughter for the mother, her need above all to understand this woman, so adored and so unavailable to her; to understand, in all complexity, the differences that separated her mother from herself.

The woman activist or artist born of a family-centered mother may in any case feel that her mother cannot understand or sympathize with the imperatives of her life; or that her mother has preferred and valued a more conventional daughter, or a son. In order to study nursing, Florence Nightingale was forced to battle, in the person of her mother, the restrictive conventions of upper-class Victorian womanhood, the destiny of a life in drawing rooms and country houses in which she saw women going mad "for want of something to do."[9] The painter Paula Modersohn-Becker was, throughout her life, concerned—and fearful—that her mother might not accept the terms of her life. Writing in 1899 of her struggles with her work, she says: "I write this especially for mother. I think she feels that my life is one long continuous egoistic drunken joyousness." On leaving her husband she writes: "I was so fearful that you might have been angry. . . . And now you are so good to me. . . . You, my dearest mother, stay by me and bless my life." And, the year before her own death in childbirth:

> . . . I am in continuous tumult, always . . . only sometimes resting, then moving again towards a goal . . . I beg of you to keep this in mind when at times I seem unloving. It means that all my strength is concentrated towards one thing only. I do not know whether this should be called egotism. If so, it is the most noble.
>
> I put my head in the lap from which I came forth, and thank you for my life.[10]

Emily Dickinson's famous statement that "I never had a mother" has been variously interpreted; but surely she meant in part that she felt herself deviant, set apart, from the kind of life her mother lived; that what most concerned her, her mother could not understand. Yet when her mother suffered a paralytic stroke in 1875, both Dickinson sisters nursed her tenderly until her death in 1882, and in a letter of that year Emily Dickinson writes:

> ... the departure of our Mother is so bleak a surprise, we are both benumbed ... only the night before she died, she was happy and hungry and ate a little Supper I made her with so much enthusiasm, I laughed with delight ...

> Wondering with sorrow, how we could spare our lost Neighbors [her correspondents] our first Neighbor, our Mother, quietly stole away.

> Plundered of her dear face, we scarcely know each other, and feel as if wrestling with a Dream, waking would dispel ...

And the daughter's letter ends with the poet's cry: "Oh, Vision of Language!"[11]

"Between Sylvia and me existed—as between my own mother and me—a sort of psychic osmosis which, at times, was very wonderful and comforting; at other times an unwelcome invasion of privacy." This is Aurelia Plath's description of the relationship between herself and her daughter Sylvia, from the other side. The intensity of the relationship seems to have disturbed some readers of Plath's *Letters Home*, an outpouring chiefly to her mother, written weekly or oftener, first from college and later from England. There is even a tendency to see this mother-daughter relationship as the source of Sylvia Plath's early suicide attempt, her relentless perfectionism and obsession with "greatness." Yet the preface to *Letters Home* reveals a remarkable woman, a true survivor; it was Plath's father who set the example of self-destructiveness. The letters are far from complete* and until many more materials are released, efforts to write Plath biography and criticism are questionable at best. But throughout runs her need to lay in her mother's lap, as it were, poems and

---

* There are many elisions and omissions, since publication had to be approved by Ted Hughes, Sylvia's husband.

prizes, books and babies, the longing for her mother when she is about to give birth, the effort to let Aurelia Plath know that her struggles and sacrifices to rear her daughter had been vindicated. In the last letters Sylvia seems to be trying to shield herself and Aurelia, an ocean away, from the pain of that "psychic osmosis." "I haven't the strength to see you for some time," she writes, explaining why she will not come to America after her divorce. "The horror of what you saw and what I saw you see last summer is between us and I cannot face you again until I have a new life . . ." (October 9, 1962). Three days later: "Do tear up my last one . . . I have [had] an incredible change of spirit. . . . Every morning, when my sleeping pill wears off, I am up about five, in my study with coffee, writing like mad— have managed a poem a day before breakfast. . . . Terrific stuff, as if domesticity had choked me. . . . Nick [her son] has two teeth, stands, and is an *angel . . .*" (October 12, 1962).[12*]

Psychic osmosis. Desperate defenses. The power of the bond often denied because it cracks consciousness, threatens at times to lead the daughter back into "those secret chambers . . . becoming, like waters poured into one jar, inextricably the same, one with the object one adored . . ."[13] Or, because there is no indifference or cruelty we can tolerate less, than the indifference or cruelty of our mothers.

In *The Well of Loneliness*, a novel by now notorious for its pathological-tragic view of lesbianism, Radclyffe Hall suggests an almost preternatural antipathy between Anna Gordon and her lesbian daughter Stephen. It is Stephen's father who—through having read Krafft-Ebbing—"understands" her, and treats her as he might a tragically maimed son. Her mother views her from the first as a stranger, an interloper, an alien creature. Radclyffe Hall's novel is painful as a revelation of the author's self-rejection, her internalizing of received opinions against her own instincts. The crux of her self-hatred lies in her imagining no possible relationship between

---

* 1986: See Alice Miller, "Sylvia Plath: An Example of Forbidden Suffering," in *For Your Own Good: Hidden Cruelty in Child-rearing and the Roots of Violence* (New York: Farrar, Straus & Giroux, 1983)..

Anna the mother and Stephen the daughter. Yet there is one passage in which she suggests the longing for and possibility of connection between mother and daughter—a connection founded on physical sensation:

> The scents of the meadows would move those two strangely. . . . Sometimes Stephen must tug at her mother's sleeve sharply—intolerable to bear that thick fragrance alone!
>
> One day she had said: "Stand still or you'll hurt it—it's all round us—it's a white smell, it reminds me of you!" And then she had flushed, and had glanced up quickly, rather frightened in case she should find Anna laughing.
>
> But her mother had looked at her curiously, gravely, puzzled by this creature who seemed all contradictions. . . . Anna had been stirred, as her child had been stirred, by the breath of the meadowsweet under the hedges; for in this way they were one, the mother and daughter . . . could they only have divined it, such simple things might have formed a link between them . . .
>
> They had gazed at each other as though asking for something . . . the one from the other; then the moment had passed—they had walked on in silence, no nearer in spirit than before.[14]

A woman who feels an unbridgeable gulf between her mother and herself may be forced to assume that her mother—like Stephen's—could never accept her sexuality. But, despite the realities of popular ignorance and bigotry about lesbians, and the fear that *she* has somehow "damaged" her daughter in the eyes of society, the mother may at some level—mute, indirect, oblique—want to confirm that daughter in her love for women. Mothers who have led perfectly traditional, heterosexual lives have welcomed their daughters' women lovers and supported their domestic arrangements, though often denying, if asked, the nature of the relationship. A woman who fully and gladly accepts her love for another woman is likely to create an atmosphere in which her mother will not reject her.* But that acceptance has first to be found in ourselves; it does not come as an act of will.

For those of us who had children, and later came to recognize and act upon the breadth and depth of our feelings for women, a complex new bond with our mothers is possible. The poet Sue Silvermarie writes:

> I find now, instead of a contradiction between lesbian and mother, there is an overlapping. What is the same between my lover and me, my mother and me, and my son and me is the motherbond—primitive, all-encompassing, and paramount.

> In loving another woman I discovered the deep urge to both be a mother to and find a mother in my lover. At first I feared the discovery. Everything around me told me it was evil. Popular Freudianism cursed it as a fixation, a sign of immaturity. But gradually I came to have faith in my own needs and desires. . . . Now I treasure and trust the drama between two loving women, in which each can become mother and each become child.

> It is most clear during lovemaking, when the separation of everyday life lifts for awhile. When I kiss and stroke and enter my lover, I am also a child re-entering my mother. I want to return to the womb-state of harmony, and also to the ancient world. I enter my lover but it is she in her orgasm who returns. I see on her face for a long moment, the unconscious bliss that an infant carries the memory of behind its shut eyes. Then when it is she who makes love to me . . . the intensity is also a pushing out, a borning! She comes in and is then identified with the

---

* 1986: This sentence seems facile to me in placing too much weight on the "self-acceptance" of the lesbian daughter and denying the mother's responsibility for her homophobia.

ecstasy that is born. . . . So I too return to the mystery of my mother, and of the world as it must have been when the motherbond was exalted.

Now I am ready to go back and understand the one whose body actually carried me. Now I can begin to learn about her, forgive her for the rejection I felt, yearn for her, ache for her. I could never want her until I myself had been wanted. By a woman. Now I know what it is to feel exposed as a newborn, to be pared down to my innocence. To lie with a woman and give her the power of my utter fragility. To have that power be cherished. Now that I know, I can return to her who could not cherish me as I needed. I can return without blame, and I can hope that she is ready for me.[15]

In studying the diaries and letters of American women of thirty-five families, from the 1760s to the 1880s, the historian Carroll Smith-Rosenberg has traced a pattern—indeed, a network—of close, sometimes explicitly sensual, long-lasting female friendships characteristic of the period. Tender, devoted, these relationships persisted through separations caused by the marriage of one or both women, in the context of a "female world" distinctly separate from the larger world of male concerns, but in which women held a paramount importance in each others' lives.

Smith-Rosenberg finds

> . . . an intimate mother-daughter relationship . . . at the heart of this female world. . . . Central to these relationships is what might be described as an apprenticeship system . . . mothers and other older women carefully trained daughters in the arts of housewifery and motherhood . . . adolescent girls temporarily took over the household . . . and helped in childbirth, nursing and weaning . . .

Daughters were born into a female world. . . . As long as the mother's domestic role remained relatively stable and few viable alternatives competed with it, daughters tended to accept their mother's world and to turn automatically to other women for support and intimacy . . .

One could speculate at length concerning the absence of that mother-daughter hostility today considered almost inevitable to an adolescent's struggle for autonomy. . . . It is possible that taboos against female aggression . . . were sufficiently strong to repress even that between mothers and their adolescent daughters. Yet these letters seem so alive and the interest of daughters in their mothers' affairs so vital and genuine that it is difficult to interpret their closeness exclusively in terms of repression and denial.[16]

What the absence of such a female world meant on the newly opening frontier can be grasped from the expressions of loneliness and nostalgia of immigrant women from Europe, who had left such networks of friends, mothers, and sisters far behind. Many of these women remained year-in, year-out on the homesteads, waiting eagerly for letters from home, fighting a peculiarly female battle with loneliness. "If I only had a few good women friends, I would be entirely satisfied. Those I miss," writes a Wisconsin woman in 1846. Instead of giving birth and raising children near her mother or other female relatives, the frontier mother had no one close to her with whom to share her womanly experiences; if cholera or diphtheria carried off a child or children, she would have to face the rituals of death and mourning on her own. Loneliness, unshared grief, and guilt often led to prolonged melancholy or mental breakdown.[17] If the frontier offered some women a greater equality and independence, and the chance to break out of more traditional roles, it also, ironically, deprived many of the emotional support and intimacy of a female community; it tore them from their mothers.

It may also seem ironic that the growth of nineteenth-century feminism, the false "liberation" (to smoke cigarettes and sleep around) of the twentieth-century flapper, the beginnings of new options for women as birth control gained in acceptance and use, may have had the initial effect of weakening the mother-daughter tie (and with it, the network of intense female friendships based on a common life-pattern and common expectancies). By the 1920s, and with the increasing pervasiveness of Freudian thought, intense female friendships could be tolerated between schoolgirls as "crushes," but were regarded as regressive and neurotic if they persisted into later life.*

4

"Matrophobia" as the poet Lynn Sukenick has termed it[18] is the fear not of one's mother or of motherhood but of *becoming one's mother.* Thousands of daughters see their mothers as having taught a compromise and self-hatred they are struggling to win free of, the one through whom the restrictions and degradations of a female existence were perforce transmitted. Easier by far to hate and reject a mother outright than to see beyond her to the forces acting upon her. But where a mother is hated to the point of matrophobia there may also be a deep underlying pull toward her, a dread that if one relaxes one's guard one will identify with her completely. An adolescent daughter may live at war with her mother yet borrow her clothes, her perfume. Her style of housekeeping when she leaves home may be a negative image of her mother's: beds never made, dishes unwashed, in unconscious reversal of the immaculately tended house of a woman from whose orbit she has to extricate herself.

While, in Grace Paley's words, "her son the doctor and her son the novelist" blame and ridicule the "Jewish mother," Jewish daughters are left with all the panic, guilt, ambivalence, and self-hatred of the woman from whom they came and the woman they may become. "Matrophobia" is a late-arrived strain in the life

---

* A woman of my mother's generation told me that her husband had effectively dampened her intimate friendship with another woman by telling her he was sure the woman was a lesbian. A hundred years before, their friendship would have been taken for granted, even to the husband's leaving the conjugal bed when a wife's woman friend came to visit, so that the two women could share as many hours, day and night, as possible.

of the Jewish daughter. Jewish women of the *shtetl* and ghetto and of the early immigrant period supported their Talmud-studying men, raised children, ran the family business, trafficked with the hostile gentile world, and in every practical and active way made possible the economic and cultural survival of the Jews. Only in the later immigrant generations, with a greater assimilationism and pressure for men to take over the economic sphere, were women expected to reduce themselves to perfecting the full-time mother-housewife role already invented by the gentile middle class.

"My mother would kill me if I didn't marry." "It would kill my mother if I didn't marry." In the absence of other absorbing and valued uses for her energy, the full-time "homemaker" has often sunk, yes, into the overinvolvement, the martyrdom, the possessive control, the chronic worry over her children, caricatured in fiction through the "Jewish mother." But the "Jewish mother" is only one creation of the enforced withdrawal of nineteenth- and twentieth-century women from all roles save one.*

Matrophobia can be seen as a womanly splitting of the self, in the desire to become purged once and for all of our mothers' bondage, to become individuated and free. The mother stands for the victim in ourselves, the unfree woman, the martyr. Our personalities seem dangerously to blur and overlap with our mothers'; and, in a desperate attempt to know where mother ends and daughter begins, we perform radical surgery.

> When her mother had gone, Martha cupped her hands protestingly over her stomach, and murmured to the creature within it that nothing would deform it, freedom would be its gift. She, Martha, the free spirit, would protect the creature from her, Martha, the maternal force; the maternal Martha, that enemy, would not be allowed to enter the picture.[19]

---

* 1986: Here is an obvious example of unstated class generalization. For large numbers of nineteenth- and twentieth-century freedwomen and immigrant women, no such withdrawal was mandated or possible.

Thus Doris Lessing's heroine, who has felt devoured by her own mother, splits herself—or tries to—when she realizes she, too, is to become a mother.

But even women with children, can exist in an uneasy wariness such as Kate Chopin depicts in *The Awakening* (1899):

> ... Mrs. Pontellier was not a mother-woman. The mother-women seemed to prevail that summer at Grand Isle. It was easy to know them, fluttering about with extended, protecting wings when any harm, real or imaginary, threatened their precious brood. They were women who idolized their children, worshipped their husbands, and esteemed it a holy privilege to efface' themselves as individuals and grow wings as ministering angels.[20]

Edna Pontellier, seeking her own pleasure and self-realization (though still entirely through men) is seen as "inadequate" as a mother, although her children are simply more independent than most. Cora Sandel sets her heroine, Alberta, against an archetypal mother-woman, Jeanne. Alberta is a writer, "haunted in recent years [by the fear] of not appearing sufficiently motherly and domesticated." She feels both reproached and wearied by the efficient, energetic Jeanne, who maintains an eye on everyone:

> "Don't forget your strengthening medicine, Pierre. Then you must lie down for awhile. You'll work all the better for it. Marthe, you've scratched yourself; don't touch anything before I've put iodine on it. You ought to look in at Mme. Poulain, Alberta, before she sells the rest of those sandshoes. . . . I don't think Tot should be in the sun for such a long time, Alberta . . .[21]

Thus, women who identify themselves primarily as mothers may seem both threatening and repellent to those who do not, or who feel unequal to the mother-role as defined by Chopin. Lily Briscoe, too, rejects this role: She does not want to *be* Mrs. Ramsay, and her discovery of this is crucial for her.

5

The loss of the daughter to the mother, the mother to the daughter, is the essential female tragedy. We acknowledge Lear (father-daughter split), Hamlet (son and mother), and Oedipus (son and mother) as great embodiments of the human tragedy; but there is no presently enduring recognition of mother-daughter passion and rapture.

There was such a recognition, but we have lost it. It was expressed in the religious mystery of Eleusis, which constituted the spiritual foundation of Greek life for two thousand years. Based on the mother-daughter myth of Demeter and Korê, this rite was the most forbidden and secret of classical civilization, never acted on the stage, open only to initiates who underwent long purification beforehand. According to the Homeric hymn to Demeter of the seventh century B.C., the mysteries were established by the goddess herself, on her reunion with her daughter Korê, or Persephone, who had been raped and abducted, in one version of the myth by Poseidon as lord of the underworld, or, in a later version, by Hades or Pluto, king of death. Demeter revenges herself for the loss of her daughter by forbidding the grain—of which she is queen—to grow.

When her daughter is restored to her—for nine months of the year only—she restores fruitfulness and life to the land for those months. But the Homeric hymn tells us that Demeter's supreme gift to humanity, in her rejoicing at Korê's return, was not the return of vegetation, but the founding of the sacred ceremonies at Eleusis.

The Eleusinian mysteries, inaugurated somewhere between 1400 and 1100 B.C., were considered a keystone to human spiritual survival. The Homeric hymn says:

> Blessed is he among men on earth who has beheld this. Never will he who has had no part in [the Mysteries] share in such things. He will be a dead man, in sultry darkness.*

* The above rendering is from C. Kerenyi's book *Eleusis*. For a verse translation of the entire hymn to Demeter, see Thelma Sargent, *The Homeric Hymns* (New York: Norton, 1973), pp. 2–14.

Pindar and Sophocles also distinguish between the initiate and "all the rest," the nonbeatified. And the Roman Cicero is quoted as saying of the Mysteries: "We have been given a reason not only to live in joy but also to die with better hope." The role played by the Mysteries of Eleusis in ancient spirituality has been compared to that of the passion and resurrection of Christ. But in the resurrection celebrated by the Mysteries, it is a mother whose wrath catalyzes the miracle, a daughter who rises from the underworld.

The rites of Eleusis were imitated and plagiarized in many parts of the ancient world. But the unique and sacred place, the *only* place where the true vision might be experienced, was the shrine at Eleusis itself. This was the site of the "Virgin's Well" or fountain where Demeter is supposed to have sat, grieving for the loss of Korê, and where she returned to establish the ceremonies. This sanctuary was destroyed, after two thousand years, when the Goths under Alaric invaded Greece in 396 A.D.

But for two thousand years, once a year in September, the *mystai* or initiands underwent purification by sea bathing, then walked in procession, carrying torches and bundles of myrtle, to Eleusis, where they finally had access to the "vision"—"the state of having seen." Pigs (animals sacred to the Great Mother) were slaughtered in sacrifice to Demeter, and eaten in her honor as a first stage in initiation. Only initiands and hierophants were allowed into the innermost shrine, where Korê appeared, called up by the voice of a thundering gong. There, in a great blaze of light, the queen of the dead, Persephone, appeared with her infant son, a sign to human beings that "birth in death *is* possible . . . if they had faith in the Goddess." The real meaning of the Mysteries was this reintegration of death and birth, at a time when patriarchal splitting may have seemed about to sever them entirely.

At the end of the ceremonies, according to C. Kerenyi, whose study of Eleusis I have drawn on for most of the above, the hierophant turned to the initiates and showed them a cut-off ear of grain:

> All who had "seen" turned, at the sight of this "concrete thing,"
> as though turning back from the hereafter into this world, back

to the world of tangible things, including grain. The grain *was* grain and not more, but it may well have summed up for the [initiates] everything that Demeter and Persephone had given to mankind: Demeter food and wealth, Persephone birth under the earth. To those who had seen Korê at Eleusis this was no mere metaphor.[22]

A marble relief of the fifth century B.C., found at Eleusis, portrays the goddesses Demeter and Korê, and between them the figure of a boy, Triptolemus. Triptolemus is the "primordial man," who must come to Demeter for her gift of the grain. According to one myth, he is converted from a violent, warlike way of life to a peaceful, agrarian one, through his initiation at Eleusis. He is supposed to have disseminated three commandments: "Honor your parents," "Honor the gods with fruits," and "Spare the animals." But Kerenyi makes clear that Triptolemus is not an essential figure at Eleusis.[23] Demeter as "tranquilly-enthroned" grain-goddess had existed in the archaic past, giver of fruits to man. But in her aspect as Goddess of the Mysteries she became much more: "she herself in grief and mourning entered upon the path of initiation and turned toward *the core of the Mysteries, namely, her quality as her daughter's mother.*" (Emphasis mine.)[24]

The separation of Demeter and Korê is an unwilling one; it is neither a question of the daughter's rebellion against the mother, nor the mother's rejection of the daughter. Eleusis seems to have been a final resurgence of the multiple aspects of the Great Goddess in the classical-patriarchal world. Rhea, the mother of Demeter, also appears in some of the myths; but also, Korê herself becomes a mother in the underworld.[25] Jane Harrison considered the Mysteries to be founded on a much more ancient women's rite, from which men were excluded, a possibility which tells us how endangered and complex the mother-daughter cathexis was, even before recorded history. Each daughter, even in the millennia before Christ, must have longed for a mother whose love for her and whose power were so great as to undo rape and bring her back from death. And every mother must have longed for the power of Demeter, the efficacy of her anger, the reconciliation with her lost self.

6

A strange and complex modern version of the Demeter-Korê myth resides in Margaret Atwood's novel, *Surfacing*. Her narrator—a woman without a name, who says of herself that she "can't love," "can't feel"—returns to the island in Canada where she and her family lived during World War II. She is searching for her father, who had been living there alone and has mysteriously disappeared. Her mother is dead. With her lover, and another couple, David and Anna—all more or less hippies in the American style, though professing hatred for all things Yankee—she returns to the place where her childhood was spent. She searches for clues to her father's whereabouts, in the surrounding woods and the neglected cabin. She finds old albums and scrapbooks of her childhood, saved by her mother; her mother's old leather jacket still swings from a hanger. She also finds sketches of Indian pictographs, made by her father. Her hippie friends are restless and bored in the primitive setting of the island, although they constantly express disgust with American technological imperialism. But it's the men in the novel—Canadian as well as Yankee—who are destroying the natural world, who kill for the sake of killing, cut down the trees; David brutally dominates Anna, sex is exploitative. Finally the narrator learns that her father's body has been found in the lake, drowned, evidently, while attempting to photograph some Indian wall-paintings. The others in her party are picked up by boat to return to civilization; she remains, determined to get back into connection with the place and its powers. She crawls naked through the woods, eating berries and roots, seeking her vision. Finally she returns to the cabin and its overgrown, half-wild garden, and there

> . . . I see her. She is standing in front of the cabin, her hand stretched out, she is wearing her grey leather jacket; her hair

is long, down to her shoulders, in the style of thirty years ago, before I was born; she is turned half away from me. I can see only the side of her face. She doesn't move, she is feeding them: one perches on her wrist, another on her shoulder.

I've stopped walking. At first I feel nothing except a lack of surprise: that is where she would be, she has been standing there all along. Then as I watch and it doesn't change I'm afraid, I'm cold with fear, I'm afraid it isn't real, paper doll cut by my eyes, burnt picture, if I blink she will vanish.

She must have sensed it, my fear. She turns her head quietly and looks at me, past me, as though she knows something is there but she can't quite see it ...

I go up to where she was. The jays are there in the trees, cawing at me; there are a few scraps on the feeding-tray still, they've knocked some to the ground. I squint up at them, trying to see her, trying to see which one she is.

Later, she has a vision of her father in the same place:

He has realized he was an intruder; the cabin, the fences, the fires and paths were violations; now his own fence excludes him, as logic excludes love. He wants it ended, the borders abolished, he wants the forest to flow back into the places his mind cleared: reparation ...

He turns toward me and it's not my father. It is what my father saw, the thing you meet when you've stayed here too long alone ...

I see now that although it isn't my father, it is what my father has become. I knew he wasn't dead ...

Atwood's last chapter begins:

This above all, to refuse to be a victim. Unless I can do that I can do nothing. I have to recant, give up the old belief that I am powerless and because of it nothing I can do will ever hurt anyone.... The word games, the winning and losing games are finished, at the moment there are no others but they will have to be invented....[26]

She is no "free woman," no feminist; her way of dealing with male-identification, the struggle with a male culture, has been to numb herself, to believe she "can't love." But *Surfacing* is not a programmatic novel. It is the work of a poet, filled with animistic and supernatural materials. The search for the father leads to reunion with the mother, who is at home in the wilderness, Mistress of the Animals. In some obscure, subconscious way, Atwood's narrator begins to recognize and accept her own power through her moment of vision, her brief, startling visitation from her mother. She has worked her way back—through fasting and sacrifice—beyond patriarchy. She cannot stay there: the primitive (her father's solution, the male—ultimately the fascist—solution) is not the answer; she has to go and live out her existence in this time. But she has had her illumination: she has seen her mother.

7

The woman who has felt "unmothered" may seek mothers all her life—may even seek them in men. In a women's group recently, someone said: "I married looking for a mother"; and a number of others in the group began agreeing with her. I myself remember lying in bed next to my husband, half-dreaming, half-believing, that the body close against mine was my mother's.* Perhaps all sexual or

---

* Simone de Beauvoir says of her mother that: "Generally speaking, I thought of her with no particular feeling. Yet in my sleep (although my father only made very rare and then insignificant appearances) she often played a most important part: she blended with Sartre, and we were happy together. And then the dream would turn into a nightmare: why was I living with her once more? How had I come to be in her power again? So our former relationship lived on in me in its double aspect—a

intimate physical contact brings us back to that first body. But the "motherless" woman may also react by denying her own vulnerability, denying she has felt any loss or absence of mothering. She may spend her life proving her strength in the "mothering" of others—as with Mrs. Ramsay, mothering men, whose weakness makes her feel strong, or mothering in the role of teacher, doctor, political activist, psychotherapist. In a sense she is giving to others what she herself has lacked; but this will always mean that she needs the neediness of others in order to go on feeling her own strength. She may feel uneasy with equals—particularly women.

Few women growing up in patriarchal society can feel mothered enough; the power of our mothers, whatever their love for us and their struggles on our behalf, is too restricted. And it is the mother through whom patriarchy early teaches the small female her proper expectations. The anxious pressure of one female on another to conform to a degrading and dispiriting role can hardly be termed "mothering," even if she does this believing it will help her daughter to survive.

Many daughters live in rage at their mothers for having accepted, too readily and passively, "whatever comes." A mother's victimization does not merely humiliate her, it mutilates the daughter who watches her for clues as to what it means to be a woman. Like the traditional foot-bound Chinese woman, she passes on her own affliction. The mother's self-hatred and low expectations are the binding-rags for the psyche of the daughter. As one psychologist has observed:

> When a female child is passed from lap to lap so that all the males in the room (father, brother, acquaintances) can get a hard-on, it is the helpless mother standing there and looking on that creates the sense of shame and guilt in the child. One woman at the recent rape conference in New York City testified that her father put a series of watermelon rinds in her vagina

subjection that I loved and hated" (*A Very Easy Death* [New York: Warner Paperback, 1973], pp. 119–20).

when she was a child to open it up to his liking, and beat her if she tried to remove them. Yet what that woman focuses her rage on today is that her mother told her, "Never say a word about it to anyone."

Another young girl was gang-raped in her freshman year of high school and her mother said to her, "You have brought disgrace on the family. You are no good anymore." . . . When she talks about these things now, the pain is as great as if it all happened yesterday.[27]

It is not simply that such mothers feel both responsible and powerless. It is that they carry their own guilt and self-hatred over into their daughters' experiences. The mother knows that if raped *she* would *feel* guilty; hence she tells her daughter she *is* guilty. She identifies intensely with her daughter, but through weakness, not through strength. Freudian psychoanalysis has viewed the rage of daughters toward their mothers as resentment for not having been given a penis. Clara Thompson, however, remarked, in a suprisingly early political view of "penis envy" that "the penis is the sign of the person in power in one particular competitive set-up in this culture, that between man and woman. . . . So, the attitude called penis envy is similar to the attitude of any underprivileged group toward those in power."[28] A contemporary psychoanalyst points out that the daughter's rage at her mother is more likely to arise from her mother having relegated her to second-class status, while looking to the son (or father) for the fulfillment of her own thwarted needs.[29] But even where there is no preferred brother or father, a daughter can feel rage at her mother's powerlessness or lack of struggle—because of her intense identification and because in order to fight for herself she needs first to have been both loved and fought for.*

* Nancy Chodorow cites examples of communities—among the Rajput and Brahmins in India—where, although sons are considered more desirable, mothers show a special attachment to their daughters, and she comments that "people in both groups say that this is out of sympathy for the future plight of their daughters, who will have to leave their natal family for a strange and usually oppressive postmarital household"

The nurture of daughters in patriarchy calls for a strong sense of *self*-nurture in the mother. The psychic interplay between mother and daughter can be destructive, but there is no reason why it is doomed to be. A woman who has respect and affection for her own body, who does not view it as unclean or as a sex-object, will wordlessly transmit to her daughter that a woman's body is a good and healthy place to live. A woman who feels pride in being female will not visit her self-depreciation upon her female child. A woman who has used her anger creatively will not seek to suppress anger in her daughter in fear that it could become, merely, suicidal.

All this is extremely difficult in a system which has persistently stolen women's bodies and egos from us. And what can we say of mothers who have not simply been robbed of their egos but who—alcoholic, drugged, or suicidal—are unavailable to their daughters? What of a woman who has to toil so hard for survival that no maternal energy remains at the end of the day, as she numbly, wearily picks up her child after work? The child does not discern the social system or the institution of motherhood, only a harsh voice, a dulled pair of eyes, a mother who does not hold her, does not tell her how wonderful she is. And what can we say of families in which the daughter feels that it was her father, not her mother, who gave her affection and support in becoming herself? It is a painful fact that a nurturing father, who replaces rather than complements a mother, *must be loved at the mother's expense*, whatever the reasons for the mother's absence. He may be doing his best, giving everything that a man can give, but the mother is twice-lost, if love for him takes the place of love for her.

"I have always gotten more support from men than from women": a cliché of token women, and an understandable one, since we do identify gratefully with anyone who seems to have strengthened us. But who has been *in a position* to strengthen us? A man often lends his

---

("Family Structure and Feminine Personality," in M. Z. Rosaldo and L. Lamphère, eds., *Woman, Culture and Society* [Stanford, Calif.: Stanford University Press, 1974], p. 47). But this kind of female bonding, though far preferable to rejection or indifference, arises from identification with the daughter's future victimization. There is no attempt on the mothers' part to change the cycle of repetitions into which the daughters' lives are being woven.

daughter the ego-support he denies his wife; he may use his daughter as stalking-horse against his wife; he may simply feel less threatened by a daughter's power, especially if she adores him. A male teacher may confirm a woman student while throttling his wife and daughters. Men have been able to give us power, support, and certain forms of nurture, as individuals, when they chose; but the power is always stolen power, withheld from the mass of women in patriarchy. And, finally, I am talking here about a kind of strength which can only be one woman's gift to another, the bloodstream of our inheritance. Until a strong line of love, confirmation, and example stretches from mother to daughter, from woman to woman across the generations, women will still be wandering in the wilderness.

8

What do we mean by the nurture of daughters? What is it we wish we had, or could have, as daughters; could give, as mothers? Deeply and primally we need trust and tenderness; surely this will always be true of every human being, but women growing into a world so hostile to us need a very profound kind of loving in order to learn to love ourselves. But this loving is not simply the old, institutionalized, sacrificial, "mother-love" which men have demanded: we want courageous mothering. The most notable fact that culture imprints on women is the sense of our limits. The most important thing one woman can do for another is to illuminate and expand her sense of actual possibilities. For a mother, this means more than contending with the reductive images of females in children's books, movies, television, the schoolroom. It means that the mother herself is trying to expand the limits of her life. *To refuse to be a victim:* and then to go on from there.

Only when we can wish imaginatively and courageously for ourselves can we wish unfetteredly for our daughters. But finally, a child is not a wish, nor a product of wishing. Women's lives—in all levels of society—have been lived too long in both depression and fantasy, while our active energies have been trained and absorbed into caring for others. It is essential, now, to begin breaking that cycle. Anyone who has read the literature in the obstetrician's waiting-room knows the child-care booklets which, at some point, confess that "you may get a fit of the blues" and suggest "having your husband take you to dinner in a French restaurant, or going shopping for a new dress." (The fiction that most women have both husbands and money is forever with us.) But the depressive mother who now and then allows herself a "vacation" or a "reward" is merely showing her daughters both that the female condition is depressing, and that there is no real way out.

As daughters we need mothers who want their own freedom and ours. We need not to be the vessels of another woman's self-denial and frustration. The quality of the mother's life—however embattled and unprotected—is her primary bequest to her daughter, because a woman who can believe in herself, who is a fighter, and who continues to struggle to create livable space around her, is demonstrating to her daughter that these possibilities exist. Because the conditions of life for many poor women demand a fighting spirit for sheer physical survival, such mothers have sometimes been able to give their daughters something to be valued far more highly than full-time mothering. But the toll is taken by the sheer weight of adversity, the irony that to fight for her child's physical survival the mother may have to be almost always absent from the child, as in Tillie Olsen's story, "I Stand Here Ironing."[30] For a child needs, as that mother despairingly knew, the care of someone for whom she is "a miracle."

Many women have been caught—have split themselves—between two mothers: one, usually the biological one, who represents the culture of domesticity, of male-centeredness, of conventional expectations, and another, perhaps a woman artist or teacher, who becomes the countervailing figure. Often this "counter-mother" is an athletics teacher who exemplifies strength and pride in her body, a freer way of being in the world; or an unmarried woman professor, alive with ideas, who represents the choice of a vigorous work life, of "living alone and liking it." This splitting may allow the young woman to fantasize alternately living as one or the other "mother," to test out two different identifications. But it can also lead to a life in which she never consciously resolves the choices, in which she alternately tries to play the hostess and please her husband as her mother did, and to write her novel or doctoral thesis. She has tried to break through the existing models, but she has not gone far enough, usually because nobody has told her how far there is to go.

The double messages need to be disentangled. "You can be anything you really want to be" is a half-truth, whatever a woman's class or economic advantages. We need to be very clear about the missing portion, rather than whisper the fearful subliminal message: "Don't go too far." A female child needs to be told, very early, the practical difficulties females have to face in even trying to imagine "what they want to be." Mothers who can talk freely with their daughters about sex, even teaching them to use contraception in adolescence, still leave them in the dark as to the expectations and stereotypes, false promises and ill-faith, awaiting them in the world. "You can be anything you really want to be"—*if* you are prepared to fight, to create priorities for yourself against the grain of cultural expectations, to persist in the face of misogynist hostility. Interpreting to a little girl, or to an adolescent woman, the kinds of treatment she encounters because she is female, is as necessary as explaining to a nonwhite child reactions based on the color of her skin.*

It is one thing to adjure a daughter, along Victorian lines, that her lot is to "suffer and be still," that woman's fate is determined. It is wholly something else to acquaint her honestly with the jeopardy all women live under in patriarchy, to let her know by word and deed that she has her mother's support, and moreover, that while it *can* be dangerous to move, to speak, to act, each time she suffers rape—physical or psychic—in silence, she is putting another stitch in her own shroud.

9

I talk with a brilliant and radical thinker, a woman scholar of my generation. She describes her early feelings when she used to find herself at conferences or parties among faculty wives, most of whom

* A woman recently described in my hearing how her friend's daughter had been on the verge of dropping out of architecture school because of the harassment she encountered there as a woman. It was her mother who urged her to stay, to fight a political battle against sexism, and get the training she wanted.

had or would have children, she the only unmarried woman in the room. She felt, then, that her passionate investigations, the recognition accorded her work, still left her the "barren" woman, the human failure, among so many women who were mothers. I ask her, "But can you imagine how some of them were envying you your freedom, to work, to think, to travel, to enter a room as yourself, not as some child's mother or some man's wife?" Yet even as I speak, I know: the gulf between "mothers" and "nonmothers" (even the term is pure negation, like "widow," meaning *without*) will be closed only as we come to understand how *both* childbearing and childlessness have been manipulated to make women into negative quantities, or bearers of evil.

In the interstices of language lie powerful secrets of the culture. Throughout this book I have been thrown back on terms like "unchilded," "childless," or "child-free"; we have no familiar, ready-made name for a woman who defines herself, by choice, neither in relation to children nor to men, who is self-identified, who has chosen herself. "Unchilded," "childless," simply define her in terms of a lack; even "child-free" suggests only that she has refused motherhood, not what she is about *in and of herself.* The notion of the "free woman" is strongly tinged with the suggestion of sexual promiscuity, of "free love," of being "free" of man's ownership; it still defines the woman by her relationships with men. The ancient meaning of the word "virgin" (she-who-is-unto-herself) is obscured by connotations of the "undeflorated" or intact hymen, or of the Roman Catholic Virgin Mother, defined entirely by her relationship to God the Son. "Amazon" suggests too narrowly the warrior-maiden who has renounced all ties with men except for procreation: again, definition through relatedness. Neither is "lesbian" a satisfactory term here; not all self-identified women would call themselves lesbians; moreover, numberless lesbians are mothers of children.

There can be no more simplistic formula for women than to escape into some polarization such as "Mothers or Amazons," "matriarchal clan or guerilleres." For one thing, in the original matriarchal clan *all* females, of whatever age, were called "mothers"—even little girls. Motherhood was a social rather than a physical function. "Women . . . were sisters to one another and mothers to all the children of the community without regard to which individual mother bore any child. . . . Aborigines describe themselves as . . . 'brotherhoods' from the standpoint of the male and 'motherhoods' from the standpoint of the female."[31] And everywhere, girl-children as young as six have cared for younger siblings.

The "childless woman" and the "mother" are a false polarity, which has served the institutions both of motherhood and heterosexuality. There are no such simple categories. There are women (like Ruth Benedict) who have tried to have children and could not. The causes may range from a husband's unacknowledged infertility to signals of refusal sent out from her cerebral cortex. A woman may have looked at the lives of women with children and have felt that, given the circumstances of motherhood, she must remain childless if she is to pursue any other hopes or aims.* As the nineteenth-century feminist Margaret Fuller wrote in an undated fragment:

> I have no child and the woman in me has so craved this experience, that it seems the want of it must paralyze me. But now as I look on these lovely children of a human birth, what slow and neutralizing cares they bring with them to the mother! The children of the muse come quicker, with less pain and disgust, rest more lightly on the bosom.†

A young girl may have lived in horror of her mother's child-worn existence and told herself, once and for all, *No, not for me.* A lesbian may have gone through abortions in early relationships with men, love children, yet still feel her life too insecure to take on the grilling of an adoption or the responsibility of an artificial pregnancy. A

---

* There are enough single women now adopting children, enough unmarried mothers keeping their children, to suggest that if mothering were not an enterprise which so increases a woman's social vulnerability, many more "childless" women would choose to have children of their own.

† She was later to bear a child, in Italy, to a man ten years younger than herself, and to die in the wreck of the ship on which she, the child, and the father were returning to America.

woman who has chosen celibacy may feel her decision entails a life without children. Ironically, it is precisely the institution of motherhood, which, in an era of birth control, has influenced women against becoming mothers. It is simply too hypocritical, too exploitative of mothers and children, too oppressive.

But is a woman who bore a baby she could not keep a "childless" woman? Am I, whose children are grown-up, who come and go as I will, unchilded as compared to younger women still pushing prams, hurrying home to feedings, waking at night to a child's cry? What makes us mothers? The care of small children? The physical changes of pregnancy and birth? The years of nurture? What of the woman who, never having been pregnant, begins lactating when she adopts an infant? What of the woman who stuffs her newborn into a bus-station locker and goes numbly back to her "child-free" life? What of the woman who, as the eldest girl in a large family, has practically raised her younger sisters and brothers, and then has entered a convent?

The woman struggling to cope with several young children, a job, and the unavailability of decent child-care and schooling, may feel pure envy (and rage) at the apparent freedom and mobility of the "child-free" woman (I have). The woman without children of her own may see, like Margaret Fuller, the "dull and neutralizing cares" of motherhood *as it is lived in the bondage of a patriarchal system* and congratulate herself on having stayed "free," not having been "brainwashed into motherhood." But these polarizations imply a failure of imagination.

Throughout recorded history the "childless" woman has been regarded (with certain specific exceptions, such as the cloistered nun or the temple virgin) as a failed woman, unable to speak for the rest of her sex,* and omitted from the hypocritical and palliative reverence accorded the mother. "Childless" women have been

---

* See, for example, Albert Memmi's criticism of Simone de Beauvoir's *The Second Sex:* she is suspect because she did not exercise what Memmi glibly describes as her "woman's right" to bear children (*Dominated Man* [Boston: Beacon, 1968], pp. 150–51).

burned as witches, persecuted as lesbians, have been refused the right to adopt children because they were unmarried. They have been seen as embodiments of the great threat to male hegemony: the woman who is not tied to the family, who is disloyal to the law of heterosexual pairing and bearing. These women have nonetheless been expected to serve their term for society as missionaries, nuns, teachers, nurses, maiden aunts; to give, rather than sell their labor if they were middle-class; to speak softly, if at all, of women's condition. Yet ironically, precisely because they were not bound to the cycle of hourly existence with children, because they could reflect, observe, write, such women in the past have given us some of the few available strong insights into the experience of women in general. Without the unacclaimed research and scholarship of "childless" women, without Charlotte Brontë (who died in her first pregnancy), Margaret Fuller (whose major work was done before her child was born), without George Eliot, Emily Brontë, Emily Dickinson, Christina Rossetti, Virginia Woolf, Simone de Beauvoir—we would all today be suffering from spiritual malnutrition as women.

The "unchilded" woman, if such a term makes any sense, is still affected by centuries-long attitudes—on the part of both women and men—towards the birthing, child-rearing function of women. Any woman who believes that the institution of motherhood has nothing to do with *her* is closing her eyes to crucial aspects of her situation.

Many of the great mothers have not been biological. The novel *Jane Eyre*, as I have tried to show elsewhere, can be read as a woman-pilgrim's progress along a path of classic female temptation, in which the motherless Jane time after time finds women who protect, solace, teach, challenge, and nourish her in self-respect.[32] For centuries, daughters have been strengthened and energized by nonbiological mothers, who have combined a care for the practical values of survival with an incitement toward further horizons, a compassion for vulnerability with an insistence on our buried strengths.*

---

* Mary Daly has suggested to me that the "nonbiological mother" is really a "spirit-sister" (a phrase which affirms her in terms of what she is rather than what she isn't).

It is precisely this that has allowed us to survive; not our occasional breakthroughs into tokendom, not our "special cases," although these have been beacons for us, illuminations of what ought to be.

We are, none of us, "either" mothers or daughters; to our amazement, confusion, and greater complexity, we are both. Women, mothers or not, who feel committed to other women, are increasingly giving each other a quality of caring filled with the diffuse kinds of identification that exist between actual mothers and daughters. Into the mere notion of "mothering" we may carry, as daughters, negative echoes of our own mothers' martyrdom, the burden of their valiant, necessarily limited efforts on our behalf, the confusion of their double messages. But it is a timidity of the imagination which urges that we can be "daughters"—therefore free spirits—rather than "mothers"—defined as eternal givers. Mothering and nonmothering have been such charged concepts for us, precisely because *whichever we did has been turned against us.*

To accept and integrate and strengthen both the mother and the daughter in ourselves is no easy matter, because patriarchal attitudes have encouraged us to split, to polarize, these images, and to project all unwanted guilt, anger, shame, power, freedom, onto the "other" woman. But any radical vision of sisterhood demands that we reintegrate them.

10

As a child raised in what was essentially the South, Baltimore in the segregated 1930s, I had from birth not only a white, but a Black mother. This relationship, so little explored, so unexpressed, still charges the relationships of Black and white women. We have not only been under slavery, lily white wife and dark, sensual concubine; victims of marital violation on the one hand and unpredictable, licensed rape on the other. We have been mothers and daughters to each other; and although, in the last few years, Black and white feminists have been moving toward a still-difficult sisterhood, there is little yet known, unearthed, of the time when we were mothers and daughters. Lillian Smith remembers:

I knew that my old nurse who had cared for me through long
months of illness, who had given me refuge when a little sister
took my place as the baby of the family, who soothed me, fed
me, delighted me with her stories and games, let me fall asleep
on her warm, deep breast, was not worthy of the passionate love
I felt for her but must be given instead a half-smiled-at affection . . . I knew but I never believed it that the deep respect I
felt for her, the tenderness, the love, was a childish thing which
every normal child outgrows . . . and that somehow—though it
seemed impossible to my agonized heart—I too must outgrow
these feelings. . . . I learned to cheapen with tears and sentimental talk of "my old mammy" one of the profound relationships of my life.[33]

My Black mother was "mine" only for four years, during which
she fed me, dressed me, played with me, watched over me, sang to
me, cared for me tenderly and intimately. "Childless" herself, she *was*
a mother. She was slim, dignified, and very handsome, and from her
I learned—nonverbally—a great deal about the possibilities of dignity in a degrading situation. After my sister's birth, though she still
worked from time to time in the house, she was no longer my care-
giver. Another nurse came, but she was not the same to me; I felt she
belonged to my sister. Twenty years later, when I left my parents'
house, expecting never to return, my Black mother told me: "Yes, I
understand how you have to leave and do what you think is right. I
once had to break somebody's heart to go and live my life." She died
a few years later; I did not see her again.

And, yes: I know what Lillian Smith describes, the confusion of
discovering that a woman one has loved and been cherished by is
somehow "unworthy" of such love after a certain age. That sense of
betrayal, of the violation of a relationship, was for years a nameless
thing, for no one yet spoke of racism, and even the concept of "prejudice" had not yet filtered into my childhood world. It was simply
"the way things were," and we tried to repress the confusion and
the shame.

When I began writing this chapter I began to remember my Black mother again: her calm, realistic vision of things, her physical grace and pride, her beautiful soft voice. For years, she had drifted out of reach, in my searches backward through time, exactly as the double silence of sexism and racism intended her to do. She was meant to be utterly annihilated.*

But, at the edge of adolescence, we find ourselves drawing back from our natural mothers as if by a similar edict. It is toward men, henceforth, that our sensual and emotional energies are intended to flow. The culture makes it clear that neither the Black mother, nor the white mother, nor any of the other mothers, are "worthy" of our profoundest love and loyalty. Women are made taboo to women—not just sexually, but as comrades, cocreators, coinspiritors. In breaking this taboo, we are reuniting with our mothers; in reuniting with our mothers, we are breaking this taboo.

* 1986: The above passage overpersonalizes and does not, it seems to me now, give enough concrete sense of the actual position of the Black domestic worker caring for white children. Whatever the white child has received both in care and caring, the Black woman has given under enormous constraints. As Trudier Harris sums it up, "Control of time, wages and work was solely in the hands of the white woman." Black women domestic workers were often statistically invisible in the labor market and were expected to behave invisibly in the white home, existing as a role and not a person: "She must maneuver . . . in order to salvage what portion of dignity she can, to resist depersonalization and dehumanization. . . . The mistress expects the maid to be a good mammy simply because, she believes, it's in her blood." (Trudier Harris, *From Mammies to Militants: Domestics in Black American Literature* [Philadelphia: Temple University Press, 1982], pp. 10, 13, 20. See also Alice Childress, *Like One of the Family . . . Conversations from a Domestic's Life* [New York: Independence, 1956].)

Blood, Bread, and Poetry

Selected Prose
1979–1985

WHAT DOES A WOMAN NEED TO KNOW? (1979)

have been very much moved that you, the class of 1979, chose me for your commencement speaker. It is important to me to be here, in part because Smith is one of the original colleges for women, but also because she has chosen to continue identifying herself as a women's college. We are at a point in history where this fact has enormous potential, even if that potential is as yet unrealized. The possibilities for the future education of women that haunt these buildings and grounds are enormous, when we think of what an independent women's college might be: a college dedicated both to teaching women what women need to know and, by the same token, to changing the landscape of knowledge itself. The germ of those possibilities lies symbolically in The Sophia Smith Collection, an archive much in need of expansion and increase, but which by its very existence makes the statement that women's lives and work are valued here and that our foresisters, buried and diminished in male-centered scholarship, are a living presence, necessary and precious to us.

Suppose we were to ask ourselves simply: What does a woman need to know to become a self-conscious, self-defining human being? Doesn't she need a knowledge of her own history, of her much-politicized female body, of the creative genius of women of the past—the skills and crafts and techniques and visions possessed by women in other times and cultures, and how they have been rendered anonymous, censored, interrupted, devalued? Doesn't she, as one of that majority who are still denied equal rights as citizens, enslaved as sexual prey, unpaid or underpaid as workers, withheld

Commencement address at Smith College, Northampton, Massachusetts, 1979.

from her own power—doesn't she need an analysis of her condition, a knowledge of the women thinkers of the past who have reflected on it, a knowledge, too, of women's world-wide individual rebellions and organized movements against economic and social injustice, and how these have been fragmented and silenced?

Doesn't she need to know how seemingly natural states of being, like heterosexuality, like motherhood, have been enforced and institutionalized to deprive her of power? Without such education, women have lived and continue to live in ignorance of our collective context, vulnerable to the projections of men's fantasies about us as they appear in art, in literature, in the sciences, in the media in the so-called humanistic studies. I suggest that not anatomy, but enforced ignorance, has been a crucial key to our powerlessness.

There is—and I say this with sorrow—there is no women's college today which is providing young women with the education they need for survival as whole persons in a world which denies women wholeness—that knowledge which, in the words of Coleridge, "returns again as power." The existence of Women's Studies courses offers at least some kind of life line. But even Women's Studies can amount simply to compensatory history; too often they fail to challenge the intellectual and political structures that must be challenged if women as a group are ever to come into collective, nonexclusionary freedom. The belief that established science and scholarship—which have so relentlessly excluded women from their making—are "objective" and "value-free" and that feminist studies are "unscholarly," "biased," and "ideological" dies hard. Yet the fact is that all science, and all scholarship, and all art are ideological; there is no neutrality in culture. And the ideology of the education you have just spent four years acquiring in a women's college has been largely, if not entirely, the ideology of white male supremacy, a construct of male subjectivity. The silences, the empty spaces, the language itself, with its excision of the female, the methods of discourse tell us as much as the content, once we learn to watch for what is left out, to listen for the unspoken, to study the patterns of established science and scholarship with an outsider's eye. One of the dangers of a privileged education for women is that we may lose the eye of the outsider and come to believe that those patterns hold for humanity, for the universal, and that they include us.

And so I want to talk today about privilege and about tokenism and about power. Everything I can say to you on this subject comes hard-won, from the lips of a woman privileged by class and skin color, a father's favorite daughter, educated at Radcliffe, which was then casually referred to as the Harvard "Annex." Much of the first four decades of my life was spent in a continuous tension between the world the Fathers taught me to see, and had rewarded me for seeing, and the flashes of insight that came through the eye of the outsider. Gradually those flashes of insight, which at times could seem like brushes with madness, began to demand that I struggle to connect them with each other, to insist that I take them seriously. It was only when I could finally affirm the outsider's eye as the source of a legitimate and coherent vision, that I began to be able to do the work I truly wanted to do, live the kind of life I truly wanted to live, instead of carrying out the assignments I had been given as a privileged woman and a token.

For women, all privilege is relative. Some of you were not born with class or skin-color privilege; but you all have the privilege of education, even if it is an education which has largely denied you knowledge of yourselves as women. You have, to begin with, the privilege of literacy; and it is well for us to remember that, in an age of increasing illiteracy, 60 percent of the world's illiterates are women. Between 1960 and 1970, the number of illiterate men in the world rose by 8 million, while the number of illiterate women rose by 40 million.[1] And the number of illiterate women is increasing. Beyond literacy, you have the privilege of training and tools which can allow you to go beyond the content of your education and re-educate yourselves—to debrief yourselves, we might call it, of the false messages of your education in this culture, the messages telling you that women have not really cared about power or learning or creative opportunities because of a psychobiological need to serve men and produce children; that only a few atypical women have been exceptions to this rule; the messages telling you that woman's experience is neither normative nor central to human experience. You have the training and the tools to do independent research, to evaluate data, to criticize, and to express in language and visual forms what you discover. This is a privilege, yes, but only if you do not give up in exchange for it the deep knowledge of the unprivileged, the knowledge that, as a woman, you have historically been viewed and still are viewed as existing, not in your own right, but in the service of men. And only if you refuse to give up your capacity to think as a woman, even though in the graduate schools and professions to which many of you will be going you will be praised and rewarded for "thinking like a man."

The word *power* is highly charged for women. It has been long associated for us with the use of force, with rape, with the stockpiling of weapons, with the ruthless accrual of wealth and the hoarding of resources, with the power that acts only in its own interest, despising and exploiting the powerless—including women and children. The effects of this kind of power are all around us, even literally in the water we drink and the air we breathe, in the form of carcinogens and radioactive wastes. But for a long time now, feminists have been talking about redefining power, about that meaning of power which returns to the root—*posse, potere, pouvoir:* to be able, to have the potential, to possess and use one's energy of creation—*transforming power.* An early objection to feminism—in both the nineteenth and twentieth centuries—was that it would make women behave like men—ruthlessly, exploitatively, oppressively. In fact, radical feminism looks to a transformation of human relationships and structures in which power, instead of a thing to be hoarded by a few, would be released to and from within the many, shared in the form of knowledge, expertise, decision making, access to tools, as well as in the basic forms of food and shelter and health care and literacy. Feminists—and many nonfeminists—are, and rightly so, still concerned with what power would mean in such a society, and with the relative differences in power among and between women here and now.

Which brings me to a third meaning of power where women are concerned: the false power which masculine society offers to a few women, on condition that they use it to maintain things as they are, and that they essentially "think like men." This is the meaning of female tokenism: that power withheld from the vast majority of women is offered to a few, so that it appears that any "truly qualified" woman can gain access to leadership, recognition, and reward; hence, that justice based on merit actually prevails. The token woman is encouraged to see herself as different from most other women, as exceptionally talented and deserving, and to separate herself from the wider female condition; and she is perceived by "ordinary" women as separate also, perhaps even as stronger than themselves.

Because you are, within the limits of all women's ultimate outsiderhood, a privileged group of women, it is extremely important for your future sanity that you understand the way tokenism functions. Its most immediate contradiction is that, while it seems to offer the individual token woman a means to realize her creativity, to influence the course of events, it also, by exacting of her certain kinds of behavior and style, acts to blur her outsider's eye, which could be her real source of power and vision. Losing her outsider's vision, she loses the insight which both binds her to other women and affirms her in herself. Tokenism essentially demands that the token deny her identification with women as a group, especially with women less privileged than she: if she is a lesbian, that she deny her relationships with individual women; that she perpetuate rules and structures and criteria and methodologies which have functioned to exclude women; that she renounce or leave undeveloped the critical perspective of her female consciousness. Women unlike herself—poor women, women of color, waitresses, secretaries, housewives in the supermarket, prostitutes, old women—become invisible to her; they may represent too acutely what she has escaped or wished to flee.

President Conway tells me that ever-increasing numbers of you are going on from Smith to medical and law schools. The news, on the face of it, is good: that, thanks to the feminist struggle of the past decade, more doors into these two powerful professions are open to women. I would like to believe that any profession would be better for having more women practicing it, and that any woman practicing law or medicine would use her knowledge and skill to work to transform the realm of health care and the interpretations of the law, to make them responsive to the needs of all those—women, people of color, children, the aged, the dispossessed—for whom they function today as repressive controls. I would like to believe this, but it will not happen even if 50 percent of the members of these professions are women, unless those women refuse to be made into token insiders, unless they zealously preserve the outsider's view and the outsider's consciousness.

For no woman is really an insider in the institutions fathered by masculine consciousness. When we allow ourselves to believe we are, we lose touch with parts of ourselves defined as unacceptable by that consciousness; with the vital toughness and visionary strength of the angry grandmothers, the shamanesses, the fierce marketwomen of the Ibo Women's War, the marriage-resisting women silkworkers of prerevolutionary China, the millions of widows, midwives, and women healers tortured and burned as witches for three centuries in Europe, the Beguines of the twelfth century, who formed independent women's orders outside the domination of the Church, the women of the Paris Commune who marched on Versailles, the uneducated housewives of the Women's Cooperative Guild in England who memorized poetry over the washtub and organized against their oppression as mothers, the women thinkers discredited as "strident," "shrill," "crazy," or "deviant" whose courage to be heretical, to speak their truths, we so badly need to draw upon in our own lives. I believe that every woman's soul is haunted by the spirits of earlier women who fought for their unmet needs and those of their children and their tribes and their peoples, who refused to accept the prescriptions of a male church and state, who took risks and resisted, as women today—like Inez Garcia, Yvonne Wanrow, Joan Little, Cassandra Peten—are fighting their rapists and batterers. Those spirits dwell in us, trying to speak to us. But we can choose to be deaf; and tokenism, the myth of the "special" woman, the unmothered Athena sprung from her father's brow, can deafen us to their voices.

In this decade now ending, as more women are entering the professions (though still suffering sexual harassment in the workplace, though still, if they have children, carrying two full-time jobs, though still vastly outnumbered by men in upper-level and decision-making jobs), we need most profoundly to remember that early insight of the feminist movement as it evolved in the late sixties: *that no woman is liberated until we all are liberated.* The media flood us with messages to the contrary, telling us that we live in an era when "alternate life styles" are freely accepted, when "marriage contracts" and "the new intimacy" are revolutionizing heterosexual relationships, that shared parenting and the "new fatherhood" will change the world. And we live in a society leeched upon by the "personal growth" and "human potential" industry, by the delusion that individual self-fulfillment can be found in thirteen weeks or a weekend, that the alienation and injustice experienced by women, by Black and Third World people, by the poor, in a world ruled by white males, in a society which fails to meet the most basic needs and which is slowly poisoning itself, can be mitigated or dispersed by Transcendental Meditation. Perhaps the most succinct expression of this message I have seen is the appearance of a magazine for women called *Self.* The insistence of the feminist movement, that each woman's selfhood is precious, that the feminine ethic of self-denial and self-sacrifice must give way to a true woman identification, which would affirm our connectedness with all women, is perverted into a commercially profitable and politically debilitating narcissism. It is important for each of you, toward whom many of these messages are especially directed, to discriminate clearly between "liberated life style" and feminist struggle, and to make a conscious choice.

It's a cliché of commencement speeches that the speaker ends with a peroration telling the new graduates that however badly past generations have behaved, their generation must save the world. I would rather say to you, women of the class of 1979: Try to be worthy of your foresisters, learn from your history, look for inspiration to your ancestresses. If this history has been poorly taught to you, if you do not know it, then use your educational privilege to learn it. Learn how some women of privilege have compromised the greater liberation of women, how others have risked their privileges to further it; learn how brilliant and successful women have failed to create a more just and caring society, precisely because they have tried to do so on terms that the powerful men around them would accept and tolerate. Learn to be worthy of the women of every class, culture, and historical age who did otherwise, who spoke boldly when women were jeered and physically harassed for speaking in public, who—like Anne Hutchinson, Mary Wollstonecraft, the Grimké sisters, Abby Kelley, Ida B. Wells-Barnett, Susan B. Anthony, Lillian Smith, Fannie Lou Hamer—broke taboos, who resisted slavery—their own and other people's. To become a token woman—whether you win the Nobel prize or merely get tenure at the cost of denying your sisters—is to become something less than a man indeed, since men are loyal at least to their own world view, their laws of brotherhood and male self-interest. I am not suggesting that you imitate male loyalties; with the philosopher Mary Daly, I believe that the bonding of women must be utterly different and for an utterly different end: not the misering of resources and power, but the release, in each other, of the yet unexplored resources and transformative power of women, so long despised, confined, and wasted. Get all the knowledge and skill you can in whatever professions you enter; but remember that most of your education must be self-education, in learning the things women need to know and in calling up the voices we need to hear within ourselves.

COMPULSORY HETEROSEXUALITY AND LESBIAN EXISTENCE (1980)

FOREWORD

I want to say a little about the way "Compulsory Heterosexuality" was originally conceived and the context in which we are now living. It was written in part to challenge the erasure of lesbian existence from so much of scholarly feminist literature, an erasure which I felt (and feel) to be not just anti-lesbian, but anti-feminist in its consequences, and to distort the experience of heterosexual women as well. It was not written to widen divisions but to encourage heterosexual feminists to examine heterosexuality as a political institution which disempowers women—and to change it. I also hoped that other lesbians would feel the depth and breadth of woman identification and woman bonding that has run like a continuous though stifled theme through the heterosexual experience, and that this would become increasingly a politically activating impulse, not simply a validation of personal lives. I wanted the essay to suggest new kinds of criticism, to incite new questions in classrooms and academic journals, and to sketch, at least, some bridge over the gap between *lesbian* and *feminist*. I wanted, at the very least, for feminists to find it less possible to read, write, or teach from a perspective of unexamined heterocentricity.

Within the three years since I wrote "Compulsory Heterosexuality"—with this energy of hope and desire—the pres-

Originally written in 1978 for the "Sexuality" issue of *Signs*, this essay was published there in 1980. In 1982 Antelope Publications reprinted it as part of a feminist pamphlet series. Rich provided some additional notes when it was reprinted in *Blood, Bread, and Poetry* (1986). The foreword was written for the pamphlet.

sures to conform in a society increasingly conservative in mood
have become more intense. The New Right's messages to women
have been, precisely, that we are the emotional and sexual property of men, and that the autonomy and equality of women threaten
family, religion, and state. The institutions by which women have
traditionally been controlled—patriarchal motherhood, economic
exploitation, the nuclear family, compulsory heterosexuality—are
being strengthened by legislation, religious fiat, media imagery, and
efforts at censorship. In a worsening economy, the single mother
trying to support her children confronts the feminization of poverty which Joyce Miller of the National Coalition of Labor Union
Women has named one of the major issues of the 1980s. The lesbian,
unless in disguise, faces discrimination in hiring and harassment
and violence in the street. Even within feminist-inspired institutions
such as battered-women's shelters and Women's Studies programs,
open lesbians are fired and others warned to stay in the closet. The
retreat into sameness—assimilation for those who can manage it—is
the most passive and debilitating of responses to political repression,
economic insecurity, and a renewed open season on difference.

I want to note that documentation of male violence against
women—within the home especially—has been accumulating rapidly in this period (see pages 375–76, note 9). At the same time, in the
realm of literature which depicts woman bonding and woman identification as essential for female survival, a steady stream of writing
and criticism has been coming from women of color in general and
lesbians of color in particular—the latter group being even more profoundly erased in academic feminist scholarship by the double bias
of racism and homophobia.[1]

There has recently been an intensified debate on female sexuality
among feminists and lesbians, with lines often furiously and bitterly
drawn, with *sadomasochism* and *pornography* as key words which
are variously defined according to who is talking. The depth of wom-
en's rage and fear regarding sexuality and its relation to power and
pain is real, even when the dialogue sounds simplistic, self-righteous,
or like parallel monologues.

Because of all these developments, there are parts of this essay that I would word differently, qualify, or expand if I were writing it today. But I continue to think that heterosexual feminists will draw political strength for change from taking a critical stance toward the ideology which *demands* heterosexuality, and that lesbians cannot assume that we are untouched by that ideology and the institutions founded upon it. There is nothing about such a critique that requires us to think of ourselves as victims, as having been brainwashed or totally powerless. Coercion and compulsion are among the conditions in which women have learned to recognize our strength. Resistance is a major theme in this essay and in the study of women's lives, if we know what we are looking for.

I

Biologically men have only one innate orientation—a sexual one that draws them to women,—while women have two innate orientations, sexual toward men and reproductive toward their young.[2]

I was a woman terribly vulnerable, critical, using femaleness as a sort of standard or yardstick to measure and discard men. Yes—something like that. I was an Anna who invited defeat from men without ever being conscious of it. (But I am conscious of it. And being conscious of it means I shall leave it all behind me and become—but what?) I was stuck fast in an emotion common to women of our time, that can turn them bitter, or Lesbian, or solitary. Yes, that Anna during that time was ...

[Another blank line across the page:][3]

The bias of compulsory heterosexuality, through which lesbian experience is perceived on a scale ranging from deviant to abhorrent or simply rendered invisible, could be illustrated from many texts other than the two just preceding. The assumption made by Rossi, that women are "innately" sexually oriented only toward men, and that made by Lessing, that the lesbian is simply acting out of her bitterness toward men, are by no means theirs alone; these assumptions are widely current in literature and in the social sciences.

I am concerned here with two other matters as well: first, how and why women's choice of women as passionate comrades, life partners, co-workers, lovers, community has been crushed, invalidated, forced into hiding and disguise; and second, the virtual or total neglect of lesbian existence in a wide range of writings, including feminist scholarship. Obviously there is a connection here. I believe that much feminist theory and criticism is stranded on this shoal.

My organizing impulse is the belief that it is not enough for feminist thought that specifically lesbian texts exist. Any theory or cultural/political creation that treats lesbian existence as a marginal or less "natural" phenomenon, as mere "sexual preference," or as the mirror image of either heterosexual or male homosexual relations is profoundly weakened thereby, whatever its other contributions. Feminist theory can no longer afford merely to voice a toleration of "lesbianism" as an "alternative life style" or make token allusion to lesbians. A feminist critique of compulsory heterosexual orientation for women is long overdue. In this exploratory paper, I shall try to show why.

I will begin by way of examples, briefly discussing four books that have appeared in the last few years, written from different viewpoints and political orientations, but all presenting themselves, and favorably reviewed, as feminist.[4] All take as a basic assumption that the social relations of the sexes are disordered and extremely problematic, if not disabling, for women; all seek paths toward change. I have learned more from some of these books than from others, but on this I am clear: each one might have been more accurate, more powerful, more truly a force for change had the author dealt with lesbian existence as a reality and as a source of knowledge and power available to women, or with the institution of heterosexuality itself as a beachhead of male dominance.[5] In none of them is the question ever raised as to whether, in a different context or other things being equal, women would *choose* heterosexual coupling and marriage; heterosexuality is presumed the "sexual preference" of "most women," either implicitly or explicitly. In none of these books, which concern themselves with mothering, sex roles, relationships, and societal prescriptions for women, is compulsory heterosexuality ever examined as an institution powerfully affecting all these, or the idea of "preference" or "innate orientation" even indirectly questioned.

In *For Her Own Good: 150 Years of the Experts' Advice to Women* by Barbara Ehrenreich and Deirdre English, the authors' superb pamphlets *Witches, Midwives and Nurses: A History of Women Healers* and *Complaints and Disorders: The Sexual Politics of Sickness* are developed into a provocative and complex study. Their thesis in this book is that the advice given to American women by male health professionals, particularly in the areas of marital sex, maternity, and child care, has echoed the dictates of the economic marketplace and the role capitalism has needed women to play in production and/or reproduction. Women have become the consumer victims of various cures, therapies, and normative judgments in different periods (including the prescription to middle-class women to embody and preserve the sacredness of the home—the "scientific" romanticization of the home itself). None of the "experts'" advice has been either particularly scientific or women-oriented; it has reflected male needs, male fantasies about women, and male interest in controlling women—particularly in the realms of sexuality and motherhood—fused with the requirements of industrial capitalism. So much of this book is so devastatingly informative and is written with such lucid feminist wit, that I kept waiting as I read for the basic proscription against lesbianism to be examined. It never was.

This can hardly be for lack of information. Jonathan Katz's *Gay American History*[6] tells us that as early as 1656 the New Haven Colony prescribed the death penalty for lesbians. Katz provides many suggestive and informative documents on the "treatment" (or torture) of lesbians by the medical profession in the nineteenth and twentieth centuries. Recent work by the historian Nancy Sahli documents the crackdown on intense female friendships among college women at the turn of the present century.[7] The ironic title *For Her Own Good* might have referred first and foremost to the economic imperative to heterosexuality and marriage and to the sanctions imposed against single women and widows—both of whom have been and still are viewed as deviant. Yet, in this often enlightening Marxist-feminist overview of male prescriptions for female sanity and health, the economics of prescriptive heterosexuality go unexamined.[8]

Of the three psychoanalytically based books, one, Jean Baker Miller's *Toward a New Psychology of Women*, is written as if lesbians simply do not exist, even as marginal beings. Given Miller's title, I find this astonishing. However, the favorable reviews the book has received in feminist journals, including *Signs* and *Spokeswoman*, suggest that Miller's heterocentric assumptions are widely shared. In *The Mermaid and the Minotaur: Sexual Arrangements and the Human Malaise*, Dorothy Dinnerstein makes an impassioned argument for the sharing of parenting between women and men and for an end to what she perceives as the male/female symbiosis of "gender arrangements," which she feels are leading the species further and further into violence and self-extinction. Apart from other problems that I have with this book (including her silence on the institutional and random terrorism men have practiced on women—and children—throughout history,[9] and her obsession with psychology to the neglect of economic and other material realities that help to create psychological reality), I find Dinnerstein's view of the relations between women and men as "a collaboration to keep history mad" utterly ahistorical. She means by this a collaboration to perpetuate social relations which are hostile, exploitative, and destructive to life itself. She sees women and men as equal partners in the making of "sexual arrangements," seemingly unaware of the repeated struggles of women to resist oppression (their own and that of others) and to change their condition. She ignores, specifically, the history of women who—as witches, *femmes seules,* marriage resisters, spinsters, autonomous widows, and/or lesbians—have managed on varying levels *not* to collaborate. It is this history, precisely, from which feminists have so much to learn and on which there is overall such blanketing silence. Dinnerstein acknowledges at the end of her book that "female separatism," though "on a large scale and in the long run wildly impractical," has something to teach us: "Separate, women could in principle set out to learn from scratch—undeflected by the opportunities to evade this task that men's presence has so far offered—what intact self-creative humanness is."[10] Phrases like "intact self-creative humanness" obscure the question of what the many forms of female separatism have actually been addressing. The fact is that women in every culture and throughout history *have* undertaken the task of independent, nonheterosexual, woman-connected existence, to the extent made possible by their context, often in the belief that they were the "only ones" ever to have done so. They have undertaken it even though few women have been in an economic position to resist marriage altogether, and even though attacks against unmarried women have ranged from aspersion and mockery to deliberate gynocide, including the burning and torturing of millions of widows and spinsters during the witch persecutions of the fifteenth, sixteenth, and seventeenth centuries in Europe.

Nancy Chodorow does come close to the edge of an acknowledgment of lesbian existence. Like Dinnerstein, Chodorow believes that the fact that women, and women only, are responsible for child care in the sexual division of labor has led to an entire social organization of gender inequality, and that men as well as women must become primary carers for children if that inequality is to change. In the process of examining, from a psychoanalytic perspective, how mothering by women affects the psychological development of girl and boy children, she offers documentation that men are "emotionally secondary" in women's lives, that "women have a richer, ongoing inner world to fall back on . . . men do not become as emotionally important to women as women do to men."[11] This would carry into the late twentieth century Smith-Rosenberg's findings about eighteenth- and nineteenth-century women's emotional focus on women. "Emotionally important" can, of course, refer to anger as well as to love, or to that intense mixture of the two often found in women's relationships with women—one aspect of what I have come to call the "double life of women" (see below). Chodorow concludes that because women have women as mothers, "the mother remains a primary internal object [*sic*] to the girl, so that heterosexual relationships are on the model of a nonexclusive, second relationship for her, whereas for the boy they re-create an exclusive, primary relationship." According to

Chodorow, women "have learned to deny the limitations of masculine lovers for both psychological and practical reasons."[12]

But the practical reasons (like witch burnings, male control of law, theology, and science, or economic nonviability within the sexual division of labor) are glossed over. Chodorow's account barely glances at the constraints and sanctions which historically have enforced or ensured the coupling of women with men and obstructed or penalized women's coupling or allying in independent groups with other women. She dismisses lesbian existence with the comment that "lesbian relationships do tend to re-create mother-daughter emotions and connections, but most women are heterosexual" (implied: more mature, having developed beyond the mother-daughter connection?). She then adds: "This heterosexual preference and taboos on homosexuality, in addition to objective economic dependence on men, make the option of primary sexual bonds with other women unlikely—though more prevalent in recent years."[13] The significance of that qualification seems irresistible, but Chodorow does not explore it further. Is she saying that lesbian existence has become more *visible* in recent years (in certain groups), that economic and other pressures have changed (under capitalism, socialism, or both), and that consequently more women are rejecting the heterosexual "choice"? She argues that women want children because their heterosexual relationships lack richness and intensity, that in having a child a woman seeks to re-create her own intense relationship with her mother. It seems to me that on the basis of her own findings, Chodorow leads us implicitly to conclude that heterosexuality is *not* a "preference" for women, that, for one thing, it fragments the erotic from the emotional in a way that women find impoverishing and painful. Yet her book participates in mandating it. Neglecting the covert socializations and the overt forces which have channeled women into marriage and heterosexual romance, pressures ranging from the selling of daughters to the silences of literature to the images of the television screen, she, like Dinnerstein, is stuck with trying to reform a man-made institution—compulsory heterosexuality—as if, despite profound emotional impulses and complementarities drawing women toward women, there is a mystical/biological heterosexual inclination, a "preference" or "choice" which draws women toward men.

Moreover, it is understood that this "preference" does not need to be explained unless through the tortuous theory of the female Oedipus complex or the necessity for species reproduction. It is lesbian sexuality which (usually, and incorrectly, "included" under male homosexuality) is seen as requiring explanation. This assumption of female heterosexuality seems to me in itself remarkable: it is an enormous assumption to have glided so silently into the foundations of our thought.

The extension of this assumption is the frequently heard assertion that in a world of genuine equality, where men are nonoppressive and nurturing, everyone would be bisexual. Such a notion blurs and sentimentalizes the actualities within which women have experienced sexuality; it is a liberal leap across the tasks and struggles of here and now, the continuing process of sexual definition which will generate its own possibilities and choices. (It also assumes that women who have chosen women have done so simply because men are oppressive and emotionally unavailable, which still fails to account for women who continue to pursue relationships with oppressive and/or emotionally unsatisfying men.) I am suggesting that heterosexuality, like motherhood, needs to be recognized and studied as a *political institution*—even, or especially, by those individuals who feel they are, in their personal experience, the precursors of a new social relation between the sexes.

II

If women are the earliest sources of emotional caring and physical nurture for both female and male children, it would seem logical, from a feminist perspective at least, to pose the following questions: whether the search for love and tenderness in both sexes does not originally lead toward women; *why in fact women would ever redirect that search;* why species survival, the means of impregnation, and emotional/erotic relationships should ever have become so rigidly identified with each other; and why such violent strictures should be found necessary to enforce women's total emotional, erotic loyalty and subservience to men. I doubt that enough feminist scholars and theorists have taken the pains to acknowledge the societal forces which wrench women's emotional and erotic energies away from themselves and other women and from woman-identified values. These forces, as I shall try to show, range from literal physical enslavement to the disguising and distorting of possible options.

I do not assume that mothering by women is a "sufficient cause" of lesbian existence. But the issue of mothering by women has been much in the air of late, usually accompanied by the view that increased parenting by men would minimize antagonism between the sexes and equalize the sexual imbalance of power of males over females. These discussions are carried on without reference to compulsory heterosexuality as a phenomenon, let alone as an ideology. I do not wish to psychologize here, but rather to identify sources of male power. I believe large numbers of men could, in fact, undertake child care on a large scale without radically altering the balance of male power in a male-identified society.

In her essay "The Origin of the Family," Kathleen Gough lists eight characteristics of male power in archaic and contemporary societies which I would like to use as a framework: "men's ability to deny women sexuality or to force it upon them; to command or exploit their labor to control their produce; to control or rob them of their children; to confine them physically and prevent their movement; to use them as objects in male transactions; to cramp their creativeness; or to withhold from them large areas of the society's knowledge and cultural attainments."[14] (Gough does not perceive these power characteristics as specifically enforcing heterosexuality, only as producing sexual inequality.) Below, Gough's words appear in italics; the elaboration of each of her categories, in brackets, is my own.

Characteristics of male power include *the power of men*

1. *to deny women* [their own] *sexuality*—[by means of clitoridectomy and infibulation; chastity belts; punishment, including

death, for female adultery; punishment, including death, for lesbian sexuality; psychoanalytic denial of the clitoris; strictures against masturbation; denial of maternal and postmenopausal sensuality; unnecessary hysterectomy; pseudolesbian images in the media and literature; closing of archives and destruction of documents relating to lesbian existence]

2. *or to force it* [male sexuality] *upon them*—[by means of rape (including marital rape) and wife beating; father-daughter, brother-sister incest; the socialization of women to feel that male sexual "drive" amounts to a right;[15] idealization of heterosexual romance in art, literature, the media, advertising, etc.; child marriage; arranged marriage; prostitution; the harem; psychoanalytic doctrines of frigidity and vaginal orgasm; pornographic depictions of women responding pleasurably to sexual violence and humiliation (a subliminal message being that sadistic heterosexuality is more "normal" than sensuality between women)]

3. *to command or exploit their labor to control their produce*—[by means of the institutions of marriage and motherhood as unpaid production; the horizontal segregation of women in paid employment; the decoy of the upwardly mobile token woman; male control of abortion, contraception, sterilization, and childbirth; pimping; female infanticide, which robs mothers of daughters and contributes to generalized devaluation of women]

4. *to control or rob them of their children*—[by means of father right and "legal kidnapping";[16] enforced sterilization; systematized infanticide; seizure of children from lesbian mothers by the courts; the malpractice of male obstetrics; use of the mother as "token torturer"[17] in genital mutilation or in binding the daughter's feet (or mind) to fit her for marriage]

5. *to confine them physically and prevent their movement*—[by means of rape as terrorism, keeping women off the streets; purdah; foot binding; atrophying of women's athletic capabilities; high heels and "feminine" dress codes in fashions; the

veil; sexual harassment on the streets; horizontal segregation of women in employment; prescriptions for "full-time" mothering at home; enforced economic dependence of wives]

6. *to use them as objects in male transactions*—[use of women as "gifts"; bride price; pimping; arranged marriage; use of women as entertainers to facilitate male deals—e.g., wife-hostess, cocktail waitress required to dress for male sexual titillation, call girls, "bunnies," geisha, *kisaeng* prostitutes, secretaries]

7. *to cramp their creativeness*—[witch persecutions as campaigns against midwives and female healers, and as pogrom against independent, "unassimilated" women;[18] definition of male pursuits as more valuable than female within any culture, so that cultural values become the embodiment of male subjectivity; restriction of female self-fulfillment to marriage and motherhood; sexual exploitation of women by male artists and teachers; the social and economic disruption of women's creative aspirations;[19] erasure of female tradition][20]

8. *to withhold from them large areas of the society's knowledge and cultural attainments*—[by means of noneducation of females; the "Great Silence" regarding women and particularly lesbian existence in history and culture;[21] sex-role tracking which deflects women from science, technology, and other "masculine" pursuits; male social/professional bonding which excludes women; discrimination against women in the professions]

These are some of the methods by which male power is manifested and maintained. Looking at the schema, what surely impresses itself is the fact that we are confronting not a simple maintenance of inequality and property possession, but a pervasive cluster of forces, ranging from physical brutality to control of consciousness, which suggests that an enormous potential counterforce is having to be restrained.

Some of the forms by which male power manifests itself are more easily recognizable as enforcing heterosexuality on women than are others. Yet each one I have listed adds to the cluster of forces within which women have been convinced that marriage and sexual orientation toward men are inevitable—even if unsatisfying or oppressive—components of their lives. The chastity belt; child marriage; erasure of lesbian existence (except as exotic and perverse) in art, literature, film; idealization of heterosexual romance and marriage—these are some fairly obvious forms of compulsion, the first two exemplifying physical force, the second two control of consciousness. While clitoridectomy has been assailed by feminists as a form of woman torture,[22] Kathleen Barry first pointed out that it is not simply a way of turning the young girl into a "marriageable" woman through brutal surgery. It intends that women in the intimate proximity of polygynous marriage will not form sexual relationships with each other, that—from a male, genital-fetishist perspective—female erotic connections, even in a sex-segregated situation, will be literally excised.[23]

The function of pornography as an influence on consciousness is a major public issue of our time, when a multibillion-dollar industry has the power to disseminate increasingly sadistic, women-degrading visual images. But even so-called soft-core pornography and advertising depict women as objects of sexual appetite devoid of emotional context, without individual meaning or personality—essentially as a sexual commodity to be consumed by males. (So-called lesbian pornography, created for the male voyeuristic eye, is equally devoid of emotional context or individual personality.) The most pernicious message relayed by pornography is that women are natural sexual prey to men and love it, that sexuality and violence are congruent, and that for women sex is essentially masochistic, humiliation pleasurable, physical abuse erotic. But along with this message comes another, not always recognized: that enforced submission and the use of cruelty, if played out in heterosexual pairing, is sexually "normal," while sensuality between women, including erotic mutuality and respect, is "queer," "sick," and either pornographic in itself or not very exciting compared with the sexuality of whips and bondage.[24] Pornography does not simply create a climate in which sex and violence are interchangeable; *it widens the range of behavior considered acceptable from men in heterosexual intercourse*—behavior which reiteratively strips women of their autonomy, dignity, and sexual potential, including the potential of loving and being loved by women in mutuality and integrity.

In her brilliant study *Sexual Harassment of Working Women: A Case of Sex Discrimination*, Catharine A. MacKinnon delineates the intersection of compulsory heterosexuality and economics. Under capitalism, women are horizontally segregated by gender and occupy a structurally inferior position in the workplace. This is hardly news, but MacKinnon raises the question why, even if capitalism "requires some collection of individuals to occupy low-status, low-paying positions . . . such persons must be biologically female," and goes on to point out that "the fact that male employers often do not hire qualified women, *even when they could pay them less than men* suggests that more than the profit motive is implicated" [emphasis added].[25] She cites a wealth of material documenting the fact that women are not only segregated in low-paying service jobs (as secretaries, domestics, nurses, typists, telephone operators, child-care workers, waitresses), but that "sexualization of the woman" is part of the job. Central and intrinsic to the economic realities of women's lives is the requirement that women will "market sexual attractiveness to men, who tend to hold the economic power and position to enforce their predilections." And MacKinnon documents that "sexual harassment perpetuates the interlocked structure by which women have been kept sexually in thrall to men at the bottom of the labor market. Two forces of American society converge: men's control over women's sexuality and capital's control over employees' work lives."[26] Thus, women in the workplace are at the mercy of sex as power in a vicious circle. Economically disadvantaged, women—whether waitresses or professors—endure sexual harassment to keep their jobs and learn to behave in a complaisantly and ingratiatingly heterosexual manner because they discover this is their true qualification for employment, whatever the job description. And, MacKinnon notes, the woman who too decisively resists sexual overtures in the workplace is accused of being "dried up" and sexless, or lesbian. This raises a specific difference between the experiences of lesbians and homosexual men. A lesbian, closeted on her job because of heterosexist prejudice, is not simply forced into denying the truth of her outside relationships or private life. Her job depends on her pretending to be not merely heterosexual, but a heterosexual *woman* in terms of dressing and playing the feminine, deferential role required of "real" women.

MacKinnon raises radical questions as to the qualitative differences between sexual harassment, rape, and ordinary heterosexual intercourse. ("As one accused rapist put it, he hadn't used 'any more force than is usual for males during the preliminaries.'") She criticizes Susan Brownmiller[27] for separating rape from the mainstream of daily life and for her unexamined premise that "rape is violence, intercourse is sexuality," removing rape from the sexual sphere altogether. Most crucially she argues that "taking rape from the realm of 'the sexual,' placing it in the realm of 'the violent,' allows one to be against it without raising any questions about the extent to which the institution of heterosexuality has defined force as a normal part of 'the preliminaries.' "[28] "Never is it asked whether, under conditions of male supremacy, the notion of 'consent' has any meaning."[29]

The fact is that the workplace, among other social institutions, is a place where women have learned to accept male violation of their psychic and physical boundaries as the price of survival; where women have been educated—no less than by romantic literature or by pornography—to perceive themselves as sexual prey. A woman seeking to escape such casual violations along with economic disadvantage may well turn to marriage as a form of hoped-for protection, while bringing into marriage neither social nor economic power, thus entering that institution also from a disadvantaged position. MacKinnon finally asks:

> What if inequality is built into the social conceptions of male and female sexuality, of masculinity and femininity, of sexiness and heterosexual attractiveness? Incidents of sexual harassment suggest that male sexual desire itself may be aroused by female vulnerability.... Men feel they can take advantage, so they want to, so they do. Examination of sexual harassment, precisely because the episodes appear commonplace, forces one to confront the fact that sexual intercourse normally occurs

between economic (as well as physical) unequals . . . the apparent legal requirement that violations of women's sexuality appear out of the ordinary before they will be punished helps prevent women from defining the ordinary conditions of their own consent.[30]

Given the nature and extent of heterosexual pressures—the daily "eroticization of women's subordination," as MacKinnon phrases it[31]—I question the more or less psychoanalytic perspective (suggested by such writers as Karen Horney, H. R. Hayes, Wolfgang Lederer, and, most recently, Dorothy Dinnerstein) that the male need to control women sexually results from some primal male "fear of women" and of women's sexual insatiability. It seems more probable that men really fear not that they will have women's sexual appetites forced on them or that women want to smother and devour them, but that women could be indifferent to them altogether, that men could be allowed sexual and emotional—therefore economic— access to women *only* on women's terms, otherwise being left on the periphery of the matrix.

The means of assuring male sexual access to women have recently received searching investigation by Kathleen Barry.[32] She documents extensive and appalling evidence for the existence, on a very large scale, of international female slavery, the institution once known as "white slavery" but which in fact has involved, and at this very moment involves, women of every race and class. In the theoretical analysis derived from her research, Barry makes the connection between all enforced conditions under which women live subject to men: prostitution, marital rape, father-daughter and brother-sister incest, wife beating, pornography, bride price, the selling of daughters, purdah, and genital mutilation. She sees the rape paradigm— where the victim of sexual assault is held responsible for her own victimization—as leading to the rationalization and acceptance of other forms of enslavement where the woman is presumed to have "chosen" her fate, to embrace it passively, or to have courted it perversely through rash or unchaste behavior. On the contrary, Barry maintains, "female sexual slavery is present in ALL situations where women or girls cannot change the conditions of their existence; where regardless of how they got into those conditions, e.g., social pressure, economic hardship, misplaced trust or the longing for affection, they cannot get out; and where they are subject to sexual violence and exploitation."[33] She provides a spectrum of concrete examples, not only as to the existence of a widespread international traffic in women, but also as to how this operates—whether in the form of a "Minnesota pipeline" funneling blonde, blue-eyed midwestern runaways to Times Square, or the purchasing of young women out of rural poverty in Latin America or Southeast Asia, or the providing of *maisons d'abattage* for migrant workers in the eighteenth arrondissement of Paris. Instead of "blaming the victim" or trying to diagnose her presumed pathology, Barry turns her floodlights on the pathology of sex colonization itself, the ideology of "cultural sadism" represented by the pornography industry and by the overall identification of women primarily as "sexual beings whose responsibility is the sexual service of men."[34]

Barry delineates what she names a "sexual domination perspective" through whose lens sexual abuse and terrorism of women by men has been rendered almost invisible by treating it as natural and inevitable. From its point of view, women are expendable as long as the sexual and emotional needs of the male can be satisfied. To replace this perspective of domination with a universal standard of basic freedom for women from gender-specific violence, from constraints on movement, and from male right of sexual and emotional access is the political purpose of her book. Like Mary Daly in *Gyn/Ecology*, Barry rejects structuralist and other cultural-relativist rationalizations for sexual torture and anti-woman violence. In her opening chapter, she asks of her readers that they refuse all handy escapes into ignorance and denial. "The only way we can come out of hiding, break through our paralyzing defenses, is to know it all— the full extent of sexual violence and domination of women. . . . In *knowing,* in facing directly, we can learn to chart our course out of this oppression, by envisioning and creating a world which will preclude sexual slavery."[35]

"Until we name the practice, give conceptual definition and

form to it, illustrate its life over time and in space, those who are its most obvious victims will also not be able to name it or define their experience."

But women are all, in different ways and to different degrees, its victims; and part of the problem with naming and conceptualizing female sexual slavery is, as Barry clearly sees, compulsory heterosexuality.[36] Compulsory heterosexuality simplifies the task of the procurer and pimp in world-wide prostitution rings and "eros centers," while, in the privacy of the home, it leads the daughter to "accept" incest/rape by her father, the mother to deny that it is happening, the battered wife to stay on with an abusive husband. "Befriending or love" is a major tactic of the procurer, whose job it is to turn the runaway or the confused young girl over to the pimp for seasoning. The ideology of heterosexual romance, beamed at her from childhood out of fairy tales, television, films, advertising, popular songs, wedding pageantry, is a tool ready to the procurer's hand and one which he does not hesitate to use, as Barry documents. Early female indoctrination in "love" as an emotion may be largely a Western concept; but a more universal ideology concerns the primacy and uncontrollability of a male sexual drive. This is one of many insights offered by Barry's work:

> As sexual power is learned by adolescent boys through the social experience of their sex drive, so do girls learn that the locus of sexual power is male. Given the importance placed on the male sex drive in the socialization of girls as well as boys, early adolescence is probably the first significant phase of male identification in a girl's life and development.... As a young girl becomes aware of her own increasing sexual feelings ... she turns away from her heretofore primary relationships with girlfriends. As they become secondary to her, recede in importance in her life, her own identity also assumes a secondary role and she grows into male identification.[37]

We still need to ask why some women never, even temporarily, turn away from "heretofore primary relationships" with other females. And why does male identification—the casting of one's social, political, and intellectual allegiances with men—exist among lifelong sexual lesbians? Barry's hypothesis throws us among new questions, but it clarifies the diversity of forms in which compulsory heterosexuality presents itself. In the mystique of the overpowering, all-conquering male sex drive, the penis-with-a-life-of-its-own, is rooted the law of male sex right to women, which justifies prostitution as a universal cultural assumption on the one hand, while defending sexual slavery within the family on the basis of "family privacy and cultural uniqueness" on the other.[38] The adolescent male sex drive, which, as both young women and men are taught, once triggered cannot take responsibility for itself or take no for an answer, becomes, according to Barry, the norm and rationale for adult male sexual behavior: a condition of *arrested sexual development*. Women learn to accept as natural the inevitability of this "drive" because they receive it as dogma. Hence, marital rape; hence, the Japanese wife resignedly packing her husband's suitcase for a weekend in the *kisaeng* brothels of Taiwan; hence, the psychological as well as economic imbalance of power between husband and wife, male employer and female worker, father and daughter, male professor and female student.

The effect of male identification means

> internalizing the values of the colonizer and actively partici-
> pating in carrying out the colonization of one's self and one's
> sex. . . . Male identification is the act whereby women place men
> above women, including themselves, in credibility, status, and
> importance in most situations, regardless of the comparative
> quality the women may bring to the situation. . . . Interaction
> with women is seen as a lesser form of relating on every level.[39]

What deserves further exploration is the doublethink many women engage in and from which no woman is permanently and utterly free: However woman-to-woman relationships, female support networks, a female and feminist value system are relied on and cherished, indoctrination in male credibility and status can still create synapses in thought, denial of feeling, wishful thinking, a profound sexual and intellectual confusion.[40] I quote here from a letter I received the day I was writing this passage: "I have had very bad relationships with men—I am now in the midst of a very painful separation. I am trying to find my strength through women—without my friends, I could not survive." How many times a day do women speak words like these or think them or write them, and how often does the synapse reassert itself?

Barry summarizes her findings:

> Considering the arrested sexual development that is understood to be normal in the male population, and considering the numbers of men who are pimps, procurers, members of slavery gangs, corrupt officials participating in this traffic, owners, operators, employees of brothels and lodging and entertainment facilities, pornography purveyors, associated with prostitution, wife beaters, child molesters, incest perpetrators, johns (tricks) and rapists, one cannot but be momentarily stunned by the enormous male population engaging in female sexual slavery. The huge number of men engaged in these practices should be cause for declaration of an international emergency, a crisis in sexual violence. But what should be cause for alarm is instead accepted as normal sexual intercourse.[41]

Susan Cavin, in a rich and provocative, if highly speculative, dissertation, suggests that patriarchy becomes possible when the original female band, which includes children but ejects adolescent males, becomes invaded and outnumbered by males; that not patriarchal marriage, but the rape of the mother by the son, becomes the first act of male domination. The entering wedge, or leverage, which allows this to happen is not just a simple change in sex ratios; it is also the mother-child bond, manipulated by adolescent males in order to remain within the matrix past the age of exclusion. Maternal affection is used to establish male right of sexual access, which, however, must ever after be held by force (or through control of consciousness) since the original deep adult bonding is that of woman for woman.[42] I find this hypothesis extremely suggestive, since one form of false consciousness which serves compulsory heterosexuality is the maintenance of a mother-son relationship between women and men, including the demand that women provide maternal solace, nonjudgmental nurturing, and compassion for their harassers, rapists, and batterers (as well as for men who passively vampirize them).

But whatever its origins, when we look hard and clearly at the extent and elaboration of measures designed to keep women within a male sexual purlieu, it becomes an inescapable question whether the issue feminists have to address is not simple "gender inequality" nor the domination of culture by males nor mere "taboos against homosexuality," but the enforcement of heterosexuality for women as a means of assuring male right of physical, economic, and emotional access.[43] One of many means of enforcement is, of course, the rendering invisible of the lesbian possibility, an engulfed continent which rises fragmentedly into view from time to time only to become submerged again. Feminist research and theory that contribute to lesbian invisibility or marginality are actually working against the liberation and empowerment of women as a group.[44]

The assumption that "most women are innately heterosexual" stands as a theoretical and political stumbling block for feminism. It remains a tenable assumption partly because lesbian existence has been written out of history or catalogued under disease, partly because it has been treated as exceptional rather than intrinsic, partly because to acknowledge that for women heterosexuality may not be a "preference" at all but something that has had to be imposed, managed, organized, propagandized, and maintained by force is an immense step to take if you consider yourself freely and "innately" heterosexual. Yet the failure to examine heterosexuality as an institution is like failing to admit that the economic system called capitalism or the caste system of racism is maintained by a variety of forces, including both physical violence and false consciousness. To take the step of questioning heterosexuality as a "preference" or "choice" for women—and to do the intellectual and emotional work that follows—will call for a special quality of courage in heterosexually identified feminists, but I think the rewards will be great: a freeing-up of thinking, the exploring of new paths, the shattering of another great silence, new clarity in personal relationships.

III

I have chosen to use the terms *lesbian existence* and *lesbian continuum* because the word *lesbianism* has a clinical and limiting ring. *Lesbian existence* suggests both the fact of the historical presence of lesbians and our continuing creation of the meaning of that existence. I mean the term *lesbian continuum* to include a range—through each woman's life and throughout history—of woman-identified experience, not simply the fact that a woman has had or consciously desired genital sexual experience with another woman. If we expand it to embrace many more forms of primary intensity between and among women, including the sharing of a rich inner life, the bonding against male tyranny, the giving and receiving of practical and political support, if we can also hear it in such associations as *marriage resistance* and the "haggard" behavior identified by Mary Daly (obsolete meanings: "intractable," "willful," "wanton," and "unchaste," "a woman reluctant to yield to wooing"),[45] we begin to grasp breadths of female history and psychology which have lain out of reach as a consequence of limited, mostly clinical, definitions of *lesbianism*.

Lesbian existence comprises both the breaking of a taboo and the rejection of a compulsory way of life. It is also a direct or indirect attack on male right of access to women. But it is more than these, although we may first begin to perceive it as a form of naysaying to patriarchy, an act of resistance. It has, of course, included isolation, self-hatred, breakdown, alcoholism, suicide, and intrawoman violence; we romanticize at our peril what it means to love and act against the grain, and under heavy penalties; and lesbian existence has been lived (unlike, say, Jewish or Catholic existence) without access to any knowledge of a tradition, a continuity, a social underpinning. The destruction of records and memorabilia and letters documenting the realities of lesbian existence must be taken very seriously as a means of keeping heterosexuality compulsory for women, since what has been kept from our knowledge is joy, sensuality, courage, and community, as well as guilt, self-betrayal, and pain.[46]

Lesbians have historically been deprived of a political existence through "inclusion" as female versions of male homosexuality. To equate lesbian existence with male homosexuality because each is stigmatized is to erase female reality once again. Part of the history of lesbian existence is, obviously, to be found where lesbians, lacking a coherent female community, have shared a kind of social life and common cause with homosexual men. But there are differences: women's lack of economic and cultural privilege relative to men; qualitative differences in female and male relationships—for example, the patterns of anonymous sex among male homosexuals, and the pronounced ageism in male homosexual standards of sexual attractiveness. I perceive the lesbian experience as being, like motherhood, a profoundly *female* experience, with particular oppressions, meanings, and potentialities we cannot comprehend as long as we simply bracket it with other sexually stigmatized existences. Just as the term *parenting* serves to conceal the particular and significant reality of being a parent who is actually a mother, the term *gay* may serve the purpose of blurring the very outlines we need to discern, which are of crucial value for feminism and for the freedom of women as a group.[47]

As the term *lesbian* has been held to limiting, clinical associations in its patriarchal definition, female friendship and comradeship have been set apart from the erotic, thus limiting the erotic itself. But as we deepen and broaden the range of what we define as lesbian existence, as we delineate a lesbian continuum, we begin to discover the erotic in female terms: as that which is unconfined to any single part of the body or solely to the body itself; as an energy not only diffuse but, as Audre Lorde has described it, omnipresent in "the sharing of joy, whether physical, emotional, psychic," and in the sharing of work; as the empowering joy which "makes us less willing to accept powerlessness, or those other supplied states of being which are not native to me, such as resignation, despair, self-effacement, depression, self-denial."[48] In another context, writing of women and work, I quoted the autobiographical passage in which the poet H.D.

described how her friend Bryher supported her in persisting with the visionary experience which was to shape her mature work:

> I knew that this experience, this writing-on-the-wall before me, could not be shared with anyone except the girl who stood so bravely there beside me. This girl said without hestita-tion, "Go on." It was she really who had the detachment and integrity of the Pythoness of Delphi. But it was I, battered and dissociated . . . who was seeing the pictures, and who was read-ing the writing or granted the inner vision. Or perhaps, in some sense, we were "seeing" it together, for without her, admittedly, I could not have gone on.[49]

If we consider the possibility that all women—from the infant suckling at her mother's breast, to the grown woman experiencing orgasmic sensations while suckling her own child, perhaps recall-ing her mother's milk smell in her own, to two women, like Virginia Woolf's Chloe and Olivia, who share a laboratory,[50] to the woman dying at ninety, touched and handled by women—exist on a lesbian continuum, we can see ourselves as moving in and out of this contin-uum, whether we identify ourselves as lesbian or not.

We can then connect aspects of woman identification as diverse as the impudent, intimate girl friendships of eight or nine year olds and the banding together of those women of the twelfth and fif-teenth centuries known as Beguines who "shared houses, rented to one another, bequeathed houses to their room-mates . . . in cheap subdivided houses in the artisans' area of town," who "practiced Christian virtue on their own, dressing and living simply and not associating with men," who earned their livings as spinsters, bakers, nurses, or ran schools for young girls, and who managed—until the Church forced them to disperse—to live independent both of mar-riage and of conventual restrictions.[51] It allows us to connect these women with the more celebrated "Lesbians" of the women's school around Sappho of the seventh century B.C., with the secret sorori-ties and economic networks reported among African women, and with the Chinese marriage-resistance sisterhoods—communities of women who refused marriage or who, if married, often refused to consummate their marriages and soon left their husbands, the only women in China who were not footbound and who, Agnes Smedley tells us, welcomed the births of daughters and organized success-ful women's strikes in the silk mills.[52] It allows us to connect and compare disparate individual instances of marriage resistance: for example, the strategies available to Emily Dickinson, a nineteenth-century white woman genius, with the strategies available to Zora Neale Hurston, a twentieth-century Black woman genius. Dickinson never married, had tenuous intellectual friendships with men, lived self-convented in her genteel father's house in Amherst, and wrote a lifetime of passionate letters to her sister-in-law Sue Gilbert and a smaller group of such letters to her friend Kate Scott Anthon. Hurston married twice but soon left each husband, scrambled her way from Florida to Harlem to Columbia University to Haiti and finally back to Florida, moved in and out of white patronage and poverty, professional success, and failure; her survival relationships were all with women, beginning with her mother. Both of these women in their vastly different circumstances were marriage resisters, com-mitted to their own work and selfhood, and were later characterized as "apolitical." Both were drawn to men of intellectual quality; for both of them women provided the ongoing fascination and suste-nance of life.

If we think of heterosexuality as *the* natural emotional and sexual inclination for women, lives such as these are seen as deviant, as pathological, or as emotionally and sensually deprived. Or, in more recent and permissive jargon, they are banalized as "life styles." And the work of such women, whether merely the daily work of individ-ual or collective survival and resistance or the work of the writer, the activist, the reformer, the anthropologist, or the artist—the work of self-creation—is undervalued, or seen as the bitter fruit of "penis envy" or the sublimation of repressed eroticism or the mean-ingless rant of a "man-hater." But when we turn the lens of vision and consider the degree to which and the methods whereby het-erosexual "preference" has actually been imposed on women, not only can we understand differently the meaning of individual lives and work, but we can begin to recognize a central fact of women's history: that women have always resisted male tyranny. A feminism of action, often though not always without a theory, has constantly re-emerged in every culture and in every period. We can then begin to study women's struggle against powerlessness, women's radical rebellion, not just in male-defined "concrete revolutionary situations"[53] but in all the situations male ideologies have not perceived as revolutionary—for example, the refusal of some women to produce children, aided at great risk by other women;[54] the refusal to produce a higher standard of living and leisure for men (Leghorn and Parker show how both are part of women's unacknowledged, unpaid, and ununionized economic contribution). We can no longer have patience with Dinnerstein's view that women have simply collaborated with men in the "sexual arrangements" of history. We begin to observe behavior, both in history and in individual biography, that has hitherto been invisible or misnamed, behavior which often constitutes, given the limits of the counterforce exerted in a given time and place, radical rebellion. And we can connect these rebellions and the necessity for them with the physical passion of woman for woman which is central to lesbian existence: the erotic sensuality which has been, precisely, the most violently erased fact of female experience.

Heterosexuality has been both forcibly and subliminally imposed on women. Yet everywhere women have resisted it, often at the cost of physical torture, imprisonment, psychosurgery, social ostracism, and extreme poverty. "Compulsory heterosexuality" was named as one of the "crimes against women" by the Brussels International Tribunal on Crimes against Women in 1976. Two pieces of testimony from two very different cultures reflect the degree to which persecution of lesbians is a global practice here and now. A report from Norway relates:

> A lesbian in Oslo was in a heterosexual marriage that didn't work, so she started taking tranquillizers and ended up at the health sanatorium for treatment and rehabilitation.... The moment she said in family group therapy that she believed she

was a lesbian, the doctor told her she was not. He knew from "looking into her eyes," he said. She had the eyes of a woman who wanted sexual intercourse with her husband. So she was subjected to so-called "couch therapy." She was put into a comfortably heated room, naked, on a bed, and for an hour her husband was to . . . try to excite her sexually. . . . The idea was that the touching was always to end with sexual intercourse. She felt stronger and stronger aversion. She threw up and sometimes ran out of the room to avoid this "treatment." The more strongly she asserted that she was a lesbian, the more violent the forced heterosexual intercourse became. This treatment went on for about six months. She escaped from the hospital, but she was brought back. Again she escaped. She has not been there since. In the end she realized that she had been subjected to forcible rape for six months.

And from Mozambique:

I am condemned to a life of exile because I will not deny that I am a lesbian, that my primary commitments are, and will always be to other women. In the new Mozambique, lesbianism is considered a left-over from colonialism and decadent Western civilization. Lesbians are sent to rehabilitation camps to learn through self-criticism the correct line about themselves. . . . If I am forced to denounce my own love for women, if I therefore denounce myself, I could go back to Mozambique and join forces in the exciting and hard struggle of rebuilding a nation, including the struggle for the emancipation of Mozambiquan women. As it is, I either risk the rehabilitation camps, or remain in exile.[55]

Nor can it be assumed that women like those in Carroll Smith-Rosenberg's study, who married, stayed married, yet dwelt in a profoundly female emotional and passional world, "preferred" or "chose" heterosexuality. Women have married because it was necessary, in order to survive economically, in order to have children who would not suffer economic deprivation or social ostracism, in order to remain respectable, in order to do what was expected of women, because coming out of "abnormal" childhoods they wanted to feel "normal" and because heterosexual romance has been represented as the great female adventure, duty, and fulfillment. We may faithfully or ambivalently have obeyed the institution, but our feelings—and our sensuality—have not been tamed or contained within it. There is no statistical documentation of the numbers of lesbians who have remained in heterosexual marriages for most of their lives. But in a letter to the early lesbian publication *The Ladder*, the playwright Lorraine Hansberry had this to say:

> I suspect that the problem of the married woman who would prefer emotional-physical relationships with other women is proportionally much higher than a similar statistic for men. (A statistic surely no one will ever really have.) This because the estate of woman being what it is, how could we ever begin to guess the numbers of women who are not prepared to risk a life alien to what they have been taught all their lives to believe was their "natural" destiny—AND—their only expectation for ECONOMIC security. It seems to be that this is why the question has an immensity that it does not have for male homosexuals. . . . A woman of strength and honesty may, if she chooses, sever her marriage and marry a new male mate and society will be upset that the divorce rate is rising so—but there are few places in the United States, in any event, where she will be anything remotely akin to an "outcast." Obviously this is not true for a woman who would end her marriage to take up life with another woman.[56]

This *double life*—this apparent acquiescence to an institution founded on male interest and prerogative—has been characteristic of female experience: in motherhood and in many kinds of heterosexual behavior, including the rituals of courtship; the pretense of asexuality by the nineteenth-century wife; the simulation of orgasm by the prostitute, the courtesan, the twentieth-century "sexually liberated" woman.

Meridel LeSueur's documentary novel of the Depression, *The Girl*, is arresting as a study of female double life. The protagonist, a waitress in a St. Paul working-class speakeasy, feels herself passionately attracted to the young man Butch, but her survival relationships are with Clara, an older waitress and prostitute, with Belle, whose husband owns the bar, and with Amelia, a union activist. For Clara and Belle and the unnamed protagonist, sex with men is in one sense an escape from the bedrock misery of daily life, a flare of intensity in the gray, relentless, often brutal web of day-to-day existence:

> It was like he was a magnet pulling me. It was exciting and powerful and frightening. He was after me too and when he found me I would run, or be petrified, just standing in front of him like a zany. And he told me not to be wandering with Clara to the Marigold where we danced with strangers. He said he would knock the shit out of me. Which made me shake and tremble, but it was better than being a husk full of suffering and not knowing why.[57]

Throughout the novel the theme of double life emerges; Belle reminisces about her marriage to the bootlegger Hoinck:

> You know, when I had that black eye and said I hit it on the cupboard, well he did it the bastard, and then he says don't tell anybody. . . . He's nuts, that's what he is, nuts, and I don't see why I live with him, why I put up with him a minute on this earth. But listen kid, she said, I'm telling you something. She looked at me and her face was wonderful. She said, Jesus Christ, Goddam him I love him that's why I'm hooked like this all my life, Goddam him I love him.[58]

After the protagonist has her first sex with Butch, her women friends care for her bleeding, give her whiskey, and compare notes.

My luck, the first time and I got into trouble. He gave me a little money and I come to St. Paul where for ten bucks they'd stick a huge vet's needle into you and you start it and then you were on your own. . . . I never had no child. I've just had Hoinck to mother, and a hell of a child he is.[59]

Later they made me go back to Clara's room to lie down. . . . Clara lay down beside me and put her arms around me and wanted me to tell her about it but she wanted to tell about herself. She said she started it when she was twelve with a bunch of boys in an old shed. She said nobody had paid any attention to her before and she became very popular. . . . They like it so much, she said, why shouldn't you give it to them and get presents and attention? I never cared anything for it and neither did my mama. But it's the only thing you got that's valuable.[60]

Sex is thus equated with attention from the male, who is charismatic though brutal, infantile, or unreliable. Yet it is the women who make life endurable for each other, give physical affection without causing pain, share, advise, and stick by each other. (*I am trying to find my strength through women—without my friends, I could not survive.*) LeSueur's *The Girl* parallels Toni Morrison's remarkable *Sula*, another revelation of female double life:

Nel was the one person who had wanted nothing from her, who had accepted all aspects of her. . . . Nel was one of the reasons Sula had drifted back to Medallion. . . . The men . . . had merged into one large personality: the same language of love, the same entertainments of love, the same cooling of love. Whenever she introduced her private thoughts into their rubbings and goings, they hooded their eyes. They taught her nothing but love tricks, shared nothing but worry, gave nothing but money. She had been looking all along for a friend, and it took her a while to discover that a lover was not a comrade and could never be—for a woman.

But Sula's last thought at the second of her death is "Wait'll I tell Nel." And after Sula's death, Nel looks back on her own life:

> "All that time, all that time, I thought I was missing Jude." And the loss pressed down on her chest and came up into her throat. "We was girls together," she said as though explaining something. "O Lord, Sula," she cried, "Girl, girl, girlgirlgirl!" It was a fine cry—loud and long—but it had no bottom and it had no top, just circles and circles of sorrow.[61]

The Girl and *Sula* are both novels which examine what I am calling the lesbian continuum, in contrast to the shallow or sensational "lesbian scenes" in recent commercial fiction.[62] Each shows us woman identification untarnished (till the end of LeSueur's novel) by romanticism; each depicts the competition of heterosexual compulsion for women's attention, the diffusion and frustration of female bonding that might, in a more conscious form, reintegrate love and power.

IV

Woman identification is a source of energy, a potential springhead of female power, curtailed and contained under the institution of heterosexuality. The denial of reality and visibility to women's passion for women, women's choice of women as allies, life companions, and community, the forcing of such relationships into dissimulation and their disintegration under intense pressure have meant an incalculable loss to the power of all women *to change the social relations of the sexes, to liberate ourselves and each other.* The lie of compulsory female heterosexuality today afflicts not just feminist scholarship, but every profession, every reference work, every curriculum, every organizing attempt, every relationship or conversation over which it hovers. It creates, specifically, a profound falseness, hypocrisy, and hysteria in the heterosexual dialogue, for every heterosexual relationship is lived in the queasy strobe light of that lie. However we choose to identify ourselves, however we find ourselves labeled, it flickers across and distorts our lives.[63]

The lie keeps numberless women psychologically trapped, trying to fit mind, spirit, and sexuality into a prescribed script because they cannot look beyond the parameters of the acceptable. It pulls on the energy of such women even as it drains the energy of "closeted" lesbians—the energy exhausted in the double life. The lesbian trapped in the "closet," the woman imprisoned in prescriptive ideas of the "normal" share the pain of blocked options, broken connections, lost access to self-definition freely and powerfully assumed.

The lie is many-layered. In Western tradition, one layer—the romantic—asserts that women are inevitably, even if rashly and tragically, drawn to men; that even when that attraction is suicidal (e.g., *Tristan and Isolde*, Kate Chopin's *The Awakening*), it is still an organic imperative. In the tradition of the social sciences it asserts that primary love between the sexes is "normal"; that women *need* men as social and economic protectors, for adult sexuality, and for psychological completion; that the heterosexually constituted family is the basic social unit; that women who do not attach their primary intensity to men must be, in functional terms, condemned to an even more devastating outsiderhood than their outsiderhood as women. Small wonder that lesbians are reported to be a more hidden population than male homosexuals. The Black lesbian-feminist critic Lorraine Bethel, writing on Zora Neale Hurston, remarks that for a Black woman—already twice an outsider—to choose to assume still another "hated identity" is problematic indeed. Yet the lesbian continuum has been a life line for Black women both in Africa and the United States.

> Black women have a long tradition of bonding together . . . in a Black/women's community that has been a source of vital survival information, psychic and emotional support for us. We have a distinct Black woman-identified folk culture based on our experiences as Black women in this society; symbols, language and modes of expression that are specific to the realities of our lives. . . . Because Black women were rarely among those Blacks and females who gained access to literary and other

acknowledged forms of artistic expression, this Black female bonding and Black woman-identification has often been hidden and unrecorded except in the individual lives of Black women through our own memories of our particular Black female tradition.[64]

Another layer of the lie is the frequently encountered implication that women turn to women out of hatred for men. Profound skepticism, caution, and righteous paranoia about men may indeed be part of any healthy woman's response to the misogyny of male-dominated culture, to the forms assumed by "normal" male sexuality, and to *the failure even of "sensitive" or "political" men to perceive or find these troubling*. Lesbian existence is also represented as mere refuge from male abuses, rather than as an electric and empowering charge between women. One of the most frequently quoted literary passages on lesbian relationship is that in which Colette's Renée, in *The Vagabond*, describes "the melancholy and touching image of two weak creatures who have perhaps found shelter in each other's arms, there to sleep and weep, safe from man who is often cruel, and there to taste *better than any pleasure, the bitter happiness of feeling themselves akin, frail and forgotten* [emphasis added]."[65] Colette is often considered a lesbian writer. Her popular reputation has, I think, much to do with the fact that she writes about lesbian existence as if for a male audience; her earliest "lesbian" novels, the Claudine series, were written under compulsion for her husband and published under both their names. At all events, except for her writings on her mother, Colette is a less reliable source on the lesbian continuum than, I would think, Charlotte Brontë, who understood that while women may, indeed must, be one another's allies, mentors, and comforters in the female struggle for survival, there is quite extraneous delight in each other's company and attraction to each others' minds and character, which attend a recognition of each others' strengths.

By the same token, we can say that there is a *nascent* feminist political content in the act of choosing a woman lover or life partner in the face of institutionalized heterosexuality.[66] But for lesbian existence to realize this political content in an ultimately liberating form, the erotic choice must deepen and expand into conscious woman identification—into lesbian feminism.

The work that lies ahead, of unearthing and describing what I call here "lesbian existence," is potentially liberating for all women. It is work that must assuredly move beyond the limits of white and middle-class Western Women's Studies to examine women's lives, work, and groupings within every racial, ethnic, and political structure. There are differences, moreover, between "lesbian existence" and the "lesbian continuum," differences we can discern even in the movement of our own lives. The lesbian continuum, I suggest, needs delineation in light of the "double life" of women, not only women self-described as heterosexual but also of self-described lesbians. We need a far more exhaustive account of the forms the double life has assumed. Historians need to ask at every point how heterosexuality as institution has been organized and maintained through the female wage scale, the enforcement of middle-class women's "leisure," the glamorization of so-called sexual liberation, the withholding of education from women, the imagery of "high art" and popular culture, the mystification of the "personal" sphere, and much else. We need an economics which comprehends the institution of heterosexuality, with its doubled workload for women and its sexual divisions of labor, as the most idealized of economic relations.

The question inevitably will arise: Are we then to condemn all heterosexual relationships, including those which are least oppressive? I believe this question, though often heartfelt, is the wrong question here. We have been stalled in a maze of false dichotomies which prevents our apprehending the institution as a whole: "good" versus "bad" marriages; "marriage for love" versus arranged marriage; "liberated" sex versus prostitution; heterosexual intercourse versus rape; *Liebeschmerz* versus humiliation and dependency. Within the institution exist, of course, qualitative differences of experience; but the absence of choice remains the great unacknowledged reality, and in the absence of choice, women will remain dependent upon the chance or luck of particular relationships and will have no collective power to determine the meaning and place of sexuality in their lives. As we address the institution itself, moreover, we begin to perceive a history of female resistance which has never fully understood itself because it has been so fragmented, miscalled, erased. It will require a courageous grasp of the politics and economics, as well as the cultural propaganda, of heterosexuality to carry us beyond individual cases or diversified group situations into the complex kind of overview needed to undo the power men everywhere wield over women, power which has become a model for every other form of exploitation and illegitimate control.

AFTERWORD

In 1980, Ann Snitow, Christine Stansell, and Sharon Thompson, three Marxist-feminist activists and scholars, sent out a call for papers for an anthology on the politics of sexuality. Having just finished writing "Compulsory Heterosexuality" for *Signs,* I sent them that manuscript and asked them to consider it. Their anthology, *Powers of Desire,* was published by the Monthly Review Press New Feminist Library in 1983 and included my paper. During the intervening period, the four of us were in correspondence, but I was able to take only limited advantage of this dialogue due to ill health and resulting surgery. With their permission, I reprint here excerpts from that correspondence as a way of indicating that my essay should be read as one contribution to a long exploration in progress, not as my own "last word" on sexual politics. I also refer interested readers to *Powers of Desire* itself.

Dear Adrienne,
　... In one of our first letters, we told you that we were finding parameters of left-wing/feminist sexual discourse to be far broader than we imagined. Since then, we have perceived what we believe to be a crisis in the feminist movement about sex, an intensifying debate (although not always an explicit one), and a questioning of assumptions once taken for granted. While we fear the link between

sex and violence, as do Women Against Pornography, we wish we better understood its sources in ourselves as well as in men. In the Reagan era, we can hardly afford to romanticize any old norm of a virtuous and moral sexuality.

In your piece, you are asking the question, what would women choose in a world where patriarchy and capitalism did *not* rule? We agree with you that heterosexuality is an institution created between these grind stones, but we don't conclude, therefore, that it is entirely a male creation. You only allow for female historical agency insofar as women exist on the lesbian continuum while we would argue that women's history, like men's history, is created out of a dialectic of necessity and choice.

All three of us (hence one lesbian, two heterosexual women) had questions about your use of the term "false consciousness" for women's heterosexuality. In general, we think the false-consciousness model can blind us to the necessities and desires that comprise the lives of the oppressed. It can also lead to the too easy denial of others' experience when that experience is different from our own. We posit, rather, a complex social model in which all erotic life is a continuum, one which therefore includes relations with men.

Which brings us to this metaphor of the continuum. We know you are a poet, not an historian, and we look forward to reading your metaphors all our lives—and standing straighter as feminists, as women, for having read them. But the metaphor of the lesbian continuum is open to all kinds of misunderstandings, and these sometimes have odd political effects. For example, Sharon reports that at a recent meeting around the abortion-rights struggle, the notions of continuum arose in the discussion several times and underwent divisive transformation. Overall, the notion that two ways of being existed on the same continuum was interpreted to mean that those two ways were the *same*. The sense of range and gradation that your description evokes disappeared. Lesbianism and female friendship became exactly the same thing. Similarly, heterosexuality and rape became the same. In one of several versions of the continuum that evolved, a slope was added, like so:

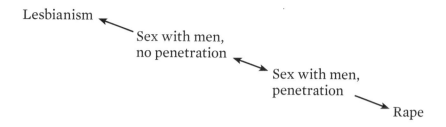

This sloped continuum brought its proponents to the following conclusion: An appropriate, workable abortion-rights strategy is to inform all women that heterosexual penetration is rape, whatever their subjective experience to the contrary. All women will immediately recognize the truth of this and opt for the alternative of non-penetration. The abortion-rights struggle will thus be simplified into a struggle against coercive sex and its consequences (since no enlightened woman would voluntarily undergo penetration unless her object was procreation—a peculiarly Catholic-sounding view).

The proponents of this strategy were young women who have worked hard in the abortion-rights movement for the past two or more years. They are inexperienced but they are dedicated. For this reason, we take their reading of your work seriously. We don't think, however, that it comes solely, or even at all, from the work itself. As likely a source is the tendency to dichotomize that has plagued the women's movement. The source of that tendency is harder to trace.

In that regard, the hints in "Compulsory" about the double life of women intrigue us. You define the double life as "the apparent acquiescence to an institution founded on male interest and prerogative." But that definition doesn't really explain your other references—to, for instance, the "intense mixture" of love and anger in lesbian relationships and to the peril of romanticizing what it means "to love and act against the grain." We think these comments raise extremely important issues for feminists right now; the problem of division and anger among us needs airing and analysis. Is this, by any chance, the theme of a piece you have in the works?

. . . We would still love it if we could have a meeting with you in the next few months. Any chance? ... Greetings and support from us—in all your undertakings.

We send love,
Sharon, Chris, and Ann

New York City
April 19, 1981

Dear Ann, Chris, and Sharon,

... It's good to be back in touch with you, you who have been so unfailingly patient, generous, and persistent. Above all, it's important to me that you know that ill health, not a withdrawal because of political differences, delayed my writing back to you. ...

"False consciousness" can, I agree, be used as a term of dismissal for any thinking we don't like or adhere to. But, as I tried to illustrate in some detail, there is a real, identifiable system of heterosexual propaganda, of defining women as existing for the sexual use of men, which goes beyond "sex role" or "gender" stereotyping or "sexist imagery" to include a vast number of verbal and nonverbal messages. And this I call "control of consciousness." The possibility of a woman who does not exist sexually for men—the lesbian possibility—is buried, erased, occluded, distorted, misnamed, and driven underground. The feminist books—Chodorow, Dinnerstein, Ehrenreich and English, and others—which I discuss at the beginning of my essay contribute to this invalidation and erasure, and as such are part of the problem.

My essay is founded on the belief that we all think from within the limits of certain solipsisms—usually linked with privilege, racial, cultural, and economic as well as sexual—which present themselves as "the universal," "the way things are," "all women," etc., etc. I wrote it equally out of the belief that in becoming conscious of our solipsisms we have certain kinds of choices, that we can and must re-educate ourselves. I never have maintained that heterosexual feminists are walking about in a state of "brainwashed" false consciousness. Nor have such phrases as "sleeping with the enemy" seemed to me either profound or useful. *Homophobia* is too diffuse a term and does not go very far in helping us identify and talk about the sexual solipsism of heterosexual feminism. In this paper I was trying to ask heterosexual feminists to examine their experience of heterosexuality critically and antagonistically, to critique the institution of which they are a part, to struggle with the norm and its implications for women's freedom, to become more open to the considerable resources offered by the lesbian-feminist perspective, to refuse to settle for the personal privilege and solution of the individual "good relationship" within the institution of heterosexuality.

As regards "female historical agency," I wanted, precisely, to suggest that the victim model is insufficient; that there *is* a history of female agency and choice which has actually challenged aspects of male supremacy; that, like male supremacy, these can be found in many different cultures. . . . It's not that I think all female agency has been solely and avowedly lesbian. But by erasing lesbian existence from female history, from theory, from literary criticism . . . from feminist approaches to economic structure, ideas about "the family," etc., an enormous amount of female agency is kept unavailable, hence unusable. I wanted to demonstrate that that kind of obliteration continues to be acceptable in seriously regarded feminist texts. What surprised me in the responses to my essay, including your notes, is how almost every aspect of it has been considered, except this—to me—central one. I was taking a position which was neither lesbian/separatist in the sense of dismissing heterosexual women nor a "gay civil rights" plea for . . . openness to lesbianism as an "option" or an "alternate life style." I was urging that lesbian *existence* has been an unrecognized and unaffirmed claiming by women of their sexuality, thus a pattern of resistance, thus also a kind of borderline position from which to analyze and challenge the relationship of heterosexuality to male supremacy. And that lesbian existence, when recognized, demands a conscious restructuring of feminist analysis and criticism, not just a token reference or two.

I certainly agree with you that the term *lesbian continuum* can be misused. It was, in the example you report of the abortion-rights meeting, though I would think anyone who had read my work from *Of Woman Born* onward would know that my position on abortion and sterilization abuse is more complicated than that. My own problem with the phrase is that it can be, is, used by women who have not yet begun to examine the privileges and solipsisms of heterosexuality, as a safe way to describe their felt connections with women, without having to share in the risks and threats of lesbian existence. What I had thought to delineate rather complexly as a continuum has begun to sound more like "life-style shopping." *Lesbian continuum*—the phrase—came from a desire to allow for the greatest possible variation of female-identified experience, while paying a different kind of respect to *lesbian existence*—the traces and knowledge of women who have made their primary erotic and emotional choices for women. If I were writing the paper today, I would still want to make this distinction, but would put more caveats around *lesbian continuum*. I fully agree with you that Smith-Rosenberg's "female world" is not a social ideal, enclosed as it is within prescriptive middle-class heterosexuality and marriage.

My own essay could have been stronger had it drawn on more of the literature by Black women toward which Toni Morrison's *Sula* inevitably pointed me. In reading a great deal more of Black women's fiction I began to perceive a different set of valences from those found in white women's fiction for the most part: a different quest for the woman hero, a different relationship both to sexuality with men and to female loyalty and bonding.

You comment briefly on your reactions to some of the radical-feminist works I cited in my first footnote.[67] I am myself critical of some of them even as I found them vitally useful. What most of them share is a taking seriously of misogyny—of organized, institutionalized, normalized hostility and violence against women. I feel no "hierarchy of oppressions" is needed in order for us to take misogyny as seriously as we take racism, anti-Semitism, imperialism. To take misogyny seriously needn't mean that we perceive women merely as victims, without responsibilities or choices; it does mean recognizing the "necessity" in that "dialectic of necessity and choice"— identifying, describing, refusing to turn aside our eyes. I think that some of the apparent reductiveness, or even obsessiveness, of some white radical-feminist theory derives from racial and/or class solipsism, but also from the immense effort of trying to render woman hating visible amid so much denial. . . .

Finally, as to poetry and history: I want both in my life; I need to see through both. If metaphor can be misconstrued, history can also lead to misconstrual when it obliterates acts of resistance or rebellion, wipes out transformational models, or sentimentalizes power relationships. I know you know this. I believe we are all trying to think and write out of our best consciences, our most open consciousness. I expect that quality in this book which you are editing, and look forward with anticipation to the thinking—and the actions—toward which it may take us.

In sisterhood,
Adrienne

Montague, Massachusetts
November 1981

SPLIT AT THE ROOT

An Essay on Jewish Identity (1982)

For about fifteen minutes I have been sitting chin in hand in front of the typewriter, staring out at the snow. Trying to be honest with myself, trying to figure out why writing this seems to be so dangerous an act, filled with fear and shame, and why it seems so necessary. It comes to me that in order to write this I have to be willing to do two things: I have to claim my father, for I have my Jewishness from him and not from my gentile mother; and I have to break his silence, his taboos; in order to claim him I have in a sense to expose him.

And there is, of course, the third thing: I have to face the sources and the flickering presence of my own ambivalence as a Jew; the daily, mundane anti-Semitisms of my entire life.

These are stories I have never tried to tell before. Why now? Why, I asked myself sometime last year, does this question of Jewish identity float so impalpably, so ungraspably around me, a cloud I can't quite see the outlines of, which feels to me to be without definition?

And yet I've been on the track of this longer than I think.

•

In a long poem written in 1960, when I was thirty-one years old, I described myself as "Split at the root, neither Gentile nor Jew, / Yankee nor Rebel."[1] I was still trying to have it both ways: to be neither/nor, trying to live (with my Jewish husband and three children

I wrote this essay in 1982 for Evelyn Torton Beck's *Nice Jewish Girls: A Lesbian Anthology*. It was later reprinted in *Fathers*, an anthology edited by Ursula Owen for Virago Ltd., in London, and published in the United States by Pantheon.

more Jewish in ancestry than I) in the predominantly gentile Yankee academic world of Cambridge, Massachusetts.

But this begins, for me, in Baltimore, where I was born in my father's workplace, a hospital in the Black ghetto, whose lobby contained an immense white marble statue of Christ.

•

My father was then a young teacher and researcher in the department of pathology at the Johns Hopkins Medical School, one of the very few Jews to attend or teach at that institution. He was from Birmingham, Alabama; his father, Samuel, was Ashkenazic, an immigrant from Austria-Hungary and his mother, Hattie Rice, a Sephardic Jew from Vicksburg, Mississippi. My grandfather had had a shoe store in Birmingham, which did well enough to allow him to retire comfortably and to leave my grandmother income on his death. The only souvenirs of my grandfather, Samuel Rich, were his ivory flute, which lay on our living-room mantel and was not to be played with; his thin gold pocket watch, which my father wore; and his Hebrew prayer book, which I discovered among my father's books in the course of reading my way through his library. In this prayer book there was a newspaper clipping about my grandparents' wedding, which took place in a synagogue.

My father, Arnold, was sent in adolescence to a military school in the North Carolina mountains, a place for training white southern Christian gentlemen. I suspect that there were few, if any, other Jewish boys at Colonel Bingham's, or at "Mr. Jefferson's university" in Charlottesville, where he studied as an undergraduate. With whatever conscious forethought, Samuel and Hattie sent their son into the dominant southern WASP culture to become an "exception," to enter the professional class. Never, in describing these experiences, did he speak of having suffered—from loneliness, cultural alienation, or outsiderhood. Never did I hear him use the word *anti-Semitism.*

•

It was only in college, when I read a poem by Karl Shapiro beginning "To hate the Negro and avoid the Jew / is the curriculum," that it flashed on me that there was an untold side to my father's story of his student years. He looked recognizably Jewish, was short and slender in build with dark wiry hair and deep-set eyes, high forehead and curved nose.

My mother is a gentile. In Jewish law I cannot count myself a Jew. If it is true that "we think back through our mothers if we are women" (Virginia Woolf)—and I myself have affirmed this—then even according to lesbian theory, I cannot (or need not?) count myself a Jew.

The white southern Protestant woman, the gentile, has always been there for me to peel back into. That's a whole piece of history in itself, for my gentile grandmother and my mother were also frustrated artists and intellectuals, a lost writer and a lost composer between them. Readers and annotators of books, note takers, my mother a good pianist still, in her eighties. But there was also the obsession with ancestry, with "background," the southern talk of family, not as people you would necessarily know and depend on, but as heritage, the guarantee of "good breeding." There was the inveterate romantic heterosexual fantasy, the mother telling the daughter how to attract men (my mother often used the word "fascinate"); the assumption that relations between the sexes could only be romantic, that it was in the woman's interest to cultivate "mystery," conceal her actual feelings. Survival tactics of a kind, I think today, knowing what I know about the white woman's sexual role in the southern racist scenario. Heterosexuality as protection, but also drawing white women deeper into collusion with white men.

It would be easy to push away and deny the gentile in me—that white southern woman, that social christian. At different times in my life I have wanted to push away one or the other burden of inheritance, to say merely *I am a woman; I am a lesbian.* If I call myself a Jewish lesbian, do I thereby try to shed some of my southern gentile white woman's culpability? If I call myself only through my mother, is it because I pass more easily through a world where being a lesbian often seems like outsiderhood enough?

According to Nazi logic, my two Jewish grandparents would have made me a *Mischling, first-degree*—nonexempt from the Final Solution.

•

The social world in which I grew up was christian virtually without needing to say so—christian imagery, music, language, symbols, assumptions everywhere. It was also a genteel, white, middle-class world in which "common" was a term of deep opprobrium. "Common" white people might speak of "niggers"; *we* were taught never to use that word—*we* said "Negroes" (even as we accepted segregation, the eating taboo, the assumption that Black people were simply of a separate species). Our language was more polite, distinguishing us from the "red-necks" or the lynch-mob mentality. But so charged with negative meaning was even the word "Negro" that as children we were taught never to use it in front of Black people. We were taught that any mention of skin color in the presence of colored people was treacherous, forbidden ground. In a parallel way, the word "Jew" was not used by polite gentiles. I sometimes heard my best friend's father, a Presbyterian minister, allude to "the Hebrew people" or "people of the Jewish faith." The world of acceptable folk was white, gentile (christian, really), and had "ideals" (which colored people, white "common" people, were not supposed to have). "Ideals" and "manners" included not hurting someone's feelings by calling her or him a Negro or a Jew—naming the hated identity. This is the mental framework of the 1930s and 1940s in which I was raised.

(Writing this, I feel dimly like the betrayer: of my father, who did not speak the word; of my mother, who must have trained me in the messages; of my caste and class; of my whiteness itself.)

Two memories: I am in a play reading at school of *The Merchant of Venice.* Whatever Jewish law says, I am quite sure I was *seen* as Jewish (with a reassuringly gentile mother) in that double vision that bigotry allows. I am the only Jewish girl in the class, and I am playing Portia. As always, I read my part aloud for my father the night before, and he tells me to convey, with my voice, more scorn and contempt with the word "Jew": "Therefore, Jew . . ." I have to say the word out, and say it loudly. I was encouraged to pretend to be a non-Jewish child acting a non-Jewish character who has to speak the word "Jew" emphatically. Such a child would not have had trouble with the part. But *I* must have had trouble with the part, if only because the word itself was really taboo. I can see that there was a kind of terrible, bitter bravado about my father's way of handling this. And who would not dissociate from Shylock in order to identify with Portia? As a Jewish child who was also a female, I loved Portia—and, like every other Shakespearean heroine, she proved a treacherous role model.

A year or so later I am in another play, *The School for Scandal*, in which a notorious spendthrift is described as having "many excellent friends . . . among the Jews." In neither case was anything explained, either to me or to the class at large, about this scorn for Jews and the disgust surrounding Jews and money. Money, when Jews wanted it, had it, or lent it to others, seemed to take on a peculiar nastiness; Jews and money had some peculiar and unspeakable relation.

At this same school—in which we had Episcopalian hymns and prayers, and read aloud through the Bible morning after morning—I gained the impression that Jews were in the Bible and mentioned in English literature, that they had been persecuted centuries ago by the wicked Inquisition, but that they seemed not to exist in everyday life. These were the 1940s, and we were told a great deal about the Battle of Britain, the noble French Resistance fighters, the brave, starving Dutch—but I did not learn of the resistance of the Warsaw ghetto until I left home.

I was sent to the Episcopal church, baptized and confirmed, and attended it for about five years, though without belief. That religion seemed to have little to do with belief or commitment; it was liturgy that mattered, not spiritual passion. Neither of my parents ever entered that church, and my father would not enter *any* church for any reason—wedding or funeral. Nor did I enter a synagogue until I left Baltimore. When I came home from church, for a while, my father insisted on reading aloud to me from Thomas Paine's *The Age of Reason*—a diatribe against institutional religion. Thus, he explained, I would have a balanced view of these things, a choice. He—they—did not give me the choice to be a Jew. My mother explained to me when I was filling out forms for college that if any question was asked about "religion," I should put down "Episcopalian" rather than "none"—to seem to have no religion was, she implied, dangerous.

But it was white social christianity, rather than any particular christian sect, that the world was founded on. The very word *Christian* was used as a synonym for virtuous, just, peace-loving, generous, etc., etc.[2] The norm was christian: "religion: none" was indeed not acceptable. Anti-Semitism was so intrinsic as not to have a name. I don't recall exactly being taught that the Jews killed Jesus—"Christ killer" seems too strong a term for the bland Episcopal vocabulary—but certainly we got the impression that the Jews had been caught out in a terrible mistake, failing to recognize the true Messiah, and were thereby less advanced in moral and spiritual sensibility. The Jews had actually allowed *moneylenders in the Temple* (again, the unexplained obsession with Jews and money). They were of the past, archaic, primitive, as older (and darker) cultures are supposed to be primitive; christianity was lightness, fairness, peace on earth, and combined the feminine appeal of "The meek shall inherit the earth" with the masculine stride of "Onward, Christian Soldiers."

•

Sometime in 1946, while still in high school, I read in the newspaper that a theater in Baltimore was showing films of the Allied liberation of the Nazi concentration camps. Alone, I went downtown after school one afternoon and watched the stark, blurry, but unmistakable newsreels. When I try to go back and touch the pulse of that girl of sixteen, growing up in many ways so precocious and so ignorant, I am overwhelmed by a memory of despair, a sense of inevitability more enveloping than any I had ever known. Anne Frank's diary and many other personal narratives of the Holocaust were still unknown or unwritten. But it came to me that every one of those piles of corpses, mountains of shoes and clothing had contained, simply, individuals, who had believed, as I now believed of myself, that they were intended to live out a life of some kind of meaning, that the world possessed some kind of sense and order; yet *this* had happened to them. And I, who believed my life was intended to be so interesting and meaningful, was connected to those dead by something—not just mortality but a taboo name, a hated identity. Or was I—did I really have to be? Writing this now, I feel belated rage that I was so impoverished by the family and social worlds I lived in, that I had to try to figure out by myself what this did indeed mean for me. That I had never been taught about resistance, only about passing. That I had no language for anti-Semitism itself.

When I went home and told my parents where I had been, they were not pleased. I felt accused of being morbidly curious, not healthy, sniffing around death for the thrill of it. And since, at sixteen, I was often not sure of the sources of my feelings or of my motives for doing what I did, I probably accused myself as well. One thing was clear: there was nobody in my world with whom I could discuss those films. Probably at the same time, I was reading accounts of the camps in magazines and newspapers; what I remember were the films and having questions that I could not even phrase, such as *Are those men and women "them" or "us"?*

To be able to ask even the child's astonished question *Why do they hate us so?* means knowing how to say "we." The guilt of not knowing, the guilt of perhaps having betrayed my parents or even those victims, those survivors, through mere curiosity—these also froze in me for years the impulse to find out more about the Holocaust.

1947: I left Baltimore to go to college in Cambridge, Massachusetts, left (I thought) the backward, enervating South for the intellectual, vital North. New England also had for me some vibration of higher moral rectitude, of moral passion even, with its seventeenth-century Puritan self-scrutiny, its nineteenth-century literary "flowering," its abolitionist righteousness, Colonel Shaw and his Black Civil War regiment depicted in granite on Boston Common. At the same time, I found myself, at Radcliffe, among Jewish women. I used to sit for hours over coffee with what I thought of as the "real" Jewish students, who told me about middle-class Jewish culture in America. I described my background—for the first time to strangers—and they took me on, some with amusement at my illiteracy, some arguing that I could never marry into a strict Jewish family, some convinced I didn't "look Jewish," others that I did. I learned the names of holidays and foods, which surnames are Jewish and which are "changed names"; about girls who had had their noses "fixed," their hair straightened. For these young Jewish women, students in the late 1940s, it was acceptable, perhaps even necessary, to strive to look as gentile as possible; but they stuck proudly to being Jewish, expected to marry a Jew, have children, keep the holidays, carry on the culture.

I felt I was testing a forbidden current, that there was danger in these revelations. I bought a reproduction of a Chagall portrait of a rabbi in striped prayer shawl and hung it on the wall of my room. I was admittedly young and trying to educate myself, but I was also doing something that *is* dangerous: I was flirting with identity.

•

One day that year I was in a small shop where I had bought a dress with a too-long skirt. The shop employed a seamstress who did alterations, and she came in to pin up the skirt on me. I am sure that she was a recent immigrant, a survivor. I remember a short, dark woman wearing heavy glasses, with an accent so foreign I could not understand her words. Something about her presence was very powerful and disturbing to me. After marking and pinning up the skirt, she sat back on her knees, looked up at me, and asked in a hurried whisper: "You Jewish?" Eighteen years of training in assimilation sprang into the reflex by which I shook my head, rejecting her, and muttered, "No."

What was I actually saying "no" to? She was poor, older, struggling with a foreign tongue, anxious; she had escaped the death that had been intended for her, but I had no imagination of her possible courage and foresight, her resistance—I did not see in her a heroine who had perhaps saved many lives, including her own. I saw the frightened immigrant, the seamstress hemming the skirts of college girls, the wandering Jew. But I was an American college girl having her skirt hemmed. And I was frightened myself, I think, because she had recognized me ("It takes one to know one," my friend Edie at

Radcliffe had said) even if I refused to recognize myself or her, even if her recognition was sharpened by loneliness or the need to feel safe with me.

But why should she have felt safe with me? I myself was living with a false sense of safety.

There are betrayals in my life that I have known at the very moment were betrayals: this was one of them. There are other betrayals committed so repeatedly, so mundanely, that they leave no memory trace behind, only a growing residue of misery, of dull, accreted self-hatred. Often these take the form not of words but of silence. Silence before the joke at which everyone is laughing: the anti-woman joke, the racist joke, the anti-Semitic joke. Silence and then amnesia. Blocking it out when the oppressor's language starts coming from the lips of one we admire, whose courage and eloquence have touched us: *She didn't really mean that; he didn't really say that.* But the accretions build up out of sight, like scale inside a kettle.

•

1948: I come home from my freshman year at college, flaming with new insights, new information. I am the daughter who has gone out into the world, to the pinnacle of intellectual prestige, Harvard, fulfilling my father's hopes for me, but also exposed to dangerous influences. I have already been reproved for attending a rally for Henry Wallace and the Progressive party. I challenge my father: "Why haven't you told me that I am Jewish? Why do you never talk about being a Jew?" He answers measuredly, "You know that I have never denied that I am a Jew. But it's not important to me. I am a scientist, a deist. I have no use for organized religion. I choose to live in a world of many kinds of people. There are Jews I admire and others whom I despise. I am a person, not simply a Jew." The words are as I remember them, not perhaps exactly as spoken. But that was the message. And it contained enough truth—as all denial drugs itself on partial truth—so that it remained for the time being unanswerable, leaving me high and dry, split at the root, gasping for clarity, for air.

At that time Arnold Rich was living in suspension, waiting to be appointed to the professorship of pathology at Johns Hopkins. The appointment was delayed for years, no Jew ever having held a professional chair in that medical school. And he wanted it badly. It must have been a very bitter time for him, since he had believed so greatly in the redeeming power of excellence, of being the most brilliant, inspired man for the job. With enough excellence, you could presumably make it stop mattering that you were Jewish; you could become the *only* Jew in the gentile world, a Jew so "civilized," so far from "common," so attractively combining southern gentility with European cultural values that no one would ever confuse you with the raw, "pushy" Jews of New York, the "loud, hysterical" refugees from eastern Europe, the "overdressed" Jews of the urban South.

We—my sister, mother, and I—were constantly urged to speak quietly in public, to dress without ostentation, to repress all vividness or spontaneity, to assimilate with a world which might see us as too flamboyant. I suppose that my mother, pure gentile though she was, could be seen as acting "common" or "Jewish" if she laughed too loudly or spoke aggressively. My father's mother, who lived with us half the year, was a model of circumspect behavior, dressed in dark blue or lavender, retiring in company, ladylike to an extreme, wearing no jewelry except a good gold chain, a narrow brooch, or a string of pearls. A few times, within the family, I saw her anger flare, felt the passion she was repressing. But when Arnold took us out to a restaurant or on a trip, the Rich women were always tuned down to some WASP level my father believed, surely, would protect us all—maybe also make us unrecognizable to the "real Jews" who wanted to seize us, drag us back to the *shtetl*, the ghetto, in its many manifestations.

For, yes, that *was* a message—that some Jews would be after you, once they "knew," to rejoin them, to re-enter a world that was messy, noisy, unpredictable, maybe poor—"even though," as my mother once wrote me, criticizing my largely Jewish choice of friends in college, "some of them will be the most brilliant, fascinating people you'll ever meet." I wonder if that isn't one message of assimilation— of America—that the unlucky or the unachieving want to pull you backward, that to identify with them is to court downward mobility, lose the precious chance of passing, of token existence. There was always within this sense of Jewish identity a strong class discrimination. Jews might be "fascinating" as individuals but came with huge unruly families who "poured chicken soup over everyone's head" (in the phrase of a white southern male poet). Anti-Semitism could thus be justified by the bad behavior of certain Jews; and if you did not effectively deny family and community, there would always be a remote cousin claiming kinship with you who was the "wrong kind" of Jew.

I have always believed his attitude toward other Jews depended on who they were. . . . It was my impression that Jews of this background looked down on Eastern European Jews, including Polish Jews and Russian Jews, who generally were not as well educated. This from a letter written to me recently by a gentile who had worked in my father's department, whom I had asked about anti-Semitism there and in particular regarding my father. This informant also wrote me that it was hard to perceive anti-Semitism in Baltimore because the racism made so much more intense an impression: *I would almost have to think that blacks went to a different heaven than the whites, because the bodies were kept in a separate morgue, and some white persons did not even want blood transfusions from black donors.* My father's mind was predictably racist and misogynist; yet as a medical student he noted in his journal that southern male chivalry stopped at the point of any white man in a streetcar giving his seat to an old, weary Black woman standing in the aisle. Was this a Jewish insight—an outsider's insight, even though the outsider was striving to be on the inside?

Because what isn't named is often more permeating than what is, I believe that my father's Jewishness profoundly shaped my own identity and our family existence. They were shaped both by external anti-Semitism and my father's self-hatred, and by his Jewish pride. What Arnold did, I think, was call his Jewish pride something else: achievement, aspiration, genius, idealism. Whatever was unacceptable got left back under the rubric of Jewishness or the "wrong kind" of Jews—uneducated, aggressive, loud. The message I got was that we were really superior: nobody else's father had collected so many books, had traveled so far, knew so many languages. Baltimore was a musical city, but for the most part, in the families of my school friends, culture was for women. My father was an amateur musician, read poetry, adored encyclopedic knowledge. He prowled and pounced over my school papers, insisting I use "grown-up" sources; he criticized my poems for faulty technique and gave me books on rhyme and meter and form. His investment in my intellect and talent was egotistical, tyrannical, opinionated, and terribly wearing. He taught me, nevertheless, to believe in hard work, to mistrust easy inspiration, to write and rewrite; to feel that I *was* a person of the book, even though a woman; to take ideas seriously. He made me feel, at a very young age, the power of language and that I could share in it.

The Riches were proud, but we also had to be very careful. Our behavior had to be more impeccable than other people's. Strangers were not to be trusted, nor even friends; family issues must never go beyond the family; the world was full of potential slanderers, betrayers, *people who could not understand.* Even within the family, I realize that I never in my whole life knew what my father was really feeling. Yet he spoke—monologued—with driving intensity. You could grow up in such a house mesmerized by the local electricity, the crucial meanings assumed by the merest things. This used to seem to me a sign that we were all living on some high emotional plane. It was a difficult force field for a favored daughter to disengage from.

Easy to call that intensity Jewish; and I have no doubt that passion is one of the qualities required for survival over generations of persecution. But what happens when passion is rent from its original base, when the white gentile world is softly saying "Be more like us and you can be almost one of us"? What happens when survival seems to mean closing off one emotional artery after another? His forebears in Europe had been forbidden to travel or expelled from one country after another, had special taxes levied on them if they left the city walls, had been forced to wear special clothes and badges, restricted to the poorest neighborhoods. He had wanted to be a "free spirit," to travel widely, among "all kinds of people." Yet in his prime of life he lived in an increasingly withdrawn world, in his house up on a hill in a neighborhood where Jews were not supposed to be able to buy property, depending almost exclusively on interactions with his wife and daughters to provide emotional connectedness. In his home, he created a private defense system so elaborate that even as he was dying, my mother felt unable to talk freely with his colleagues or others who might have helped her. Of course, she acquiesced in this.

The loneliness of the "only," the token, often doesn't feel like loneliness but like a kind of dead echo chamber. Certain things that ought to don't resonate. Somewhere Beverly Smith writes of women of color "inspiring the behavior" in each other. When there's nobody to "inspire the behavior," act out of the culture, there is an atrophy, a dwindling, which is partly invisible.

•

I was married in 1953, in the Hillel House at Harvard, under a portrait of Albert Einstein. My parents refused to come. I was marrying a Jew of the "wrong kind" from an Orthodox eastern European background. Brooklyn-born, he had gone to Harvard, changed his name, was both indissolubly connected to his childhood world and terribly ambivalent about it. My father saw this marriage as my having fallen prey to the Jewish family, eastern European division.

Like many women I knew in the fifties living under a then-unquestioned heterosexual imperative, I married in part because I knew no better way to disconnect from my first family. I married a "real Jew" who was himself almost equally divided between a troubled yet ingrained Jewish identity, and the pull toward Yankee approval, assimilation. But at least he was not adrift as a single token in a gentile world. We lived in a world where there was much inter-marriage and where a certain "Jewish flavor" was accepted within the dominant gentile culture. People talked glibly of "Jewish self-hatred," but anti-Semitism was rarely identified. It was as if you could have it both ways—identity and assimilation—without having to think about it very much.

I was moved and gratefully amazed by the affection and kindliness my husband's parents showed me, the half *shiksa*. I longed to embrace that family, that new and mysterious Jewish world. It was never a question of conversion—my husband had long since ceased being observant—but of a burning desire to do well, please these new parents, heal the split consciousness in which I had been raised, and, of course, to belong. In the big, sunny apartment on Eastern Parkway, the table would be spread on Saturday afternoons with a white or an embroidered cloth and plates of coffeecake, spongecake, mohncake, cookies for a family gathering where everyone ate and drank—coffee, milk, cake—and later the talk still eddied among the women around the table or in the kitchen, while the men ended up in the living room watching the ball game. I had never known this kind of family, in which mock insults were cheerfully exchanged, secrets whispered in corners among two or three, children and grandchildren boasted about, and the new daughter-in-law openly inspected. I was profoundly attracted by all this, including the punctilious observance of *kashrut,* the symbolism lurking behind daily kitchen tasks. I saw it all as quintessentially and authentically Jewish, and I objectified both the people and the culture. My unexamined anti-Semitism allowed me to do this. But also, I had not yet recognized that as a woman I stood in a particular and unexamined relationship to the Jewish family and to Jewish culture.

There were several years during which I did not see, and barely communicated with, my parents. At the same time, my father's personality haunted my life. Such had been the force of his will in our household that for a long time I felt I would have to pay in some terrible way for having disobeyed him. When finally we were reconciled, and my husband and I and our children began to have some minimal formal contact with my parents, the obsessional power of Arnold's voice or handwriting had given way to a dull sense of useless anger and pain. I wanted him to cherish and approve of me, not as he had when I was a child, but as the woman I was, who had her own mind and had made her own choices. This, I finally realized, was not to be; Arnold demanded absolute loyalty, absolute submission to his will. In my separation from him, in my realization at what price that once-intoxicating approval had been bought, I was learning in concrete ways a great deal about patriarchy, in particular how the "special" woman, the favored daughter, is controlled and rewarded.

Arnold Rich died in 1968 after a long, deteriorating illness; his mind had gone, and he had been losing his sight for years. It was a year of intensifying political awareness for me: the Martin Luther King and Robert Kennedy assassinations, the Columbia strike. But it was not that these events, and the meetings and demonstrations that surrounded them, preempted the time of mourning for my father; I had been mourning a long time for an early, primary, and intense relationship, by no means always benign, but in which I had been ceaselessly made to feel that what I did with my life, the choices I made, the attitudes I held, were of the utmost consequence.

•

Sometime in my thirties, on visits to Brooklyn, I sat on Eastern Parkway, a baby stroller at my feet—one of many rows of young Jewish women on benches with children in that neighborhood. I used to see the Lubavitcher Hasidim—then beginning to move into the Crown Heights neighborhood—walking out on *Shabbes*, the women in their *shaytls* a little behind the men. My father-in-law pointed them out as rather exotic—too old-country, perhaps, too unassimilated even for his devout yet Americanized sense of Jewish identity. It took many years for me to understand—partly because I understood so little about class in America—how in my own family, and in the very different family of my in-laws, there were degrees and hierarchies of assimilation which looked askance upon each other—and also geographic lines of difference, as between southern Jews and New York Jews, whose manners and customs varied along class as well as regional lines.

•

I had three sons before I was thirty, and during those years I often felt that to be a Jewish woman, a Jewish mother, was to be perceived in the Jewish family as an entirely physical being, a producer and nourisher of children. The experience of motherhood was eventually to radicalize me. But before that, I was encountering the institution of motherhood most directly in a Jewish cultural version; and I felt rebellious, moody, defensive, unable to sort out what was

Jewish from what was simply motherhood or female destiny. (I lived in Cambridge, not Brooklyn; but there, too, restless, educated women sat on benches with baby strollers, half-stunned, not by Jewish cultural expectations, but by the middle-class American social expectations of the 1950s.)

My children were taken irregularly to Seders, to bar mizvahs, and to special services in their grandfather's temple. Their father lit Hanukkah candles while I stood by, having rememorized each year the English meaning of the Hebrew blessing. We all celebrated a secular, liberal Christmas. I read aloud from books about Esther and the Maccabees and Moses, and also from books about Norse trolls and Chinese grandmothers and Celtic dragon slayers. Their father told stories of his boyhood in Brooklyn, his grandmother in the Bronx who had to be visited by subway every week, of misdeeds in Hebrew school, of being a bright Jewish kid at Boys' High. In the permissive liberalism of academic Cambridge, you could raise your children to be as vaguely or distinctly Jewish as you would, but Christian myth and calendar organized the year. My sons grew up knowing far more about the existence and concrete meaning of Jewish culture than I had. But I don't recall sitting down with them and telling them that millions of people like themselves, many of them children, had been rounded up and murdered in Europe in their parents' lifetime. Nor was I able to tell them that they came in part out of the rich, thousand-year-old Ashkenazic culture of eastern Europe, which the Holocaust destroyed; or that they came from a people whose traditions, religious and secular, included a hatred of oppression and an imperative to pursue justice and care for the stranger—an antiracist, a socialist, and even sometimes a feminist vision. I could not tell them these things because these things were still too indistinct in my own mind.

•

The emergence of the Civil Rights movement in the sixties I remember as lifting me out of a sense of personal frustration and hopelessness. Reading James Baldwin's early essays in the fifties had stirred me with a sense that apparently "given" situations like racism could be analyzed and described and that this could lead to action, to change. Racism had been so utter and implicit a fact of my childhood and adolescence, had felt so central among the silences, negations, cruelties, fears, superstitions of my early life, that somewhere among my feelings must have been the hope that if Black people could become free of the immense political and social burdens they were forced to bear, I, too, could become free of all the ghosts and shadows of my childhood, named and unnamed. When "the movement" began, it felt extremely personal to me. And it was often Jews who spoke up for the justice of the cause, Jewish students and civil rights lawyers who travelled South; it was two young Jews who were found murdered with a young Black man in Mississippi: Schwerner, Goodman, Chaney.

•

Moving to New York in the mid-sixties meant being plunged almost immediately into the debate over community control of public schools, in which Black and Jewish teachers and parents were often on opposite sides of extremely militant barricades. It was easy as a white liberal to deplore and condemn the racism of middle-class Jewish parents or angry Jewish schoolteachers, many of them older women; to displace our own racism onto them; or to feel it as too painful to think about. The struggle for Black civil rights had such clarity about it for me: I knew that segregation was wrong, that unequal opportunity was wrong; I knew that segregation in particular was more than a set of social and legal rules—it meant that even "decent" white people lived in a network of lies and arrogance and moral collusion. In the world of Jewish assimilationist and liberal politics which I knew best, however, things were far less clear to me, and anti-Semitism went almost unmentioned. It was even possible to view concern about anti-Semitism as a reactionary agenda, a monomania of *Commentary* magazine or, later, the Jewish Defense League. Most of the political work I was doing in the late 1960s was on racial issues, in particular as a teacher in the City University during the struggle for open admissions. The white colleagues I thought of as allies were, I think, mostly Jewish. Yet it was easy to see other New York Jews, who had climbed out of poverty and exploitation through the public-school system and the free city colleges, as now trying to block Black and Puerto Rican students trying to do likewise. I didn't understand then that I was living between two strains of Jewish social identity: the Jew as radical visionary and activist who understands oppression firsthand, and the Jew as part of America's devouring plan in which the persecuted, called to assimilation, learn that the price is to engage in persecution.

And, indeed, there *was* intense racism among Jews as well as white gentiles in the City University, part of the bitter history of Jews and Blacks which James Baldwin had described much earlier, in his 1948 essay "The Harlem Ghetto";[3] part of the divide-and-conquer script still being rehearsed by those of us who have the least to gain from it.

•

By the time I left my marriage, after seventeen years and three children, I had become identified with the Women's Liberation movement. It was an astonishing time to be a woman of my age. In the 1950s, seeking a way to grasp the pain I seemed to be feeling most of the time, to set it in some larger context, I had read all kinds of things; but it was James Baldwin and Simone de Beauvoir who had described the world—though differently—in terms that made the most sense to me. By the end of the sixties there were two political movements—one already meeting severe repression, one just emerging—which addressed those descriptions of the world.

And there was, of course, a third movement, or a movement-within-a-movement: the early lesbian manifestoes, the new visibility and activism of lesbians everywhere. I had known very early on that the women's movement was not going to be a simple walk across an open field; that it would pull on every fiber of my existence; that it would mean going back and searching the shadows of my consciousness. Reading *The Second Sex* in the 1950s isolation of an academic housewife had felt less dangerous than reading "The Myth of Vaginal Orgasm" or "Woman-identified Woman" in a world where I was in constant debate and discussion with women over every aspect of our lives that we could as yet name. De Beauvoir had placed "The Lesbian" on the margins, and there was little in her book to suggest the power of woman bonding. But the passion of debating ideas with women was an erotic passion for me, and the risking of self with women that was necessary in order to win some truth out of the lies of the past was also erotic. The suppressed lesbian I had been carrying in me since adolescence began to stretch her limbs, and her first full-fledged act was to fall in love with a Jewish woman.

Some time during the early months of that relationship, I dreamed that I was arguing feminist politics with my lover. *Of course*, I said to her in this dream, *if you're going to bring up the Holocaust against me, there's nothing I can do.* If, as I believe, I was both myself and her in this dream, it spoke of the split in my consciousness. I had been, more or less, a Jewish heterosexual woman. But what did it mean to be a Jewish lesbian? What did it mean to feel myself, as I did, both anti-Semite and Jew? And, as a feminist, how was I charting for myself the oppressions within oppression?

The earliest feminist papers on Jewish identity that I read were critiques of the patriarchal and misogynist elements in Judaism, or of the caricaturing of Jewish women in literature by Jewish men. I remember hearing Judith Plaskow give a paper called "Can a Woman Be a Jew?" (Her conclusion was "Yes, but . . .") I was soon after in correspondence with a former student who had emigrated to Israel, was a passionate feminist, and wrote to me at length of the legal and social constraints on women there, the stirrings of contemporary Israeli feminism, and the contradictions she felt in her daily life. With the new politics, activism, literature of a tumultuous feminist movement around me, a movement which claimed universality though it had not yet acknowledged its own racial, class, and ethnic perspectives or its fears of the differences among women, I pushed aside for one last time thinking further about myself as a Jewish woman. I saw Judaism simply as another strand of patriarchy. If asked to choose, I might have said (as my father had said in other language): *I am a woman, not a Jew.* (But, I always added mentally, if Jews had to wear yellow stars again, I, too, would wear one—as if I would have the choice to wear it or not.)

•

Sometimes I feel I have seen too long from too many disconnected angles: white, Jewish, anti-Semite, racist, anti-racist, once-married, lesbian, middle-class, feminist, exmatriate southerner, *split at the root*—that I will never bring them whole. I would have liked, in this essay, to bring together the meanings of anti-Semitism and racism as I have experienced them and as I believe they intersect in the world beyond my life. But I'm not able to do this yet. I feel the tension as I think, make notes: *If you really look at the one reality, the other will waver and disperse.* Trying in one week to read Angela Davis and Lucy Davidowicz;[4] trying to hold throughout to a feminist, a lesbian, perspective—what does this mean? Nothing has trained me for this. And sometimes I feel inadequate to make any statement as a Jew; I feel the history of denial within me like an injury, a scar. For assimilation has affected *my* perceptions; those early lapses in meaning, those blanks, are with me still. My ignorance can be dangerous to me and to others.

Yet we can't wait for the undamaged to make our connections for us; we can't wait to speak until we are perfectly clear and righteous. There is no purity and, in our lifetimes, no end to this process.

This essay, then, has no conclusions: it is another beginning for me. Not just a way of saying, in 1982 Right Wing America, *I, too, will wear the yellow star.* It's a moving into accountability, enlarging the range of accountability. I know that in the rest of my life, the next half century or so, every aspect of my identity will have to be engaged. The middle-class white girl taught to trade obedience for privilege. The Jewish lesbian raised to be a heterosexual gentile. The woman who first heard oppression named and analyzed in the Black Civil Rights struggle. The woman with three sons, the feminist who hates male violence. The woman limping with a cane, the woman who has stopped bleeding are also accountable. The poet who knows that beautiful language can lie, that the oppressor's language sometimes sounds beautiful. The woman trying, as part of her resistance, to clean up her act.

THE EYE OF THE OUTSIDER

Elizabeth Bishop's Complete Poems, 1927–1979 *(1983)*

knew Elizabeth Bishop's poetry very well before I ever met her, and I always knew the poems better than the woman. I had early been drawn to the timbre of the voice in her first two books, had met her once or twice in literary groups, not the best place for breaking through shyness and differences in age and reputation. Much later, in the early 1970s, I offered her a ride from New York to Boston, where we were both then living. We found ourselves talking of the recent suicides in each of our lives, telling "how it happened" as people speak who feel they will be understood. In the course of this drive I forgot to take the turnoff at Hartford, and drove as far as Springfield without noticing. This conversation was the only one approaching intimacy I ever had with Elizabeth Bishop and almost the only time I saw her alone.

I had felt drawn, but also repelled, by Bishop's early work—I mean *repel* in the sense of refusing access, seeming to push away. In part, my difficulties with her were difficulties in the poetry, of Bishop as a young poet finding her own level and her own language. But in part they were difficulties I brought with me, as a still younger woman poet already beginning to question sexual identity, looking for a female genealogy, still not yet consciously lesbian. I had not then connected the themes of outsiderhood and marginality in her work, as well as its encodings and obscurities, with a lesbian identity. I was looking for a clear female tradition; the tradition I was discovering was diffuse, elusive, often cryptic. Yet, especially given the times

Originally published in the *Boston Review* (April 1983): 15–17.

and customs of the 1940s and 1950s, Bishop's work now seems to me remarkably honest and courageous.

Women poets searching for older contemporaries in that period were supposed to look to "Miss" Marianne Moore as the paradigm of what a woman poet might accomplish, and, after her, to "Miss" Bishop. Both had been selected and certified by the literary establishment, which was, as now, white, male, and at least ostensibly heterosexual. Elizabeth Bishop's name was spoken, her books reviewed with deep respect. But attention was paid to her triumphs, her perfections, not to her struggles for self-definition and her sense of difference. In this way, her reputation made her less, rather than more, available to me. The infrequency of her public appearances and her geographic remoteness—living for many years in Brazil, with a woman as it happened, but we didn't know that—made her an indistinct and a problematic life model for a woman poet.

Some of the poems in her first book, *North and South* (1946), I found impenetrable: intellectualized to the point of obliquity (e.g., "The Map"), or using extended metaphor to create a mask (e.g., "A Miracle for Breakfast," "The Monument," "The Imaginary Iceberg"). That first book contains traces of Miss Moore—for example, the coy use of quoted phrases within a poem, a mannerism Bishop soon discarded. And the overall strategy of many poems—the poem-about-an-artifact which becomes the poem-as-artifact—owes too much to Moore. Bishop wrote such poems later in her life (see "12 o'Clock News," for example), but not often. More and more, her poems embodied a need to place herself in the actual, to come to terms with a personal past, with family and class and race, with her presence as a poet in cities and landscapes where human suffering is not a metaphor.

I have been fascinated by the diversity of challenges that *The Complete Poems, 1927–1979* [New York: Farrar, Straus & Giroux, 1983] raises, the questions—poetic and political—that it stirs up, the opportunities that it affords. In addition to the four volumes published in her lifetime, this edition—enhanced by the work of the gifted designer Cynthia Krupat—includes late poems which appeared in magazines after *Geography III* (1976), some posthumously published late poems, eleven poems written between the ages of sixteen and twenty-two, some uncollected later poems, and translations. Part of the value of such a collection is the chance it gives to see where certain obsessions and motives begin to take hold and how they work their way through a lifetime of poems; how certain echoes sound and die away; how style metamorphoses over time. This collection offers not just challenges and questions, but very deep pleasure. In her later work especially, Bishop is difficult to quote from because her poems are so often hung on one long thread; the progression of language and images does not readily separate into extracts. By the same token she is a wonderful poet to read aloud.

Criticism of Bishop in her lifetime was mostly appreciative of her powers of observation, her carefully articulated descriptive language, her wit, her intelligence, the individuality of her voice. I want to acknowledge the distinction of all these, the marvelous flexibility and sturdiness of her writing, her lack of self-indulgence, her capacity to write of loss and of time past without pathos and with precision, as in poems like "Sestina," "The Moose," "Filling Station," "First Death in Nova Scotia," "At the Fishhouses." I want to pay this homage and go on to aspects of her work which I have not yet seen discussed. In particular I am concerned with her experience of outsiderhood, closely—though not exclusively—linked with the essential outsiderhood of a lesbian identity; and with how the outsider's eye enables Bishop to perceive other kinds of outsiders and to identify, or try to identify, with them. I believe she deserves to be read and valued not only for her language and images or for her personality within the poems, but for the way she locates herself in the world.

Elizabeth Bishop was born in Worcester, Massachusetts, in 1911, and lost her mother into a mental institution when she was five years old—a loss that was permanent. Her father was already dead. She migrated not once, but several times: first to Nova Scotia to be raised by relatives, then back to the United States, then to Brazil, then back to New England after the death of Lota de Soares. Travel—not as in "vacation," not as in "escape"—was from early on a given for her.

"Continent, city, country, society:
the choice is never wide and never free,
And here, or there. . . . No. Should we have stayed at home,
Wherever that may be?

("Questions of Travel")

The child made "different" because parentless, the emigrant who thinks she would—understandably—"rather have the iceberg than the ship," the woman writing, consciously or not, "against the male flood" (Woolf's phrase), the lesbian writing under the false universal of heterosexuality, the foreigner who can take little for granted—all inhabit Bishop's poetic voice and eye. Outsiderhood is a condition which most people spend (and are often constrained to spend) great energy trying to deny or evade, through whatever kinds of assimilation or protective coloration they can manage. Poetry, too, can serve as protective coloration; the social person who is the poet may also try to "pass," but the price of external assimilation is internal division.

The pain of division is acutely present in some of Bishop's earliest poems, notably in "A Word with You," written when she was twenty-two, a tense, panicky, one-sided conversation during which a whole menagerie gets out of control:

Look out! there's that damned ape again
sit silently until he goes
or else forgets the things he knows
(whatever they are) about us, then
we can begin to talk again.

In *North and South*, "The Weed" grows up through and divides the "frozen" heart so that it gushes two "rushing, half-clear streams." "The Gentleman of Shalott" is a half man whose other half is actually a reflection in a mirror. "The Colder the Air" and "Chemin de Fer" can be read as two bleakly counterpoised possibilities. The "huntress of the winter air" has everything under control, having reduced the world to her shooting gallery, in an icy single-mindedness; the speaker of the poem does not have such power, and beneath its frigid surface the poem quivers with barely suppressed rage. In "Chemin de Fer" the speaker is in an endangered position also, "Alone on the railroad track," while the "dirty hermit" firing his gun hits nothing, is impotent to carry through:

> "Love should be put into action!"
>   screamed the dirty hermit.
> Across the pond an echo
>   tried and tried to confirm it.

What does it mean to put love into action? Especially in isolation and in a world which does not confirm that imperative?

To know yourself as an outsider, as an "invert" in the old jargon, and to try to live and love in two worlds, is to dream of the impossible safe place, the upside-down park and fountain of "Sleeping on the Ceiling" or, in "Insomnia,"

> that world inverted
> where left is always right
> where the shadows are really the body
> where we stay awake all night,
> where the heavens are shallow as the sea
> is now deep, and you love me.

Or, in "O Breath"—one of a sequence of four short, tensely packed love poems—there is the still ambivalent evocation of

> something that maybe I   could bargain with
> and make a separate peace   beneath
> within   if never with

There is disturbance and tension in these "Four Poems," but there is also a glimpse, at least, of some kind of erotic freeing-up:

The face is pale
that tried the puzzle of their prison
and solved it with an unexpected kiss,
whose freckled unsuspected hands alit.

The first and title poem of *A Cold Spring* can be read as a record
of a slow, deliberate, erotic unfolding, with a culminating image of
"shadowy pastures" from which fireflies rise "exactly like the bub-
bles in champagne." The final poem of this collection, "Shampoo,"
celebrates a serious, tender, practical rite between two women:

The shooting stars in your black hair
in bright formation
are flocking where,
so straight, so soon?
—come, let me wash it in this big tin basin
battered and shiny like the moon.

But Bishop left behind, in the last unpublished poem of the last
year of her life, her own last word on division, decision, and questions of travel:

Caught—the bubble
in the spirit-level,
a creature divided,
and the compass needle
wobbling and wavering,
undecided.
Freed—the broken
thermometer's mercury
running away;
and the rainbow bird
from the narrow bevel
of the empty mirror,
flying wherever
it feels like, gay!
(*"Sonnet"*)

Poems examining intimate relationship are almost wholly absent from Bishop's later work. What takes their place is a series of poems examining relationships between people who are, for reasons of inequality, distanced: rich and poor, landowner and tenant, white woman and Black woman, invader and native. Even in her first book she had taken on the theme of the Black woman's existence in a white world. The poem "Cootchie" addresses the fate of a Black woman who has died, presumably by drowning, perhaps by suicide. The white woman she has worked for is literally deaf but also self-absorbed: she will not "understand." "Songs for a Colored Singer," rumored to have been written with Billie Holiday in mind, begins:

> A washing hangs upon the line
>   but it's not mine.
> None of the things that I can see
>   belong to me . . .

This is a white woman's attempt—respectful, I believe—to speak through a Black woman's voice. A risky undertaking, and it betrays the failures and clumsiness of such a position. The personae we adopt, the degree to which we use lives already ripped off and violated by our own culture, the problem of racist stereotyping in every white head, the issue of the writer's power, right, obligation to speak for others denied a voice, or the writer's duty to shut up at times or at least to make room for those who can speak with more immediate authority—these are crucial questions for our time, and questions that are relevant to much of Bishop's work. What I value is her attempt to acknowledge other outsiders, lives marginal in ways that hers is not, long before the Civil Rights movement made such awareness temporarily fashionable for some white writers.

Brazil, a multiracial yet still racist and class-fragmented country, clearly opened up a further range of understanding for Bishop. Her earliest poems about Brazil grasp the presence of colonization and enslavement:

Just so the Christians, hard as nails . . .
in creaking armor, came and found it all,
not unfamiliar. . . .
Directly after Mass . . .
they ripped away into the hanging fabric,
each out to catch an Indian for himself—
those maddening little women who kept calling,
calling to each other (or had the birds waked up?)
and retreating, always retreating, behind it.

("*Brazil, January 1, 1502*")

Some of Bishop's best Brazilian poems are exercises in coming to terms with her location as a foreign white woman living as part of a privileged class in a city of beggars and rich people. I am thinking of "Faustina," "Manuelzinho," "The Burglar of Babylon," "Pink Dog." In "Faustina" she draws the scene of a white woman dying in her "crazy house," with her white hair, among "white disordered sheets," in a white "chamber of bleached flags," tended by a Black woman servant. The narrator is confronted by the "conundrum" of white power, the history of what whites have done to Black people, and the vulnerability of this particular dying old woman. It is a poem of contradictions and about extremes of possibility between the two women: a dream of "freedom at last, a lifelong / . . . dream of protection and rest" versus the "unimaginable nightmare / that never before dared last / more than a second." Extremes defined from a white woman's perspective, but at least *acknowledging* the "acuteness of the question." I cannot think of another poem by a white woman, until some feminist poetry of the last few years, in which the servant-mistress dynamic between Black and white women has received unsentimental attention.[1]

Bishop precedes "Manuelzinho" with the note "A friend of the writer is speaking," as if partly to dissociate herself from the speaker, a liberal landowner addressing a squatter-tenant. Manuelzinho, the tenant, is seen as improvident, touching, exasperating, picturesque—qualities traditionally attributed to the colonized; the landowner is essentially benign, ruefully resigned to the balance of power in which

Manuelzinho must cajole and beg for handouts. In this poem, Bishop places herself between, but not equidistant from, landowner and tenant. There is no way for her to be equidistant: the poem reads, after all, from the landowner's point of view, even though it also exposes her or him. The poem explores that perspective, leaving the reader free to accept or reject it. By contrast, we live through much of "The Burglar of Babylon" in the Burglar's skin; and it's clear that despite the poem's deadpan tone, we are not invited to stay neutral: Micuçu, three times escaped from jail, with a vague array of charges against him, is ambushed by the militia and shot. Soon after his death the soldiers are out on the hills again, searching for two more "enemies of society." The police overkill is ridiculous, the drama recounted in flat-voiced meters. No heroes to this ballad, only victims. Burglars are caught and killed; the essential state of things remains the same:

> On the fair green hills of Rio
>   There grows a fearful stain:
> The poor who come to Rio
>   And can't go home again. . . .
>
> There's the hill of Kerosene,
>   And the hill of the Skeleton,
> The hill of Astonishment,
>   And the hill of Babylon.

Finally, there is the 1979 poem "Pink Dog," subtitled in brackets "Rio de Janeiro"—a brilliantly bitter, indignant satire on the notion that the wretched of the earth are themselves to blame for their misery and should try to disguise themselves (or assimilate) for their own survival. The hairless female dog with scabies is advised to dress up in a carnival costume and dance the samba:

> (A nursing mother, by those hanging teats.)
> In what slum have you hidden them, poor bitch,
> while you go begging, living by your wits? . . .

If they do this to anyone who begs,
drugged, drunk, or sober, with or without legs,
what would they do to sick, four-leggèd dogs?

In selecting the poems I have discussed here, in limited space, I
have reluctantly neglected the marvelous Nova Scotia poems as well
as many others even better known, such as "Roosters," "The Fish,"
"Visits to St. Elizabeths" (also a seriously political poem), "In the
Waiting Room," "One Art." But it seems to me that Bishop's value for
us is more complex and multifaceted than we may have been aware,
and I have wanted to suggest new ways of entering her work. Moreover, it is only now, with a decade of feminist and lesbian poetry
and criticism behind us and with the publication of these *Complete
Poems*, that we can read her as part of a female and lesbian tradition rather than simply as one of the few and "exceptional" women
admitted to the male canon. Too often, the "exceptional" or token
outsider is praised for her skill and artistry while her deep and troubled connections with other outsiders are ignored. (This is itself part
of the imperative to be assimilated.) It is important to me to know
that, through most of her life, Bishop was critically and consciously
trying to explore marginality, power and powerlessness, often in
poetry of great beauty and sensuousness. That not all these poems
are fully realized or satisfying simply means that the living who care
that art should embody these questions have still more work to do.

BLOOD, BREAD, AND POETRY

The Location of the Poet (1984)

The Miami airport, summer 1983: a North American woman says to me, "You'll love Nicaragua: everyone there is a poet." I've thought many times of that remark, both while there and since returning home. Coming from a culture (North American, white- and male-dominated) which encourages poets to think of ourselves as alienated from the sensibility of the general population, which casually and devastatingly marginalizes us (so far, no slave labor or torture for a political poem—just dead air, the white noise of the media jamming the poet's words)—coming from this North American dominant culture which so confuses us, telling us poetry is neither economically profitable nor politically effective and that political dissidence is destructive to art, coming from this culture that tells me I am destined to be a luxury, a decorative garnish on the buffet table of the university curriculum, the ceremonial occasion, the national celebration—what am I to make, I thought, of that remark? *You'll love Nicaragua: everyone there is a poet.* (Do I love poets in general? I immediately asked myself, thinking of poets I neither love nor would wish to see in charge of my country.) Is being a poet a guarantee that I will love a Marxist-Leninist revolution? Can't I travel simply as an American radical, a lesbian feminist, a citizen who opposes her government's wars against its own people and its intervention in other people's lands? And what effectiveness has the testimony of a poet returning from a revolution where "everyone is

Talk given for the Institute for the Humanities, University of Massachusetts, Amherst, series "Writers and Social Responsibility," 1983. Originally published in the *Massachusetts Review*.

a poet" to a country where the possible credibility of poetry is not even seriously discussed?

Clearly, this well-meant remark triggered strong and complex feelings in me. And it provided, in a sense, the text on which I began to build my talk here tonight.

I was born at the brink of the Great Depression; I reached sixteen the year of Nagasaki and Hiroshima. The daughter of a Jewish father and a Protestant mother, I learned about the Holocaust first from newsreels of the liberation of the death camps. I was a young white woman who had never known hunger or homelessness, growing up in the suburbs of a deeply segregated city in which neighborhoods were also dictated along religious lines: Christian and Jewish. I lived sixteen years of my life secure in the belief that though cities could be bombed and civilian populations killed, the earth stood in its old indestructible way. The process through which nuclear annihilation was to become a part of all human calculation had already begun, but we did not live with that knowledge during the first sixteen years of my life. And a recurrent theme in much poetry I read was the indestructibility of poetry, the poem as a vehicle for personal immortality.

I had grown up hearing and reading poems from a very young age, first as sounds, repeated, musical, rhythmically satisfying in themselves, and the power of concrete, sensuously compelling images:

All night long they hunted
    And nothing did they find
But a ship a-sailing,
    A-sailing with the wind.
One said it was a ship,
    The other he said, Nay,
The third said it was a house
    With the chimney blown away;
And all the night they hunted
    And nothing did they find
But the moon a-gliding
    A-gliding with the wind. . . .

Tyger! Tyger! burning bright
    In the forest of the night,
What immortal hand or eye
    Dare frame thy fearful symmetry?

But poetry soon became more than music and images; it was also revelation, information, a kind of teaching. I believed I could learn from it—an unusual idea for a United States citizen, even a child. I thought it could offer clues, intimations, keys to questions that already stalked me, questions I could not even frame yet: *What is possible in this life? What does "love" mean, this thing that is so important? What is this other thing called "freedom" or "liberty"—is it like love, a feeling? What have human beings lived and suffered in the past? How am I going to live my life?* The fact that poets contradicted themselves and each other didn't baffle or alarm me. I was avid for everything I could get; my child's mind did not shut down for the sake of consistency.

I was angry with my friend,
I told my wrath, my wrath did end.
I was angry with my foe,
I told it not, my wrath did grow.

As an angry child, often urged to "curb my temper," I used to ponder those words of William Blake, but they slid first into my memory through their repetitions of sound, their ominous rhythms.

Another poem that I loved first as music, later pondered for what it could tell me about women and men and marriage, was Edwin Arlington Robinson's "Eros Turannos":

She fears him, and will always ask
    What fated her to choose him;
She meets in his engaging mask
    All reasons to refuse him;
But what she meets and what she fears
    Are less than are the downward years,

Drawn slowly to the foamless weirs
  Of age, were she to lose him. . . .

And, of course, I thought that the poets in the anthologies were the only real poets, that their being in the anthologies was proof of this, though some were classified as "great" and others as "minor." I owed much to those anthologies: *Silver Pennies;* the constant out-flow of volumes edited by Louis Untermeyer; *The Cambridge Book of Poetry for Children;* Palgrave's *Golden Treasury;* the *Oxford Book of English Verse.* But I had no idea that they reflected the taste of a particular time or of particular kinds of people. I still believed that poets were inspired by some transcendent authority and spoke from some extraordinary height. I thought that the capacity to hook syllables together in a way that heated the blood was the sign of a universal vision.

Because of the attitudes surrounding me, the aesthetic ideology with which I grew up, I came into my twenties believing in poetry, in all art, as the expression of a higher world view, what the critic Edward Said has termed "a quasi-religious wonder, instead of a human sign to be understood in secular and social terms."[1] The poet achieved "universality" and authority through tapping his, or occasionally her, own dreams, longings, fears, desires, and, out of this, "speaking as a man to men," as Wordsworth had phrased it. But my personal world view at sixteen, as at twenty-six, was itself being created by political conditions. I was not a man; I was white in a white-supremacist society; I was being educated from the perspective of a particular class; my father was an "assimilated" Jew in an anti-Semitic world, my mother a white southern Protestant; there were particular historical currents on which my consciousness would come together, piece by piece. My personal world view was shaped in part by the poetry I had read, a poetry written almost entirely by white Anglo-Saxon men, a few women, Celts and Frenchmen notwithstanding. Thus, no poetry in the Spanish language or from Africa or China or the Middle East. My personal world view, which like so many young people I carried as a conviction of my own uniqueness, was not original with me, but was, rather, my untutored and half-conscious rendering of the facts of blood and bread, the social and political forces of my time and place.

I was in college during the late 1940s and early 1950s. The thirties, a decade of economic desperation, social unrest, war, and also of affirmed political art, was receding behind the fogs of the Cold War, the selling of the nuclear family with the mother at home as its core, heightened activity by the FBI and CIA, a retreat by many artists from so-called "protest" art, witch-hunting among artists and intellectuals as well as in the State Department, anti-Semitism, scapegoating of homosexual men and lesbians, and with a symbolic victory for the Cold War crusade in the 1953 electrocution of Ethel and Julius Rosenberg.

Francis Otto Matthiessen, a socialist and a homosexual, was teaching literature at Harvard when I came there. One semester he lectured on five poets: Blake, Keats, Byron, Yeats, and Stevens. That class perhaps affected my life as a poet more than anything else that happened to me in college. Matthiessen had a passion for language, and he read aloud, made us memorize poems and recite them to him as part of the course. He also actually alluded to events in the outside world, the hope that eastern Europe could survive as an independent socialist force between the United States and the Soviet Union; he spoke of the current European youth movements as if they should matter to us. Poetry, in his classroom, never remained in the realm of pure textual criticism. Remember that this was in 1947 or 1948, that it was a rare teacher of literature at Harvard who referred to a world beyond the text, even though the classrooms were full of World War II veterans studying on the G.I. Bill of Rights—men who might otherwise never have gone to college, let alone Harvard, at all. Matthiessen committed suicide in the spring of my sophomore year.

Because of Yeats, who by then had become my idea of the Great Poet, the one who more than others could hook syllables together in a way that heated my blood, I took a course in Irish history. It was taught by a Boston Irish professor of Celtic, one of Harvard's tokens, whose father, it was said, had been a Boston policeman. He read poetry aloud in Gaelic and in English, sang us political ballads, gave us what amounted to a mini-education on British racism and imperialism, though the words were never mentioned. He also slashed at Irish self-romanticizing. People laughed about the Irish history course, said it must be full of football players. In and out of the Harvard Yard, the racism of Yankee Brahmin toward Boston Irish was never questioned, laced as it was with equally unquestioned class arrogance. Today, Irish Boston both acts out and takes the weight of New England racism against Black and Hispanic people. It was, strangely enough, through poetry that I first began to try to make sense of these things.

"Strangely enough," I say, because the reading of poetry in an elite academic institution is supposed to lead you—in the 1980s as back there in the early 1950s—not toward a criticism of society, but toward a professional career in which the anatomy of poems is studied dispassionately. Prestige, job security, money, and inclusion in an exclusive fraternity are where the academic study of literature is supposed to lead. Maybe I was lucky because I had started reading poetry so young, and not in school, and because I had been writing poems almost as long as I had been reading them. I should add that I was easily entranced by pure sound and still am, no matter what it is saying; and any poet who mixes the poetry of the actual world with the poetry of sound interests and excites me more than I am able to say. In my student years, it was Yeats who seemed to do this better than anyone else. There were lines of Yeats that were to ring in my head for years:

Many times man lives and dies
Between his two eternities,
That of race and that of soul,
And ancient Ireland knew it all....

Did she in touching that lone wing
Recall the years before her mind
Became a bitter, an abstract thing
Her thought some popular enmity:
Blind and leader of the blind
Drinking the foul ditch where they lie?

I could hazard the guess that all the most impassioned, seductive arguments against the artist's involvement in politics can be found in Yeats. It was this dialogue between art and politics that excited me in his work, along with the sound of his language—never his elaborate mythological systems. I know I learned two things from his poetry, and those two things were at war with each other. One was that poetry can be "about," can root itself in, politics. Even if it is a defense of privilege, even if it deplores political rebellion and revolution, it can, may have to, account for itself politically, consciously situate itself amid political conditions, without sacrificing intensity of language. The other, that politics leads to "bitterness" and "abstractness" of mind, makes women shrill and hysterical, and is finally a waste of beauty and talent: "Too long a sacrifice / can make a stone of the heart." There was absolutely nothing in the literary canon I knew to counter the second idea. Elizabeth Barrett Browning's anti-slavery and feminist poetry, H.D.'s anti-war and woman-identified poetry, like the radical—yes, revolutionary—work of Langston Hughes and Muriel Rukeyser, were still buried by the academic literary canon. But the first idea was extremely important to me: a poet—one who was apparently certified—could actually write about political themes, could weave the names of political activists into a poem:

MacDonagh and MacBride
And Connally and Pearce
Now and in time to come
Wherever green is worn
Are changed, changed utterly:
A terrible beauty is born.

As we all do when young and searching for what we can't even name yet, I took what I could use where I could find it. When the ideas or forms we need are banished, we seek their residues wherever we can trace them. But there was one major problem with this. I had been born a woman, and I was trying to think and act as if poetry—and the possibility of making poems—were a universal—a gender-neutral—realm. In the universe of the masculine paradigm, I naturally absorbed ideas about women, sexuality, power from the subjectivity of male poets—Yeats not least among them. The dissonance between these images and the daily events of my own life demanded a constant footwork of imagination, a kind of perpetual translation, and an unconscious fragmentation of identity: woman from poet. Every group that lives under the naming and image-making power of a dominant culture is at risk from this mental fragmentation and needs an art which can resist it.

But at the middle of the fifties I had no very clear idea of my positioning in the world or even that such an idea was an important resource for a writer to have. I knew that marriage and motherhood, experiences which were supposed to be truly womanly, often left me feeling unfit, disempowered, adrift. But I had never had to think about bread itself as a primary issue; and what I knew of blood was that mine was white and that white was better off. Much as my parents had worried about questions of social belonging and acceptability, I had never had to swallow rage or humiliation to earn a paycheck. The literature I had read only rarely suggested that for many people it is a common, everyday fact of life to be hungry. I thought I was well educated. In that Cold War atmosphere, which has never really ended, we heard a lot about the "indoctrinating" of people in the Soviet Union, the egregious rewriting of history to conform to Communist dogma. But, like most Americans, I had been taught a particular version of our history, the version of the proper-tied white male; and in my early twenties I did not even realize this. As a younger and then an older woman, growing up in the white mainstream American culture, I was destined to piece together, for the rest of my life, laboriously and with much in my training against me, the history that really concerned me, on which I was to rely as a poet, the only history upon which, both as a woman and a poet, I could find any grounding at all: the history of the dispossessed.

It was in the pain and confusion of that inward wrenching of the self, which I experienced directly as a young woman in the fifties, that I started to feel my way backward to an earlier splitting, the covert and overt taboos against Black people, which had haunted my earliest childhood. And I began searching for some clue or key to life, not only in poetry but in political writers. The writers I found were Mary Wollstonecraft, Simone de Beauvoir, and James Baldwin. Each of them helped me to realize that what had seemed simply "the way things are" could actually be a social construct, advantageous to some people and detrimental to others, and that these constructs could be criticized and changed. The myths and obsessions of gender, the myths and obsessions of race, the violent exercise of power in these relationships could be identified, their territories could be mapped. They were not simply part of my private turmoil, a secret misery, an individual failure. I did not yet know what I, a white woman, might have to say about the racial obsessions of white consciousness. But I did begin to resist the apparent splitting of poet from woman, thinker from woman, and to write what I feared was political poetry. And in this I had very little encouragement from the literary people I knew, but I did find courage and vindication in words like Baldwin's: "Any real change implies the breakup of the world as one has always known it, the loss of all that gave one an identity, the end of safety." I don't know why I found these words encouraging—perhaps because they made me feel less alone.

Mary Wollstonecraft had seen eighteenth-century middle-class Englishwomen brain-starved and emotionally malnourished through denial of education; her plea was to treat women's minds as respectfully as men's—to admit women as equals into male culture. Simone de Beauvoir showed how the male perception of Woman as Other dominated European culture, keeping "woman" entrapped in myths which robbed her of her independent being and value. James Baldwin insisted that *all* culture was politically significant, and described the complexity of living with integrity as a Black person, an artist in a white-dominated culture, whether as an Afro-American growing up in Harlem, U.S.A., or as an African in a country emerging from a history of colonialism. He also alluded to "that as yet unwritten history of the Negro woman"; and he wrote in 1954 in an essay on Gide that "when men [heterosexual or homosexual] can no longer love women they also cease to love or respect or trust each other, which makes their isolation complete." And he was the first writer I read who suggested that racism was poisonous to white as well as destructive to Black people.

The idea of freedom—so much invoked during World War II—had become pretty abstract politically in the fifties. Freedom—then as now—was supposed to be what the Western democracies believed in and the "Iron Curtain" Soviet-bloc countries were deprived of. The existentialist philosophers who were beginning to be read and discussed among young American intellectuals spoke of freedom as something connected with revolt. But in reading de Beauvoir and Baldwin, I began to taste the concrete reality of being unfree, how continuous and permeating and corrosive a condition it is, and how it is maintained through culture as much as through the use of force.

I am telling you this from a backward perspective, from where I stand now. At the time I could not have summed up the effect these writers had on me. I only knew that I was reading them with the same passion and need that I brought to poetry, that they were beginning to penetrate my life; I was beginning to feel as never before that I had some foothold, some way of seeing, which helped me to ask the questions I needed to ask.

But there were many voices then, as there are now, warning the North American artist against "mixing politics with art." I have been trying to retrace, to delineate, these arguments, which carry no weight for me now because I recognize them as the political declarations of privilege. There is the falsely mystical view of art that assumes a kind of supernatural inspiration, a possession by universal forces unrelated to questions of power and privilege or the artist's relation to bread and blood. In this view, the channel of art can only become clogged and misdirected by the artist's concern with merely temporary and local disturbances. The song is higher than the struggle, and the artist must choose between politics—here defined as earth-bound factionalism, corrupt power struggles—and art, which exists on some transcendent plane. This view of literature has dominated literary criticism in England and America for nearly a century. In the fifties and early sixties there was much shaking of heads if an

artist was found "meddling in politics"; art was mystical and universal, but the artist was also, apparently, irresponsible and emotional
and politically naïve.

In North America, moreover, "politics" is mostly a dirty word,
associated with low-level wheeling and dealing, with manipulation.
(There is nothing North Americans seem to fear so much as manipulation, probably because at some level we know that we belong to a
deeply manipulative system.) "Politics" also suggested, certainly in
the fifties, the Red Menace, Jewish plots, spies, malcontents conspir-
ing to overthrow democracy, "outside agitators" stirring up perfectly
contented Black and/or working people. Such activities were dangerous and punishable, and in the McCarthy era there was a great
deal of fear abroad. The writer Meridel LeSueur was blacklisted,
hounded by the FBI, her books banned; she was dismissed from job
after job—teaching, waitressing—because the FBI intimidated her
students and employers. A daughter of Tillie Olsen recalls going with
her mother in the 1950s to the Salvation Army to buy heavy winter
clothes because the family had reason to believe that Leftists in the
San Francisco Bay Area would be rounded up and taken to detention
camps farther north. These are merely two examples of politically
committed writers who did survive that particular repression—
many never recovered from it.

Perhaps many white North Americans fear an overtly political art
because it might persuade us emotionally of what we think we are
"rationally" against; it might get to us on a level we have lost touch
with, undermine the safety we have built for ourselves, remind us of
what is better left forgotten. This fear attributes real power to the
voices of passion and of poetry which connect us with all that is not
simply white chauvinist/male supremacist/straight/puritanical—
with what is "dark," "effeminate," "inverted," "primitive," "volatile," "sinister." Yet we are told that political poetry, for example,
is doomed to grind down into mere rhetoric and jargon, to become
one-dimensional, simplistic, vituperative; that in writing "protest literature"—that is, writing from a perspective which may not be male,
or white, or heterosexual, or middle-class—we sacrifice the "universal"; that in writing of injustice we are limiting our scope, "grinding

a political axe." So political poetry is suspected of immense subversive power, yet accused of being, by definition, bad writing, impotent, lacking in breadth. No wonder if the North American poet finds herself or himself slightly crazed by the double messages.

By 1956, I had begun dating each of my poems by year. I did this because I was finished with the idea of a poem as a single, encapsulated event, a work of art complete in itself; I knew my life was changing, my work was changing, and I needed to indicate to readers my sense of being engaged in a long, continuing process. It seems to me now that this was an oblique political statement—a rejection of the dominant critical idea that the poem's text should be read as separate from the poet's everyday life in the world. It was a declaration that placed poetry in a historical continuity, not above or outside history.

In my own case, as soon as I published—in 1963—a book of poems which was informed by any conscious sexual politics, I was told, in print, that this work was "bitter," "personal"; that I had sacrificed the sweetly flowing measures of my earlier books for a ragged line and a coarsened voice. It took me a long time not to hear those voices internally whenever I picked up my pen. But I was writing at the beginning of a decade of political revolt and hope and activism. The external conditions for becoming a consciously, self-affirmingly political poet were there, as they had not been when I had begun to publish a decade earlier. Out of the Black Civil Rights movement, amid the marches and sit-ins in the streets and on campuses, a new generation of Black writers began to speak—and older generations to be reprinted and reread; poetry readings were infused with the spirit of collective rage and hope. As part of the movement against United States militarism and imperialism, white poets also were writing and reading aloud poems addressing the war in Southeast Asia. In many of these poems you sensed the poet's desperation in trying to encompass in words the reality of napalm, the "pacification" of villages, trying to make vivid in poetry what seemed to have minimal effect when shown on television. But there was little location of the self, the poet's own identity as a man or woman. As I wrote in another connection, "The enemy is always outside the self, the struggle somewhere else." I had—perhaps through reading de Beauvoir and Baldwin—some nascent idea that "Vietnam and the lovers' bed," as I phrased it then, were connected; I found myself, in the late sixties, trying to describe those relations in poetry. Even before I called myself a feminist or a lesbian, I felt driven—for my own sanity—to bring together in my poems the political world "out there"—the world of children dynamited or napalmed, of the urban ghetto and militarist violence, and the supposedly private, lyrical world of sex and of male/female relationships.

I began teaching in an urban subway college, in a program intended to compensate ghetto students for the inadequacy of the city's public schools. Among staff and students, and in the larger academic community, there were continual debates over the worth and even the linguistic existence of Black English, the expressive limits and social uses of Standard English—the politics of language. As a poet, I had learned much about both the value and the constraints of convention: the reassurances of traditional structures and the necessity to break from them in recognition of new experience. I felt more and more urgently the dynamic between poetry as language and poetry as a kind of action, probing, burning, stripping, placing itself in dialogue with others out beyond the individual self.

By the end of the 1960s an autonomous movement of women was declaring that "the personal is political." That statement was necessary because in other political movements of that decade the power relation of men to women, the question of women's roles and men's roles, had been dismissed—often contemptuously—as the sphere of personal life. Sex itself was not seen as political, except for interracial sex. Women were now talking about domination, not just in terms of economic exploitation, militarism, colonialism, imperialism, but within the family, in marriage, in child rearing, in the heterosexual act itself. Breaking the mental barrier that separated private from public life felt in itself like an enormous surge toward liberation. For a woman thus engaged, every aspect of her life was on the line. We began naming and acting on issues we had been told were trivial, unworthy of mention: rape by husbands or lovers; the boss's hand groping the employee's breast; the woman beaten in her home with no place to go; the woman sterilized when she sought an abortion; the lesbian penalized for her private life by loss of her child, her lease, her job. We pointed out that women's unpaid work in the home is central to every economy, capitalist or socialist. And in the crossover between personal and political, we were also pushing at the limits of experience reflected in literature, certainly in poetry.

To write directly and overtly as a woman, out of a woman's body and experience, to take women's existence seriously as theme and source for art, was something I had been hungering to do, needing to do, all my writing life. It placed me nakedly face to face with both terror and anger; it did indeed *imply the breakdown of the world as I had always known it, the end of safety*, to paraphrase Baldwin again. But it released tremendous energy in me, as in many other women, to have that way of writing affirmed and validated in a growing political community. I felt for the first time the closing of the gap between poet and woman.

Women have understood that we needed an art of our own: to remind us of our history and what we might be; to show us our true faces—all of them, including the unacceptable; to speak of what has been muffled in code or silence; to make concrete the values our movement was bringing forth out of consciousness raising, speak-outs, and activism. But we were—and are—living and writing not only within a women's community. We are trying to build a political and cultural movement in the heart of capitalism, in a country where racism assumes every form of physical, institutional, and psychic violence, and in which more than one person in seven lives below the poverty line. The United States feminist movement is rooted in the United States, a nation with a particular history of hostility both to art and to socialism, where art has been encapsulated as a commodity, a salable artifact, something to be taught in MFA programs, that requires a special staff of "arts administrators"; something you "gotta have" without exactly knowing why. As a lesbian-feminist poet and writer, I need to understand how this *location* affects me, along with the realities of blood and bread within this nation.

"As a woman I have no country. As a woman I want no country. As a woman my country is the whole world." These words, written by Virginia Woolf in her feminist and antifascist book *Three Guineas*, we dare not take out of context to justify a false transcendence, an irresponsibility toward the cultures and geopolitical regions in which we are rooted. Woolf was attacking—as a feminist—patriotism, nationalism, the values of the British patriarchal establishment for which so many wars have been fought all over the world. Her feminism led her by the end of her life to anti-imperialism. As women, I think it essential that we admit and explore our cultural identities, our national identities, even as we reject the patriotism, jingoism, nationalism offered to us as "the American way of life." Perhaps the most arrogant and malevolent delusion of North American power— of white Western power—has been the delusion of destiny, that white is at the center, that white is endowed with some right or mission to judge and ransack and assimilate and destroy the values of other peoples. As a white feminist artist in the United States, I do not want to perpetuate that chauvinism, but I still have to struggle with its pervasiveness in culture, its residues in myself.

Working as I do in the context of a movement in which artists are encouraged to address political and ethical questions, I have felt released to a large degree from the old separation of art from politics. But the presence of that separation "out there" in North American life is one of many impoverishing forces of capitalist patriarchy. I began to sense what it might be to live, and to write poetry, as a woman, in a society which took seriously the necessity for poetry, when I read Margaret Randall's anthology of contemporary Cuban women poets *Breaking the Silences*. This book had a powerful effect on me—the consistently high level of poetry, the diversity of voices, the sense of the poets' connections with world and community, and, in their individual statements, the affirmation of an organic relation between poetry and social transformation:

Things move so much around you.
Even your country has changed. You yourself have
changed it.

And the soul, will it change? You must change it.
Who will tell you otherwise?
Will it be a desolate journey?
Will it be tangible, languid
without a hint of violence?
As long as you are the person you are today
being yesterday's person as well,
you will be tomorrow's . . .
the one who lives and dies
to live like this.[2]

It was partly because of that book that I went to Nicaragua. I seized the opportunity when it arose, not because I thought that everyone would be a poet, but because I had been feeling more and more ill informed, betrayed by the coverage of Central America in the United States media. I wanted to know what the Sandinistas believed they stood for, what directions they wanted to take in their very young, imperiled revolution. But I also wanted to get a sense of what art might mean in a society committed to values other than profit and consumerism. What was constantly and tellingly manifested was a *belief* in art, not as commodity, not as luxury, not as suspect activity, but as a precious resource to be made available to all, one necessity for the rebuilding of a scarred, impoverished, and still-bleeding country. And returning home I had to ask myself: What happens to the heart of the artist, here in North America? What toll is taken of art when it is separated from the social fabric? How is art curbed, how are we made to feel useless and helpless, in a system which so depends on our alienation?

Alienation—not just from the world of material conditions, of power to make things happen or stop happening. Alienation from our own roots, whatever they are, the memories, dreams, stories, the language, history, the sacred materials of art. In *A Gathering of Spirit*, an anthology of writing and art by North American Indian women, a poem by the Chicana/American Indian poet Anita Valerio[3] reasserts the claim to a complex historical and cultural identity, the selves who are both of the past and of tomorrow:

There is the cab driver root and elevator
root, there is the water
root of lies   The root of speech hidden in the secretary's
marinated tongue   There is the ocean
root and seeing
root, heart and belly root, antelope
roots hidden in hills   There is the root
of the billy club/beginning with electric drums . . .
            root of hunters   smoky
ascensions into heaven   trails
            beat out of ice   There is the root
of homecoming   The house my grandfather built first   I see
him   standing in his black
hat beating the snake with a stick
            There is the root shaped
by spirits speaking
in the lodge   There is the root you don't
want to hear and the one that hides
from you under the couch. . . .

            Root of teeth and
the nape of the goat   oranges,   fog
written on a camera   There is the carrot owl hunting
for her hat in the wind   moccasins
                                    of the blue deer
    flashing
in the doorknob. . . .
            There is the root of sex eating
pound cake in the kitchen   crumbs
                                    crumbs
                                        alibis
crumbs
a convict astroprojects   She is
picking up her torches, picking up her psalms, her
necklaces[4]

I write in full knowledge that the majority of the world's illiterates are women, that I live in a technologically advanced country where 40 percent of the people can barely read and 20 percent are functionally illiterate.[5] I believe that these facts are directly connected to the fragmentations I suffer in myself, that we are all in this together. Because I can write at all—and I think of all the ways women especially have been prevented from writing—because my words are read and taken seriously, because I see my work as part of something larger than my own life or the history of literature, I feel a responsibility to keep searching for teachers who can help me widen and deepen the sources and examine the ego that speaks in my poems—not for political "correctness," but for ignorance, solipsism, laziness, dishonesty, automatic writing. I look everywhere for signs of that fusion I have glimpsed in the women's movement, and most recently in Nicaragua. I turn to Toni Cade Bambara's *The Salt Eaters* or Ama Ata Aidoo's *Our Sister Killjoy* or James Baldwin's *Just above My Head*; to paintings by Frida Kahlo or Jacob Lawrence; to poems by Dionne Brand or Judy Grahn or Audre Lorde or Nancy Morejón; to the music of Nina Simone or Mary Watkins. This kind of art—like the art of so many others uncanonized in the dominant culture—is not produced as a commodity, but as part of a long conversation with the elders and with the future. (And, yes, I do live and work believing in a future.) Such artists draw on a tradition in which political struggle and spiritual continuity are meshed. Nothing need be lost, no beauty sacrificed. The heart does not turn to a stone.

What Is
Found There

Notebooks on
Poetry and Politics
(1993, 2003)

WOMAN AND BIRD

January 1990. I live on a street of mostly older, low-lying little houses in a straggling, villagelike, "unincorporated" neighborhood between two small towns on the California coast. There are a few old palms, apple, guava, quince, plum, lemon, and walnut trees, here and there old roses, climbing a fence or freestanding. One garden boasts an ancient, sprawling prickly pear. An elementary school accounts for most of the traffic, mornings and midafternoons. Pickup trucks and boats on trailers sit for days or weeks or months in front yards; old people and children walk in the road, while the serious traffic moves along the frontage road and the freeway. It's an ordinary enough place, I suppose, yet it feels fragile, as condominiums and automobile plazas multiply up and down the coast.

Around the house I live in there are trees enough—Monterey pines, acacias, a big box elder, fruit trees, two Italian cypresses, an eastern maple—so that mockingbirds, finches, doves, Steller's jays, hummingbirds are drawn to come and feed on plums and ollalieberries, honeysuckle and fuchsia during the warm months of the year. There's almost always a gull or two far overhead. Somebody keeps chickens; a rooster crows at dawn.

Today I returned from an errand, parked the car behind the house. Opening the car door I saw and heard the beating of enormous wings taking off from the deck. At first I thought: a very big gull, or even a raven. Then it alighted on the low roof of the house next door, stretched its long body, and stood in profile to me. It was a Great Blue Heron.

I had never seen one from below or from so near: usually from a car window on a road above a small bay or inlet. I had not seen

one many times at all. I was not sure. Poised there on the peak of
the roof, it looked immense, fastidious, apparently calm. It turned a
little; seemed to gaze as far into the blue air as the curve of the earth
would allow; took a slow, ritualistic, provocative step or two. I could
see the two wirelike plumes streaming from the back of its head.

I walked quietly into the garden toward the fence between the
two houses, speaking to it in a low voice. I told it that I thanked it
for having come; that I wanted it to be safe. I moved backward again
a little to look at it better. Suddenly it was in air, had flapped out
of sight.

It would be easy to call this apparition "dreamlike," but it did not
feel so. After some moments I went into the house. I wanted to be
sure I could name what I had seen; to stay with what I had seen. I
pulled from the bookcase a guide to Pacific Coast ecology. The color
plate of the Great Blue Heron confirmed my naming.

Then, as I sat there, my eye began to travel the margins of the
book, along the names and habitats of creatures and plants of the
4,000-mile Pacific coastline of North America. It was an idle enough
activity at first, the kind that sometimes plays upon other, subterra-
nean activities of the mind, draws thinking and unfiltered feelings
into sudden dialogue. Of late, I had been consciously thinking about
the decade just beginning, the last of the twentieth century, and the
great movements and shudderings of the time; about the country
where I am a citizen, and what has been happening in our social
fabric, our emotional and sensual life, during that century. Somewhere beneath these conscious speculations lay a vaguer desire: to
feel the pull of the future, to possess the inner gift, the unsentimen-
tality, the fortitude, to see into it—if only a little way.

But I found myself pulled by names: Dire Whelk, Dusky Tegula,
Fingered Limpet, Hooded Puncturella, Veiled Chiton, Bat Star, By-
the-Wind Sailor, Crumb-of-Bread Sponge, Eye Fringed Worm, Sugar
Wrack, Frilled Anemone, Bull Kelp, Ghost Shrimp, Sanderling, Wall-
eye Surfperch, Volcano Barnacle, Stiff-footed Sea Cucumber, Leather
Star, Innkeeper Worm, Lug Worm. And I felt the names drawing me
into a state of piercing awareness, a state I associate with reading
and writing poems. These names—by whom given and agreed on?—

these names work as poetry works, enlivening a sensuous reality through recognition or through the play of sounds (the short *i*'s of Fingered Limpet, the open vowels of Bull Kelp, Hooded Puncturella, Bat Star); the poising of heterogeneous images (*volcano* and *barnacle*, *leather* and *star*, *sugar* and *wrack*) to evoke other worlds of meaning. Sugar Wrack: a foundered ship in the Triangle Trade? Volcano Barnacle: tiny unnoticed undergrowth with explosive potential? Who saw the bird named Sanderling and gave it that caressive, diminutive name? Or was Sanderling the name of one who saw it? These names work as poetry works in another sense as well: they make something unforgettable. You will remember the pictorial names as you won't the Latin, which, however, is more specific as to genus and species. Human eyes gazed at each of all these forms of life and saw resemblance in difference—the core of metaphor, that which lies close to the core of poetry itself, the only hope for a humane civil life. The eye for likeness in the midst of contrast, the appeal to recognition, the association of thing to thing, spiritual fact with embodied form, begins here. And so begins the suggestion of multiple, many-layered, rather than singular, meanings, wherever we look, in the ordinary world.

I began to think about the names, beginning with the sound and image delivered in the name "Great Blue Heron," as tokens of a time when naming was poetry, when connections between things and living beings, or living things and human beings, were instinctively apprehended. By "a time" I don't mean any one historical or linguistic moment or period. I mean *all* the times when people have summoned language into the activity of plotting connections between, and marking distinctions among, the elements presented to our senses.

This impulse to enter, with other humans, through language, into the order and disorder of the world, is poetic at its root as surely as it is political at its root. Poetry and politics both have to do with description and with power. And so, of course, does science. We might hope to find the three activities—poetry, science, politics— triangulated, with extraordinary electrical exchanges moving from each to each and through our lives.[1] Instead, over centuries, they have become separated—poetry from politics, poetic naming from scientific naming, an ostensibly "neutral" science from political questions, "rational" science from lyrical poetry—nowhere more than in the United States over the past fifty years.

•

The Great Blue Heron is not a symbol. Wandered inadvertently or purposefully inland, maybe drought-driven, to a backyard habitat, it is a bird, *Ardea herodias*, whose form, dimensions, and habits have been described by ornithologists, yet whose intangible ways of being and knowing remain beyond my—or anyone's—reach. If I spoke to it, it was because I needed to acknowledge in words the rarity and signifying power of its appearance, not because I thought it had come to me. The tall, foot-poised creature had a life, a place of its own in the manifold, fragile system that is this coastline; a place of its own in the universe. Its place, and mine, I believe, are equal and interdependent. Neither of us—woman or bird—is a symbol, despite efforts to make us that. But I needed to acknowledge the heron with speech, and by confirming its name. To it I brought the kind of thing my kind of creature does.

A Mohawk Indian friend says she began writing "after a motor trip through the Mohawk Valley, when a Bald Eagle flew in front of her car, sat in a tree, and instructed her to write."[2] Very little in my own heritage has suggested to me that a wild living creature might come to bring me a direct personal message. And I know too that a complex humor underlies my friend's statement (I do not mean it is a joke). I am suspicious—first of all, in myself—of adopted mysticisms, of glib spirituality, above all of white people's tendency to sniff and taste, uninvited, and in most cases to vampirize American Indian, or African, or Asian, or other "exotic" ways of understanding. I made no claim upon the heron as my personal instructor. But our trajectories crossed at a time when I was ready to begin something new, the nature of which I did not clearly see. And poetry, too, begins in this way: the crossing of trajectories of two (or more) elements that might not otherwise have known simultaneity. When this happens, a piece of the universe is revealed as if for the first time.

VOICES FROM THE AIR

On a bleak December night in 1967, I lay awake in a New York City hospital, in pain from a newly operated knee in traction. It was too soon for the next pain-dulling injection; I was in the depression of spirits that follows anesthesia, unable to sleep or to discover in myself any thread that might lead me back to a place I used to recognize as "I." Turning the dial of my bedside radio for music, I came upon a speaking voice, deep, a woman's.

"Who am I?" it asked.[1]

Thou art a box of worme-seede, at best, but a salvatory of greene mummey: what's this flesh? a little cruded milke, phantastical puff-paste: our bodies are weaker than those paper prisons boys use to keep flies in: more contemptible: since ours is to preserve earthwormes: didst thou ever see a Larke in a cage? such is the soule in the body. . . .

Am not I, thy Duchess?

Thou art some great woman, sure, for riot begins to sit on thy fore-head (clad in gray haires) twenty years sooner, then on a merry milkmaydes. Thou sleepst worse, then if a mouse should be forc'd to take up her lodging in a cats eare: a little infant, that breedes it's teeth, should it lie with thee, would crie out, as if thou wert the more unquiet bedfellow.

I am Duchess of Malfy still.

That makes thy sleepes so broken:
Glories (like glow-wormes) afarre off, shine bright
But look'd to neere, have neither heate, nor light.

It does not seem strange to me now—it did not seem so then—that this dialogue, in which the opposition of flesh and spirit is so brutally vaunted, and which ends in the strangling of the Duchess, could, crystallized out of the airwaves on an icy night, solace my consciousness to the point of relief. For that is one property of poetic language: to engage with states that themselves would deprive us of language and reduce us to passive sufferers.

•

Thirteen years later, a different night, another radio. Driving over the mountains from upstate New York into Massachusetts, once more twisting a dial, I brought in not music, but a voice, speaking words I had read many times:

The house was quiet and the world was calm.
The reader became the book; and summer night

Was like the conscious being of the book.
The house was quiet and the world was calm.

The words were spoken as if there was no book,
Except that the reader leaned above the page,

Wanted to lean, wanted much most to be
The scholar to whom his book is true, to whom

The summer night is like perfection of thought.
The house was quiet because it had to be.

The quiet was part of the meaning, part of the mind:
The access of perfection to the page.

And the world was calm. The truth in a calm world,
In which there is no other meaning, itself

Is calm, itself is summer and night, itself
Is the reader leaning late and reading there.[2]

Wallace Stevens, reading his poetry on a recording. And for those
moments, on a mountain road on a calm night, for two listeners in a
world we knew to be in fracture, the words—Stevens at his plainest
and most mantralike—rose in that flat, understated, actuarial voice
to bind the actual night, the moving car, the two existences, almost
as house, reader, meaning, truth, summer, and night are bound in the
poem. For a few moments, we could believe in it all.

But what is a poem like this doing in a world where even the sem-
blance of calm is a privilege few can afford? Another scenario: Your
sister, stabbed in the early morning hours by her boyfriend ("lover"
is not the word, "domestic partner" is not the word), called you at
1:30 A.M. You were back from the evening shift at the nursing home;
your children and your mother, who lives with you, were asleep.
You had just looked in at the children, turned to the refrigerator to
pack their lunches for morning. As you searched for cold cuts, the
phone rang; it was Connie—Can you drive me to the emergency? he's
taken my car. You have had to do this before, you are enraged though
differently at both of them; but she's your sister, and you scrawl a
note to your mother, push the food back in the refrigerator, and run
for the car. On the highway you twist the radio dial for late-night
music. There are words, coming through suddenly clear: *house . . .
quiet . . . calm . . . summer night . . . book . . . quiet . . . truth.* What
would make your hand pause on the dial, why would these words
hold you? What, of the world the poem constructs, would seem anything more than suburban separatism, the tranquil luxury of a complacent man? If you go on listening, if the words can draw you in,
it's surely for their music as much as for meaning—music that calls
up the state of which the words are speaking. You are drawn in not
because this is a description of your world, but because you begin to
be reminded of your own desire and need, because the poem is not

about integration and fulfillment, but about the desire (*That makes thy sleepes so broken*) for those conditions. You listen, if you do, not simply to the poem, but to a part of you reawakened by the poem, momentarily made aware, a need both emotional and physical, that can for a moment be affirmed there. And, maybe, because the phrase "summer night" calls up more than a time and a season.

•

A poem can't free us from the struggle for existence, but it can uncover desires and appetites buried under the accumulating emergencies of our lives, the fabricated wants and needs we have had urged on us, have accepted as our own. It's not a philosophical or psychological blueprint; it's an instrument for embodied experience. But we seek that experience, or recognize it when it is offered to us, because it reminds us in some way of our need. After that rearousal of desire, the task of acting on that truth, or making love, or meeting other needs, is ours.

THE DISTANCE BETWEEN
LANGUAGE AND VIOLENCE

She's calling from Hartford: another young dark-skinned man has been killed—shot by police in the head while lying on the ground. Her friend, riding the train up from New York, has seen overpass after overpass spraypainted: "KKK—Kill Niggers." It's Black History Month.

But this is white history.

White hate crimes, white hate speech. I still try to claim I wasn't brought up to hate. But hate isn't the half of it. I grew up in the vast encircling presumption of whiteness—that primary quality of being which knows itself, its passions, only against an otherness that has to be dehumanized. I grew up in white silence that was utterly obsessional. Race was the theme whatever the topic.

In the case of my kin the word sprayed on the overpasses was unspeakable, part of a taboo vocabulary. *That* word was the language of "rednecks." My parents said "colored," "Negro," more often "They," even sometimes, in French, *"les autres."*

Such language could dissociate itself from lynching, from violence, from such a thing as hatred.

•

A poet's education. A white child growing into her powers of language within white discourse. Every day, when she is about five years old, her father sets her a few lines of poetry to copy into a ruled notebook as a handwriting lesson:

A thing of beauty is a joy forever;
Its loveliness increases . . .[1]

Tyger, Tyger, burning bright,
In the forests of the night;
What immortal hand or eye,
Could frame thy fearful symmetry?[2]

She receives a written word in her notebook as grade: "Excellent,"
"Very good," "Good," "Fair," "Poor." The power of words is enormous; the rhythmic power of verse, rhythm meshed with language,
excites her to imitation. Later, she begins reading in the books of
poetry from which she copied her lessons. Blake, especially, she
loves. She has no idea whether he, or Keats, or any of the poets is
alive or dead, or where they wrote from: poetry, for her, is now and
here. The "Songs of Innocence" seem both strange and familiar:

When the voices of children are heard on the green
And laughing is heard on the hill,
My heart is at rest within my breast
And everything else is still.

And.

My mother bore me in the southern wild,
And I am black, but O! my soul is white;
White as an angel is the English child:
But I am black, as if bereav'd of light.

This poem disturbs her faintly, not because it in any way con-
tradicts the white discourse around her, but because it seems to
approach the perilous, forbidden theme of color, the endless under-
tone of that discourse.

She is not brought up to hate; she is brought up within the circum-
ference of white language and metaphor, a space that looks and feels
to her like freedom. Early on, she experiences language, especially
poetry, as power: an elemental force that is *with* her, like the wind at
her back as she runs across a field.

Only much later she begins to perceive, reluctantly, the relationships of power sketched in her imagination by the language she loves and works in. How hard, against others, that wind can blow.

•

White child growing into her whiteness. Tin shovel flung by my hand at the dark-skinned woman caring for me, summer 1933, soon after my sister's birth, my mother ill and back in the hospital. A half-effaced, shamed memory of a bleeding cut on her forehead. I am reprimanded, made to say I'm sorry. I have "a temper," for which I'm often punished; but this incident remains vivid while others blur. The distance between language and violence has already shortened. Violence becomes a language. If I flung words along with the shovel, I can't remember them. Then, years later, I do remember. *Negro! Negro!* The polite word becomes epithet, stands in for the evil epithet, the taboo word, the curse.

•

A white child's anger at her mother's absence, already translated (some kind of knowledge makes this possible) into a racial language. That *They* are to blame for whatever pain is felt.

•

This is the child we needed and deserved, my mother writes in a notebook when I'm three. My parents require a perfectly developing child, evidence of their intelligence and culture. I'm kept from school, taught at home till the age of nine. My mother, once an aspiring pianist and composer who earned her living as a piano teacher, need not—and must not—work for money after marriage. Within this bubble of class privilege, the child can be educated at home, taught to play Mozart on the piano at four years old. She develops facial tics, eczema in the creases of her elbows and knees, hay fever. She is prohibited confusion: her lessons, accomplishments, must follow a clear trajectory. For her parents she is living proof. A Black woman cleans the apartment, cooks, takes care of the child when the child isn't being "educated."

Mercifully, I had time to imagine, fantasize, play with paper dolls and china figurines, inventing and resolving their fates. The best times were times I was ignored, could talk stories under my breath, loving my improvised world almost as much as I loved reading.

•

Popular culture entered my life as Shirley Temple, who was exactly my age and wrote a letter in the newspapers telling how her mother fixed spinach for her, with lots of butter. There were paper-doll books of her and of the Dionne quintuplets—five identical girls born to a French-Canadian family—and of the famous dollhouse of the actress Colleen Moore, which contained every luxury conceivable in perfect miniature, including a tiny phonograph that played Gershwin's *Rhapsody in Blue*. I was impressed by Shirley Temple as a little girl my age who had power: she could write a piece for the newspapers and have it printed in her own handwriting. I must have seen her dancing with Bill "Bojangles" Robinson in *The Littlest Rebel,* but I remember her less as a movie star than as a presence, like President Roosevelt, or Lindbergh, whose baby had been stolen; but she was a little girl whose face was everywhere—on glass mugs and in coloring books as well as in the papers.

Other figures peopling my childhood: the faceless, bonneted woman on the Dutch Cleanser can, Aunt Jemima beaming on the pancake box, "Rastus" the smiling Black chef on the Cream of Wheat box, the "Gold Dust Twins" capering black on orange on soap boxes, also in coloring books given as premiums with the soap powder. (The white obsession wasn't silent where advertising logos were concerned.) The Indian chief and the buffalo, "vanished" but preserved on the nickel. Characters in books read aloud: Little Black Sambo, Uncle Remus—with accompanying illustrations. Hiawatha. The Ten Little Indians, soon reduced to none, in the counting-backward rhyme.

•

In 1939 came the New York World's Fair. Our family, including my paternal grandmother, took the train from Baltimore and stayed two or three nights at the Hotel Pennsylvania in New York, across the street from Pennsylvania Station. We saw the Rockettes at Radio City Music Hall, spent a day in Flushing Meadows at the Fair, with its Trylon and Perisphere of which we had heard so much. We went to Atlantic City for a day, chewed its saltwater taffy, were pushed in wicker chairs along the boardwalk (a favorite tourist ride in Atlantic City in those days—hard to fathom its appeal to a child). My sister and I had our portraits sketched in pastel by a boardwalk artist. Under her picture he wrote, "Dad's Pride," and under mine, "Miss America, 1949."

It was going to be a long way to 1949. In a month war would be declared in Europe; soon the Atlantic Ocean would be full of convoys, submarines, and torpedoes; in Baltimore we would have blackouts, and air-raid drills at school. I would become part of the first American "teenage" generation, while people my age in Europe were, unbeknownst to me, being transported east in cattle cars, fighting as partisans, living in hiding, sleeping underground in cratered cities. Pearl Harbor would call in the wrath of the United States.

I was keeping a "Line-A-Day" diary and wrote of the World's Fair: "The greatest part was the World of Tomorrow. Men and women of Tomorrow appeared in the sky and sang." Some early version of big-screen vision and sound must have been projected on the dome of the Perisphere, celebrating the World of Tomorrow with its material goods, miracle conveniences, freeways, skyways, aerial transport. No World War II, no Final Solution, no Hiroshima. The men and women of Tomorrow marched with energetic and affirming tread. Whatever they sang, it wasn't the "Internationale"—more like a hymn to American technology and free enterprise. The Depression was still on, the Nazi invasion of Czechoslovakia only a few weeks away. But the World of Tomorrow—capitalist kitsch—inspired a nine-year-old girl, who, decades later, remembers but one other moment from the New York World's Fair of 1939: a glassblower blew, over live fire, a perfect glass pen and nib in translucent blue-green, and handed it over to her to keep, and she did keep it, for many years.

•

Mercifully, at last, I was sent to school, to discover other, real children, born into other families, other kinds of lives. Not a wide range, at a private school for white girls. Still, a new horizon.

Mercifully, I discovered *Modern Screen, Photoplay,* Jack Benny, "Your Hit Parade," Frank Sinatra, "The Romance of Helen Trent," "Road of Life." The war was under way; I learned to swing my hips to "Don't Sit under the Apple Tree," "Deep in the Heart of Texas," "Mairzy Doats," "Don't Get Around Much Anymore." I loved Walter Pidgeon and the singing of the miners in *How Green Was My Valley*, Irene Dunne in *The White Cliffs of Dover*. I learned to pick out chords for "Smoke Gets in Your Eyes" and "As Time Goes By" on the keyboard devoted to Mozart.

•

A poet's education. Most of the poetry she will read for many years, when poetry is both sustenance and doorway, is not only written by white men, but frames an all-white world; its images and metaphors are not "raceless," but rooted in an apartheid of the imagination. In college, for a seminar in modern American poetry that includes no Black (and almost no women) poets, she reads one of Allen Tate's "Sonnets at Christmas":

Ah, Christ, I love you rings to the wild sky
And I must think a little of the past:
When I was ten I told a stinking lie
That got a black boy whipped; but now at last
The going years, caught in an accurate glow,
Reverse like balls englished upon green baize—
Let them return, let the round trumpets blow
The ancient crackle of the Christ's deep gaze.
Deafened and blind, with senses yet unfound,
Am I, untutored to the after-wit
Of knowledge, knowing a nightmare has no sound;
Therefore with idle hands and head I sit
In late December before the fire's daze
Punished by crimes of which I would be quit.[3]

This girl, this student, this poet is only barely learning that poetry occurs in "periods" and "movements." She is still trying to read the way she always has: in the here and now, what makes you shudder with delight or trouble, what keeps you reading, what's boring? But she's hearing about a southern poetry (she who grew up in the city of

Edgar Allan Poe and Sidney Lanier) that calls itself Fugitive, Agrarian. Nothing helps her to connect these literary movements with southern history, with her own history. Tate's sonnet leaps out at her because it breaks, or seems to break, a silence—at very least it seems to point to something under the surface, the unspeakability of which her pulse is tracking as it flickers through the poem. She is studying in New England, now, joking about her southern heritage, there are a few African-American students (still known as "Negroes") in her classes, she knows now that "segregation" (a name for the laws she grew up under) and "prejudice" (a vaguer notion) are retrograde; the freshman sister assigned to her by the college is the daughter of a famous international diplomat, later a Nobel laureate: a distinguished Negro. She takes her light-skinned, serious "sister" out for lunches and coffee, is supposed to guide her with sisterly advice. How is she equipped for this, in the presumption of whiteness? Some years later, she hears that this young woman, whose unsmiling ivory face and dark, back-strained hair have become a perplexing memory, is a suicide.

Tate's poem teaches her nothing except the possibility that race can be a guilty burden on white people, leading them to Christmas Eve depression, and (more usefully) that a phrase like "stinking lie" can effectively be inserted in an elegant modern sonnet. Only years later will she learn that the writer of the poem, aristocrat of the world of southern letters, was, at the very least, and as part of his literary politics, a segregationist and supporter of the Ku Klux Klan.

––––––

[2003] In his strangely awkward, sometimes incoherent essay, "Remarks on the Southern Religion," in the Fugitive anthology, *I'll Take My Stand*, Tate wrote:

> The South would not have been defeated had it possessed a sufficient faith in its own kind of God. It would not have been defeated, in other words, had it been able to bring out a body of doctrine setting forth its true conviction that the ends of man require more for their realization than politics. The setback of the war was, of itself, a very trivial one.
>
> We are very near an answer to our question—How may the Southerner take hold of his Tradition?
>
> The answer is, by violence.
>
> For this answer is inevitable.... Since he cannot bore from within, he has left the sole alternative of boring from without. This method is political, active, and, in the nature of the case, violent and revolutionary.[4]

NOT HOW TO WRITE POETRY,
BUT WHEREFORE

M*asters.* For all the poetry I grew up with—the Blake, the Keats, the Swinburne and the Shelley, the Elizabeth Barrett Browning, the Whitman, the domesticated versions of Dickinson—in my twenties a greater ocean fell open before me, with its contradictory currents and undertows. Frost, Wylie, Millay seemed like shoreline tidal pools: out beyond lay fogs, reefs, wrecks, floating corpses, kelp forests, sargasso silences, moonlit swells, dolphins, pelicans, icebergs, suckholes, hunting grounds. Young, hungry, I was searching, within the limits of time and place and sex, for words to match and name desire.

Rilke's poem, the antique marble torso of Apollo glinting at the passerby through its pectorals like eyes, saying: *Du musst dein Leben ändern, You have to change your life.*[1] Finding J. B. Leishman and Stephen Spender's translations of Rilke in a bookstore in Harvard Square (at first, thinking this Rainer Maria might be a woman). *Du musst dein Leben ändern.* No poem had ever said it quite so directly. At twenty-two it called me out of a kind of sleepwalking. I knew, even then, that for me poetry wasn't enough as something to be appreciated, finely fingered: it could be a fierce, destabilizing force, a wave pulling you further out than you thought you wanted to be. *You have to change your life.*

•

In his editor's foreword to my first book of poems, published in 1951, W. H. Auden praised my "talent for versification" and "craftsmanship," while explaining to and of my poetic generation:

Radical changes and significant novelty in artistic style can only occur when there has been a radical change in human sensibility to require them. The spectacular events of the present time [did he mean the revelations of the Holocaust? the unleashing of nuclear weapons? the dissolution of the old colonial empires?] must not blind us to the fact that we are living not at the beginning but in the middle of a historical epoch; they are not novel but repetitions on a vastly enlarged scale and at a violently accelerated tempo of events which took place long since.

Every poet under fifty-five cherishes, I suspect, a secret grudge against Providence for not getting him [*sic*] born earlier.[2]

If anything, I cherished a secret grudge against Auden—not because he didn't proclaim me a genius, but because he proclaimed so diminished a scope for poetry, including mine. I had little use for his beginnings and middles. Yet he was one of the masters. I had read his much-quoted lines:

> . . . poetry makes nothing happen; it survives
> In the valley of its saying where executives
> Would never want to tamper; it flows south
> From ranches of isolation and the busy griefs,
> Raw towns that we believe and die in; it survives,
> A way of happening, a mouth.[3]

Auden had written that in January 1939, elegizing W. B. Yeats. He ended it with a charge to living poets (or so I read it; maybe he was still talking to Yeats):

> In the nightmare of the dark
> All the dogs of Europe bark,
> And the living nations wait,
> Each sequestered in its hate;

Intellectual disgrace
Stares from every human face,
And the seas of pity lie
Locked and frozen in each eye.

Follow, poet, follow right
To the bottom of the night,
With your unconstraining voice
Still persuade us to rejoice.

With the farming of a verse
Make a vineyard of the curse,
Sing of human unsuccess
In a rapture of distress;

In the deserts of the heart
Let the healing fountain start,
In the prison of his days
Teach the free man how to praise.[4]

But I was growing up in a postwar world where executives were increasingly tampering with everything, not least the valleys of saying. And in that world—or in the sector of it I could perceive around me—both women and poetry were being redomesticated.

•

Masters. In my college years T. S. Eliot was the most talked-of poet. *The Cocktail Party* played on Broadway at that time; his name and work were already part of student conversations, alluded to in courses. I listened to lectures on *The Waste Land,* the *Four Quartets*, earnestly taking notes, trying to grasp the greatness. I came to Eliot's poetry with the zeal of a young neophyte discovering the new and admired.

I came to it also as a young person utterly disaffected from Christianity and from organized religion in general. My experience of the suburban Protestant Church was that it had nothing whatsoever to do with changing one's life. Its images and rituals were wedded to a world I was trying to escape, the world of passionless respectability. I wanted nothing more to do with it. But how could an eighteen-year-old girl from Baltimore critique the fact that the greatest modern poet in English (as everyone seemed to agree) was a High Church Anglican? In my lecture notes, penciled on the endpapers of the copy of *Four Quartets* that I still have, I find: "This = problem of a Christian poem in a secular age—you can't accept it unless you accept Christian religion." The lecturer was F. O. Matthiessen, one of Eliot's earliest interpreters, who one year later, in a suicide note, described himself as a Christian and a socialist. He was also a homosexual.

My Jewish father, calling himself a Deist, my Protestant-born mother, secular by default (as, perhaps, married to a Christian, she'd have been Christian, without strong convictions either way), had sent me to church for several years as a kind of social validation, mainly as protection against anti-Semitism. I learned nothing there about spiritual passion or social ethics. If the liturgy found me, it was through the Book of Common Prayer, mostly the poetry of the King James Bible contained in it. I used to walk home from church feeling that I must be at fault: surely, if I were truly receptive, I would feel "something" when the wafer was given, the chalice touched to my lips. What I felt was that I was acting—we were all in a pageant or a play. Nor was this theater magical. Christianity as thus enacted felt like a theological version of a social world I already knew I had to leave. Sometimes, having to pull away from a world of coldness, you end up feeling you yourself are cold. I wrote this disaffection into an early poem, "Air without Incense."[5]

Christianity aside, there was for me a repulsive quality to Eliot's poetry: an aversion to ordinary life and people. I couldn't have said that then. I tried for some time to admire the structure, the learnedness, the cadences of the poems, but the voice overall sounded dry and sad to me. Eliot was still alive, and I did not know how much his poetry had been a struggle with self-hatred and breakdown; nor was I particularly aware that his form of Christianity, like the religion I had rejected, was aligned with a reactionary politics. He was supposed to be a master, but, as the young woman I was, seeking possibilities—and responsibilities—of existence in poetry, I felt he was useless for me.

•

What I lacked was even the idea of a twentieth-century tradition of radical or revolutionary poetics as a stream into which a young poet could dip her glass. Among elders, William Carlos Williams wrote from the landscape of ordinary urban, contemporary America, of ordinary poor and working people, and in a diction of everyday speech, plainspoken yet astonishingly musical and flexible. But I don't recall being taken out of my skin by any Williams poem, though later I would work with his phrasing and ways of breaking a line as a means of shedding formal metrics. Muriel Rukeyser, the most truly experimental and integratedly political poet of her time, was unknown to me except by her name in a list of former Yale Younger Poets. I don't recall the publication of *The Life of Poetry* in 1949. No one—professor or fellow student—ever said to me that this was a book I needed. And not even the name of Thomas McGrath, the great midwestern working-class poet, was known to me. His chapbooks and small-press editions were not published or discussed by critics in the East; he was himself on the McCarthyite blacklist. Even the Left and Communist journals had trouble with his poetry, finding it "difficult" and unorthodox.[6] In fact, I was to discover Rukeyser only in the late 1960s with the poetry readings against the Vietnam War and, soon after, with the rising women's movement in which she was, late in her life, a powerful voice. I did not read McGrath until the 1980s, when his long historical and autobiographical "Letter to an Imaginary Friend" became available in its entirety. But, in my early twenties, was my life ready for Rukeyser and McGrath? Perhaps not. Yet each of them was asking urgent questions about the place of poetry, questions I had as yet no language for.

•

I was exceptionally well grounded in formal technique, and I loved the craft. What I was groping for was something larger, a sense of vocation, what it means to live as a poet—not how to write poetry, but wherefore. In my early twenties I took as guide a poet of extreme division, an insurance executive possessed by the imagination. But if I was going to have to write myself out of my own divisions, Wallace Stevens wasn't the worst choice I could have made.

"ROTTED NAMES"

A few years ago, in the early California spring, I put my typewriter, suitcase, and a copy of Steven's *Collected Poems* into the trunk of my car and drove to the town of Twentynine Palms, at the edge of the Joshua Tree National Monument. The town clung along a rough strip, supported largely by a Marine Corps base. Off the main route, behind a bank of pines and oleanders, I found a little motel built around a courtyard with a swimming pool, banksia rose trees, and palm trees. My room had a kitchenette with a table where I could type and read. Daytimes I drove and walked in the desert among the hairy, mad-hermit shapes of the Joshua trees, sat among gray and gold rocks grizzled with lichen, against whose epochal scale tiny lives played out their dramas—lizards, wasps, butterflies, burrowing bugs, red and gilt flies. I stood at the edge of a lake bed, waterless for centuries, a vast bowl rimmed by mountains, brimming with silence. The Joshua trees were starting to open their creamy, almost shocking blooms. It was still cool in the desert through midday. Late afternoons I went back to the motel and sat on the patio—usually empty—reading Stevens straight through, something I had never done before.

I hadn't been writing poems for a while. I had known I was at the end of a cycle, that were I to write anything it would be a poetry of the past—my own past—that I was unready to write what was still strange and unformed in me, the poetry of the future. It seemed as good a time as any to come to terms with Stevens.

•

"I didn't think much of him when I read him in graduate school," a younger friend of mine, a political activist and passionate reader of poetry, commented recently. I had started reading Stevens in college, but not really as a student. I read all the "modern" poets I encountered (later they would be labeled "modernist") as an apprentice, though a wayward one. I picked and chose with sublime pigheadedness what I thought could help me live and write. Never having been a graduate student, I was never compelled to spend hours and days fettered to the explication of works that felt deadening or alien to me. It was another young poet, David Ferry, who told me I should read a poem called "The Man with the Blue Guitar," and from there I went on, buying the separate volumes as I found them in secondhand bookshops.

From the first I was both attracted and repelled by different Stevens poems, sometimes by different parts of a single poem. I was attracted first by the music, by the intense familiarity yet strangeness of lines like

She sang beyond the genius of the sea

and

It was her voice that made
The sky acutest at its vanishing.
She measured to the hour its solitude.
She was the single artificer of the world
In which she sang . . .
Then we,
As we beheld her striding there alone,
Knew that there never was a world for her
Except the one she sang and, singing, made.[1]

The metrics and diction were familiar, that "high" tone at the intersection of Victorian and modern poetic English. But "The Idea of Order at Key West" offered me something absolutely new: a conception of a woman maker, singing and striding beside the ocean, creating her own music, separate from yet bestowing its order upon *the meaningless plunges of water and the wind.* This image entered me, in the 1950s, an era of feminist retrenchment and poetic diminishment, as an image of my tongue-tied desire that a woman's life, a poet's work, should amount to more than the measured quantities I saw around me.

> Now grapes are plush upon the vines.
> A soldier walks before my door.
>
> The hives are heavy with the combs.
> Before, before, before my door.
>
> And seraphs cluster on the domes,
> And saints are brilliant in fresh cloaks.
>
> Before, before, before my door.
> The shadows lessen on the walls.
>
> The bareness of the house returns.
> An acid sunlight fills the halls.
>
> Before, before. Blood smears the oaks.
> A soldier stalks before my door.[2]

If I first loved that poem for its sound, I later loved it for its soundings—its prescience, its concentrated fusion of fulfillment and disaster, autumn and war and death, the stripping down from combs full of honey to acid light, the figure of the soldier, unaccounted for, from the first couplet, so that right away you feel him there, only walking at first, but *stalking* by the end past the blood-smeared oaks. There are many poems of Stevens that have lasted for me in this way.

And there were others that, from the first, I found—and still find—irritating and alienating in tone, mere virtuosity carrying on at great length, like "The Comedian As the Letter C," which begins:

Nota: man is the intelligence of his soil,
The sovereign ghost. As such, the Socrates
Of snails, musician of pears, principium
And lex. Sed quaeritur: is this same wig
Of things, this noncompated pedagogue,
Preceptor to the sea?[3]

I can allow that Stevens—disappointed husband of a beautiful woman, successful insurance lawyer, fugitive in the imagination—was shoring up around him a self-protective, intellectual wit, that his desperation must have needed the excess of virtuosity displayed in many of his poems. But it's a voice of elegance straining against bleakness, renunciation, and truncation much of the time, ending suddenly and bitterly: *So may the relation of each man be clipped.*

Still, as a young woman, impatiently skimming the poem, I found passages that corresponded to my own moments of self-consciousness, of self-questioning: What was *I* really doing as a poet?

The book of moonlight is not written yet
Nor half begun, but, when it is, leave room
For Crispin, fagot in the lunar fire,
Who, in the hubbub of his pilgrimage
Through sweating changes, never could forget
That wakefulness or meditating sleep,
In which the sulky strophes willingly
Bore up, in time, the somnolent, deep songs . . .

How many poems he denied himself
In his observant progress, lesser things
Than the relentless contact he desired . . .[4]

Of the modern poets I read in my twenties, Stevens was the liberator. Yes: Stevens, whom I found so vexing and perplexing, so given sometimes to cake-decoration, affectations in French, yet also capable of shedding any predictable music to write poems like "Dry Loaf" or "The Dwarf," which force you to hear music of their own, or *The skreak and skritter of evening gone.* It was Stevens who told me, in "Of Modern Poetry":

> It has to be living, to learn the speech of the place.
> It has to face the men of the time and to meet
> The women of the time. It has to think about war
> And it has to find what will suffice.[5]

I took this quite literally. It was he who said to me, *Ourselves in poetry must take their place,* who told me that poetry must change, our ideas of order, of the romantic, of language itself must change:

> Throw away the lights, the definitions
> And say of what you see in the dark
>
> That it is this or it is that,
> But do not use the rotted names.[6]

The last line in the *Collected Poems* is *A new knowledge of reality.*

I felt these were messages left along the trail for me. I was going on pure desire; I had no means of fathoming how life and work as a woman poet would force me to rethink ideas of order surrounding me and within me, ideas about scope and destiny, about the place of poetry in a life still so unrealized, so vaguely aware, so conventional. I was to carry Stevens with me into places neither of us could have foreknown, places as dense, implacable, and intricate as the desert at Joshua Tree.

•

In the last days I spent at Twentynine Palms, I thought I was coming down with 'flu. I ached, felt chilled at night; the desert wind seemed to blow across my bed. Mornings, I'd stand a long time in the hot shower, then make my instant coffee and sit on at the kitchenette table staring at the pines across the parking lot, hearing the United States flag whipping in the wind, an arrhythmic, riptide sound. Some days the desert was so dun, so coldly lit I could hardly bear it. My heart quailed and expanded under influences I couldn't trace.

One evening I drove to an Italian restaurant on the strip to eat dinner, thinking to lift my spirits. I had lasagna, fries and salad, and a glass of ice-cold Chianti in a room otherwise occupied by a table of very young marines, teenagers, heads half-shaved (close over ears and necks, slightly longer on top). They had a bottle of wine, seemed out for a good time, but depressed, ill at ease with each other. I felt their physical strength—a terribly young, uninformed strength— were these kids descendants of European workers on the land, whose forefathers had been foot soldiers in war after war? Generations without education or control over the time and products of their labor?

The young recruits I saw that evening were all apparently white. At the motel, a weekend earlier, an African-American officer and his family had been swimming in the pool, later carried drinks to the patio. Our hosts had seemed to welcome them, but they were soon gone. Almost everyone I had seen hiking or rock climbing in the National Monument appeared to be white except for a Mexican family at one campsite among the rocks. Beyond the strip lay a kind of desert barrio of vaguely marked dirt roads leading to earth-colored shacks.

More than ever in my life I had been taking in the multivarious shadings of human life in the American landscape. Feeling how long whiteness had kept me from seeing that variety—or, in some places, noticing its lack—because whiteness—as a mindset—is bent only on distinguishing discrete bands of color from itself. That is its obsession—to distinguish, discriminate, categorize, exclude on the basis of clearly defined color. What else is the function of being white? The iris of actual light, the colors seen in a desert shower or rainbow, or in the streets of a great metropolis, speak for continuum, spectrum, inclusion as laws of life.

I have come, through many turnings of life and through many willing and reluctant mentors, to understand that there is no study of race—only of racism. It's a bitter, violent, nauseating study, the study of racism. Race itself is a meaningless category. But people have defined themselves as white, over and against darkness, with disastrous results for human community.

And for poetry?

•

Why, I was asking myself, was that "master" of my youth, that liberatory spokesman for the imagination, that mentor who warned *Do not use the rotted names,* so attracted and compelled by old, racist configurations? How, given the sweep of his claims for the imagination, for poetry as that which gives sanction to life, his claims for modernity, could he accept the stunting of his own imagination by the repetitions of a mass imaginative failure, by nineteenth-century concepts of "civilized" and "savage," by compulsive reiterations of the word "nigger"? Why does the image and rhyming sound of the offensive word "negress" dominate one poem ("The Virgin Carrying a Lantern") and slide, for no apparent reason, into *The Auroras of Autumn*? What impelled him to address the haunting poem "Two at Norfolk" to "darkies" mowing grass in a cemetery? And why should an abstract "black man," a "woollen massa" be summoned up as interlocutors in the two epigrams "Nudity in the Colonies" and "Nudity at the Capitol"? What are these "frozen metaphors,"[7] as Aldon Nielsen calls them, doing in his work?

Reading Stevens in other years I had tried to write off that deliberately racial language as a painful but encapsulated lesion on the imagination, a momentary collapse of the poet's intelligence. I treated those figures—not that far removed from Rastus and Aunt Jemima—as happenstance, accidental. There in the high desert I finally understood: *This is a key to the whole. Don't try to extirpate, censor, or defend it.* Stevens's reliance on one-dimensional and abstract images of African-Americans is a watermark in his poetry. To understand how he places himself in relation to these and other dark-skinned figments of his mind—often Latin American and Caribbean lay figures—is to understand more clearly the meanings of North and South in Stevens's poetry, the riven self, the emotionally unhappy white man with a "fairly substantial income,"[8] the fugitive

in the imagination who is repeatedly turned back by a wall of mir-
rors, whose immense poetic gift is thus compelled to frustrate itself.
It's to grasp the deforming power of racism—or what Toni Morrison
has named "Africanism"[9]—over the imagination—not only of this
poet, but of the collective poetry of which he was a part, the poetry
in which I, as a young woman, had been trying to take my place.

A POET'S EDUCATION

Diane Glancy: "The poet writes as [s]he is written by circumstance and environment."[1] And "I . . . feel I must make use of myself as a found object."[2] Glancy: a woman of the Plains, of Cherokee and poor white "Arkansas backhill culture."[3] Driving hundreds of miles to teach poetry in the public schools of Arkansas and Oklahoma, she keeps a kind of journal, a series of meditations on place, poetry, literacy, oral tradition, words, religion. She has written one of the new sourcebooks brought forth in this country today by poets for whose parents or grandparents literacy or English was not a given. It's a lie that poetry is only read by or "speaks to" people in the universities or elite intellectual circles; in many such places, poetry barely speaks at all.

Poems are written and absorbed, silently and aloud, in prisons, prairie kitchens, urban basement workshops, branch libraries, battered women's shelters, homeless shelters, offices, a public hospital for disabled people, an HIV support group. A poet can be born in a house with empty bookshelves. Sooner or later, s/he will need books. But books are not genes.

•

A poet's education.

Before I was eighteen, I was arrested on suspicion of murder after refusing to explain a deep cut on my forearm. With shocking speed I found myself handcuffed to a chain gang . . . and bussed to a holding facility to await trial. There I met men, prisoners, who read aloud to each other the works of Neruda,

Paz, Sabines, Nemerov, and Hemingway. Never had I felt such freedom as in that dormitory.... While I listened to the words of the poets, the alligators slumbered powerless in their lairs. Their language was the magic that could liberate me from myself....

And when they closed the books, these Chicanos, and went into their own Chicano language, they made barrio life come alive for me in the fullness of its vitality. I began to learn my own language, the bilingual words and phrases explaining to me my own place in the universe....

Two years passed. I was twenty now, and behind bars again ... One night on my third month in the county jail ... [s]ome detectives had kneed an old drunk and handcuffed him to the booking bars. His shrill screams raked my nerves like hacksaw on bone, the desperate protest of his dignity against their inhumanity.... When they went to the bathroom to pee and the desk attendant walked to the file cabinet to pull the arrest record, I shot my arm through the bars, grabbed one of the attendant's university textbooks, and tucked it in my over-alls. It was the only way I had of protesting.

It was late when I returned to my cell. Under my blanket I switched on a pen flashlight and opened the thick book at random, scanning the pages.... Slowly I enunciated the words ... p-o-n-d, ri-pple. It scared me that I had been reduced to this to find comfort. I always had thought reading a waste of time, that nothing could be gained by it. Only by action, by moving out into the world and confronting and challenging the obstacles, could one learn anything worth knowing.

Even as I tried to convince myself that I was merely curious, I became so absorbed in how the sounds created music in me, and happiness, I forgot where I was.... For a while, a deep sadness overcame me, as if I had chanced on a long-lost friend and mourned the years of separation. But soon the heartache of having missed so much of life, that had numbed me since I was a child, gave way, as if a grave illness had lifted itself from me and I was cured, innocently believing in the beauty of life again.

I stumblingly repeated the author's name as I fell asleep, saying
it over and over in the dark: Words-worth,

Words-worth....

Days later, with a stub pencil I whittled sharp with my teeth,
I propped a Red Chief notebook on my knees and wrote my first
words. From that moment, a hunger for poetry possessed me.[4]

Jimmy Santiago Baca writes of poetry as a birth into the self out of
a disarticulated, violently unworded condition, the Chicano taught
to despise his own speech, the male prisoner *in a world ... run by
men's rules and maintained by men's anger and brutish will to survive,*[5] forced to bury his feminine heart save in the act of opening a
letter or in writing poems. *Every poem is an infant labored into birth
and I am drenched with sweating effort. Tired from the pain and hurt
of being a man, in the poem I transform myself into woman.*[6] Released
from the anguish of speechlessness (*There was nothing so humiliating
as being unable to express myself, and my inarticulateness increased
my sense of jeopardy, of being endangered*),[7] Baca transforms himself into a woman who has transcended the pain and hurt of being
female, who has actually given birth to words, not to a living, crying,
shitting child. But how balance the hard labor of bearing a poem
against the early depletion of uneducated women bearing children
year after year? Or against the effort for speech by a woman who
culture has determined that women shall be silent?

En boca cerrada no entran moscas. "Flies don'ts enter a closed
mouth" is a saying I kept hearing when I was a child. *Ser habla-
dora* was to be a gossip and a liar, to talk too much. *Muchachi-
tas bien criadas,* well-bred girls don't answer back. *Es una falta
de respeto* to talk back to one's mother or father.... *Hociona,
repelona, chismosa,* having a big mouth, questioning, carrying
tales are all signs of being *mal criada.* In my culture they are
all words that are derogatory if applied to women—I've never
heard them applied to men.[8]

Gloria Anzaldúa, disentangling the heavy hanging strands fringing the cave of mestiza consciousness, finds speechlessness compounded by femaleness, and both by the fact of being alien, "queer," not a woman in her culture's eyes. Her sense of identity is more complicated than Baca's because she's forced to transform many layers of negativity surrounding femaleness itself—images of *Malintzin*, the Indian woman as betrayer, of *la chingada*, the Indian woman as the fucked-one, of *la Llorona*, eternally mourning, long-suffering mother—and to confront the despot duality of simplistic masculine/feminine: *I, like other queer people, am two in one body, both male and female. I am the embodiment of the hieros gamos: the coming together of opposite qualities within.*[9]

A poet's education.

> In the 1960s, I read my first Chicano novel. It was *City of Night* by John Rechy, a gay Texan, son of a Scottish father and a Mexican mother. For days I walked around in stunned amazement that a Chicano could write and get published. When I read *I Am Joaquín* I was surprised to see a bilingual book by a Chicano in print. When I saw poetry written in Tex-Mex for the first time, a feeling of pure joy flashed through me. . . .
>
> Even before I read books by Chicanos or Mexicans, it was the Mexican movies I saw at the drive-in—the Thursday night special of $1.00 a car—that gave me a sense of belonging. *Vámonos a las vistas*, my mother would call out and we'd all—grandmother, brothers, sister and cousins—squeeze into the car. We'd wolf down cheese and bologna white bread sandwiches while watching Pedro Infante in melodramatic tearjerkers like *Nosotros los pobres*, the first "real" Mexican movie (that was not an imitation of European movies). . . . I remember the singing type "westerns" of Jorge Negrete and Miguel Aceves Mejia. . . .
>
> The whole time I was growing up, there was *norteño* music, sometimes called North Mexican border music, or Tex Mex music, or Chicano music, or *cantina* (bar) music. I grew up

listening to conjuntos, three- or four-piece bands made up of folk musicians playing guitar, *bajo sexto*, drums and button accordion, which Chicanos had borrowed from the German immigrants who had come to Central Texas and Mexico to farm and build breweries. . . .

I remember the hot, sultry evenings when *corridos*— songs of love and death on the Texas-Mexican borderlands— reverberated out of cheap amplifiers from the local *cantinas* and wafted in through my bedroom window.

Corridos first became widely used along the South Texas/ Mexican border during the early conflict between Chicanos and Anglos. The *corridos* are usually about Mexican heroes who do valiant deeds against the Anglo oppressors. Pancho Villa's song *"La cucaracha,"* is the most famous one. *Corridos* of John F. Kennedy and his death are still very popular in the Valley. Older Chicanos remember Lydia Mendoza, one of the great border *corrido* singers who was called *la Gloria de Tejas.* Her "El tango negro," sung during the Great Depression, made her a singer of the people. The everpresent *corridos* narrated one hundred years of border history, bringing news of events as well as entertainment. These folk musicians and folk songs are our chief cultural mythmakers, and they made our hard lives seem bearable.[10]

A poet's education.

After the divorce, I had new territory, much like the Oklahoma land run when a piece of land was claimed & had to be set- tled. I had spent years hiding behind my husband, the children & housework. Now the land & sky were open. That's what's frightening about the prairie at first \ its barrenness & lack of shelter. I had always written, but now my sense of place was defined by whatever mattered. I picked up my Indian heritage & began a journey toward ani-yun-wiyu, translated from the Cherokee, 'real people.'

I read journals \ magazines. Poetry \ some fiction. I saw that feelings could be expressed in writing. Feelings of bewilderment & fear. Especially anger. It was a trend in women's writing \ the pulley I needed out of the separation & isolation I felt without the surroundings of family. I saw women come to grips with themselves. The vulnerability, the struggle, the agonizing choices. I had to find a homestead within myself, or invent one. I dug a potato cellar.

Family had covered the fissures in my life. Now I had fragments \ shards \ whatever the territory offered. My poems & writing were the land I cultivated. I moved toward 'being' in poetry. A struggle for survival. My purpose was to find the truth of what I was \ my voice. What I had to offer. I could not have done it without the other voices\ the sun & rain & soil for myself as a person. The pleasure of being a woman.

I found that I weathered the prairie storms & the limitations that come with the territory. I found acceptance of myself\ the strength to travel prairie roads & talk about poetry in towns where farmers in the cafés stare. I relived the struggle to claim the land \ establish a sod house\ plow the fields\ milk the cow. The rest will come. All this is an internal land, of course. I started late with only a map given to me by other women who said the territory was there. It was a fertile landscape just inside the head. I had only to load the wagon, hitch the horses. A journey which my mother never made before she folded up her camp.

I learned to trust images. I could even experiment with words. Put muffler, glass packs on the wagon. Mud flaps if I wanted. I have what men have had\ liberty to be myself. Maybe women had it too & I just never knew. Wrong \ wright \ whatever. Now I could throw out the ice cubes \ find my severed limbs \ sew them on instead of giving heart & arms & lungs away. I have use for them on the edge of the frontier\ saw-edge after saw-edge.

The glory of the plain self in search of words to say, 'the self' / the delight of it. The birth \ the shedding of invisibility. The pursuit of she-pleasure. SHEDONISM.

The themes \ form \ experimental forms. Words as house & shed & outbuildings on the land. The urgency. The cessation of pounding myself \ hanging my separate parts to dry on low branches & rocks. It's women who influenced my work. Their courage \ their trend toward revelation. I am on the journey to the ani-yun-wiyu.[11]

TOURISM AND PROMISED LANDS

Tourism. Can be a trap for poets, especially poets of North America who may elect to be escapist, breezy, about our empire, the sands we are lying on.

Poems decorated with brilliantly colored flowers, fronds, views from the cabana or through louvered shutters, dark silhouettes gutting fish, bearing mounds of fruit on their heads.

White poetry of the islands: no clue that there are poets, born and living there, who are building literary movements, who are part of an anticolonial resistance. The people of the fabulous realm: abstract figures on a simplified ground.

The exotic—that way of viewing a landscape, people, a culture as escape from our carefully constructed selves, our "real" lives—a trap for poets.

•

In my twenties, soon after World War II, I viewed Western Europe like that. The dollar was high, and college students from the United States could travel and study abroad with a sense of being on cultural holiday. Coming from our unscorched earth, our unblasted cities, we sought not the European present, traumatized and hectically rebuilding, but the European past of our schoolbooks. Being mostly white, we saw European culture as the ancestor of ours: we romanticized that ancestry, half in awe at its artifacts, half convinced of our own national superiority. In essence, Europe's glorious past had been saved from barbarism by us and for us: a huge outdoor museum.

Many of the poems in my second book were poems of such tourism. It was a difficult, conflicted time in my own life, from which I

gladly fled into poems about English or Italian landscape and architecture. Only once, in a poem called "The Tourist and the Town," I
tried to place myself as I was, alongside an acknowledgment that life
in the foreign town was as "ordinary" as anywhere else.

Poems of tourism: like travel snapshots taken compulsively, a
means of capturing, collecting, framing the ruins, the exotic street,
the sacred rocks, the half-naked vending child, the woman setting
forth under her colorful burden. A means of deflecting the meanings
of the place, the meaning of the tourist's presence, in a world economy in which tourism has become a major industry for poor countries and in which a different kind of travel—immigration in search
of work—is the only option facing a majority of the inhabitants of
those countries.

June Jordan turns this genre inside out in a poem called "Solidarity." She balances the spoken word "terrorist" against the unspoken
word "tourist." But the tourists here are four women of color visiting Paris:

Even then
in the attenuated light
of the Church of le Sacre Coeur
(early evening and folk songs
on the mausoleum steps)
and armed
only with 2 instamatic cameras
(not a terrorist among us)
even there
in that Parisian downpour
four
Black women (2 of Asian 2
of African descent)
could not catch a taxi
and
I wondered what umbrella
would be big enough to stop
the shivering

of our collective impotence
up
against such negligent
assault
And I wondered
who would build that shelter
who will build and lift it
high and wide
above
such loneliness[1]

•

Poems of the artists' colony: poems about grass being cut a long way off, poetry of vacation rather than vocation, poems written on retreat, like poems written at court, treating the court as the world.

This is not to deplore the existence of artists' colonies, but rather the way they exist in a society where the general maldistribution of opportunity (basic needs) extends to the opportunity (basic need) to make art. Most of the people who end up at artists' colonies, given this maldistribution, are relatively well educated, have had at least the privilege of thinking that they might create art. Imagine a society in which strong arts programs were integral elements of a free public education. Imagine a society in which, upon leaving school, any worker was eligible, as part of her or his worker's benefits, to attend free arts workshops, classes, retreats, both near the workplace and at weekend or summer camps. The values embodied in existing public policy are oppositional to any such vision. One result is that art produced in an exceptional, rarefied situation like an artists' colony for the few can become rarefied, self-reflecting, complicit with the circumstances of its making, cut off from a larger, richer, and more disturbing life.

•

Who is to dictate what may be written about and how? Isn't that what everybody fears—the prescriptive, the demand that we write out of certain materials, avoid others?

No one is to dictate. But if many, many poems written and published in this country are shallow, bland, fluent without intensity, timorous, and docile in their undertakings, must we assume that it's only natural? Isn't there something that points a finger in the direction of blandness, of fluency, something that rewards those qualities?

What is it that allows many poets in the United States, their critics and readers, to accept the view of poetry as a luxury (Audre Lorde's term) rather than a food for all, food for the heart and senses, food of memory and hope? Why do poets ever fawn or clown or archly undercut their work when reading before audiences, as if embarrassed by their own claims to be heard, by poetry's function as witness? Why do some adopt a self-conscious snake-oil shamanism, as if the electrical thread from human being through poem to other human beings weren't enough? Why are literary journals full of poems that sound as if written by committee in a department of comparative literature, or by people still rehearsing Ezra Pound's long-ago groan *I cannot make it cohere*—a groan that, after so many repetitions, becomes a whine? Why do so many poems full of liberal or radical hope and outrage fail to lift off the ground, for which "politics" is blamed rather than a failure of poetic nerve? Why have poets in the United States (I include myself) so often accepted that so little was being asked of us? asked so little of each other and ourselves?

The reviewer of a recent anthology of Los Angeles poets comments:

> This book is not a response to public life, although it does share the despair and helplessness of the 1990's, which the riots have helped crystallize. No: The burning here originates in the personal isolation into which these poets have plunged themselves, who appear to choose loneliness and self-pity as guides through their individual pain. . . . [S]uch wounds result not in any explosion, but in uneasy confessions. . . . Predictably, some poems do little more than photograph frustration and numbness. A poetry of stunned realizations, of therapy, it speaks of art as mere self-disclosure: We tell about our troubles, and we feel better.[2]

Isn't there something that points a finger in the direction of mere self-disclosure, telling our troubles, as an end in itself? From television talk shows to the earnest confessions of political candidates, isn't there a shunting off of any collective vitality and movement that might rise from all these disclosures? *We feel better,* then worse again, we go back to the therapeutic group, the people who understand us, we do not trouble the waters with a language that exceeds the prescribed common vocabulary, we try to "communicate," to "dialogue," to "share," to "heal" in the holding patterns of capitalistic self-help—we pull further and further away from poetry.

The reviewer goes on to criticize the nervelessness of form that accompanies this attitude toward the materials: a "lackadaisical" craft. But even a highly crafted poem may evoke little more than a life of resigned interiority.

Interiority *was* the material for Emily Dickinson, yet she turned her lens both on her personal moment and on eternity. She had to make herself like that, embracing her own authority and linguistic strangeness, or she'd have joined the ranks of sad, fluent female singers of her North American century. She wanted more for poetry than that. More for herself.

•

In a time of great and mostly terrible uprootings, no "promised land" is a land for poetry. For Poetry the Immigrant, surrounded by her hastily crammed bags and baskets, there is no final haven. In its mixture of the ancient and the unthought-of, the well-loved and the unthinkable, its strange tension between conservation and radical excavation, poetry is continually torn between its roots, the bones of the ancestors, and its bent beyond the found, toward the future.

Raya Dunayevskaya wrote of revolution that while "great divides in epochs, in cognition, in personality, are crucial," we need to understand the moment of discontinuity—the break in the pattern—itself as part of a continuity, for it to become a turning point in human history.[3]

Poetry wrenches around our ideas about our lives as it grows alongside other kinds of human endeavor. But it also recalls us to ourselves—to memory, association, forgotten or forbidden languages.

Poetry will not fly across the sea, against the storms, to any "new world," any "promised land," and then fold its wings and sing. Poetry is not a resting on the given, but a questing toward what might otherwise be. It will always pick a quarrel with the found place, the refuge, the sanctuary, the revolution that is losing momentum. Even though the poet, human being with many anxious fears, might want just to rest, acclimate, adjust, become naturalized, learn to write in a new landscape, a new language. Poetry will go on harassing the poet until, and unless, it is driven away.

SIX MEDITATIONS IN PLACE
OF A LECTURE

I

Let me begin with a dream. I have been invited to give a lecture. Increasingly the expected format—the presentation of previously worked-out ideas—has become problematic for me. It rises up as a blockage to expression, a resistance to meaning. In the dream I am making the effort once more. What comes to me is the opening of Robert Duncan's "A Poem Beginning with a Line by Pindar," the first line of which reads:

The light foot hears you and the brightness begins

Still dreaming, my mind becomes active, playing with the vowel sounds of the title and first line, hearing, in a state of peculiar happiness, recurrent *I* sounds, both short and long: "beginning with a line by Pindar," the open vowels of the word "poem," the long *A* of "Pindar," the internal rhyming of "light" and "brightness," the echo of "beginning" in "the brightness begins." And the dream elides into another poem, from *the middle range of the Nineteenth century in the New World: a strange, unloosen'd, wondrous time* as the poet called it:

Out of the cradle, endlessly rocking,
Out of the mocking-bird's throat, the musical shuttle,
Out of the Ninth-month midnight,
Over the sterile sands and the fields beyond, where the child
    leaving his bed wander'd alone. . . .[1]

First given as the Clark Lecture at Trinity College, Cambridge, England, in 2002.

Walt Whitman's meditation on eros and death. A poem beginning with the cradle and the ninth month—not only September but
the month of delivery, of birth—a poem that ends with the figure of
"an old crone, rocking the cradle." *O*'s and *U*'s and long *I*'s. *N*'s and
M's. Out . . . out . . . out . . . and over. Mockingbird syllables: *Soothe!
Soothe! Soothe! . . . Loud, loud, loud! . . . Loved! loved! loved! loved!
loved!* In the dream I do not intellectualize, I do not explicate, I listen
to the liquidity of the language.

On waking I make a few notes: "Vowel sounds: first sounds we
make at birth, perhaps the last we make at death." "A poem begins
in the ear not in the mind." But these observations seem obvious
and deadweight to me, not nearly as compelling as the language of
the dream. The deadline for the lecture has weighed upon me; the
dream and its poetry haunt me.

"Before I bring this poor, badly constructed lecture to a close. . . ."
That's Federico García Lorca, speaking in Spain in 1922 of the *cante
jondo,* songs it was believed the Gypsies brought into Andalusia from
ancient sources, music rapidly going to the grave with its aging singers, replaced in popular culture by flamenco and other forms, and
derogated by the elite culture. He pleads for the preservation and
dignifying of this "deep song," and for support for the Festival of
Cante Jondo he and the composer Manuel de Falla have organized.
His motive is passionate, his words eloquent. Still, he apologizes—
perhaps part nervously, part ironically—for the faulty formal construction of his lecture. Almost a decade later, in Buenos Aires, he
would admit to his audience:

"From 1918, when I entered the Residencia de Estudiantes in
Madrid, until 1928, when I finished my studies in Philosophy and
Letters and left, I attended, in that elegant salon . . . around one
thousand lectures.

"Hungry for air and for sunlight, I used to grow so bored as to
feel myself covered by a light film of ash about to turn into sneez-
ing powder.

"And that is why I promise never to let the terrible bot-fly of boredom into *this* room, stringing your heads together on the fine thread
of sleep and putting tiny pins and needles in your eyes."[2]

To learn by going where I have to go, in Theodore Roethke's words. The power and significance of an emerging consciousness, of form discovering its meaning, form indissoluble from meaning, is the process art (as creative change) depends on—and embodies. If this was perhaps not always so, in the past century it has been an unavoidable condition of making art.

"What are your poems about?" a stranger will sometimes ask. I don't say, "About finding form," since that would imply that form is my only concern. But without the intuition and mutation, in each poem yet again, of what its form will be, I have no poem, no subject, no meaning.

Even for poets like Pindar—in ages and cultures where the occasion for the poem is formal, ritualized, the poetry—if it is poetry—will tend to go its own way. Pindar wrote and declaimed his odes for the athletic games of Greece, which have come down to us as the modern "Olympics" for which nations and cities now contend, vying for enrichment of civic coffers, infrastructural development, nationalist prestige, global advertising. Poetry need not apply. Odd as it may or may not seem, the poet chosen to praise the victorious athletes of the various Greek games was a sought-after figure, honored as the athletes themselves. The odes were prescribed in form, but Pindar was outrageous, Pindar invented out beyond the forms, Pindar was accused by later critics as too far-out, over-the-top—but also praised for the richness and complexity of his work.

A poem beginning with a line by Pindar, written by a twentieth-century poet (Robert Duncan) who was, himself, to be accused by some critics of being too far-out, too over-the-top:

The light foot hears you and the brightness begins

Feet that hear? Who or what is that "you"? It's the lyre of Apollo, music, measure: the source of poetry.

The light foot hears you and the brightness begins
god-step at the margins of thought,
     quick adulterous tread at the heart.

Who is it that goes there?
    Where I see your quick face
notes of an old music pace the air,
    torso-reverberations of a Grecian lyre.

Poetry, for Duncan, is an erotic pull "at the margins of thought," adulterous in its wandering from the intellectual straight and narrow. Even the shape of the Greek lyre becomes a torso, as if the "you" of poetry dissolves into the "you" of a male lover. And, as Duncan tells us in a later essay, "In Pindar it is the harp of Apollo that the light foot of the dancer hears, but *something had intruded, a higher reality for me* [italics mine], and it was the harp that heard the dancer. 'Who is it that goes there?' the song cried out."[3]

Who is it that goes there? "at the margins of thought"? And now I begin to see the path for which the dream has acted as trailhead.

II

On my worktable are two books, each with a title containing the word *poetics*. One is Smadar Lavie's *The Poetics of Military Occupation*, a woman anthropologist's study of the Mzeini Bedouin dwelling on the south Sinai peninsula in the 1970s and 1980s.[4] The other is the Martinican writer Édouard Glissant's visionary work, *The Poetics of Relation*. Each author has reached for an unconventional form: Glissant's a layered, spiraling meditation on Antillean language, Creole patois, and especially poetry as a world-embracing reality—an aesthetics of recognition of the Other. Writing in French, an imposed colonial language, Glissant invents his own vocabulary for human dispersions, voluntary and enforced: "I build my language with rocks," he says.

Lavie, a Sephardic/Ashkenazic Israeli, doing years of fieldwork in a Bedouin and Muslim tribal ethos long penetrated by foreign military powers, most recently Israeli, and by the incursions of foreign tourism, seeks to traverse gender and ethnic lines in a strongly gendered and self-conscious culture, writing both as "the anthropologist" who observes, makes notes, tape-records and photographs, produces rational text, and as the "I" who reacts, feels, brings her own life to her experiences: the woman participant-observer who faints at a ritual female circumcision.

But what is this word *poetics*? In its narrowest sense it is taken as a descriptive, normative criticism of what poetry is. But really, there can be no definition of poetry except in actual poems—which are as disparate and various (and interlinked) as people and cultures are. Poetics, we could say, refer to and describe the heterogeneous expressive, linguistic means by which we human beings survive and interpret our collective and individual lives—but even this falls short.

Lavie witnesses to how the Mzeini Bedouin, under first Egyptian and then Israeli military occupation—invaded also by hippie culture imported from America via Europe and Israel, by filmmakers intent on their exotic representations, by Egyptian drug-smuggling operations—struggle to make sense of their historical being, their contemporary identity, through poetry, proverbs, song, oral allegorical stories, and spontaneous performances. Her account illuminates the resources of language for people without material power, negotiating their ways with the foreigner as they must, but for whom the central question, after physical survival, is: *Who are we?* Where herding and date harvesting have given way to day labor on the occupier's roads, smuggling hashish, picking up the garbage left by seasonal tourists on the beaches, what does it mean to be Bedouin? Where hospitality to the stranger has been a core point of honor and pride, what does it mean to open your house to the exploiter and the occupier? Where the keeping private of women has required veiling, how regard the unveiled anthropologist, the naked Western backpackers screwing each other on the beach? Lavie discovers the imagination and wit—and sometimes the formal silences—that continually re-create self-meaning among people whose traditions include the arguing of cases at trial in "improvised rhymed poetry ... dense, and therefore short and pungent."

For both Glissant and Lavie, poetics does not imply simply literary

---

*"Poetics is the continuation of poetry by other means. Just as poetry is the continuation of politics by other means. ... Some tactics of poetics include hyperbole (though

criticism or a treatise on poetry. For Glissant it becomes a means of referring to a kind of expressive consciousness, embedded in language, a movement toward coexistence and connection. He does not minimize the risks and difficulties of such a consciousness. One way or another, the emotional apartheid of domination is a legacy of global history. For Caribbean peoples it has been that of the Plantation; for most people at most times some version of the apartheid of power: between the imposers of hierarchy, the violent censors of other languages and lives, the appropriators of culture, and those who have—not without resisting—been silenced and penalized for their languages, their art, their selves. Pervasive throughout, as Amartya Sen has shown, lies that rift of inequality between the freedoms implied by wealth and the absence of freedom intrinsic to poverty.[5] Glissant opens a huge window onto the possibility of another model: the "human imaginary" he calls Relation.

Relation for Glissant is not a panacea or a utopia or any pseudo solidarity.[6] It is not comfortable and sweet; as Gerard Manley Hopkins said of Peace, "It does not come to coo." Relation is turbulence, exposure, an identity not of roots but of meeting places; not a lingua franca but a multiplicity of languages, articulations, messages. It can appear to us, accustomed as we are to thinking in terms of separate and unequal nations, ethnicities, religions, tribes (and, I would add, genders), as "indecipherable magma." We fear it means chaos. But it is a transformational mode of apprehending.

Lavie's work, neither as ambitious nor as mature as Glissant's, nonetheless provides an instance of the problematics of Relation and its poetics. The conjunctions of the Mzeini with foreign incursions

---

personally I would never exaggerate), understatement, metonymy, evasion, paranoia, aphorism, assonance, cacophony, caesura, rime, mosaic, blurring. . . . Poetics makes explicit what is otherwise inexplicit and, perhaps more important, makes unexplicit what is otherwise explicit." (Charles Bernstein, *A Poetics* [Cambridge, Mass.: Harvard University Press, 1992], p. 160.) To which it must be added that military occupation is the continuation of war by any means possible: humiliations, detentions without charges, searches and seizures, censorship, rape, demolition of homes, destruction of harvests, withholding of medical supplies, and so on.

and with the anthropologist from the occupying nation who feels marginalized in her own country as a dark-skinned woman, the paradoxes of these conjunctions, create occasions for their questioning who is Other, and where, and when, and how the questions can be framed, if not answered, in poetry and performance. Lavie leaves us, as she is left, with these questions. But her book helps us perceive a poetics as something essential to any humanity refusing to accept the muted condition of an imposed Otherness.

III

I was starting to write this early in the Ninth month, month of the Jewish New Year, in the second year of the Palestinian Al-Aqsa intifada. The time of year—the season and its Jewish inflection—never fails to give me pause, though I am a secular Jew. Each year, among the powerful questions of early autumn, I am caught by the sharpening light, the shortening days, the silver eyelash of a crescent moon in the west, the sense that, indeed, this is a time of reckoning, and it is brief. In Judaism it's a season for recognition of self and other, acknowledging our violations against others, forgiving and asking forgiveness, for changing our ways of being in the world, recognizing that in the coming year some will live and some will die, wishing to be reinscribed in the Book of Life, wishing the coming months to be sweet and not bitter. And I think of Rainer Maria Rilke's poem "Autumn Day," which ends,

> Whoever has no house now will not build one anymore.
> Whoever is alone now will remain so for a long time,
> will stay up, read, write long letters,
> and wander the avenues, up and down
> restlessly, while the leaves are blowing.[7]

Rilke sets the unbuilt house—the house that will not get built after all—in conjunction with aloneness (a condition he knew well). What is this house? Surely in the largest sense it's whatever we mean by the soul. And if a house is a space indicating relatedness, not just a shelter but a place inhabited with others, a site of both intimacy and hospitality, an unbuilt house suggests relation not accomplished.

Early last September, for me, the thought inevitably followed of long-inhabited houses bulldozed, villages strafed, orchards and avenues obliterated—the antipoetics of a military occupation, force that can destroy but is unable to build, the absolute negation of relatedness.

IV

I left, at this point, my subversion of a lecture, my computer screen, my desk, my house, to fly to the Midwest for a couple of poetry readings. While eating breakfast in a Missouri motel I learned that the two tallest skyscrapers in New York had been demolished in a terrorist attack, with still untold losses of lives, and that all the airports in the country were shut down. Subsequently that day I was driven by a car service up through the heart of the United States to Minneapolis. My driver and companion was a retired fireman from St. Louis, and for eleven hours we listened to the radio, talked, and drove, up through Missouri, Iowa, Minnesota, stopping for gas and snacks, trying to make sense of what we were hearing. The fields around us were voluble in harvest, the rivers glittered, the interstate highways swooped over the cities—a landscape not without its aggressive billboards marketing both religion and property, but overall a scene of apparent peace and plenty. The driver was an ordinary, acute, reflective man who was interested in politics, read newspapers and magazines; we soon trusted each other, as strangers, with our deep distrust of the Bush administration and what it would make of the disaster. At our final rest stop somewhere in southern Minnesota, while he smoked a pipe, we sat looking up at the enormous prairie sky, dark by now, pulsing with the constellations and the Milky Way.

It soon became a media and pundit cliché in the United States to say that on September 11 "everything changed." Certainly the fireman and I were as shocked and stunned that day as any two people distant from lower Manhattan could be. But I also felt like someone who has been watching a reckless, stoned driver take off in his expensive car again and again, and who hears on the news that he has had a fatal crash. As the days and weeks and months passed, as I traded phone calls and visits and e-mails and letters with friends and political comrades and fellow artists, with neighbors and acquaintances, as we learned that "America has gone to war" and that unheard-of military and security measures must and would be taken for the protection of our victimized nation, as the Stars and Stripes flew from the radio antennae of enormous private vehicles and appeared in the anxious windows of small immigrant shops, as the bombing of an already suffering and impoverished country became our American twenty-first-century crusade, our mission, as that crusade was declared to extend to the entire globe, as news of domestic corruption on a seemingly unheard of scale (because so many of us did not know our economic history) vied on television with our vaunted military prowess against evil, as private and public grief for civilian losses from many cultures and nations at the World Trade Center had to make way for the patriotic imperative to spend, consume, rescue the economy for profiteering and militarization, as fear was sowed broadside by our government as well as by lethal extremist acts—I can only say that in this pressure chamber of history and politics, a great many elements previously held to be separate began to mix and fuse.

For an American poet, an unrepentant socialist and feminist, a critic of her government and its lamentable record of service to the country, it was not that "everything had changed" but that everything had been flung into sharper relief. The nation had in fact been riven within and whirling in megalomaniac violence abroad and for a long time, fantasizing itself safe behind the electronic fences and stockpiled resources of a gated community. In a newspaper column on September 30, 2001, the poet David Budbill observed: "Some people have been saying that the American age of innocence is over. What is over is the American age of impunity."[8]

Now, a government that had seized power through a corrupt

electoral process bade us draw together for security under the flag
of national unity. Dissent was collaboration with evil. We were citizens of a body insulted and wounded, and endless war would be the
nostrum of our pain.

But there was nothing sudden about this. Writing in the late
1940s, the poet Muriel Rukeyser had warned that

> American poetry has been part of a culture in conflict. . . . We
> are people tending toward democracy at the level of hope; on
> another level, the economy of the nation, the empire of busi-
> ness within the republic, both include in their basic premise the
> concept of perpetual warfare. It is the history of the idea of war
> that is beneath our other histories.[9]

Since September 11, 2001, that idea of perpetual war has simply been
made explicit policy—foreign and domestic.

A poet friend, Ed Pavlić, sent me, in late September 2001, a passage from James Baldwin's 1961 novel, *Another Country:*

> A sign advertised the chewing gum which would help one to
> relax and keep smiling. A hotel's enormous neon name chal-
> lenged the starless sky. So did the names of movie stars and
> people currently appearing or scheduled to appear on Broad-
> way, along with the mile-high names of the vehicles which
> would carry them into immortality. The great buildings, unlit,
> blunt like the phallus or sharp like the spear, guarded the city
> which never slept.
>
> Beneath them Rufus walked, one of the fallen—for the
> weight of this city was murderous—one of those who had been
> crushed on the day, which was every day, these towers fell.
> Entirely alone, and dying of it, he was part of an unprecedented
> multitude.[10]

A century before, Walt Whitman, sometimes taken as the voice of
American optimism and overreaching destiny, was in fact continu-

ally bringing up short, accusing, the complacencies of national chauvinism. Let several instances stand for many: some passages from his *Democratic Vistas:*

> In vain have we annex'd Texas, California, Alaska, and reach north for Canada and south for Cuba. It is as if we were somehow being endow'd with a vast and more and more thoroughly appointed body, and then left with little or no soul. . . .
>
> The great word Solidarity has arisen. Of all dangers to a nation, as things exist in our day, there can be no greater one than having certain portions of the people set off from the rest by a line drawn—they not privileged as others, but degraded, humiliated, made of no account. Much quackery teems, of course, even on democracy's side, yet does not really affect the orbic quality of the matter. . . .
>
> We have frequently printed the word Democracy. Yet I cannot too often repeat that it is a word the real gist of which still sleeps, quite unawaken'd, notwithstanding the resonances and the many angry tempests out of which its syllables have come, from pen or tongue. It is a great word, whose history, I suppose, remains unwritten, because that history has yet to be enacted.[11]

Whitman's sweeping, peopled landscapes are vistas of possibility, not odes to empire.

The poet Michael Harper has written of the early 1960s as "a promissory note and the first harbinger of a failed notion of freedom and the institutions that needed replenishing over the long haul. . . . I began to write poems because I could not see those elements of my life that I considered sacred reflected in my courses of study: scientific, linguistic, and literary. . . . I set out on a path to document those elements of contradiction most salient to my antenna and to find a speech that would have some influence on the world I was forced to live in." He alludes to an "element of foreboding" in this poetic process.[12]

Foreboding and warning: a multiplicity of American artists have
seismically registered the fault lines and shifting plates of the republic and of its foreign adventures. Many have been written off as
ideologues, leftists, treasonable to their nation and to their art; or,
especially in the case of African Americans, selectively ignored. But
I would claim that an engaged and freely ranging imagination will
be stubbornly resistant to institutions and governments that inflict
enormous divisions and suppress enormous human possibilities. It is
in fact through art that those possibilities continually reembody and
reiterate themselves and, like William Carlos Williams's saxifrage
flower, split the rocks.

V

To reread Duncan's poems was to be reminded of this. "A Poem
Beginning with a Line by Pindar"[13] is a long and complex work, from
which I must reluctantly excerpt. Moving from the classical lyre of
Apollo and the myth of Cupid and Psyche (eros and soul), it becomes
a poem distinctively of the United States. And Duncan turns from
the Greek celebration of aesthetic male youth to two aging American poets, Walt Whitman and Ezra Pound, Pound in his late "Pisan
Cantos," Whitman in his old age, stricken in language.

> In time we see a tragedy, a loss of beauty
>   the glittering youth
> of the god retains—but from this threshold
>   it is age
> that is beautiful. It is toward the old poets
>   we go, to their faltering,
> their unfaltering wrongness that has style,
>   their variable truth,
>   the old faces,
> words shed like tears from
> a plenitude of powers time stores.

Whitman groping for words:

A stroke. These little strokes. A chill.
  The old man, feeble, does not recoil.
Recall. A phase so minute,
  only part of the word in- jerrd.
damerging a nuv. A nerb.
  The Present dented of the U
nighted stayd. States. The heavy clod?
  Cloud. Invades the brain. What
   if lilacs last in *this* dooryard bloomd?

"When Lilacs Last in the Dooryard Bloom'd"—Whitman's elegy for Abraham Lincoln. And so Duncan moves into a bitterly decelebrating roster of American presidents:

Hoover, Roosevelt, Truman, Eisenhower—
where among these did the power reside
that moves the heart? What flower of the nation
bride-sweet broke to the whole rapture?
Hoover, Coolidge, Harding, Wilson
hear the factories of human misery turning out commodities.
For whom are the holy matins of the heart ringing?
Noble men in the quiet of morning hear
Indians singing the continent's violent requiem.
Harding, Wilson, Taft, Roosevelt,
idiots fumbling at the bride's door,
hear the cries of men in meaningless debt and war.
Where among these did the spirit reside
that restores the land to productive order?
McKinley, Cleveland, Harrison, Arthur,
Garfield, Hayes, Grant, Johnson,
dwell in the roots of the heart's rancor.
How sad "amid lanes and through old woods"
  echoes Whitman's love for Lincoln!
There is no continuity then. Only a few
  posts of the good remain. I too
that am a nation sustain the damage

where smokes of continual ravage
obscure the flame.
                              It is across great scars of wrong
     I reach toward the song of kindred men
     and strike again the naked string
old Whitman sang from. Glorious mistake!
     that cried:

     "The theme is creative and has vista."
     "He is the president of regulation."*

     I see always the under side turning,
fumes that injure the tender landscape.
     From which up break
lilac blossoms of courage in daily act
     striving to meet a natural measure

But the poem doesn't end here. Duncan rejoins it with the classic myth, the task set Psyche by jealous Aphrodite, the sorting of millions of seeds:

     These are the old tasks.
     You've heard them before.

     They must be impossible. Psyche
     must despair, be brought to her
                                   insect instructor;
     must obey the counsels of the green reed;

---

* Duncan is quoting from the 1855 Preface to *Leaves of Grass,* in which Whitman extols the futurity of American poetry: "Let the age and wars of other nations be chanted and their eras and characters be illustrated and that finish the verse. Not so the great psalm of the republic. Here the theme is creative and has vista. Here comes one among the wellbeloved stonecutters and plans with decision and science and sees the solid and beautiful forms of the future where there are now no solid forms." Further on, Whitman continues: "The greatest poet . . . is not one of the chorus. . . . He does not stop for regulation . . . he is the president of regulation." (Walt Whitman, *Complete Poetry and Prose* [New York: Library of America, 1982], pp. 8, 10.)

saved from suicide by a tower speaking,
    must follow to the letter
    freakish instructions.

In the story the ants help. The old man at Pisa
    mixd in whose mind
(to draw the sorts) are all seeds
    as a lone ant from a broken ant-hill
had part restored by an insect, was
    upheld by a lizard . . .

Ezra Pound at Pisa.

Pound's fascism-crazed mind; Whitman's stroke. The old poets in their "glorious mistakes." A mixed bag, the "freakish instructions" we take from the forerunners, certainly in the United States.

                   West
From east   men push.
            The islands are blessd
(cursed) that swim below the sun,

man upon whom the sun has gone down!

Finally, by a winding route, the poem ends like this:

(An ode? Pindar's art, the editors tell us, was not a statue but
a mosaic, an accumulation of metaphor. But if he was archaic,

---

Charles Bernstein offers this commentary on Pound's "freakish instructions": "When Pound the great artist is excused for his politics, fascism has won. When Pound's politics are used to categorically discredit the compositional methods of his poetry, fascism has won. When Pound's poetry is exalted and his politics are dismissed as largely irrelevant to his achievement, fascism has won. When Pound's politics are condemned, his poetry acknowledged or ignored in passing, but sanitized forms of his ideas prevail—the virtue of authority, property and the homestead ("family values"), the sanctity of the classics, the condemnation of the nonstandard in favor of the plain sense of the word and the divine right of the West (or East) to harness and bleed the rest of the world—fascism has won."(Bernstein, p. 126.)

not classic, a survival of obsolete mode, there may have been old voices in the survival that directed the heart. So, a line from a hymn came in a novel I was reading to help me. Psyche, poised to leap—and Pindar too, the editors write, goes too far, topples over—listened to a tower that said, *Listen to Me!* The oracle had said, *Despair! The Gods themselves abhor his power.* And then the virgin flower of the dark falls back flesh of our flesh from which everywhere. . . .

> the information flows
>   that is yearning. A line of Pindar
> moves from the area of my lamp
>   toward morning.

> In the dawn that is nowhere
>   I have seen the willful children

> clockwise and counter-clockwise turning.

I want to say a word about Duncan's bitter litany of the names of American presidents. It's catalyzed by Whitman's elegy for Lincoln. Lincoln, who signed the Emancipation Proclamation with racist mental reservations, determined to hold together the Union at any cost, became and for many remains an iconic figure in American history, a marker of leadership and a marble monument, a

---

Hans Magnus Enzensberger has observed that in Europe after the eighteenth century nothing definable as a poem could be written in praise of a ruler or statesman or national hero. Till then, court poetry, the eulogy for the prince or patron, was a common Western poetic genre, coming down from the Greek panegyric. He fixes this endpoint for German poetry in an 1809 poem by Heinrich von Kleist, in which it's the God of History, not the dynast in question, who is invoked as the enduring power.

Enzensberger maintains that poetry can no longer either praise or condemn a ruler; its power lies neither in the zone of bourgeois aesthetics that deny it all social efficacy nor in the realm of propaganda. Rather, it's an imagination of the future. (H. M. Enzensberger, "Poetry and Politics," in *The Consciousness Industry: On Literature, Politics and the Media* [New York: Seabury Press, 1974].)

democratic figure unlike the property- and slave-owning "founding fathers." And a great rhetorician. Duncan isn't enumerating
the names of "Hoover, Roosevelt, Truman, Eisenhower" et cetera
in the simplistic search for a great man to whom a great poem might
be written. He is calling up history as schoolchildren have learned
it by rote, via the names and dates of presidents; but in visionary
indignation, not the patriotism of the schoolroom.

If we look to American poetry, as Duncan reminds us, Whitman's
elegy for Lincoln is unique as an artistically and emotionally memo-
rable document. Yet "When Lilacs Last in the Dooryard Bloom'd" *is*
an elegy, not a eulogy; the people of the United States, the mourners,
are where the life continues and the social power resides.

The landscape of language is—as Wittengenstein has it—like the
oldest part of a city, original trails and cow paths interlacing as streets,
a map determined not by preconceptions of urban order but by the
intricate tracings of the human brain—and voice. A poem emerges
as language, and the poems that most interest and engage me are
poems in which several kinds of language impel you along a twisting path, as Duncan draws his from the aural and visual synthesis
of a Greek myth toward his own leap of imagination. That myth (of
betrayal, despair, rescue through insects and tutelary voices) leads
by poetic synapse into the formative legend of the United States, the
Western frontier, Duncan's own relation to that legend and to his own
tutelary voices—the aging poets Whitman and Pound in *their unfal-
tering wrongness that has style / their variable truth*, back and around
through his indictment of the history underlying the false myths
of the nation (*I too / that am a nation sustain the damage*) back into
childhood and a final image of children playing in a ring *clockwise and
counter-clockwise turning*. That image reappears in another Duncan
poem, "Often I Am Permitted to Return to a Meadow": *a children's
game / of ring a round the roses told*. . . . That rhyme goes back to the
Black Plague and the burning of the dead: *Ashes, ashes, all fall down*.

Are these children simply caught in the circles of an old game, or
are they a glimpse of something new?

I return now to my dream into which Duncan's poem came

as intervention, interrupting the task of a lecture to be given, in which the sound of the first lines melted into the music of Whitman's "Out of the Cradle, Endlessly Rocking." I did not deliberately choose "A Poem Beginning with a Line by Pindar" as an exemplary poem about which to build a lecture. To say that it came to me in a dream is merely to underscore the element of chance and associative method in poetry. It has certainly been exemplary for me, in its open lines marked by varying musics, its complex undertaking, its sense of history as profoundly personal. I have read it many times in my life, coming to it slowly with an increasing sense of the possibilities it offered: I have talked about it here as a poet who reads other poets for such possibilities, not in the effort to grasp and fix a poem but to attend to it intensely and with what, in a scientific context, has been called "a feeling for the organism."[14]

VI

Poets are often asked how they start to write a poem, whether with an idea or a chosen form, or what? Once as a young neophyte and apprentice I thought that poems were like jewel boxes that contained, literally, ideas to be inscribed in given forms—this was my earliest training. By my mid-twenties I was breaking from that training. At the "margins of thought" flickered the question *Who is it that goes there?*—something, a brushing past of syllables, indecipherable perceptions, memories, musical phrases, plasmic sensations, not to be named but rather rendered in words, allowed to gather and configure themselves on the page, into a more deliberate act of making. I have experienced this process as active yet receptive, engaged even as it requires solitude, dialectical since it does not allow disconnection of self from world yet is psychologically intense: the state of making poetry.

This loosening of the bonds of linear thought, this psychological intensity, has been sought and chemically induced by many poets of the last two centuries, from Coleridge and Poe to Rimbaud to the Beats and most of my contemporaries and the poets of the 1960s and beyond. If the desired poetry has sometimes eluded its devotees, perhaps it's because (as poet and translator Clayton Eshleman has reminded me) Rimbaud's famous edict was for the *rational* derangement of all the senses, and many poets and would-be poets have followed it only partway.*

Certainly the divided condition of mind/sensation, flesh/spirit, sense splintered from sense is inimical to poetry and to a larger poetics of relation. What's also incompatible with such a poetics—with the nature of poetry itself—is the professional project of defining, labeling, categorizing, historicizing, ranking, instrumentalizing the poem. Yes, the history of the art is needed, along with other historical and material context; yes, engaged and astute social criticism is wanted; but the rush to theory, the use of the work of art simply as a springboard to intellectual acrobatics and intramural academic debates, the psychobiographizing of the imagination, has been a fever to colonize and commoditize, not unlike the fever to convert wilderness or desert or productive farmland into profitable real estate. It would subvert the agency and potency of poetry in the life of collective transformation.

This agency of art in transformational social processes throughout the world is negatively reflected in the fear and hatred of art's freedom by authoritarian, theocratic, and militaristic powers, including those that wear the alias of democracy, including those that wear the robes of the academy.

I began with music: the sound of some lines from Duncan and

---

* Needless to say, a "derangement of the senses" in desire for another sexual being has induced poetry in every culture and in every kind of voice, from traditional (and unconventional) heterosexual love poems to the poetry of Sappho, Cavafy or Pasolini, of Whitman's "Calamus," of Muriel Rukeyser, Melvin Dixon, Judy Grahn, June Jordan, among others. And I would add to this an erotics located, not out-of-time, out-of-place, but in a landscape of circumstances suffered and resisted and countered with others, in mutual recognition and desire. An erotics beyond the couple, though aroused in the double body. Desire that enlarges the theater of desire. Once again, a poetics of relation. "In touch with the erotic," wrote Audre Lorde, "I become less willing to accept powerlessness, or those other supplied states of being which are not native to me, such as resignation, despair, self-effacement, depression, self-denial." And "... the erotic is not a question only of what we do; it is a question of how acutely and fully we can feel in the doing." (Audre Lorde, "Uses of the Erotic: The Erotic as Power," in *Sister Outsider* [Trumansburg, N.Y.: Crossing Press, 1984] pp. 58, 54.)

Whitman. In more ways than one, poetry must recall us to our senses—our bodily sensual life and our sense of other and different human presences. The oceanic multiplicities of this art call us toward possibilities of relation still very much alive in a world where violent material power can speak only to and of itself, yet in which— in the words of the Salvadorean revolutionary poet Roque Dalton— "poetry, like bread is for everyone."

Arts of the
Possible
(2001)

MURIEL RUKEYSER

Her Vision (1993)

To enter her work is to enter a life of tremendous scope, the consciousness of a woman who was a full actor and creator in her time. But in many ways Muriel Rukeyser was beyond her time— and seems, at the edge of the twenty-first century, to have grasped resources we are only now beginning to reach for: connections between history and the body, memory and politics, sexuality and public space, poetry and physical science, and much else. She spoke as a poet, first and foremost; but she spoke also as a thinking activist, biographer, traveler, explorer of her country's psychic geography.

It's no exaggeration to say that in the work of Muriel Rukeyser we discover new and powerful perspectives on the culture of the United States in the twentieth century, "the first century of world wars," as she called it. Her lifetime spanned two of them, along with the Spanish Civil War, the trial of the anarchists Sacco and Vanzetti, the Depression, the New Deal, the Holocaust, the Cold War and McCarthy years, the Vietnam War, the renewal of radicalism in the 1960s, the women's liberation movement of the late '60s and '70s, and, throughout, the movements of African-Americans and of working people for survival and dignity. All these informed her life and her art, as did other arts: film, painting, theater, the music of the blues and jazz, of classical orchestras, popular song. From a young age she seems to have understood herself as living in history—not as a static pattern but as a confluence of dynamic currents, always

Written as introduction to the Norton *Muriel Rukeyser Reader*, edited by Jan Heller Levi.

changing yet faithful to sources, a fluid process that is constantly shaping us and that we have the possibility of shaping.

The critic Louise Kertesz, a close reader of Rukeyser and her context, notes that "no woman poet makes the successful fusion of personal and social themes in a modern prosody before Rukeyser."[1] She traces a North American white women's tradition in Lola Ridge, Marya Zaturenska and Genevieve Taggard, all born at the end of the nineteenth century and all struggling to desentimentalize the personal lyric and to write from urban, revolutionary, and working-class experience. In her earliest published poetry, Rukeyser writes herself into the public events unfolding from the year of her birth, and into the public spaces of a great, expansive city. "The city rises in its light. Skeletons of buildings; the orange-peel cranes; highways put through; the race of skyscrapers. And you are part of this."[2]

Rukeyser grew up on Riverside Drive in an upwardly mobile Jewish family—her mother a bookkeeper from Yonkers who counted the poet-scholar-martyr Akiba among her legendary forebears, her father a concrete salesman from Wisconsin who became partner in a sand-and-gravel company. Both loved music and opera, but the house was sparsely supplied with books—"except in the servants' rooms: what do you hear there? *The Man with the Hoe, The Ballad of Reading Gaol.* The little five-cent books . . . read and reread."[3] Rukeyser was sent to Ethical Culture schools and to Vassar, but her father's financial difficulties forced her to leave college. "I was expected to grow up and become a golfer," she recalled—a suburban matron. "There was no idea at that point of a girl growing up to write poems." But she was writing poetry seriously by high school. She was also leading a secret life with the children in her neighborhood, playing in the basements and tunnels beneath the apartment buildings, and noting "the terrible, murderous differences between the ways people lived."[4]

Rukeyser was twenty-one when her *Theory of Flight* received the Yale Younger Poets Prize. Two crucial motifs of her life and work were already unmistakable: the book's title suggests how early she embraced the realm of the technological and scientific imagination; and the opening "Poem out of Childhood" points to her lifelong project of knitting together personal experience with politics. "Knitting together" is the wrong phrase here; in her words, she simply did not allow them to be torn apart.

Any sketch of her life (and here I have space for the merest) suggests the vitality of a woman who was by nature a participant, as well as an inspired observer, and the risk-taking of one who trusted the unexpected, the fortuitous, without relinquishing choice or sense of direction. In 1933, having left Vassar, she went to Alabama and was arrested while reporting on the Scottsboro case.[5] In the years to come she traveled as a journalist to Spain on the eve of the Civil War; to Gauley Bridge, West Virginia, for hearings on a silicon mining disaster; to the opening of the Golden Gate Bridge; to North Vietnam and to South Korea on political journeys. She was disinherited by her family, had a two-months'—long, annulled marriage, bore a son by a different man and raised him in single motherhood. She worked in film and theater, taught at Vassar, the California Labor School, and Sarah Lawrence College, and was a consultant for the Exploratorium, a museum of science and the arts in San Francisco. A wealthy California woman, out of admiration for her work and recognition of her struggles to earn a living as a single mother, provided an anonymous annual stipend, which Rukeyser gave up after seven years once she held a steady teaching job. She edited a "review of Free Culture" called *Decision,* was hunted as a Communist, was attacked both by conservative New Critics and "proletarian" writers, continued productive as writer and filmmaker, underwent a stroke but survived to write poems about it, and to see her poetry rediscovered by a younger generation of women poets and her *Collected Poems* in print. In 1978 she agreed to speak on a "Lesbians and Literature" panel at the annual convention of the Modern Language Association, but illness precluded her appearing.

Rukeyser's work attracted slashing hostility and scorn (of a kind that suggests just how unsettling her work and her example could be) but also honor and praise. Kenneth Rexroth, patriarch of the San Francisco Renaissance, called her "the best poet of her exact generation." At the other end of the critical spectrum, for the *London Times Literary Supplement* she was "one of America's greatest living poets."

She received the Copernicus Prize of the American Academy and Institute of Arts and Letters, and wrote "The Backside of the Academy," celebrating "my street . . . the street I live and write in," its urban vitality and human possibilities unencouraged by the locked doors and formal rituals of the Academy. In her lifetime she was a teacher of many poets, and readers of poetry, and some scientists paid tribute to her vision of science as inseparable from art and history. But she has largely been read and admired in pieces—in part because most readers come to her out of the very separations that her work, in all its phases, steadfastly resists. We read as feminists, or as literary historians, or we are searching for a viable Left tradition, and we sift her pages for our concerns; or we are students of poetry who assume a scientific biography is irrelevant to us; or we are trapped in ideas of genre that Rukeyser was untroubled by: what are passages of poetry doing in a serious political biography? (She called her life of Wendell Willkie "a story and a song.") Or, meeting her only in anthologies, we meet only the shorter poems of a great practitioner of the long poem, and meet her prose not at all. We call her prose "poetic" without referring to her own definitions of what poetry actually is—an *exchange of energy*, a *system of relationships*.

Rukeyser was unclassifiable, thus difficult for canon-makers and anthologists. She was not a "left wing" poet simply, though her sympathies more often than not intersected with those of the organized left, or the various lefts, of her time. Her insistence on the value of the unquantifiable and unverifiable ran counter to mainstream "scientific attitudes" and to plodding forms of materialism. She explored and valued myth but came to recognize that mythologies can rule us unless we pierce through them, that we need to criticize them in order to move beyond them. She wrote at the age of thirty-one: "My themes and the use I have made of them have depended on my life as a poet, as a woman, as an American, and as a Jew."[6] She saw the self-impoverishment of assimilation in her family and in the Jews she grew up among; she also recognized the vulnerability and the historical and contemporary "stone agonies" endured by the Jewish people. She remained a secular visionary with a strongly political sense of her Jewish identity. She wrote out of a woman's sexual longings, pregnancy, night-feedings, in a time when it was courageous to do so, especially as she did it—unapologetically, as a big woman alive in mind and body, capable of violence and despair as well as desire.

In a very real sense, we learn to read Rukeyser by reading her. She "scatters clews," as she wrote of the charismatic labor organizer Anne Burlak, "clews" that take light from each other, clews that reunite pieces of our experience and thought that we have mistrusted, forgotten, or allowed to be torn from each other. Much that we are taught, much that we live, is of this description. When Rukeyser said that she wrote the biography of the physicist Willard Gibbs because it was a book she needed to read, she could have been speaking of her work as a whole. She wanted to be able to read the life and research of a physicist against the background of the slave trade, of nineteenth-century industrial expansion and urban violence, of the lives of women—intellectuals and factory hands—of Emily Dickinson's poetry and Edison's invention, of Gibbs's own resonances with Melville and Whitman. She wanted to be able to write her own poems in full recognition of the language and imagery of the scientific imagination, the "traces" of the splitting she deplored. Her work was always a process of testing, by the written word and in the most concrete and risk-taking ways, her instincts, making their foundations and meanings visible, first to herself, then to the world.

When Rukeyser is, or appears, "difficult," this may be partly due to resistances stored in us by our own social and emotional training. But it's also true that while she can be direct and linear, she often builds on a nonlogical accumulation of images, glimpses, questions, a process resembling the way our apparently unrelated experiences can build into insight, once connected. This can be an accumulation within a given poem or book of poems, within a prose book, or in the undivided stream of her poetry and her prose. She isn't a writer with a few "gems" that can be extracted from the rest; of all twentieth-century writers, her work repays full reading.

I myself first read Rukeyser in the early 1950s. Like her, I had won the Yale Younger Poets Prize at the age of twenty-one, and I was curious to see what a woman poet, at my age, now ahead of me on the path, had written in her first book. I remember the extraordinary force of the first poem in *Theory of Flight*, how it broke over me, and my envy of the sweeping lines, the authority in that poem. But I was not yet ready to learn from her. *The Life of Poetry* had been published in 1949, the year I began to take myself seriously as a poet, or at least as an apprentice to poetry. No one in the literary world of Cambridge, Massachusetts, where I was a student, spoke of that book as an important resource; young poets were reading Empson's *Seven Types of Ambiguity*, Eliot's *Tradition and the Individual Talent*, I. A. Richards's *Practical Criticism*. Of my professors, only the brilliant and volatile F. O. Matthiessen spoke of Rukeyser, but the poets he taught in his seminar were Eliot, Pound, Williams, Stevens, Marianne Moore, E. E. Cummings. I came to Rukeyser in my maturity, as my own life opened out and I began to trust the directions of my own work. Gradually I found her to be the poet I most needed in the struggle to make my poems and live my life. In the past quarter century, as many silenced voices—especially women's voices—began to bear witness, the prescience and breadth of her vision came clearer to me—for it is a peculiarly relevant vision for our lives on this continent now.

In the 1960s and early '70s Rukeyser and I, together with other poets, often found ourselves on the same platform at readings for groups like RESIST and the Angry Arts Against the War in Vietnam. I never came to know her well; New York has a way of sweeping even the like-spirited into different scenes. But there was an undeniable sense of female power that came onto any platform along with Muriel Rukeyser. She carried her large body and strongly molded head with enormous pride, and stood with presence behind her words. Her poems ranged from political witness to the erotic to the mordantly witty to the visionary. Even struggling back from a stroke, she appeared inexhaustible.

She was, in the originality of her nature and achievement, as much an American classic as Melville, Whitman, Dickinson, Du Bois, or Hurston. It's to be hoped that more of her books will soon be back in print, and still-unpublished writings collected for the first time.[7]

WHY I REFUSED THE NATIONAL MEDAL FOR THE ARTS (1997)

July 3, 1997
Jane Alexander, Chair
The National Endowment for the Arts
1100 Pennsylvania Avenue
Washington, D.C. 20506

Dear Jane Alexander,
I just spoke with a young man from your office, who informed me that I had been chosen to be one of twelve recipients of the National Medal for the Arts at a ceremony at the White House in the fall. I told him at once that I could not accept such an award from President Clinton or this White House because the very meaning of art, as I understand it, is incompatible with the cynical politics of this administration. I want to clarify to you what I meant by my refusal.

Anyone familiar with my work from the early sixties on knows that I believe in art's social presence—as breaker of official silences, as voice for those whose voices are disregarded, and as a human birthright. In my lifetime I have seen the space for the arts opened by movements for social justice, the power of art to break despair. Over the past two decades I have witnessed the increasingly brutal impact of racial and economic injustice in our country.

There is no simple formula for the relationship of art to justice. But I

After the text of my letter to Jane Alexander, then chair of the National Endowment for the Arts, had been fragmentarily quoted in various news stories, Steve Wasserman, editor of the *Los Angeles Times Book Review*, asked me for an article expanding on my reasons. Herewith the letter and the article.

do know that art—in my own case the art of poetry—means nothing if it simply decorates the dinner table of power that holds it hostage. The radical disparities of wealth and power in America are widening at a devastating rate. A president cannot meaningfully honor certain token artists while the people at large are so dishonored.

I know you have been engaged in a serious and disheartening strug-gle to save government funding for the arts, against those whose fear and suspicion of art is nakedly repressive. In the end, I don't think we can separate art from overall human dignity and hope. My concern for my country is inextricable from my concerns as an artist. I could not participate in a ritual that would feel so hypocritical to me.
Sincerely,
Adrienne Rich

cc: *President Clinton*

•

The invitation from the White House came by telephone on July 3. After several years' erosion of arts funding and hostile pro-paganda from the religious right and the Republican Congress, the House vote to end the National Endowment for the Arts was loom-ing. That vote would break as news on July 10; my refusal of the National Medal for the Arts would run as a sidebar story alongside in the *New York Times* and the *San Francisco Chronicle*.

In fact, I was unaware of the timing. My refusal came directly out of my work as a poet and essayist and citizen drawn to the interfold of personal and public experience. I had recently been thinking and writing about the shrinking of the social compact, of whatever it was this country had ever meant when it called itself a democracy: the shredding of the vision of *government of the people, by the people, for the people.*

"We the people—still an excellent phrase," said the playwright Lorraine Hansberry in 1962, well aware who had been excluded, yet believing the phrase might someday come to embrace us all. And I had for years been feeling both personal and public grief, fear, hunger, and the need to render this, my time, in the language of my art.

Whatever was "newsworthy" about my refusal was not about a single individual—not myself, not President Clinton. Nor was it about a single political party. Both major parties have displayed a crude affinity for the interests of corporate power, while deserting the majority of the people, especially the most vulnerable. Like so many others, I've watched the dismantling of our public education, the steep rise in our incarceration rates, the demonization of our young black men, the accusations against our teen-age mothers, the selling of healthcare—public and private—to the highest bidders, the export of subsistence-level jobs in the United States to even lower-wage countries, the use of below-minimum-wage prison labor to break strikes and raise profits, the scapegoating of immigrants, the denial of dignity and minimal security to working and poor people. At the same time, we've witnessed the acquisition of publishing houses, once risk-taking conduits of creativity, by conglomerates driven single-mindedly to fast profits, the acquisition of major communications and media by those same interests, the sacrifice of the arts and public libraries in stripped-down school and civic budgets, and, most recently, the evisceration of the National Endowment for the Arts. Piece by piece the democratic process has been losing ground to the accumulation of private wealth.

There is no political leadership in the White House or the Congress that has spoken to and for the people who, in a very real sense, have felt abandoned by their government.

Lorraine Hansberry spoke her words about government during the Cuban missile crisis, at a public meeting in New York to abolish the House Un-American Activities Committee. She also said in that speech, "My government is wrong." She did not say, I abhor all government. She claimed her government as a citizen, African American, and female, and she challenged it. (I listened to her words again, on an old vinyl recording, this past Fourth of July.)

In a similar spirit many of us today might wish to hold government accountable, to challenge the agendas of private power and wealth that have displaced historical tendencies toward genuinely representative government in the United States. We might still wish to claim our government, to say, *This belongs to us*—we, the people, as we are now.

We would have to start asking questions that have been defined as nonquestions—or as naive, childish questions. In the recent official White House focus on race, it goes consistently unsaid that the all-embracing enterprise of our early history was the slave trade, which left nothing, no single life, untouched, and was, along with the genocide of the native population and the seizure of their lands, the foundation of our national prosperity and power. Promote dialogues on race? apologize for slavery? We would need to perform an autopsy on capitalism itself.

Marxism has been declared dead. Yet the questions Marx raised are still alive and pulsing, however the language and the labels have been co-opted and abused. What is social wealth? How do the conditions of human labor infiltrate other social relationships? What would it require for people to live and work together in conditions of radical equality? How much inequality will we tolerate in the world's richest and most powerful nation? Why and how have these and similar questions become discredited in public discourse?

And what about art? Mistrusted, adored, pietized, condemned, dismissed as entertainment, commodified, auctioned at Sotheby's, purchased by investment-seeking celebrities, it dies into the "art object" of a thousand museum basements. It's also reborn hourly in prisons, women's shelters, small-town garages, community-college workshops, halfway houses, wherever someone picks up a pencil, a wood-burning tool, a copy of *The Tempest*, a tag-sale camera, a whittling knife, a stick of charcoal, a pawnshop horn, a video of *Citizen Kane*, whatever lets you know again that this deeply instinctual yet self-conscious expressive language, this regenerative process, could help you save your life. "If there were no poetry on any day in the world," the poet Muriel Rukeyser wrote, "poetry would be invented that day. For there would be an intolerable hunger."[1] In an essay on the Caribbean poet Aimé Césaire, Clayton Eshleman names this hunger as "the desire, the need, for a more profound and ensouled world."[2] There is a continuing dynamic between art repressed and art reborn, between the relentless marketing of the superficial and the "spectral and vivid reality that employs all means" (Rukeyser again) to reach through armoring, resistances, resignation, to recall us to desire.

Art is both tough and fragile. It speaks of what we long to hear and what we dread to find. Its source and native impulse, the imagination, may be shackled in early life, yet may find release in conditions offering little else to the spirit. For a recent document on this, look at Phyllis Kornfeld's *Cellblock Visions: Prison Art in America*, notable for the variety and emotional depth of the artworks reproduced, the words of the inmate artists, and for Kornfeld's unsentimental and lucid text. Having taught art to inmates for fourteen years, in eighteen institutions (including maximum-security units), she sees recent incarceration policy as rapidly devolving from rehabilitation to dehumanization, including the dismantling of prison arts programs.[3]

Art can never be totally legislated by any system, even those that reward obedience and send dissident artists to hard labor and death; nor can it, in our specifically compromised system, be really free. It may push up through cracked macadam, by the merest means, but it needs breathing space, cultivation, protection to fulfill itself. Just as people do. New artists, young or old, need education in their art, the tools of their craft, chances to study examples from the past and meet practitioners in the present, get the criticism and encouragement of mentors, learn that they are not alone. As the social compact withers, fewer and fewer people will be told *Yes, you can do this; this also belongs to you.* Like government, art needs the participation of the many in order not to become the property of a powerful and narrowly self-interested few.

Art is our human birthright, our most powerful means of access to our own and another's experience and imaginative life. In continually rediscovering and recovering the humanity of human beings, art is crucial to the democratic vision. A government tending further and further away from the search for democracy will see less and less "use" in encouraging artists, will see art as obscenity or hoax.

In 1987, the late Justice William Brennan spoke of "formal reason severed from the insights of passion" as a major threat to due-process principles. "Due process asks whether government has treated someone fairly, whether individual dignity has been honored, whether the worth of an individual has been acknowledged. Officials cannot always silence these questions by pointing to rational action taken according to standard rules. They must plumb their conduct more deeply, seeking answers in the more complex equations of human nature and experience."[4]

It is precisely where fear and hatred of art join the pull toward quantification and abstraction, where the human face is mechanically deleted, that human dignity disappears from the social equation. Because it is to those "complex equations of human nature and experience" that art addresses itself.

In a society tyrannized by the accumulation of wealth as Eastern Europe was tyrannized by its own false gods of concentrated power, recognized artists have, perhaps, a new opportunity: to work out our connectedness, *as artists,* with other people who are beleaguered, suffering, disenfranchised—precariously employed workers, trashed elders, rejected youth, the "unsuccessful," and the art they too are nonetheless making and seeking.

I wish I didn't feel the necessity to say here that none of this is about imposing ideology or style or content on artists; it's about the inseparability of art from acute social crisis in this century and the one now approaching.

We have a short-lived model, in our history, for the place of art in relation to government. During the Depression of the 1930s, under New Deal legislation, thousands of creative and performing artists were paid modest stipends to work in the Federal Writers Project, the Federal Theatre Project, the Federal Art Project. Their creativity, in the form of novels, murals, plays, performances, public monuments, the providing of music and theater to new audiences, seeded the art and the consciousness of succeeding decades. By 1939 this funding was discontinued.

Federal funding for the arts, like the philanthropy of private arts patrons, can be given and taken away. In the long run art needs to grow organically out of a social compost nourishing to everyone, a literate citizenry, a free, universal, public education complex with art as an integral element, a society honoring both human individuality and the search for a decent, sustainable common life. In such conditions, art would still be a voice of hunger, desire, discontent, passion, reminding us that the democratic project is never-ending.

For that to happen, what else would have to change?

ARTS OF THE POSSIBLE (1997)

I appreciate this opportunity to pull together and present some issues I've been wrestling with over the past couple of years. In fact, I confess that I've kept for more than eighteen months a folder labeled "Troy Lecture" into which I've been sliding handwritten and typewritten notes, made in various states of intense reflection, disquietude, and hope. When I shook this folder out on the kitchen table last January, its contents did not miraculously assemble themselves into the outline of a lecture, as the mountain of peas, beans, and grains sorted themselves out for Psyche in the Greek myth. But they did remind me how persistently certain realities and urgencies had been haunting me over a period of time, ineluctable visitors it seemed.

Psyche's task was to separate legume from groat, millet grain from lentil. I see mine, rather, as a work of connection.

Let me first sketch out some of my concerns, then try to show how I think they inhere with this lectureship's focus on art, the humanities, and public education—and with conditions facing all of us, but especially the young who are trying to make sense of their lives in this time.

I begin with the abrupt reshuffling of our once apparently consensual national project: a democratic republic with a large and growing middle class, and equality of opportunity as its great hope. Over the past two decades or less, we have become a pyramidic society of the omnivorously acquisitive few, an insecure, dwindling middle

Given as the Troy Lecture, University of Massachusetts, Amherst, in April 1997. First published in the *Massachusetts Review*, autumn 1997.

class, and a multiplying number of ill-served, throwaway citizens and workers—finally, a society accused by the highest incarceration rate in the world. We dangle over an enormous gap between national propaganda and the ways most people are actually living: a cognitive and emotional dissonance, a kind of public breakdown, with symptoms along a spectrum from acute self-involvement to extreme anxiety to individual and group violence.

Along with this crisis in our own country I have been thinking about the self-congratulatory self-promotion of capitalism as a global, transnational order, superseding governments and the very meaning of free elections. I have especially been noting the corruptions of language employed to manage our perceptions of all this. Where democracy becomes "free enterprise," individual rights the self-interest of capital, it's no wonder that the complex of social policies needed to further democratic equality is dismissed as a hulk of obsolete junk known as "big government." In the vocabulary kidnapped from liberatory politics, no word has been so pimped as *freedom*.

I've been struck by the presumption, endlessly issuing from the media, in academic discourse, and from liberal as well as conservative platforms, that the questions raised by Marxism, socialism, and communism must inexorably be identified with their use and abuse by certain repressively authoritarian regimes of the twentieth century: therefore they are henceforth to be nonquestions. That because Marxism, socialism, communism were aliases employed by certain stagnating, cruel, and unscrupulous systems, they have and shall have no other existence than as masks for those systems. That American capitalism is the liberatory force of the future with a transnational mission to quench all efforts to keep these questions alive. That capitalism's violence and amorality are somehow non-accountable. That communist or socialist parties all over the world, including those of India and South Africa, imitate the degraded communisms of eastern Europe and China.

In this particular presumption, or dogma, capitalism represents itself as a law of history or, rather, a law beyond history, beneath which history now lies, corroding like the *Titanic*. Or, capitalism presents itself as obedience to a law of nature, man's "natural" and overwhelming predisposition toward activity that is competitive, aggressive, and acquisitive. Where capitalism invokes freedom, it means the freedom of capital. Where, in any mainstream public discourse, is this self-referential monologue put to the question?

The monologue may claim to be transnational, but its roots are in Western Europe and the United States, and in the United States we have our own idioms. We're still rehearsing an old, disabling rhetoric, invoking the "free" climate and virgin resources awaiting the first Europeans on this continent, the "free" spirit of individualism and laissez-faire that allowed penniless new arrivals to acquire lands and fortunes. Generally speaking, we don't trace American opportunity, prosperity, and global power to the genocide of millions of Indians, the claiming and contaminating of Indian lands and natural resources, the presently continuing repression of Indian life and leadership; nor to that Atlantic slave trade which underwrote the wealth of Europe by introducing a captive labor force into both Americas and the Caribbean, and brought the "New World" into the international economy.

We may have heard that the era of modern slavery is finished, is "history," that the genocide against tribal peoples and the expropriation of land held in trust by them are over and done with along with the last wagon trains. But such institutions and policies do not die—they mutate—and we are living them still: they are the taproots of the economic order that has taken "democracy" as its alias. Our past is seeded in our present and is trying to become our future.

These concerns engage me as a citizen, feeling daily in my relationships with my fellow citizens the effects of a system based in the accumulation of wealth—the value against which all other values must justify themselves. We all feel these effects, almost namelessly, as we go about our individual lives and as the fragments of a still ill-defined people.

But these are also my concerns as a poet, as the practitioner of an ancient and severely tested art. In a society in such extreme pain, I think these are any writer's, any artist's, concerns: the unnamed harm to human relationships, the blockage of inquiry, the oblique contempt with which we are depicted to ourselves and to others, in prevailing image making; a malnourishment that extends from the body to the imagination itself. Capital vulgarizes and reduces complex relations to a banal iconography. There is hate speech, but there is also a more generally accepted language of contempt and self-contempt—the term *baby boomers,* for instance, infantilizes and demeans an entire generation. In the interests of marketing, distinctions fade and subtleties vanish.

This devaluation of language, this flattening of images, results in a massive inarticulation, even among the educated. Language itself collapses into shallowness. Everything indeed tends toward becoming a *thing* until people can speak only in terms of the *thing,* the inert and always obsolescent commodity. We are, whatever our generation, marked as "consumers"—but what of the human energy we put forth, the actual needs we feel as distinct from the pursuit of consumption? What about the hunger no commodity can satisfy because it is not a hunger for something on a shelf? Or the hunger forced to *consume* the throwaway dinners in a fast-food restaurant dumpster?

Any artist faces the necessity to explore, by whatever means, human relationships—which may or may not be perceived as political. But there are also, and always, the changing questions of the medium itself, the craft and its demands.

The study of silence has long engrossed me. The matrix of a poet's work consists not only of what *is there* to be absorbed and worked on, but also of what is missing, *desaparecido,* rendered unspeakable, thus unthinkable. It is through these invisible holes in reality that poetry makes its way—certainly for women and other marginalized subjects and for disempowered and colonized peoples generally, but ultimately for all who practice any art at its deeper levels. The impulse to create begins—often terribly and fearfully—in a tunnel of silence. Every real poem is the breaking of an existing silence, and the first question we might ask any poem is, *What kind of voice is breaking silence, and what kind of silence is being broken?*

And yet I need to say here that silence is not always or necessarily oppressive, it is not always or necessarily a denial or extinguishing of some reality. It can be fertilizing, it can bathe the imagination, it can, as in great open spaces—I think of those plains stretching far below the Hopi mesas in Arizona—be the nimbus of a way of life, a condition of vision. Such living silences are more and more endangered throughout the world, by commerce and appropriation. Even in conversation, here in North America, we who so eagerly unpack our most private concerns before strangers dread the imaginative space that silence might open between two people or within a group. Television, obviously, abhors such silence.

But the silence I abhor is dead silence, like a dead spot in an auditorium, a dead telephone, silence where language needed to be and was prevented. I am talking about the silence of a Lexan-sealed isolation cell in a maximum security prison, of evidence destroyed, of a language forbidden to be spoken, a vocabulary declared defunct, questions forbidden to be asked. I am also thinking of the dead sound of senseless noise, of verbal displacement, when a rich and active idiom is replaced by banal and inoffensive speech, or words of active courage by the bluster of false transgression, crudely offensive yet finally impotent.

Never has the silence of displacement been so deafening and so omnipresent. Poetic language lives, labors, amid this displacement; and so does political vision.

I've been reflecting—not so much nostalgically as critically—on the early 1970s, when the emergent women's liberation movement was pouring its vitality into a great many channels: organizing, theorizing, institution building, communications, the arts, research, and journalism. For most of the women engaged with that movement, at least for a while, there was an unforgettable sense of coming alive, of newness and connectedness. You could feel the power of a social critique, a politics, that seemed capable of clarifying previously mystified and haunted terrain. Seeded for over a century in the continuity of other movements for justice—labor, anti-lynching, civil rights, anti-imperialism, antimilitarism, socialism—it called those movements to account for perpetuating old injuries of misogyny, old sexual divisions of power.

A certain elasticity of economic opportunities and means in that period, combined with intense intellectual and creative ferment, made it possible to imagine hitherto nonexistent resources and then work to realize them: women's centers for politics and culture, rape-crisis hotlines and counseling, action groups for reproductive rights, safe houses for battered women and their children, feminist health clinics and credit unions, and also feminist and lesbian presses, newspapers, arts journals, bookstores, theater, film and video collectives, cultural workshops and institutes. As always, the new liberatory politics broke open new cultural and intellectual space. For a period at least, political analysis and activism were interactive with cultural work, and "women's culture" had not broken itself off from "women's liberation."

Quite apart from the media's brief blaze of attention on a few white faces, the movement created its own spaces for dissent and disputation. The very idea of a monolithic movement was disputed early on by working-class women, by socialist feminists, by women of color, by lesbians, by women who were all of these. There were confrontations about hierarchy and democracy, about which women speak for women and how and why; about sexuality; about how racial and class separations frame what we see and how we set about organizing. There were the tenacity and courage of those who stood up in meeting after meeting to say again what others did not want to hear: that the basic facts of inequality and power in North America cannot be addressed in gender terms only.

Granting authority to women's experience as that which has been disprized, distorted, obliterated, this movement also had to reckon with the fact that on the other side of silence women have enormous *differences* of experience.

"Identity politics" was one attempt to address this contradiction. I first encountered the term in a much-discussed and widely reprinted black feminist manifesto, the Combahee River Collective statement, first published in 1977.[1] This "identity politics" was a necessary response to the devaluation and invisibility of African American women in all movements, but it was implicitly and explicitly seen as moving toward solidarity. The project of changing structures of inequality would be carried on from a self-conscious and analytic knowledge of one's own location in the intersections of gender, race, class, sexual orientation. This self-consciousness was a necessary step toward the self-definition of African American women against both white and male self-universalizing, but it was not an end in itself. The collective voiced its own "need to do political work and to move beyond consciousness-raising and serving exclusively as an emotional support group."

Had such a reading of "identity politics" been responsively taken up by a critical mass of white women, it might have led us to see—and act on—the racialization of *our* lives, how our experiences of color and class were shaped by capitalist patriarchy's variant and contradictory uses for different female identities. As the 1980s wore on, "identity" became a synonym for "safe space" in which alikeness rather than difference could be explored. An often stifling self-reference and narrow group chauvinism developed.

Meanwhile, capitalism lost no time in rearranging itself around this phenomenon called "feminism," bringing some women closer to centers of power while extruding most others at an accelerating rate. A narrow identity politics could easily be displayed on a buffet table of lifestyles by the caterers of personal solutions. We are learning that only a politics of the whole society can resist such assimilation.

I have focused briefly on the women's liberation movement both because of my own ongoing stake in it and because it embodied for a while the kind of creative space a liberatory political movement can make possible: "a visionary relation to reality."[2] Why this happens has something to do with the sheer power of a collective imagining of change and a sense of collective hope. Coming together with others to define common desires and needs, and to identify the forces that frustrate them, can be a strong tonic for the imagination. And there has been a vital dynamic between art—here I speak particularly of writing, a seizing of language, a transformation of subjectivity—and the continuing life of movements for social transformation. Where language and images help us name and recognize ourselves and our condition, and practical activity for liberation renews and challenges art, there is a complementarity as necessary as the circulation of the blood. Liberatory politics is, after all, not simply opposition but an expression of the impulse to create the new, an expanding sense of what's *humanly possible.*

The movements of the 1960s and the 1970s in the United States were openings out of apertures previously sealed, into collective imagination and hope. They wore their own blinders, made their own misjudgments. They have been relentlessly trivialized, derided, and demonized by the Right and by what's now known as the political center. They have also been disparaged, as Aijaz Ahmad notes, in many of the texts of postmodernism, as mere "false consciousness" or "folly," while in academic critical theory Marxist or socialist thought may be dismissed outright or treated "as a method primarily of *reading.*"[3]

In this time of manic official optimism and much public denial and despair, I know that the present generation of students must and will negotiate their own ways among such claims. Yet when I think of the political education of students now in college, I have to think of the political silences and displacements of the past twenty years. I think of the fabric of discussion, the great rents in that fabric, about the packaging and marketing of each generation's prefabricated desires and needs.

I have deplored the retreat into the personal as a current fetish of mass-market culture. The conglomerate publishing industry stays afloat in part on a blurry slick of heavily promoted self-help literature, personal memoirs by early bloomers, celebrity biographies, the packaging of authors complete with sex scandals and lawsuits. From television talk shows and interviews you might deduce that all human interactions are limited to individual predicaments, family injuries, personal confessions and revelations.

The relationship of the individual to a community, to social power, and to the great upheavals of collective human experience will always be the richest and most complex of questions. The blotted-out question might well be: With any personal history, what is to be done? What do we know when we know your story? *With whom do you believe your lot is cast?*

If I seem to come down hard on "the personal," it's not because I undervalue individual experience, or the human impulse to narrative, or because I believe in any kind of simplistic "universal"—male or female, old or new. Garrett Hongo gives an eloquent account of the personal essay as one means for a community to come to know itself, to reject both external and internal stereotyping, to hear "stories that are somehow forbidden and tagged as aberrational, as militant, as depraved."

> For a writer, as you live in this kind of silence, in this kind of misery, not knowing quite what it is that the world is not giving you, . . . that your work cannot address as yet, you are at the beginning of a critique of culture and society. It is the moment when powerful personal alienation slips into critical thinking— the origin of imagination. It is this initial step of intellection that enables the emergence of new, transformative, even revolutionary creativity. It occurs at the juncture between the production of art and the exercise of deep critical thought.[4]

Conglomerate publishing and marketing have little interest in such junctures.

I have been trying to decipher the moral ecology of this non-accountable economy, this old order calling itself new. What are its effects on our emotional and affectional and intellectual life? Over the past decade I would have found it harder to look steadily and long at the scene around us without using Marx's perception that economic relationships—the relationships of production—will, unchecked, infiltrate all other social relationships at the public and the most private levels. Not that Marx thought that feelings, spirit, human relationships are just inert products of the economy. Rather, he was outraged by capital's treatment of human labor and human energy as a means, its hostility to the development of the whole person, its reduction of the entire web of existence to commodity: what can be produced and sold for profit. *In place of all the physical and spiritual senses,* he tells us, *there is the sense of possession, which is the alienation of all these senses.*[5] Marx was passionate about the insensibility of a system that must extract ever more humanity from the human being: time and space for love, for sleep and dreaming, time to create art, time for both solitude and communal life, time to explore the idea of an expanding universe of freedom.

For a few years now, the Republican Congress and the Right have been repetitiously characterized by the term *mean-spirited*. By extension, the same phrase has been used to describe the mood of the disgruntled American voter. I have always found this term suspiciously off the mark. If it were only a matter of spirits! Mean-spiritedness has been as American as cherry pie—alongside other tendencies: it has designated a parochial or provincial strain in a greater social texture.

Mean-spiritedness as a generalized social symptom suggests an inexplicable national mood, a bad attitude, a souring of social conscience and compassion. But people don't succumb to sourness, resentment, and fear for no reason. The phrase directs us toward social behavior but not to the economic relationships that Marx perceived as staining all social behavior. It refers to attitude but not to policies and powers and the interests they serve. It's a diversionary piece of cant that obscures the lived impact of increasingly cruel legislation and propaganda against poor people, immigrants, women, children, youth, the old, the sick—all who are at risk to begin with—and that also masks the erosion of modest middle-class hopes, in the name of the market or of a chimera known as the balanced budget.

We have all seen attempts to graph numerically the effects of these policies: numbers of people who have slid from apartments or rented rooms or splintered households into the streets; a population of working people without health care, child care, safe and affordable shelter. But each of these people is more than a body to be counted: each is a mind and a soul. Numbers of children left alone or in the care of other children so parents can work; of children doing time in schools that are no more than holding pens for youth and lethal for many. Each of these children possesses an intelligence, creative urge, and capacity that cannot be accounted for by quantifying. Numbers of working people, blue-collar and white-collar, who have lost full-time jobs with pensions to so-called downsizing and restructuring and the export of the production process—working several jobs piecemeal for ever-sinking wages and with mandatory overtime. Each of these people is more than a pinpoint on a chart: each was born to her or his own usefulness and uniqueness. Numbers of prisons now under construction—a "growth industry" in this country, whose public schools and urban hospitals are disintegrating. These prisons, too, are holding pens for youth, disproportionately so for young African American men. The prison as shadow factory, where inmates assemble, at 35 cents an hour, parts for cars and computers, or take telephone reservations for TWA and Best Western—a captive cheap labor force. Women—of all colors—are the fastest growing incarcerated group, two-thirds being mothers of dependent children. A growing population of lifers and people on death row. A death-penalty system tabulated strenuously to race. In the words of the death-row journalist Mumia Abu-Jamal, "the barest illusion of rehabilitation [is being] replaced by dehumanization by design"[6] in the maximum-security, sensory-deprivation units of the penal system in the United States, and in prison policies overall.

Each of these women and men "inside" has, or once had, a self to offer the world, a presence. And the slippage toward prison of those "outside"—so many of them young—who feel themselves becoming social and economic discards, is a process obscured by catchwords like *drugs* and *crime*. We are supposed to blink away from that reality. But what happens behind bars, in any country, isn't sealed off from the quality of civil life. "Dehumanization by design" cannot take place behind bars without also occurring in public space at large. In the public spaces of the wealthiest, most powerful of all nations, ours.

Against a background and foreground of crisis, of technology dazzling in means and maniacally violent in substance, among declarations of resignation and predictions of social chaos, I have from time to time—I know I'm not alone in this—felt almost unbearable foreboding, a terrifying loss of gravity, and furious grief. I'm a writer in a country where native-born fascistic tendencies, allied to the practices of free marketing, have been trying to eviscerate language of meaning. I have often felt doubly cut off: that I cannot effectively be heard, and that those voices I need most to hear are being cut off from me. Any writer has necessary questions as to whether her words deserve to stand, whether his are worth reading. But it's also been a question, for me, of feeling that almost everything that has fertilized and sustained my work is in danger. I have known that this is, in fact, the very material I have to work with: it is not "in spite of the times" that I will write, but I will try to write, in both senses, *out of my time.*

(There is a 1973 painting by Dorothea Tanning in which the arm of the woman painter literally breaks through the canvas: we don't see the brush, we see the arm up to the wrist, and the gash in the material. That, viscerally, depicts what it means to me, to try to write *out of one's time.*)

I have stayed connected with activism and with people whose phoenix politics are reborn continually out of the nest charred by hostility and lying. I have talked long with other friends. I have searched for words—my own and those of other writers. I've been drawn to those writers, in so many world locations, who have felt the need to question the very activity their lives had been shaped around: to interrogate the value of the written word in the face of many kinds of danger, enormous human needs. I wasn't looking for easy reassurances but rather for evidence that others, in other societies, also had to struggle with that question.

Whatever her or his social identity, the writer is, by the nature of the act of writing, someone who strives for communication and connection, someone who searches, through language, to keep alive the conversation with what Octavio Paz has called "the lost community." Even if what's written feels like a note thrust into a bottle to be thrown into the sea. The Palestinian poet Mahmoud Darwish writes of the incapacity of poetry to find a linguistic equivalent to conditions such as the 1982 Israeli shelling of Beirut: *We are now not to describe, as much as we are to be described. We're being born totally, or else dying totally.* In his remarkable prose-meditation on that war, he also says, *Yet I want to break into song. . . . I want to find a language that transforms language itself into steel for the spirit—a language to use against these sparkling silver insects, these jets. I want to sing. I want a language that I can lean on and that can lean on me, that asks*

*me to bear witness and that I can ask to bear witness, to what power
there is in us to overcome this cosmic isolation.*[7]

Darwish writes from the heart of a military massacre. The
Caribbean-Canadian poet Dionne Brand writes from colonial diaspora: *I've had moments when the life of my people has been so overwhelming to bear that poetry seemed useless, and I cannot say that
there is any moment when I do not think that now.* Yet finally, she
admits, like Darwish: *Poetry is here, just here. Something wrestling
with how we live, something dangerous, something honest.*[8]

I've gone back many times to Eduardo Galeano's essay "In Defense
of the Word," in which he says:

> I do not share the attitude of those writers who claim for them-
> selves divine privileges not granted to ordinary mortals, nor
> of those who beat their breasts and rend their clothes as they
> clamor for public pardon for having lived a life devoted to serv-
> ing a useless vocation. Neither so godly, nor so contemptible. . . .
>
> The prevailing social order perverts or annihilates the cre-
> ative capacity of the immense majority of people and reduces
> the possibility of creation—an age-old response to human
> anguish and the certainty of death—to its professional exer-
> cise by a handful of specialists. How many "specialists" are we
> in Latin America? For whom do we write, whom do we reach?
> Where is our real public? (Let us mistrust applause. At times we
> are congratulated by those who consider us innocuous.)
>
> To claim that literature on its own is going to change reality
> would be an act of madness or arrogance. It seems to me no less
> foolish to deny that it can aid in making this change.[9]

Galeano's "defense" was written after his magazine, *Crisis,* was
closed down by the Argentine government. As a writer in exile, he
has continued to interrogate the place of the written word, of literature, in a political order that forbids literacy and creative expression
to so many; that denies the value of literature as a vehicle for social
change even as it fears its power. Like Nadine Gordimer in South
Africa, he knows that censorship can assume many faces, from the

shutting down of magazines and the banning of books by some writers, to the imprisonment and torture of others, to the structural censorship produced by utterly unequal educational opportunities and by restricted access to the means of distribution—both features of North American society that have become more and more pronounced over the past two decades.

I question the "free" market's devotion to freedom of expression. Let's bear in mind that when threats of violence came down against the publication and selling of Salman Rushdie's *Satanic Verses,* the chain bookstores took it off their shelves, while independent booksellers continued to stock it. The various small, independent presses in this country, which have had an integral relationship with the independent booksellers, are walking a difficult and risky edge as costs rise, support funding dwindles, and corporate distribution becomes more monolithic. The survival of a great diversity of books, and of work by writers far less internationally notable than Rushdie, depends on diverse interests having the means to make such books available.

It also means a nonelite but educated audience, a population who are literate, who read and talk to each other, who may be factory workers or bakers or bank tellers or paramedicals or plumbers or computer consultants or farmworkers, whose first language may be Croatian or Tagalog or Spanish or Vietnamese but who are given to critical thinking, who care about art, an intelligentsia beyond intellectual specialists.

I have encountered a bracingly hard self-questioning and self-criticism in politically embattled writers, along with their belief that language can be a vital instrument in combating unreality and lies. I have been grateful for their clarity, whether as to Latin America, South Africa, the Caribbean, North America, or the Middle East, about the systems that abuse and waste the majority of human lives. Overall, there is the conviction—and these are writers of poetry, fiction, travel, fantasy—that the writer's freedom to communicate can't be severed from universal public education and universal public access to the word.

Universal public education has two possible—and contradictory—

missions. One is the development of a literate, articulate, and well-informed citizenry so that the democratic process can continue to evolve and the promise of radical equality can be brought closer to realization. The other is the perpetuation of a class system dividing an elite, nominally "gifted" few, tracked from an early age, from a very large underclass essentially to be written off as alienated from language and science, from poetry and politics, from history and hope, an underclass to be funneled—whatever its dreams and hopes—toward low-wage temporary jobs. The second is the direction our society has taken. The results are devastating in terms of the betrayal of a generation of youth. The loss to the whole society is incalculable.

But to take the other direction, to choose an imaginative, highly developed, educational system that would serve all citizens at every age—a vast, shared, public schooling in which each of us felt a stake, as with public roads, there when needed, ready when you choose to use them—this would mean changing almost everything else.

It would mean refusing, categorically, the shallow premises of official pieties and banalities. As Jonathan Kozol writes in a "Memo to President Clinton":

> You have spoken at times of the need to put computers into ghetto schools, to set up zones of enterprise in ghetto neighborhoods, and to crack down more aggressively on crime in ghetto streets. Yet you have never asked the nation to consider whether ghetto schools and the ghetto itself represent abhorrent, morally offensive institutions. Is the ghetto . . . to be accepted as a permanent cancer on the body of American democracy? Is its existence never to be challenged? Is its persistence never to be questioned? Is it the moral agenda of our President to do no more than speak about more comely versions of apartheid, of entrepreneurial segregation . . . ?[10]

Well, but of course, voices are saying, we're now seeing the worst of breakaway capitalism, even one or two millionaires are wondering if things haven't gone far enough. Perhaps the thing can be restructured, reinvented? After all, it's all we've got, the only system we in this country have ever known! Without capitalism's lure of high stakes and risk, its glamour of individual power, how could we have conceived, designed, developed the astonishing technological fireworks of the end of this century—this technology with the power to generate ever more swiftly obsolescent products for consumption, ever more wondrous connections among the well connected?

Other voices speak of a technology that can redeem or rescue us. Some who are part of this pyrotechnic moment see it as illuminating enormous possibilities—in education, for one instance. Yet how will this come about without consistent mentoring and monitoring by nontechnical, nonprofit-oriented interests? And where will such mentoring come from? whose power will validate it?

Is technology, rather than democracy, our destiny? Who, what groups, give it direction and purpose? To whom does it really belong? What should be its content? With spectacular advances in medical technology, why not free universal health care? If computers in every ghetto school, why ghettos at all? and why not classroom teachers who are well trained and well paid? If national defense is the issue, why not, as poet-activist Frances Payne Adler suggests, a "national defense" budget that defends the people through affordable health, education, and shelter for everyone? *Why should such minimal social needs be so threatening*? Technology—magnificent, but merely a means after all—will not of itself resolve questions like these.

We need to begin changing the questions. To become less afraid to ask the still-unanswered questions posed by Marxism, socialism and communism. Not to interrogate old, corrupt hierarchical systems, but to ask anew, for our own time: What constitutes ownership? What is work? How can people be assured of a just share in the products of their precious human exertions? How can we move from a production system in which human labor is merely a disposable means to a process that depends on and expands connective relationships, mutual respect, the dignity of work, the fullest possible development of the human subject? How much inequality will we go on tolerating in the world's richest and most powerful nation? What, anyway, is social wealth? Is it only to be defined as private ownership? What does the much abused and trampled word *revolution* mean to us? How can revolutions be prevented from locking in on themselves? how can women and men together imagine "revolution in permanence," continually unfolding through time?

And if we are writers writing first of all from our own desire and need, if this is irresistible work for us, if in writing we experience certain kinds of power and freedom that may be unavailable to us in other ways—surely it would follow that we would want to make that kind of forming, shaping, naming, telling, accessible for anyone who can use it. It would seem only natural for writers to care passionately about literacy, public education, public libraries, public opportunities in all the arts. But more: if we care about the freedom of the word, about language as a liberatory current, if we care about the imagination, we will care about economic justice.

For the pull and suck of Capital's project tend toward reducing, not expanding, overall human intelligence, wit, expressiveness, creative rebellion. If free enterprise is to be totalizingly free, a value in and for itself, it can have no stake in other realms of value. It may pay lip service to charitable works, but its drive is toward what works for the accumulation of wealth; this is a monomaniacal system. Certainly it cannot enrich the realm of the social imagination, least of all the imagination of solidarity and cooperative human endeavor, the unfulfilled imagination of radical equality.

In a poem written in the early 1970s in Argentina, just as the political ground was shifting to a right-wing consolidation, military government, torture, disappearances and massacres, the poet Juan Gelman reflects on delusions of political compromise. The poem is called "Clarities":

> who has seen the dove marry the hawk
> mistrust affection the exploited the exploiter? false
> are such unspeakable marriages
> disasters are born of such marriages discord sadness

how long can the house of such a marriage last?
> wouldn't

the least breeze grind it down destroy it the sky crush it
> to ruins? oh, my country!

sad! enraged! beautiful! oh my country facing the firing
> squad!

stained with revolutionary blood!

the parrots the color of mitre
that go clucking in almost every tree
and courting on every branch
are they more alone? less alone? lonely? for

who has seen the butcher marry the tender calf
tenderness marry capitalism? false
are such unspeakable marriages
disasters are born of such marriages discord sadness
> clarities such as

the day itself spinning in the iron cupola
above this poem[11]

I have talked at some length about capitalism's drive to disenfranchise and dehumanize, to invade the very zones of feeling and relationship we deal with as writers—which Marx described long ago—because those processes still need to be described as doing what they still do. I have spoken from the perspective of a writer and a longtime teacher, trying to grasp the ill winds and the sharp veerings of her time—a human being who thinks of herself as an artist, and then must ask herself what that means.

I want to end by saying this to you: We're not simply trapped in the present. We are not caged within a narrowing corridor at "the end of history." Nor do any of us have to windsurf on the currents of a system that depends on the betrayal of so many others. We do have choices. We're living through a certain part of history that

needs us to live it and make it and write it. We can make that history with many others, people we will never know. Or, we can live
in default, under protest perhaps, but neutered in our senses and in
our sympathies.

We have to keep on asking the questions still being defined as
nonquestions—the ones beginning *Why* . . . ? *What if* . . . ? We will be
told these are childish, naive, "pre-postmodern" questions. They are
the imagination's questions.

Many of you in this audience are professional intellectuals, or
studying to become so, or are otherwise engaged in the activities
of a public university. Writers and intellectuals can name, we can
describe, we can depict, we can witness—without sacrificing craft,
nuance, or beauty. Above all, and at our best, we may sometimes help
question the questions.

Let us try to do this, if we do it, without grandiosity. Let's recognize too, without false humility, the limits of the zone in which we
work. Writing and teaching are kinds of work, and the relative creative freedom of the writer or teacher depends on the conditions of
human labor overall and everywhere.

For what are we, anyway, at our best, but one small, persistent
cluster in a greater ferment of human activity—still and forever turning toward, tuned for, the possible, the unrealized and irrepress-
ible design?

A Human Eye
(2009)

PERMEABLE MEMBRANE (2005)

1

Poetic imagination or intuition is never merely unto itself, free-floating, or self-enclosed. It's radical, meaning root-tangled in the grit of human arrangements and relationships: *how we are with each other.*

The medium is language intensified, intensifying our sense of possible reality.

2

Ghostly touch on the shoulder: dust motes of air inhaled, snatch of talk heard boarding a plane, music stored in memory. A smell provokes another sensation, a half-forgotten scene. Dream remnant. "Room sound," as in audio recording.

Working on a draft, I move by touch through what I can't see clearly. My finger on the shoulder of the ghost who first touched mine. As my eyes adjust to dimness, the shape of what I'm doing declares itself. The poem makes its needs felt, becomes both my guide and my critic.

Behind and overall there's the interpenetration of subjectivity and social being. Gleaning, not at first consciously selecting. Dissatisfaction, impulse to look at the world anew, scrape at the wounds, refuse popular healings and panaceas, official concoctions. I've learnt how

This appeared in a symposium on my work in the *Virginia Quarterly Review* (Spring 2006): 208–210, and is here slightly revised.

much this work depends on knowing myself—including how astray I can go, have gone, but also trusting how certain poetic choices have taken me beyond any conscious knowing.

I've wanted to write subjective visions of objective conditions. But this sounds like a program. Say rather: Poems become suffused, as the existence, the inner life of the maker must, with what's going on, the breaks in the assumed fabric. The makings of art are rooted in non-art labors—repetitive, toxic, body-breaking, minimum wage or less or none—that everywhere underlie those privileged creations. What you do and don't see. What is seeing you. Eyes in the thicket, eyes in the street.

I need to reach beyond interior decoration, biography. Art is a way of melting out through one's own skin. "What, who is this about?" is not the essential question. A poem is not *about*; it is *out of* and *to*. Passionate language in movement. The deep structure is always musical, and physical—as breath, as pulse.

3

In the culturally stunned, dystopic states of North America a poet needs a different (though no greater) kind of faith and commitment from that of poets under other cruel and t/ruthless political regimes. Faith in poetry itself, more perhaps than has been required in other, older societies. Commitment to a poetics not defined by the market, not complacent courtier verse or prose cut by template. A poetics of longing, of organic necessity.

Mayakovsky: **The presence of a problem in society, the solution of which is conceivable only in poetic terms. A social command.**[1] I read him as saying that for the poet the problem is insoluble by her or him alone, yet he or she feels an urgency to meet it with poetry.

That urgency—emotional as a love affair—is finally the source and meaning of my work. Why go for anything less?

Mayakovsky was writing about making poetry within a socialist revolution: a moment, as it seemed, of widening hopes for human possibilities. The battering of those hopes, both from within and without, was an international tragedy. Here, as "winners" of the Cold War, we're watchers at the bedside of a sick democracy, trans-fixed and emotionally paralyzed. Public conversation stripped of a common imagination of what's "humanly possible," of human soli-darity, of motives other than fear, shopping, and disgust.

In the doorway hovers a waiting dictatorship; let us listen to its language: **We also have to work, though, sort of, the dark side . . . use any means at our disposal, basically, to achieve our objective.**[2]

We want to believe the fever can break, the sick body politic come back to life.

In such a crisis the efficacy of any art is not measurable by its quantifiable mass distribution. If it ever was.

4

There's a permeable membrane between art and society. A continu-ous dialectical motion. Tides brining the estuary. River flowing into sea. A writer describes the landmass-"stained" current of the Congo River as discernible three hundred miles out on the ocean.[3] Like-wise: the matter of art enters the bloodstream of social energy. Call and response. The empathetic imagination can transform, but we can't identify precise loci of transformation, can't track or quantify the moments. Nor say how or when they lead, through innumerable unpredictable passageways toward re-creating survival, undermin-ing illegimate power and its cruelties.

Nor how newly unlocked social energies, movements of people, demand a renewed social dialogue with art: a spontaneous release of language and forms.

René Char: **The poet bursts the bonds of what he touches. He does not teach the end of bonds.**[4]

She cannot teach the end of bonds; but she can refuse to justify, accord with, ignore their existence.

POETRY AND THE
FORGOTTEN FUTURE (2006)

1

Poets, readers of poetry, strangers, and friends, I'm honored and glad to be here among you.

There's an invisible presence in this room whom I want to invoke: the great Scottish Marxist bard Hugh MacDiarmid. I'll begin by reading from his exuberant, discursive manifesto called, bluntly, "The Kind of Poetry I Want." I'll offer a few extracts and hope you'll read the whole poem for yourselves:

> A poetry the quality of which
> Is a stand made against intellectual apathy,
> Its material founded, like Gray's, on difficult knowledge
> And its metres those of a poet
> Who has studied Pindar and Welsh poetry,
> But, more than that, its words coming from a mind
> Which has experienced the sifted layers on layers
> Of human lives—aware of the innumerable dead
> And the innumerable to-be-born . . .
> A speech, a poetry, to bring to bear upon life
> The concentrated strength of all our being . . .

Plenary Lecture, Conference on Poetry and Politics, University of Stirling, Scotland, July 13, 2006. First published in 2007 as *Poetry and Commitment*, a chapbook, by W. W. Norton & Company.

Is not this what we require?— ...
A fineness and profundity of organization
Which is the condition of a variety enough
To express all the world's ...

In photographic language, "wide-angle" poems ...
A poetry like an operating theatre
Sparkling with a swift, deft energy,
Energy quiet and contained and fearfully alert,
In which the poet exists only as a nurse during an operation

. . . .

A poetry in which the images
Work up on each other's shoulders like Zouave acrobats,
Or strange and fascinating as the Javanese dancer,
Retna Mohini, or profound and complicated
Like all the work of Ram Gopal and his company ...

Poetry of such an integration as cannot be effected
Until a new and conscious organization of society
Generates a new view
Of the world as a whole ...

—A learned poetry wholly free
of the brutal love of ignorance;
And the poetry of a poet with no use
For any of the simpler forms of personal success.

A manifesto of desire for "a new and conscious organization of society" and a poetic view to match it. A manifesto that acknowledges the scope, tensions, and contradictions of the poet's undertaking. Let's bear in mind the phrases "difficult knowledge," "the concentrated strength of all our being," the poem as "wide-angled," but also the image of the poet as nurse in the operating theater: "fearfully alert."

2

What I'd like to do here is touch on some aspects of poetry as it's created and received in an even more violently politicized and brutally divided world than the one MacDiarmid knew. This won't be a shapely lecture; rather, I'll be scanning the terrain of poetry and commitment with many jump-cuts, hoping some of this may rub off in other sessions and conversations.

To begin: what do I mean by commitment?

I'll flash back to 1821: Shelley's claim, in "The Defence of Poetry," that "poets are the unacknowledged legislators of the world." Piously overquoted, mostly out of context, it's taken to suggest that simply by virtue of composing verse, poets exert some exemplary moral power—in a vague, unthreatening way. In fact, in his earlier political essay "A Philosophic View of Reform," Shelley had written that "Poets *and philosophers* [italics mine] are the unacknowledged" etc. The philosophers he was talking about were revolutionary-minded: Thomas Paine, William Godwin, Voltaire, Mary Wollstonecraft.

And Shelley was, no mistake, out to change the legislation of his time. For him there was no contradiction among poetry, political philosophy, and active confrontation with illegitimate authority. This was perfectly apparent to the reviewer in the *High Tory Quarterly* who mocked him as follows:

> Mr. Shelley would abrogate our laws. . . . He would abolish the rights of property. . . . He would pull down our churches, level our Establishment, and burn our bibles. . . .

His poem "Queen Mab," denounced and suppressed when first printed, was later pirated in a kind of free-speech movement and sold in cheap editions on street stalls in the industrial neighborhoods of Manchester, Birmingham, and London. There, it found plenty of enthusiastic readers among a literate working and middle class of trade unionists and Chartists. In it, Queen Mab surveys the world's disorders and declares:

This is no unconnected misery,
Nor stands uncaused and irretrievable.
Man's evil nature, that apology
Which kings who rule and cowards who crouch, set up
For their unnumbered crimes, sheds not the blood
Which desolates the discord-wasted land.

. . . .

NATURE!—No!
Kings, priests and statesmen blast the human flower. . . .

Shelley, in fact, saw powerful institutions, not original sin or "human nature," as the source of human misery. For him, art bore an integral relationship to the "struggle between Revolution and Oppression." His West Wind was the "trumpet of a prophecy," driving "dead thoughts . . . like withered leaves, to quicken a new birth."

He did *not* say, "Poets are the unacknowledged interior decorators of the world."

3

Pursuing this theme of the committed poet and the action of poetry in the world: two interviews, both from 1970.

A high official of the Greek military junta asks the poet Yannis Ritsos, then under house arrest: "You are a poet. Why do you get mixed up in politics?"

Ritsos answers, "A poet is the first citizen of his country and for this very reason it is the duty of the poet to be concerned about the politics of his country."

A Communist, he had been interned in fascist prison camps from 1947 to 1953; one of his books was publicly burned. For most of his countrymen he was indeed a "first citizen," a voice for a nation battered by invasion, occupation, and civil war—in poems of densely figurative beauty. As such, he was also a world citizen. His long poem "Romiosini," from its own place and era, speaks to the wars

and military occupations of the twenty-first century (I extract from
Kimon Friar's translation):

> This landscape is as harsh as silence,
> it hugs to its breast the scorching stones,
> clasps in the light its orphaned olive trees and vineyards,
> clenches its teeth. There is no water. Light only.
> Roads vanish in light and the shadow of the sheepfold is
>   made of iron.
>
> Trees, rivers, and voices have turned to stone in the sun's
>   quicklime.
> Roots trip on marble. Dust-laden lentisk shrubs.
> Mules and rocks. All panting. There is no water.
> All are parched. For years now. All chew a morsel of sky to
>   choke down
>   their bitterness. . . .
>
> In the field the last swallow had lingered late,
> balancing in the air like a black ribbon on the sleeve of
>   autumn.
> Nothing else remained. Only the burned houses
>   smouldering still.
>
> The others left us some time ago to lie under the stones,
> with their torn shirts and their vows scratched on the fallen
>   door.
> No one wept. We had no time. Only the silence grew deeper
>   still. . . .
> It will be hard for us to forget their hands,
> it will be hard for hands calloused on a trigger to question a
>   daisy. . . .
>
> Every night in the fields the moon turns the magnificent
>   dead over on their backs,

searching their faces with savage, frozen fingers to find her
  son
by the cut of his chin and his stony eyebrows,
searching their pockets. She will always find something.
  There is
               always something to find.
A locket with a splinter of the Cross. A stubbed-out
  cigarette.
A key, a letter, a watch stopped at seven.
We wind up the watch again. The hours plod on . . .

This was Greece speaking; today it could be Gaza or Iraq, Afghanistan or Lebanon.

Second interview. The South African poet Dennis Brutus, when asked about poetry and political activity: "I believe that the poet—as a poet—has no obligation to be committed, but the man—as a man—has an obligation to be committed. What I'm saying is that I think everybody ought to be committed and the poet is just one of the many 'everybodies.' "

Dennis Brutus wrote, acted on, was imprisoned then exiled for his opposition to the South African apartheid regime. And he continues to act and write in the international sphere in movements for global economic justice. I'll read one epigrammatically terse poem—not typical of his work but expressing a certain point:

An old black woman,
suffering,
tells me I have given her
"new images"

—a father bereaved
by radical heroism
finds consolation
in my verse.

then I know
these are those I write for
and my verse works.

My verse works. In two senses: as participant in political struggle, and at the personal, visceral level where it's received and its
witness acknowledged. These are two responses to the question
of poetry and commitment, which I take as complementary, not in
opposition.

What's at stake here is the recognition of poetry as what James
Scully calls "social practice." He distinguishes between "protest
poetry" and "dissident poetry": Protest poetry is "conceptually shallow," "reactive," predictable in its means, too often a hand-wringing
from the sidelines.

Dissident poetry, however [he writes] **does not respect boundaries between private and public, self and other. In breaking
boundaries, it breaks silences, speaking for, or at best, with,
the silenced; opening poetry up, putting it into the middle of
life. . . . It is a poetry that talks back, that would act as part of
the world, not simply as a mirror of it.**

4

I'm both a poet and one of the "everybodies" of my country. I live, in
poetry and daily experience, with manipulated fear, ignorance, cultural confusion, and social antagonism huddling together on the fault
line of an empire. In my lifetime I've seen the breakdown of rights
and citizenship where ordinary "everybodies," poets or not, have left
politics to a political class bent on shoveling the elemental resources,
the public commons of the entire world, into private control. Where
democracy has been left to the raiding of "acknowledged" legislators, the highest bidders. In short, to a criminal element.

Ordinary, comfortable Americans have looked aside when our
fraternally-twinned parties—Democrat and Republican—have
backed dictatorships against popular movements abroad; as their
covert agencies, through torture and assassination, through supplied

weapons and military training, have propped up repressive parties and regimes in the name of anticommunism and our "national interests." Why did we think fascistic methods, the subversion of civil and human rights, would be contained somewhere else? Because as a nation, we've clung to a self-righteous false innocence, eyes shut to our own scenario, our body politic's internal bleeding.

But internal bleeding is no sudden symptom. That uncannily prescient African American writer James Baldwin asked his country, a quarter century ago: "If you don't know my father, how can you know the people in the streets of Tehran?"

This year, a report from the Bureau of Justice Statistics finds that 1 out of every 136 residents of the United States is behind bars: many in jails, unconvicted. That the percentage of black men in prison or jail is almost 12 to 1 over white male prisoners. That the states with the highest rates of incarceration and execution are those with the poorest populations.

We often hear that—by contrast with, say, Nigeria or Egypt, China or the former Soviet Union—the West doesn't imprison dissident writers. But when a nation's criminal justice system imprisons so many—often on tawdry evidence and botched due process—to be tortured in maximum security units or on death row, overwhelmingly because of color and class, it is in effect—and intention—silencing potential and actual writers, intellectuals, artists, journalists: a whole intelligentsia. The internationally known case of Mumia Abu-Jamal is emblematic but hardly unique. The methods of Abu Ghraib and Guantánamo have long been practiced in the prisons and policing of the United States.

What has all this to do with poetry? Would we have come here, from so many directions, to such a conference if "all this" had nothing to do with poetry? (We can also imagine others who might be here if not for the collision of politics with literature.) In the words of Brecht's Galileo, addressed to scientists in a newly commercial age, but equally challenging for artists: What are we working *for*?

But—let's never discount it—within every official, statistical, designated nation, there breathes another nation: of unappointed, unappeased, unacknowledged clusters of people who daily, with fierce imagination and tenacity, confront cruelties, exclusions, and indignities, signaling through those barriers—which are often literal cages—in poetry, music, street theater, murals, videos, Web sites—and through many forms of direct activism.

And this keeps happening: I began making notes for this talk last March, on a day of cold wind, flattened white light overhanging the coast where I live. Raining for almost a month. A numbing sense of dead-end, endless winter, endless war.

In the last week of March, a punitive and cynical anti-immigrant bill is introduced in Congress and passed by the House of Representatives. As most of you know, essential sectors of the Western economies depend on the low-wage labor and social vulnerability of economic refugees—especially, in the United States, from south of the border. That bill would make it a felony not just to employ, but to give medical aid, even food or water, to an "illegal" immigrant. Between the United States and Mexico, a walled, armed border would turn back those economic refugees. The hypocrisy and flagrant racism of that bill arouses a vast population. Community leaders put out the word, call the Spanish-language radio stations to announce protest gatherings. Suddenly—though such events are never really sudden—a massive series of oppositional marches pours into the streets of Los Angeles, Chicago, New York, Detroit, Atlanta, Denver, Houston, and other large and smaller cities and towns—the largest demonstrations in the history of many of those cities. Not only people from Mexico and Central America, but immigrant groups from Asia, Africa, the Caribbean, the Philippines, from Arab-American communities: families, students, activists, unions, clergy, many at risk of firing or deportation, opposing that bill. Millions of people. A working-class movement different from earlier movements. A new articulation of dignity and solidarity. And a new politicized generation growing in part out of those marches—in, for example, a coalition of young Latinos and African Americans.

Of course, there's the much larger political resistance heating up—let me simply mention Chiapas, Seattle, Buenos Aires, Genoa, Porto Alegre, Caracas, Mumbai, the streets of Paris and other European cities—not to mention worldwide women's and indigenous people's movements, which have never gone away—and the gay and lesbian liberation movements allied with, and often emerging from, these.

5

I hope never to idealize poetry—it has suffered enough from that. Poetry is not a healing lotion, an emotional massage, a kind of linguistic aromatherapy. Neither is it a blueprint, nor an instruction manual, nor a billboard. There is no universal Poetry anyway, only poetries and poetics, and the streaming, intertwining histories to which they belong. There is room, indeed necessity, for both Neruda and César Vallejo, for Pier Paolo Pasolini and Alfonsina Storni, for Audre Lorde and Aimé Césaire, for both Ezra Pound and Nelly Sachs. Poetries are no more pure and simple than human histories are pure and simple. Poetry, like silk or coffee or oil or human flesh, has had its trade routes. And there are colonized poetics and resilient poetics, transmissions across frontiers not easily traced.

Walt Whitman never separated his poetry from his vision of American democracy—a vision severely tested in a Civil War fought over the economics of slavery. Late in life he called "poetic lore . . . a conversation overheard in the dusk, from speakers far or hid, of which we get only a few broken murmurs"—the obscurity, we might think now, of democracy itself.

But also of those "dark times" in and about which Bertolt Brecht assured us there would be songs.

Poetry has been charged with "aestheticizing," thus being complicit in, the violent realities of power, of practices like collective punishment, torture, rape, and genocide. This accusation was famously invoked in Adorno's "after the Holocaust lyric poetry is impossible"—which Adorno later retracted and which a succession of Jewish poets have in their practice rejected. I'm thinking now not only of post–World War II poets like Paul Celan, Edmond Jabès, Nelly Sachs, Kadia Molodowsky, Muriel Rukeyser, Irena Klepfisz. I'm also thinking of contemporary poems in a recent collection from Israel that I've been reading in translation: *With an Iron Pen: Twenty Years of Hebrew Protest Poetry,* ignited by the atrocious policies and

practices of Israel's occupation of Palestine. There, poems of disso-
nant, harsh beauty, some thrusting images of the Occupation into
the very interior of Israeli domestic life:

> ... I open the refrigerator door
> and see a weeping roll,
> see a piece of bleeding cheese,
> a radish forced to sprout
> by shocks from wires
> and blows from fists.
> The meat on its plate
> tells of placentas
> cast aside by roadblocks. ...
>
> —*Aharon Shabtai, "The Fence," trans. Peter Cole*

—or suggesting how the poem itself endures its own knowledge:

> The poem isn't served meat and fruit
> on a silver platter at night,
> and by day its mouth does not long
> for a golden spoon or communion wafers.
> Lost, it wanders the roads of Beit Jala,
> sways like a drunk through the streets of Bethlehem,
> seeking you along the way in vain,
> searching for your shadow's shadow in the shrubs.
>
> Close to the breast, the soul sits
> curled up like a boy in a sleeping bag
> dry as a flower bulb buried in the middle of the throat.
> Then the poem feels it can't go on any longer
> wandering towards the refugee camp,
> toward the fugitives' cradle
> in the Promised Land's heavy summer
> on the path to disaster
>
> —*Rami Saari, "Searching the Land," trans. Lisa Katz*

Do poems like these "work"? How do we calculate such a thing on a day when Israel is battering its way into Gaza, bombing Lebanon? Like the activist, the poet (who may be both) has to reckon with disaster, desperation, and exhaustion—these, too, are the materials.

And in such a time—when water is poisoned, when sewage flows into houses, when air becomes unbreathable from the dust of blasted schools and hospitals—poetry must gasp for breath.

But if poetry had gone mute after every genocide in history, there would be no poetry left in the world, and this conference might have a different theme: "The Death of the Poem" perhaps?

If to "aestheticize" is to glide across brutality and cruelty, treat them merely as dramatic occasions for the artist rather than structures of power to be revealed and dismantled—much hangs on the words "merely" and "rather than." Opportunism isn't the same as committed attention. But we can also define the "aesthetic" not as a privileged and sequestered rendering of human suffering, but as news of an awareness, a resistance, that totalizing systems want to quell: art reaching into us for what's still passionate, still unintimidated, still unquenched.

Poetry has been written off on other counts: (1) it's not a mass-market "product": it doesn't get sold on airport news-stands or in supermarket aisles; (2) the actual consumption figures for poetry can't be quantified at the checkout counter; (3) it's too "difficult" for the average mind; (4) it's too elite, but the wealthy don't bid for it at Sotheby's. It is, in short, redundant. This might be called the free-market critique of poetry.

There's actually an odd correlation between these ideas: poetry is either inadequate, even immoral, in the face of human suffering, or it's unprofitable, hence useless. Either way, poets are advised to hang our heads or fold our tents. Yet in fact, throughout the world, transfusions of poetic language can and do quite literally keep bodies and souls together—and more.

Two items from recent news. One is a headline from the *San Francisco Chronicle* of July 17, 2005:

Writing Poetry Was the Balm
That Kept Guantanamo Prisoners
from Going Mad

The story follows of a Pakistani Muslim, Abdul Rahim Dost, arrested in Afghanistan and held without charges in the American detention camp at Guantánamo. There he wrote thousands of lines in Pashto, translated Arabic poetry into Pashto, at first scratching lines with his fingernail into Styrofoam cups. His brother and fellow inmate is quoted as saying that "poetry was our support and psychological uplift. . . . Many people have lost their minds there. I know 40 or 50 prisoners who are mad."

These men, detained as terrorists (released after three years), turned to poetry in the depths of Guantánamo to keep themselves sane, hold onto a sense of self and culture. So, too, the Chinese immigrants to California in the early twentieth century, detained in barracks on an island in San Francisco Bay, traced their ideograms of anger and loneliness on the walls of that prison.

But poetry sometimes also finds those who weren't looking for it.

From the Israeli newspaper *Haaretz* of November 7, 2004, comes an article by David Zonsheine, a former commander in the Israel Defense Force who became organizer and leader of the anti-Occupation movement within the IDF, the Courage to Refuse. Zonsheine comes by chance upon some lines from a poem of Yitzhak Laor and finds that

> reading these lines a moment after a violent month of reserve duty, which was full of a sense of the righteousness of the way, was no easy thing. I remember that for one alarming moment I felt that I was looking at something I was forbidden to see. What this thing was I did not know, but on that same Friday afternoon I went out to look for every book by Yitzhak Laor that I could find in the shops.

Zonsheine continues,

The sense of mission with which I enlisted in the IDF was based . . . on . . . the painfully simple message that we shall not allow the Holocaust of the Jews to repeat itself no matter what the costs, and when the moral price became more severe, the sense of mission only increased . . . I am a freedom fighter . . . not an occupier, not cruel, certainly not immoral . . .

Something in Laor's texts spoke to me about the place inside me that had been closed and denied until then . . .

Here I am, 28 years old, returning home from another month of reserve duty in Gaza and suddenly asking myself questions that are beginning to penetrate even the armor of the righteousness . . . in which they had dressed me years ago. And Laor's strong words return to echo in my ears: "With such obedience? With such obedience? With such obedience?"

Ever since I refused to serve in the territories and the Ometz Lesarev (Courage to Refuse) movement was established, I have returned again and again to Laor's texts . . .

. . . The voice is that of a poetic persona through whose life the "situation" passes and touches everything he has, grasping and refusing to let go. The child, the wife, the hours of wakefulness alone at night, memory, the very act of writing—everything is political. And from the other extreme, every terror attack, every act of occupation, every moral injustice—everything is completely personal.

. . . This is . . . a poetry that does not seek parental approval or any other approval, a poetry that liberates from the limitations of criticism of the discourse, and a poetry that . . . finds the independent place that revolts and refuses.

Did Laor's poetry "work"? Did Zonsheine's commitment "work"? In either sense of the word, at any given moment, how do we measure? If we say no, does that mean we give up on poetry? On resistance? With such obedience?

"Something I was forbidden to see."

6

Critical discourse about poetry has said little about the daily conditions of our material existence, past and present: how they imprint the life of the feelings, of involuntary human responses—how we glimpse a blur of smoke in the air, look at a pair of shoes in a shop window, at a woman asleep in her car or a group of men on a street corner, how we hear the whir of a helicopter or rain on the roof or music on the radio upstairs, how we meet or avoid the eyes of a neighbor or a stranger. That pressure bends our angle of vision whether we recognize it or not. A great many well-wrought, banal poems, like a great many essays on poetry and poetics, are written as if such pressures didn't exist. But this only reveals their existence.

It's sometimes taken that politicized emotions belong solely to the "oppressed" or "disenfranchised" or "outraged," or to a facile liberalism. Can it still be controversial to say that an apparently disengaged poetics may also speak a political language—of self-enclosed complacency, passivity, opportunism, false neutrality—or that such poetry can simply be, in Mayakovsky's phrase, a "cardboard horse"?

But when poetry lays its hand on our shoulder, as Yitzhak Laor's poem did for David Zonsheine, we are, to an almost physical degree, touched and moved. The imagination's roads open before us, giving the lie to that slammed and bolted door, that razor-wired fence, that brute dictum *"There is no alternative."*

Of course, like the consciousness behind it, behind any art, a poem can be deep or shallow, visionary or glib, prescient or stuck in an already lagging trendiness. What's pushing the grammar and syntax, the sounds, the images—is it the constriction of literalism, fundamentalism, professionalism—a stunted language? Or is it the great muscle of metaphor, drawing strength from resemblance in difference? The great muscle of the unconstricted throat?

I'd like to suggest this: If there's a line to be drawn, it's not so much between secularism and belief as between those for whom language has metaphoric density and those for whom it is merely formulaic—to be used for repression, manipulation, empty certitudes to ensure obedience.

And such a line can also be drawn between ideologically obedient hack verse and an engaged poetics that endures the weight of the unknown, the untracked, the unrealized, along with its urgencies for and against.

7

Antonio Gramsci wrote of the culture of the future that "new" individual artists can't be manufactured: art is a part of society—but that to imagine a new socialist society is to imagine a new kind of art that we can't foresee from where we now stand. "One must speak," Gramsci wrote, "of a struggle for a new culture, that is, for a new moral life that cannot but be intimately connected to a new intuition of life, until it becomes a new way of feeling and seeing reality and, therefore, a world intimately ingrained in 'possible artists' and 'possible works of art.'"

In any present society, a distinction needs to be made between the "avant-garde that always remains the same"—what a friend of mine has called "the poetry of false problems"—and a poetics searching for transformative meaning on the shoreline of what can now be thought or said. Adonis, writing of Arab poetry, reminds Arab poets that "modernity should be a creative vision, or it will be no more than a fashion. Fashion grows old from the moment it is born, while creativity is ageless. Therefore not all modernity is creativity, but creativity is eternally modern."

For now, poetry has the capacity—in its own ways and by its own means—to remind us of something we are forbidden to see. A forgotten future: a still-uncreated site whose moral architecture is founded not on ownership and dispossession, the subjection of women, torture and bribes, outcast and tribe, but on the continuous redefining of freedom—that word now held under house arrest by the rhetoric of the "free" market. This ongoing future, written off over and over, is still within view. All over the world its paths are being rediscovered and reinvented: through collective action, through many kinds of art. Its elementary condition is the recovery and redistribution of the world's resources that have been extracted from the many by the few.

There are other ghostly presences here along with Hugh Mac-Diarmid: Qaifi Azami. William Blake. Bertolt Brecht. Gwendolyn Brooks. Aimé Césaire. Hart Crane. Roque Dalton. Rubén Darío. Robert Duncan. Faiz Ahmed Faiz. Forugh Farrokhzad. Robert Hayden. Nazim Hikmet. Billie Holiday. June Jordan. Federico García Lorca. Audre Lorde. Bob Marley. Vladimir Mayakovsky. Thomas McGrath. Pablo Neruda. Lorine Niedecker. Charles Olson. George Oppen. Wilfred Owen. Pier Paolo Pasolini. Dahlia Ravikov-itch. Edwin Rolfe. Muriel Rukeyser. Léopold Senghor. Nina Simone. Bessie Smith. César Vallejo.

I don't speak these names, by the way, as a canon: they are voices mingling in a long conversation, a long turbulence, a great, vexed, and often maligned tradition, in poetry as in politics. The tradi-tion of radical modernism, which crosses and recrosses the map of poetry. The tradition of those who have written against the silences of their time and location. Without it—in poetry as in politics—our world is unintelligible.

A friend asks: And what about Baudelaire, Emily Dickinson, T. S. Eliot, Gerard Manley Hopkins, D. H. Lawrence, Montale, Plath, Ezra Pound, Rilke, Rimbaud, Wallace Stevens, Yeats? In the con-text of that conversation, their poems flare up anew, signals flashing across contested, even infected waters. I'm not talking about literary "intertextuality" or a "world poetry" but about what Muriel Rukey-ser said poetry can be: *an exchange of energy,* which, in changing consciousness, can effect *change in existing conditions.*

Translation can both betray and make possible that exchange of energy. I've relied—both today and in my lifelong sense of what poetry can be—on translation: the carrying-over, the trade routes of language and literature. And the questions of who is translated, who are the translators, how and by whom the work is done and distrib-uted are also, in a world of imbalanced power and language, political questions. Let's bear in mind the Triangle Trade as a quintessential agony of translation.

In his *Poetics of Relation* Édouard Glissant meditates on the trans-mutations opening out of that abyss of the Middle Passage. He writes of the Caribbean that though this experience [of the abyss] made you, original victim ... an exception, it became something shared, and made us, the descendants, one people among others. Peoples do not live on exception. Relation is not made up of things that are foreign but of shared knowledge. ...

This is why we stay with poetry. ... We know ourselves as part and as crowd, in an unknown that does not terrify. We cry our cry of poetry. Our boats are open, and we sail them for everyone.

Finally: there is always that in poetry which will not be grasped, which cannot be described, which survives our ardent attention, our critical theories, our classrooms, our late-night arguments. There is always (I am quoting the poet/ translator Américo Ferrari) "an unspeakable where, perhaps, the nucleus of the living relation between the poem and the world resides."

The living relation between the poem and the world: difficult knowledge, operating theater where the poet, committed, goes on working.

Notes

On Lies, Secrets, and Silence: Selected Prose 1966–1978

"When We Dead Awaken: Writing as Re-Vision" (1971)

1 G. B. Shaw, *The Quintessence of Ibsenism* (New York: Hill & Wang, 1922), p. 139.

2 J. G. Stewart, *Jane Ellen Harrison: A Portrait from Letters* (London: Merlin, 1959), p. 140.

3 Henry James, "Notes on Novelists," in *Selected Literary Criticism of Henry James*, Morris Shapira, ed. (London: Heinemann, 1963), pp. 157–58.

4 A. R., 1978: This intuition of mine was corroborated when, early in 1978, I read the correspondence between Woolf and Dame Ethel Smyth (Henry W. and Albert A. Berg Collection, The New York Public Library, Astor, Lenox and Tilden Foundations); in a letter dated June 8, 1933, Woolf speaks of having kept her own personality out of *A Room of One's Own* lest she not be taken seriously: ". . . how personal, so will they say, rubbing their hands with glee, women always are; *I even hear them as I write.*" (Italics mine.)

5 A. R., 1978: Yet I spent months, at sixteen, memorizing and writing imitations of Millay's sonnets; and in notebooks of that period I find what are obviously attempts to imitate Dickinson's metrics and verbal compression. I knew H.D. only through anthologized lyrics; her epic poetry was not then available to me.

6 A. R., 1978: Texts of poetry quoted herein can be found in A. R., *Poems Selected and New: 1950–1974* (New York: Norton, 1975).

7 A. R., 1978: When I dreamed that dream, was I wholly ignorant of the tradition of Bessie Smith and other women's blues lyrics which transcended victimization to sing of resistance and independence?

8 Mary Daly, *Beyond God the Father: Towards a Philosophy of Women's Liberation* (Boston: Beacon, 1973).

"Jane Eyre: The Temptations of a Motherless Woman" (1973)

1 Virginia Woolf, *The Common Reader* (New York: Harcourt Brace, 1948), pp. 221–22. A. R., 1978: Her *Common Reader* essays, so many of which were on women writers, bear nonetheless the marks of her struggle with masculine ideas of what is important, appropriate, or valid (a struggle eloquently described in her speech before the London/National Society for Women's Service, 1931, reprinted with Woolf's own manuscript revisions in *The Pargiters*, Mitchell Leaska, ed. [New York: NYPL/Readex Books, 1977]). So, in 1925, writing of *Jane Eyre*, the future author of *To the Lighthouse* (1927), *A Room of One's Own* (1929), and *Three Guineas* (1938) was able to declare that "Charlotte Brontë does not attempt to solve the problems of human life. She is even unaware that such problems exist." Woolf herself still meets with similar incomprehension today.

2 Q. D. Leavis, Introduction to *Jane Eyre* (Baltimore: Penguin, 1966), p. 11.

3 A. R., 1978: Ground-breaking as *Women and Madness* (1972) was in its documentation of the antiwoman bias of the psychoanalytic and psychotherapeutic professions, Chesler oversimplified, I believe, the mother-daughter relationship, perceiving it as almost entirely, if tragically, negative. To a large extent she resorts to "blaming the mother" for the daughter's disadvantaged position in patriarchy. The more we learn of actual female history (to take but one example, of the history of black women) the less we can generalize about the failure of mothers to cherish and inspirit daughters in a strong, female tradition.

4 Gaston Bachelard, *The Poetics of Space* (Boston: Beacon, 1967), pp. 17–18.

5 Erich Neumann, *The Great Mother* (Princeton, N. J.: Princeton University, 1972), pp. 55–59.

"Vesuvius at Home: The Power of Emily Dickinson" (1975)

1 "The Female World of Love and Ritual: Relations between Women in Nineteenth-Century America," *Signs*, vol. 1, no. 1.

2 Hughes, ed., *A Choice of Emily Dickinson's Verse* (London: Faber & Faber, 1968), p. 11.

Of Woman Born: Motherhood as Experience and Institution (1976)

"Foreword"

1   "Rape: The All-American Crime," in Jo Freeman, ed., *Women: A Feminist Perspective* (Stanford, Calif.: Mayfield Publishing, 1975).

2   *Against Our Will: Men, Women and Rape* (New York: Simon and Schuster, 1975). Reviewing Brownmiller's book, a feminist newsletter commented: "It would be extreme and contentious . . . to call mothers rape victims in general; probably only a small percentage are. But rape is the crime that can be committed because women are vulnerable in a special way; the opposite of 'vulnerable' is 'impregnable.' Pregnability, to coin a word, has been the basis of female identity, the limit of freedom, the futility of education, the denial of growth." ("Rape Has Many Forms," review in *The Spokeswoman* 6, no. 5 [November 15, 1975].)

3   To these American capitalism is adding a third: the profit motive. Franchised, commercially operated child-care centers have become "big business." Many such centers are purely custodial; overcrowding limits physical and educational flexibility and freedom; the centers are staffed almost entirely by women, working for a minimum salary. Operated under giant corporations such as Singer, Time Inc., and General Electric, these profit-making preschools can be compared to commercial nursing homes in their exploitation of human needs and of the most vulnerable persons in the society. See Georgia Sassen, Cookie Arvin, and the Corporations and Child Care Research Project, "Corporate Child Care," *The Second Wave: A Magazine of the New Feminism* 3, no. 3, pp. 21–23, 38–43.

4   "Placing Women in History: Definitions and Challenges," in *Feminist Studies* 3, no. 1–2 (Fall 1975), pp. 8, 13.

"Anger and Tenderness"

1   Arthur W. Calhoun, *A Social History of the American Family from Colonial Times to the Present* (Cleveland: 1917). See also Gerda Lerner, *Black Women in White America: A Documentary History* (New York: Vintage, 1973), pp. 149–50 ff.

"Motherhood and Daughterhood"

Epigraph from "Mother and Child," in *Like the Iris of an Eye*, by Susan Griffin (New York: Harper and Row, 1976).

1   Alice Rossi, "Physiological and Social Rhythms: The Study of Human Cyclicity," special lecture to the American Psychiatric Association, Detroit, Michigan, May 9, 1974; "Period Piece—Bloody but Unbowed," Elizabeth Fenton, interview with Emily Culpeper, *The Real Paper*, June 12, 1974.

2   Charles Strickland, "A Transcendentalist Father: The Child-Rearing Prac-
    tices of Bronson Alcott," *History of Childhood Quarterly: The Journal of
    Psycho-History* 1, no. 1 (Summer 1973), pp. 23, 32.

3   Midge Mackenzie, ed., *Shoulder to Shoulder* (New York: Knopf, 1975), p. 28.

4   Margaret Mead, *Male and Female* (New York: Morrow, 1975), p. 61.

5   David Meltzer, *Birth* (New York: Ballantine, 1973), pp. 3, 5, 6–8.

6   Lloyd deMause, "The Evolution of Childhood," in deMause, ed., *The His-
    tory of Childhood* (New York: Harper and Row, 1974), pp. 25–26, 120.

7   Jane Lilienfeld, "Yes, the Lighthouse Looks Like That: Marriage Victo-
    rian Style," unpublished paper, presented at the Northeast Victorian Stud-
    ies Association, Conference on the Victorian Family, April 18–20, 1975,
    Worcester, Mass.

8   Virginia Woolf, *To the Lighthouse* (New York: Harcourt, Brace, 1927), pp.
    58, 92, 126, 79, 294.

9   Cecil Woodham-Smith, *Florence Nightingale* (New York: Grosset and
    Dunlap, 1951), p. 46.

10 Diaries and letters of Paula Modersohn-Becker, translated by Liselotte
    Erlanger, unpublished manuscript, quoted by permission of the trans-
    lator. See Diane Radycki, ed., and trans., *The Letters and Journals of
    Paula Modersohn-Becker* (Metuchen, N.J., and London: The Scarecrow
    Press, 1980).

11 Thomas Johnson, ed., *The Letters of Emily Dickinson* (Cambridge, Mass.:
    Harvard University Press, 1958), III: 782.

12 Sylvia Plath, *Letters Home,* ed. Aurelia Plath (New York: Harper and Row,
    1975), pp. 32, 466.

13 Virginia Woolf, *op. cit.,* p. 79.

14 Radclyffe Hall, *The Well of Loneliness* (New York: Pocket Books, 1974), p.
    32; first published 1928.

15 Sue Silvermarie, "The Motherbond," *Women: A Journal of Liberation* 4, no.
    1, pp. 26–27.

16 Carroll Smith-Rosenberg, "The Female World of Love and Ritual: Rela-
    tions between Women in Nineteenth-Century America," *Signs* 1, no. 1, pp.
    1–29.

17 Lillian Krueger, "Motherhood on the Wisconsin Frontier," *Wisconsin, A
    Magazine of History* 29, no. 3, pp. 336–46.

18 Lynn Sukenick, "Feeling and Reason in Doris Lessing's Fiction," *Contem-
    porary Literature* 14, no. 4, p. 519.

19 Doris Lessing, *A Proper Marriage* (New York: New American Library,
    1970) p. 111.

20 Kate Chopin, *The Awakening* (New York: Capricorn, 1964), p. 14; first pub-
    lished 1899.

21 Cora Sandel, *Alberta Alone*, trans. Elizabeth Rokkan (London: Peter Owen, 1965), p. 51; first published 1939.

22 C. Kerenyi, *Eleusis: Archetypal Image of Mother and Daughter* (New York: Pantheon, 1967), pp. 13–94.

23 *Ibid.*, pp. 127–28.

24 *Ibid.*, p. 130.

25 *Ibid.*, pp. 132–33.

26 Margaret Atwood, *Surfacing* (New York: Popular Library, 1972), pp. 213–14, 218–19, 222–23.

27 Jean Mundy, Ph.D., "Rape—For Women Only," unpublished paper presented to the American Psychological Association, September 1, 1974, New Orleans, La.

28 Clara Thompson, "'Penis Envy' in Women," in Jean Baker Miller, ed., *Psychoanalysis and Women* (Baltimore: Penguin, 1973), p. 54.

29 Robert Seidenberg, "Is Anatomy Destiny?" in Miller, *op. cit.*, pp. 310–11.

30 Tillie Olsen, *Tell Me A Riddle* (New York: Delta Books, 1961), pp. 1–12.

31 Evelyn Reed, *Woman's Evolution: From Matriarchal Clan to Patriarchal Family* (New York: Pathfinder, 1975), pp. 12–14.

32 Adrienne Rich, "Jane Eyre: The Temptations of a Motherless Woman," in *On Lies, Secrets, and Silence: Selected Prose 1966–1978* (New York: Norton, 1980).

33 Lillian Smith, *Killers of the Dream* (New York: Norton, 1961), pp. 28–29.

Blood, Bread, and Poetry: Selected Prose 1979–1985

"What Does a Woman Need to Know?" (1979)

1 United Nations, Department of International Economic and Social Affairs, Statistical Office, *1977 Compendium of Social Statistics* (New York: United Nations, 1980).

"Compulsory Heterosexuality and the Lesbian Existence" (1980)

1 See, for example, Paula Gunn Allen, *The Sacred Hoop: Recovering the Feminine in American Indian Traditions* (Boston: Beacon, 1986); Beth Brant, ed., *A Gathering of Spirit: Writing and Art by North American Indian Women* (Montpelier, Vt.: Sinister Wisdom Books, 1984); Gloria Anzaldúa and Cherríe Moraga, eds., *This Bridge Called My Back: Writings by Radical Women of Color* (Watertown, Mass.: Persephone, 1981; distributed by Kitchen Table/Women of Color Press, Albany, N.Y.); J. R. Roberts, *Black Lesbians: An Annotated Bibliography* (Tallahassee, Fla.: Naiad, 1981); Barbara Smith, ed., *Home Girls: A Black Feminist Anthology* (Albany, N.Y.: Kitchen Table/Women of Color Press, 1984). As Lorraine Bethel and Barbara Smith pointed out in *Conditions* 5: *The Black Women's Issue* (1980),

a great deal of fiction by Black women depicts primary relationships between women. I would like to cite here the work of Ama Ata Aidoo, Toni Cade Bambara, Buchi Emecheta, Bessie Head, Zora Neale Hurston, Alice Walker. Donna Allegra, Red Jordan Arobateau, Audre Lorde, Ann Allen Shockley, among others, write directly as Black lesbians. For fiction by other lesbians of color, see Elly Bulkin, ed., *Lesbian Fiction: An Anthology* (Watertown, Mass.: Persephone, 1981).

See also, for accounts of contemporary Jewish-lesbian existence, Evelyn Torton Beck, ed., *Nice Jewish Girls: A Lesbian Anthology* (Watertown, Mass.: Persephone, 1982; distributed by Crossing Press, Trumansburg, N.Y. 14886); Alice Bloch, *Lifetime Guarantee* (Watertown, Mass.: Persephone, 1982); and Melanie Kaye-Kantrowitz and Irena Klepfisz, eds., *The Tribe of Dina: A Jewish Women's Anthology* (Montpelier, Vt.: Sinister Wisdom Books, 1986).

The earliest formulation that I know of heterosexuality as an institution was in the lesbian-feminist paper *The Furies,* founded in 1971. For a collection of articles from that paper, see Nancy Myron and Charlotte Bunch, eds., *Lesbianism and the Women's Movement* (Oakland, Calif.: Diana Press, 1975; distributed by Crossing Press, Trumansburg, N.Y. 14886).

2 Alice Rossi, "Children and Work in the Lives of Women," paper delivered at the University of Arizona, Tuscon, February 1976.

3 Doris Lessing, *The Golden Notebook,* 1962 (New York: Bantam, 1977), p. 480.

4 Nancy Chodorow, *The Reproduction of Mothering* (Berkeley: University of California Press, 1978); Dorothy Dinnerstein, *The Mermaid and the Minotaur: Sexual Arrangements and the Human Malaise* (New York: Harper & Row, 1976); Barbara Ehrenreich and Deirdre English, *For Her Own Good: 150 Years of the Experts' Advice to Women* (Garden City, N.Y.: Doubleday, Anchor, 1978); Jean Baker Miller, *Toward a New Psychology of Women* (Boston: Beacon, 1976).

5 I could have chosen many other serious and influential recent books, including anthologies, which would illustrate the same point: e.g., *Our Bodies, Ourselves,* the Boston Women's Health Book Collective's best seller (New York: Simon and Schuster, 1976), which devotes a separate (and inadequate) chapter to lesbians, but whose message is that heterosexuality is most women's life preference; Berenice Carroll, ed., *Liberating Women's History: Theoretical and Critical Essays* (Urbana: University of Illinois Press, 1976), which does not include even a token essay on the lesbian presence in history, though an essay by Linda Gordon, Persis Hunt, *et al.* notes the use by male historians of "sexual deviance" as a category to discredit and dismiss Anna Howard Shaw, Jane Addams, and other feminists ("Historical Phallacies: Sexism in American Historical Writing"); and Renate

Bridenthal and Claudia Koonz, eds., *Becoming Visible: Women in European History* (Boston: Houghton Mifflin, 1977), which contains three mentions of male homosexuality but no materials that I have been able to locate on lesbians. Gerda Lerner, ed., *The Female Experience: An American Documentary* (Indianapolis: Bobbs-Merrill, 1977), contains an abridgment of two lesbian-feminist–position papers from the contemporary movement but no other documentation of lesbian existence. Lerner does note in her preface, however, how the charge of deviance has been used to fragment women and discourage women's resistance. Linda Gordon, in *Woman's Body, Woman's Right: A Social History of Birth Control in America* (New York: Viking, Grossman, 1976), notes accurately that "it is not that feminism has produced more lesbians. There have always been many lesbians, despite the high levels of repression; and most lesbians experience their sexual preference as innate" (p. 410).

[A.R., 1986: I am glad to update the first annotation in this footnote. *"The New" Our Bodies, Ourselves* (New York: Simon and Schuster, 1984) contains an expanded chapter on "Loving Women: Lesbian Life and Relationships" and furthermore emphasizes *choices* for women throughout—in terms of sexuality, health care, family, politics, etc.]

6   Jonathan Katz, ed., *Gay American History: Lesbians and Gay Men in the U.S.A.* (New York: Thomas Y. Crowell, 1976).

7   Nancy Sahli, "Smashing Women's Relationships before the Fall," *Chrysalis: A Magazine of Women's Culture* 8 (1979): 17–27.

8   This is a book which I have publicly endorsed. I would still do so, though with the above caveat. It is only since beginning to write this article that I fully appreciated how enormous is the unasked question in Ehrenreich and English's book.

9   See, for example, Kathleen Barry, *Female Sexual Slavery* (Englewood Cliffs, N.J: Prentice-Hall, 1979); Mary Daly, *Gyn/Ecology: The Metaethics of Radical Feminism* (Boston: Beacon, 1978); Susan Griffin, *Woman and Nature: The Roaring inside Her* (New York: Harper & Row, 1978); Diana Russell and Nicole van de Ven, eds., *Proceedings of the International Tribunal of Crimes against Women* (Millbrae, Calif.: Les Femmes, 1976); and Susan Brownmiller, *Against Our Will: Men, Women and Rape* (New York: Simon and Schuster, 1975); *Aegis: Magazine on Ending Violence against Women* (Feminist Alliance against Rape, P.O. Box 21033, Washington, D.C. 20009).

[A.R., 1986: Work on both incest and on woman battering has appeared in the 1980s which I did not cite in the essay. See Florence Rush, *The Best-kept Secret* (New York: McGraw-Hill, 1980); Louise Armstrong, *Kiss Daddy Goodnight: A Speakout on Incest* (New York: Pocket Books, 1979); Sandra

Butler, *Conspiracy of Silence: The Trauma of Incest* (San Francisco: New Glide, 1978); F. Delacoste and F. Newman, eds., *Fight Back!: Feminist Resistance to Male Violence* (Minneapolis: Cleis Press, 1981); Judy Freespirit, *Daddy's Girl: An Incest Survivor's Story* (Langlois, Ore.: Diaspora Distribution, 1982); Judith Herman, *Father-Daughter Incest* (Cambridge, Mass.: Harvard University Press, 1981); Toni McNaron and Yarrow Morgan, eds., *Voices in the Night: Women Speaking about Incest* (Minneapolis: Cleis Press, 1982); and Betsy Warrior's richly informative, multipurpose compilation of essays, statistics, listings, and facts, the *Battered Women's Directory* (formerly entitled *Working on Wife Abuse*), 8th ed. (Cambridge, Mass.: 1982).]

10 Dinnerstein, p. 272.

11 Chodorow, pp. 197–98.

12 *Ibid.*, pp. 198–99.

13 *Ibid.*, p. 200.

14 Kathleen Gough, "The Origin of the Family," in *Toward an Anthropology of Women*, ed. Rayna [Rapp] Reiter (New York: Monthly Review Press, 1975), pp. 60–70.

15 Kathleen Barry, *Female Sexual Slavery* (Englewood Cliffs, NJ: Prentice-Hall, 1979), pp. 216–19.

16 Anna Demeter, *Legal Kidnapping* (Boston: Beacon, 1977), pp. xx, 126–28.

17 Mary Daly, *Gyn/Ecology: The Metaethics of Radical Feminism* (Boston: Beacon, 1978) pp. 139–41, pp. 163–65.

18 Barbara Ehrenreich and Deirdre English, *Witches, Midwives and Nurses: A History of Women Healers* (Old Westbury, N.Y.: Feminist Press, 1973); Andrea Dworkin, *Woman Hating* (New York: Dutton, 1974), pp. 118–54; Daly, pp. 178–222.

19 See Virginia Woolf, *A Room of One's Own* (London: Hogarth, 1929), and *id., Three Guineas* (New York: Harcourt Brace, [1938] 1966); Tillie Olsen, *Silences* (Boston: Delacorte, 1978); Michelle Cliff, "The Resonance of Interruption," *Chrysalis: A Magazine of Women's Culture* 8 (1979): 29–37.

20 Mary Daly, *Beyond God the Father* (Boston: Beacon, 1973), pp. 347–51; Olsen, pp. 22–46.

21 Daly, *Beyond God the Father*, p. 93.

22 Fran P. Hosken, "The Violence of Power: Genital Mutilation of Females," *Heresies: A Feminist Journal of Art and Politics* 6 (1979): 28–35; Diana Russell and Nicole van de Ven, eds., *Proceedings of the Informational Tribunal of Crimes Against Women* (Millbrae, Calif.: Les Femmes, 1976) pp. 194–195.

   [A.R., 1986: See especially "Circumcision of Girls," in Nawal El Saadawi, *The Hidden Face of Eve: Women in the Arab World* (Boston: Beacon, 1982), pp. 33–43.]

23 Barry, pp. 163–64.

24 The issue of "lesbian sadomasochism" needs to be examined in terms of dominant cultures teachings about the relation of sex and violence. I believe this to be another example of the "double life" of women.

25 Catharine A. MacKinnon, *Sexual Harassment of Working Women: A Case of Sex Discrimination* (New Haven, Conn.: Yale University Press, 1979), pp. 15–16.

26 *Ibid.*, p. 174.

27 Susan Brownmiller, *Against Our Will: Men, Women and Rape* (New York: Simon and Schuster, 1975).

28 MacKinnon, p. 219. Susan Schecter writes: "The push for heterosexual union at whatever cost is so intense that . . . it has become a cultural force of its own that creates battering. The ideology of romantic love and its jealous possession of the partner as property provide the masquerade for what can become severe abuse" (*Aegis: Magazine on Ending Violence against Women* [July–August 1979]: 50–51).

29 MacKinnon, p. 298.

30 *Ibid.*, p. 220.

31 *Ibid.*, p. 221.

32 Barry, *op. cit.*
    [A.R., 1986: See also Kathleen Barry, Charlotte Bunch, and Shirley Castley, eds., *International Feminism: Networking against Female Sexual Slavery* (New York: International Women's Tribune Center, 1984).]

33 Barry, p. 33.

34 *Ibid.*, p. 103.

35 *Ibid.*, p. 5.

36 *Ibid.*, p. 100.
    [A.R. 1986: This statement has been taken as claiming that "all women are victims" purely and simply, or that "all heterosexuality equals sexual slavery." I would say, rather, that all women are affected, though differently, by dehumanizing attitudes and practices directed at women as a group.]

37 *Ibid.*, p. 218.

38 *Ibid.*, p. 140.

39 *Ibid.*, p. 172.

40 Elsewhere I have suggested that male identification has been a powerful source of white women's racism and that it has often been women already seen as "disloyal" to male codes and systems who have actively battled against it (Adrienne Rich, "Disloyal to Civilization: Feminism, Racism, Gynephobia," in *On Lies, Secrets, and Silence: Selected Prose, 1966–1978* [New York: Norton, 1979]).

41 Barry, p. 220.

42 Susan Cavin, "Lesbian Origins" (Ph.D. diss., Rutgers University, 1978), unpublished, ch. 6.

    [A.R., 1986: This dissertation was recently published as *Lesbian Origins* (San Francisco: Ism Press, 1986).]

43 For my perception of heterosexuality as an economic institution I am indebted to Lisa Leghorn and Katherine Parker, who allowed me to read the unpublished manuscript of their book *Woman's Worth: Sexual Economics and the World of Women* (London and Boston: Routledge & Kegan Paul, 1981).

44 I would suggest that lesbian existence has been most recognized and tolerated where it has resembled a "deviant" version of heterosexuality— e.g., where lesbians have, like Stein and Toklas, played heterosexual roles (or seemed to in public) and have been chiefly identified with male culture. See also Claude E. Schaeffer, "The Kuterai Female Berdache: Courier, Guide, Prophetess and Warrior," *Ethnohistory* 12, no. 3 (Summer 1965): 193–236. (Berdache: "an individual of a definite physiological sex [m. or f.] who assumes the role and status of the opposite sex and who is viewed by the community as being of one sex physiologically but as having assumed the role and status of the opposite sex" [Schaeffer, p. 231].) Lesbian existence has also been relegated to an upper-class phenomenon, an elite decadence (as in the fascination with Paris salon lesbians such as Renée Vivien and Natalie Clifford Barney), to the obscuring of such "common women" as Judy Grahn depicts in her *The Work of a Common Woman* (Oakland, Calif: Diana Press, 1978) and *True to Life Adventure Stories* (Oakland, Calif.: Diana Press, 1978).

45 Daly, *Gyn/Ecology*, p. 15.

46 "In a hostile world in which women are-not supposed to survive except in relation with and in service to men, entire communities of women are simply erased. History tends to bury what it seeks to reject" (Blanche W. Cook, "'Women Alone Stir My Imagination': Lesbianism and the Cultural Tradition," *Signs: Journal of Women in Culture and Society* 4, no. 4 [Summer 1979]: 719–20). The Lesbian Herstory Archives in New York City is one attempt to preserve contemporary documents on lesbian existence— a project of enormous value and meaning, working against the continuing censorship and obliteration of relationships, networks, communities in other archives and elsewhere in the culture.

47 [A.R., 1986: The shared historical and spiritual "crossover" functions of lesbians and gay men in cultures past and present are traced by Judy Grahn in *Another Mother Tongue: Gay Words, Gay Worlds* (Boston: Beacon, 1984). I now think we have much to learn both from the uniquely female

aspects of lesbian existence and from the complex "gay" identity we share with gay men.]

48   Audre Lorde, "Uses of the Erotic: The Erotic as Power," in *Sister Outsider* (Trumansburg, N.Y.: Crossing Press, 1984).

49   Adrienne Rich, "Conditions for Work: The Common World of Women," in *On Lies, Secrets, and Silence*, p. 209; H.D., *Tribute to Freud* (Oxford: Carcanet, 1971), pp. 50–54.

50   Woolf, *A Room of One's Own*, p. 126.

51   Gracia Clark, "The Beguines: A Mediaeval Women's Community," *Quest: A Feminist Quarterly* 1, no. 4 (1975): 73–80.

52   See Denise Paulmé, ed., *Women of Tropical Africa* (Berkeley: University of California Press, 1963), pp. 7, 266–67. Some of these sororities are described as "a kind of defensive syndicate against the male element," their aims being "to offer concerted resistance to an oppressive patriarchate," "independence in relation to one's husband and with regard to motherhood, mutual aid, satisfaction of personal revenge." See also Audre Lorde, "Scratching the Surface Some Notes on Barriers to Women and Loving," in *Sister Outsider,* pp. 45–52; Marjorie Topley, "Marriage Resistance in Rural Kwangtung," in *Women in Chinese Society,* ed. M. Wolf and R. Witke (Stanford, Calif.: Stanford University Press, 1978), pp. 67–89; Agnes Smedley, *Portraits of Chinese Women in Revolution*, ed. J. MacKinnon and S. MacKinnon (Old Westbury, N.Y.: Feminist Press, 1976), pp. 103–10.

53   See Rosalind Petchesky, "Dissolving the Hyphen: A Report on Marxist-Feminist Groups 1–5," in *Capitalist Patriarchy and the Case for Socialist Feminism,* ed. Zillah Eisenstein (New York: Monthly Review Press, 1979), p. 387.

54   [A.R., 1986: See Angela Davis, *Women, Race and Class* (New York: Random House, 1981), p. 102; Orlando Patterson, *Slavery and Social Death: A Comparative Study* (Cambridge, Mass.: Harvard University Press, 1982), p. 133.]

55   Russell and van de Ven, pp. 42–43, 56–57.

56   I am indebted to Jonathan Katz's *Gay American History (op. cit.)* for bringing to my attention Hansberry's letters to *The Ladder* and to Barbara Grier for supplying me with copies of relevant pages from *The Ladder,* quoted here by permission of Barbara Grier. See also the reprinted series of *The Ladder,* ed. Jonathan Katz *et al.* (New York: Arno, 1975), and Deirdre Carmody, "Letters by Eleanor Roosevelt Detail Friendship with Lorena Hickok," *New York Times* (October 21, 1979).

57   Meridel LeSueur, *The Girl* (Cambridge, Mass.: West End Press, 1978), pp. 10–11. LeSueur describes, in an afterword, how this book was drawn from

the writings and oral narrations of women in the Workers Alliance who met as a writers' group during the Depression.

58 *Ibid.,* p. 20.

59 *Ibid.,* pp. 53–54.

60 *Ibid.,* p. 55.

61 Toni Morrison, *Sula* (New York: Bantam, 1973), pp. 103–4, 149. I am indebted to Lorraine Bethel's essay " 'This Infinity of Conscious Pain': Zora Neale Hurston and the Black Female Literary Tradition," in *All the Women Are White, All the Blacks Are Men, but Some of Us Are Brave: Black Women's Studies,* ed. Gloria T. Hull, Patricia Bell Scott, and Barbara Smith (Old Westbury, N.Y.: Feminist Press, 1982).

62 See Maureen Brady and Judith McDaniel, "Lesbians in the Mainstream: The Image of Lesbians in Recent Commercial Fiction," *Conditions* 6 (1979): 82–105.

63 See Russell and van de Ven, p. 40: "Few heterosexual women realize their lack of free choice about their sexuality, and few realize how and why compulsory heterosexuality is also a crime against them."

64 Lorraine Bethel, "This Infinity of Conscious Pain: Zora Neale Hurston and the Black Literary Female Tradition," in *All the Women Are White, All the Blacks Are Men, But Some of Us Are Brave,* eds. Gloria T. Hull, Patricia Bell Scott, and Barbara Smith (Old Westbury, NY: Feminist Press, 1982) 176–88.

65 Dorothy Dinnerstein, the most recent writer to quote this passage, adds ominously: "But what has to be added to her account is that these 'women enlaced' are sheltering each other not just from what men want to do to them, but also from what they want to do to each other" (Dinnerstein, *The Mermaid and the Minotaur: Sexual Arrangements and the Human Malaise* [New York: Harper & Row, 1976], p. 103). The fact is, however, that woman-to-woman violence is a minute grain in the universe of male-against-female violence perpetuated and rationalized in every social institution.

66 Conversation with Blanche W. Cook, New York City, March 1979.

67 See note 9, above, pp. 375–76.

"Split at the Root: An Essay on Jewish Identity" (1982)

1 Adrienne Rich, "Readings of History," in *Snapshots of a Daughter-in-Law* (New York: Norton, 1967), pp. 36–40.

2 In a similar way the phrase "That's white of you" implied that you were behaving with the superior decency and morality expected of white but not of Black people.

3 James Baldwin, "The Harlem Ghetto," in *Notes of a Native Son* (Boston: Beacon, 1955).

4 Angela Y. Davis, *Women, Race and Class* (New York: Random House, 1981);

Lucy S. Davidowicz, *The War against the Jews 1933–1945* (1975) (New York: Bantam, 1979).

"The Eye of the Outsider: Elizabeth Bishop's *Complete Poems, 1927–1979*" (1983)

1 It's worth noting that Bishop, clearly selective toward her own work, chose not to include the poem "A Norther—Key West" in her canon. In this poem, dated 1962, the observer is distanced and her perceptions distorted by an artificial and brittle tone, betraying an attempted and impossible objectivity. Nor did she include "House Guest" (pre-1969), in which the depressed live-in seamstress is surveyed much as Manuelzinho is—from a "liberal" middle-class perspective. Here, though the poet has evoked a certain tone in which domestic employers have forever discussed employees—frustrated, half-guilty, uncomprehending—she has not found a way to critique the tone and break through the inevitable stereotyping of the seamstress. I am, however, grateful to be able to read these poems and see something of the process of Bishop's own self-criticism and explorations into difficult territory.

"Blood, Bread, and Poetry: The Location of the Poet" (1984)

1 Edward Said, "Literature As Values," *New York Times Book Review* (September 4, 1983), p. 9.

2 Nancy Morejón, "Elogia de la Dialéctica," in *Breaking the Silences: Twentieth Century Poetry by Cuban Women*, ed. Margaret Randall (1982, Pulp Press, Box 3868 MPO, Vancouver, Canada V6B 3Z3).

3 [Editor's note] The author of "I Am Listening: A Lyric of Roots" is today Max Wolf Valerio, a transsexual man. See Credits, page 393.

4 Anita Valerio, "I Am Listening: A Lyric of Roots," in *A Gathering of Spirit, Sinister Wisdom* 22/23 (1983, ed. Beth Brant): 212–13.

5 See p. 373, "What Does a Woman Need to Know," note 1.

What Is Found There: Notebooks on Poetry and Politics (1993, 2003)

"Woman and Bird"

1 Muriel Rukeyser (1913–1979) is the North American poet who most intuited, explored, and, in her work, embodied this triangulation.

2 Beth Brant, *Mohawk Trail* (Ithaca, N.Y.: Firebrand, 1985), p. 96.

"Voices from the Air"

1 John Webster, *Tragedies* (London: Vision Press, 1946), p. 149.

2 Wallace Stevens, *The Collected Poems of Wallace Stevens* (New York: Knopf, 1954), p. 358.

"The Distance Between Language and Violence"

1 John Keats, "Endymion," in *The Poetical Works of John Keats,* 2 vols. (Boston: Little Brown, 1899), I, p. 85.

2 All passages from William Blake are from *The Poetry and Prose of William Blake,* ed. David Erdman (New York: Doubleday/Anchor, 1970).

3 Allen Tate, "Sonnets at Christmas," in *The Voice That Is Great within Us: American Poetry of the Twentieth Century,* ed. Hayden Carruth (New York: Bantam, 1970), p. 221.

4 Allen Tate, "Remarks on the Southern Religion," in *I'll Take My Stand: The South and the Agrarian Tradition* (1930; Baton Rouge: Louisiana State University Press, 1977), pp. 174–75.

"Not How to Write Poetry, but Wherefore"

1 Rainer Maria Rilke, *The Selected Poetry of Rainer Maria Rilke,* ed. and trans. Stephen Mitchell (New York: Random House/Vintage, 1986), pp. 60–61. "You have to change your life" is my American rendering of the line.

2 W. H. Auden, Foreword, in Adrienne Rich, *A Change of World* (New Haven: Yale University Press, 1951), p. 8.

3 W. H. Auden, "In Memory of W. B. Yeats," in his *Collected Poems* (New York: Random House, 1945), p. 50.

4 *Ibid.,* p. 51.

5 Adrienne Rich, *Collected Early Poems 1950–1970* (New York: Norton, 1993), p. 15. Muriel Rukeyser, in an essay on her Jewish identity, wrote of her childhood experience of temple services: "I think that many people brought up in reformed Judaism must go starving for two phases of religion: poetry and politics" (see "Poet . . . Woman . . . American . . . Jew," *Bridges: A Journal for Jewish Feminists and Our Friends* 1, no. 1 (Spring 1990): 23–29.

6 Reginald Gibbons and Terrence DesPres, eds., *Thomas McGrath: Life and the Poem* (Urbana and Chicago: University of Illinois Press, 1992), pp. 120–21.

" 'Rotted Names' "

1 Wallace Stevens, *The Collected Poems of Wallace Stevens* (New York: Knopf, 1955), pp. 128–30.

2 *Ibid.,* p. 266.

3 *Ibid.,* p. 27.

4 *Ibid.,* pp. 33–34.

5 *Ibid.,* pp. 239–40. Stevens's program for modern poetry implies a tradition of poetry that has failed to do these very things.

6 *Ibid.,* p. 183.

7 Aldon Lynn Nielsen, *Reading Race: White American Poets and the Racial Discourse in the Twentieth Century* (Athens and London: University of Georgia Press, 1988), p. 9. Marjorie Perloff notes, in Stevens's letters written during World War II, his dismissive labeling of various literary intellectuals, even those he admired, as "a Jew and a Communist," a "Jew and an anti-Fascist," "a Catholic," and his attempt, in the long poem "Notes toward a Supreme Fiction," (1941–1942), to construct "an elaborate and daunting rhetoric . . . designed to convince both poet and reader that, despite the daily headlines and radio bulletins, the real action takes place in the country of metaphor" (Albert J. Gelpi, ed., *Wallace Stevens: The Poetics of Modernism* [London and New York: Cambridge University Press, 1985], pp. 41–52).

8 Wallace Stevens, *Letters of Wallace Stevens,* ed. Holly Stevens (New York: Knopf, 1966), p. 321.

9 "I am using the term 'Africanism' for the denotative and connotative blackness that African peoples have come to signify, as well as the entire range of views, assumptions, readings, and misreadings that accompany Eurocentric learning about these peoples. . . . As a disabling virus within literary discourse, Africanism has become, in the Eurocentric tradition that American education favors, both a way of talking about and a way of policing matters of class, sexual license, and repression, formations and exercises of power, and meditations on ethics and accountability" (Toni Morrison, *Playing in the Dark: Whiteness and the Literary Imagination* [Cambridge, Mass.: Harvard University Press, 1992], pp. 6–7).

"A Poet's Education"

1 Diane Glancy, *Claiming Breath* (Lincoln: University of Nebraska Press, 1992), p. 85.

2 *Ibid.,* p. 23.

3 *Ibid.,* p. 22.

4 Jimmy Santiago Baca, *Working in the Dark: Reflections of a Poet of the Barrio* (Santa Fe, N.M.: Red Crane Books, 1992), pp. 4–6.

5 *Ibid.,* p. 65.

6 *Ibid.,* p. 66.

7 *Ibid.,* p. 4.

8 Gloria Anzaldúa, *Borderlands/La Frontera: The New Mestiza* (San Francisco: Spinsters/Aunt Lute Books, 1987), p. 54.

9 *Ibid.*, p. 19.

10 *Ibid.*, pp. 59–61.

11 Glancy, pp. 86–87.
    [2003: See also Linda McCarriston: "Weed," in Contemporary Authors
    Autobiography Series, vol. 28, pp. 189–229.]

"Tourism and Promised Lands"

1 June Jordan, "Solidarity," in her *Naming Our Destiny: New and Selected
   Poems* (New York: Thunder's Mouth Press, 1989), p. 171.

2 Thomas Larsen, "Uneasy Confessions," review of *Truth and Lies That
   Press for Life: Sixty Los Angeles Poets,* ed. Connie Hersheym (Concord,
   Mass.: Artifact Press, 1992), in *Poetry Flash*, no. 232 (July 1992): 1.

3 *Marxist-Humanism: A Half Century of Its World Development,* XII: *Guide
   to the Raya Dunayevskaya Collection,* ed. Raya Dunayevskaya (Detroit,
   Mich.: Wayne State University Library, 1986), p. 59. Available on micro-
   film from Wayne State University Library.

"Six Meditations in Place of a Lecture"

1 Walt Whitman, *Complete Poetry and Prose* (New York: Library of America,
   1982), pp. 388–92.

2 Federico García Lorca, *In Search of Duende* (New York: New Directions,
   1998), pp. 22, 48.

3 Robert Duncan, "Towards an Open Universe" (1964), in *A Selected Prose*
   (New York: New Directions, 1995), pp. 10–11.

4 Smadar Lavie, *The Poetics of Military Occupation* (Berkeley: University of
   California Press, 1990), p. 175.

5 Amartya Sen, *Inequality Reexamined* (Cambridge, Mass.: Harvard University Press, 1992).

6 Édouard Glissant, *Poetics of Relation,* trans. Betsy Wing (Ann Arbor: University of Michigan Press, 2000).

7 Rainer Maria Rilke, "Autumn Day," in *The Essential Rilke,* trans. Galway
   Kinnell and Hannah Liebmann (New York: Ecco, 2000), p. 5.

8 David Budbill, "An End to the Age of Impunity," *Sunday Rutland Herald/
   Times Argus* (September 30, 2001).

9 Muriel Rukeyser, *The Life of Poetry* (1949; Ashfield, Mass.: Paris Press,
   1966), p. 61.

10 James Baldwin, *Another Country* (New York: Dial, 1962), p. 4.

11 Walt Whitman, *Democratic Vistas* (1871), in *Complete Poetry and Prose,* pp.
    938, 949, 960.

12 Michael Harper, *Songlines in Michaeltree: New and Collected Poems*
    (Urbana and Chicago: University of Illinois Press, 2000), p. 372.

13 Robert Duncan, *Selected Poems,* ed. Robert J. Bertholf (New York: New Directions, 1993), pp. 64–72.

14 See Evelyn Fox Keller, *A Feeling for the Organism: The Life and Work of Barbara McClintock* (San Francisco: Freeman, 1983).

Arts of the Possible (2001)
"Muriel Rukeyser: Her Vision" (1993)

1 Louise Kertesz, *The Poetic Vision of Muriel Rukeyser* (Baton Rouge: Louisiana State University Press, 1980), pp. 78–84.

2 Muriel Rukeyser, *The Life of Poetry* (1949; Williamsburg, Mass.: Paris Press, 1996), p. 192.

3 *Ibid.,* p. 197.

4 Janet Sternburg, ed., *The Writer on Her Work,* I (New York: Norton, 1980), p. 221.

5 Nine African American youths were unjustly convicted of raping two white women, a conviction later overturned by the Supreme Court, and a landmark issue for radicals.

6 Muriel Rukeyser, "Poet . . . Woman . . . American . . . Jew," *Contemporary Jewish Record* 5, no. 7 (February 1944), repr. *Bridges: A Journal for Jewish Feminists and Our Friends* 1, no. 1 (Spring 1990): 23–29.

7 Paris Press in Williamsburg, Massachusetts, has reprinted *The Life of Poetry,* with a foreword by Jane Cooper (1996), and *The Orgy* (1965), her biomythographical novel, with a foreword by Sharon Olds (1997).

"Why I Refused the National Medal for the Arts" (1997)

1 Muriel Rukeyser, *The Life of Poetry* (1949; Williamsburg, Mass.: Paris Press, 1996), p. 159.

2 Clayton Eshleman, *Antiphonal Swing: Selected Prose 1962–1987* (Kingston, N.Y.: McPherson, 1989), p. 136.

3 Phyllis Kornfeld, *Cellblock Visions: Prison Art in America* (Princeton: Princeton University Press, 1997).

4 *New York Times,* July 25, 1997, C19.

"Arts of the Possible" (1997)

1 Barbara Smith, ed., *Home Girls: A Black Feminist Anthology* (New York: Kitchen Table/Women of Color Press, 1983), pp. 272–83. See also Zilla R. Eisenstein, ed., *Capitalist Patriarchy and the Case for Socialist Feminism* (New York: Monthly Review Press, 1978).

2 Aijaz Ahmad, *In Theory: Classes, Nations, Literatures* (New York and London: Verso, 1992), p. 154.

3 *Ibid.,* pp. 4–5, 129.

4   Garrett Hongo, ed., *Under Western Eyes: Personal Essays from Asian America* (New York: Anchor, 1995), pp. 23–24.

5   Karl Marx, as quoted by Raya Dunayevskaya, *Women's Liberation and the Dialectics of Revolution* (1985; Detroit: Wayne State University Press, 1996), p. 25. See also Karl Marx, *Karl Marx: Selected Writings*, ed. David McLellan (New York: Oxford University Press, 1977), p. 92.

6   Mumia Abu-Jamal, *Live from Death Row* (New York: Addison-Wesley, 1995), pp. 89–90.

7   Mahmoud Darwish, *Memory for Forgetfulness: August, Beirut, 1982* (Berkeley: University of California Press, 1995), pp. 65, 52.

8   Dionne Brand, *Bread Out of Stone: Recollections, Sex, Recognitions, Race, Dreaming, Politics* (Toronto: Coach House Press, 1994), pp. 182–83.

9   Eduardo Galeano, *Days and Nights of Love and War,* trans. Judith Brister (New York: Monthly Review Press, 1983), pp. 191, 185, 192.

10 Jonathan Kozol, "Two Nations, Eternally Unequal," in *Tikkun* 12, no. 1 (1996): 14.

11 Juan Gelman, *Unthinkable Tenderness: Selected Poems*, ed. and trans. Joan Lindgren (Berkeley: University of California Press, 1997), p. 12.

A Human Eye (2009)

"Permeable Membrane" (2005)

1   Vladimir Mayakovsky, *How Are Verses Made?*, trans. G. M. Hyde (London: Jonathan Cape, 1970), p. 18.

2   Vice President Dick Cheney, on NBC's *Meet the Press* (September 16, 2001).

3   Nadine Gordimer, "The Congo River," in her *The Essential Gesture: Writing, Politics, and Places,* ed. Stephen Clingman (New York: Knopf, 1988), p. 15.

4   *Selected Poems of René Char,* ed. Mary Ann Caws and Tina Jolas (New York: New Directions, 1992), p. 125: "La poète fait éclater les liens de ce qu'il touche. II n'enseigne pas la fin des liens."

"Poetry and the Forgotten Future" (2006)

Bibliography

Adonis. *An Introduction to Arab Poetics.* Trans. Catherine Cobham. Austin: University of Texas Press, 1997.

Brutus, Dennis. *Poetry and Protest: A Dennis Brutus Reader.* Ed. Lee Sustar and Aisha Karim. Chicago: Haymarket, 2006.

Cárdenas, José. "Young Immigrants Raise Voices, and Hopes." *St. Petersburg* (Florida) *Times* (May 13, 2006).

Coghlan, Thomas. "Writing Poetry Was the Balm That Kept Guantanamo Prisoners from Going Mad." *San Francisco Chronicle* (July 17, 2005).

Foot, Paul. In *International Socialist Review*, no. 46 (March–April 2006).

Franklin, H. Bruce. "The American Prison and the Normalization of Torture." http://www.historiansagainstwar.org/resources/torture/brucefranklin .html.

Glissant, Édouard. *Poetics of Relation*. Trans. Betsy Wing. Ann Arbor: University of Michigan Press, 1997.

Gramsci, Antonio. *Selections from Cultural Writings*. Ed. David Forgacs and Geoffrey Nowell-Smith. Trans. William Boelhower. Cambridge, Mass.: Harvard University Press, 1985.

Holmes, Richard. *Shelley: The Pursuit*. New ed. New York: New York Review of Books, 2003.

Lai, Him Mark, Genny Lim, and Judy Yung. *Island: Poetry and History of Chinese Immigrants on Angel Island, 1910–1940*. San Francisco: Hod Doi, 1980.

MacDiarmid, Hugh. *Collected Poems of Hugh MacDiarmid*. Ed. John C. Weston. New York: Macmillan, 1967.

Mayakovsky, Vladimir. *How Are Verses Made?* Trans. G. M. Hyde. New York: Jonathan Cape/Grossman, 1974.

Nitzan, Tal, and Rachel Tzvia Back, eds. *With an Iron Pen: Twenty Years of Hebrew Protest Poetry*. Albany: State University of New York Press, 2009.

Ritsos, Yannis. *Yannis Ritsos, Selected Poems 1938–1988*. Ed. and trans. Kimon Friar and Kostas Myrsiades. Brockport, N.Y.: BOA, 1989.

Scully, James. *Line Break: Poetry as Social Practice*. Foreword by Adrienne Rich. Willimantic, Conn.: Curbstone, 2005.

Stocking, Marion. "Books in Brief." *Beloit Poetry Journal* 56 (Summer 2006).

Vallejo, César. *Trice*. Trans. Clayton Eshleman. Intro. by Américo Ferrari. New York: Marsilio, 1992.

White, Elizabeth. "1 in 36 U.S. Residents behind Bars: U.S. Prisons, Jails Grew by 1,000 Inmates a Week from '04 to '05." Associated Press (May 22, 2006).

Whitman, Walt. *Walt Whitman: Complete Poetry and Collected Prose*. Ed. Justin Kaplan. New York: Literary Classics of the United States, Library of America, 1982.

Zonsheine, David. "A Personal and Political Moment." *Haaretz* (November 7, 2004).

Credits

GLORIA ANZALDÚA: From *Borderlands/La Frontera: The New Mestiza.* © 1987 by Gloria Anzaldua. Reprinted with permission from Aunt Lute Books.

MARGARET ATWOOD: From *Surfacing* by Margaret Atwood. Copyright © 1972, 1973 by Margaret Atwood. Reprinted with the permission of Simon & Schuster, Inc. All rights reserved. Copyright © 1972 by O.W. Toad Ltd. Reprinted by permission of Emblem/McClelland & Stewart, a division of Penguin Random House Canada Limited. From Margaret Atwood, *Surfacing.* Copyright © 1973 by Andre Deutsch. Reprinted by permission of Carlton Books Ltd.

W. H. AUDEN: From *W.H. Auden: Collected Poems* by W. H. Auden, edited by Edward Mendelson. Copyright 1940 and renewed 1968 by W. H. Auden. Reprinted by permission of Curtis Brown, Ltd.

JIMMY SANTIAGO BACA: Selection from "Coming into Language" in *Working in the Dark: Reflections of a Poet of the Barrio* (1992; Museum of New Mexico Press, 2008).

KATHLEEN BARRY: *Female Sexual Slavery* (New York University Press, 1984). Copyright © 1979 by Kathleen Barry. Used by permission of New York University Press.

CHARLES BERNSTEIN: From *A Poetics* (Harvard University Press, 1992). Copyright © 1979 by Charles Bernstein. Reprinted by permission of the author.

LORRAINE BETHEL: From "This Infinity of Conscious Pain: Zora Neale Hurston & the Black Literary Female Tradition" in *But Some of Us Are Brave* (Feminist Press/CUNY, 1993). Copyright © by Lorraine Bethel.

ELIZABETH BISHOP: Excerpts from "Brazil, January 1, 1502," "The Burglar of Babylon," "Chemin de Fer," "Faustina, or Rock Roses," "Four Poems,"

Index